DISABILITY MANAGEMENT
THEORY, STRATEGY & INDUSTRY PRACTICE

Third Edition

Dianne E.G. Dyck
BN, MSc, COHN(C), COHN-S, CRSP

with contributions by
Heidi Börner, BN, COHN(C),
Bonnie Rogers, Dr. PH, BN, MSc, FAAN,
Jane Hall, RN, MPA, CCM,
Sharon Blaney, RN, COHN(C),
Sharon Chadwick, RN, BScN, COHN(C), COHN-S,
Tony Roithmayr, MA, President, BA, MEd, Performance by Design, and
Kristine Robidoux, LL.B, ComplianceWorks

LexisNexis·

Disability Management: Theory, Strategy & Industry Practice, Third Edition
© LexisNexis 2006
April 2006

Members of the LexisNexis Group worldwide

Canada	LexisNexis Canada Inc, 123 Commerce Valley Dr. E. Suite 700, MARKHAM, Ontario
Australia	Butterworths, a Division of Reed International Books Australia Pry Ltd, CHATSWOOD, New South Wales
Austria	ARD Betriebsdienst and Verlag Orac, VIENNA
Czech Republic	Orac, sro, PRAGUE
France	Éditions du Juris-Classeur SA, PARIS
Hong Kong	Butterworths Asia (Hong Kong), HONG KONG
Hungary	Hvg Orac, BUDAPEST
India	Butterworths India, NEW DELHI
Ireland	Butterworths (Ireland) Ltd, DUBLIN
Italy	Giuffré, MILAN
Malaysia	Malayan Law Journal Sdn Bhd, KUALA LUMPUR
New Zealand	Butterworths of New Zealand, WELLINGTON
Poland	Wydawnictwa Prawnicze PWN, WARSAW
Singapore	Butterworths Asia, SINGAPORE
South Africa	Butterworth Publishers (Pty) Ltd, DURBAN
Switzerland	Stämpfli Verlag AG, BERNE
United Kingdom	Butterworths Tolley, a Division of Reed Elsevier (UK), LONDON, WC2A
USA	LexisNexis, DAYTON, Ohio

Library and Archives Canada Cataloguing in Publication

Dyck, Dianne E. G.
  Disability management: theory, strategy and industry
practice/Dianne E.G. Dyck; with contributions by Heidi
Borner ... [et al.]. — 3rd ed.

Includes index.
ISBN 978-0-433-45226-3

  1. Disability insurance claims — Canada — Management.
2. Handicapped — Employment — Canada. 3. Industrial hygiene.
4. Employee health promotion. I. Title.

HD7255.D92 2006	658.3'8	C2006-900985-6

Printed and bound in Canada.

Reprint #1.

This book is dedicated with thanks, to my parents, Alice and Don Boa who taught me:

The people who get on in the world are the people who get up and look for the circumstances that they want, and if they can't find them, make them.

George Bernard Shaw

About the Author

Dianne Dyck is an occupational health & safety (OH&S) specialist who has extensive experience in developing and managing OH&S programs. Her areas of specialization include the development and implementation of OH&S, Disability Management and Occupational Health services; auditing of OH&S-related programs, benefit programs, Disability Management programs, ergonomic programs, health data information systems, employee wellness programs, and employee assistance programs; and design and implementation of computerized occupational/health information systems. She has worked for private and public-funded agencies. Her greatest interest is in workplace illness and injury prevention. Dianne has worked in collaboration with a number of OH&S and Human Resource professionals to develop innovative ways to create supportive work environments that support worker health and safety.

Preface

The growth of disability management services in Canada is an exciting area, however as with any emerging field of practice it brings with it uncertainty as well as many opportunities. For disability management services to be practised in a responsible manner, structure, process and outcomes need to be in place. The intent of this text is to offer insight and guidance into these areas. To that end, this book was written to provide some general guidelines required for creating and managing a quality Disability Management Program.

I would like to acknowledge the contributions made by Dr. Martin Shain, Sharon Blaney, Heidi Borner, Sharon Chadwick, Jane Hall, Dr. Bonnie Rogers, Tony Roithmayr and Kristine Robidoux. Without their support, writing this resource would not have been possible.

When writing on such a dynamic subject, the process can be somewhat challenging to provide the most recent and relevant information for the readers. My hope is that *Disability Management: Theory, Strategy and Industry Practice* will meet your needs and that you will find it useful as you make your contributions towards advancing the field of disability management in Canada.

The first and second editions of *Disability Management: Theory, Strategy and Industry Practice* proved successful in providing a framework for disability management in Canada. I thank the many readers, scholars and media personnel for their interest and valuable feedback.

Dianne Dyck
March 2006

Table of Contents

Disability Management Strategy and Theory

INTRODUCTION

Disability management is still a relatively new field. For years, disability management was practised within the occupational health nursing domain. Other health care practitioners entered the disability management field as interest by employers in getting employees back to work grew. In essence, what evolved in Canada was a largely unregulated practice born out of the occupational health arena and governed by case law associated with human rights legislation (duty to accommodate). Other influences in the field of disability management were occupational health and safety legislation, provincial Workers' Compensation Acts, various professional practice standards and the Freedom of Information Acts.

Today, disability management is deemed to be a valuable asset to employees, employers and unions. It has been generally identified as being "required for legislative compliance", "a good business practice" and "the right thing to do". However, as with any new field, there remains some confusion as to the scope, intent, best practices and measurement techniques. As well, most of the industry practices in disability management came into being by trial and error, as opposed to being clinically researched, and were dependent on the organizational setting in which they originated. The result is that disability management best practices are still evolving and are in a state of flux.

CHALLENGES

Many challenges exist in the field of disability management. They stem from the evolving legislation, differences in the interpretation of the legislative decisions, gaps between employer activities and insurance benefit plan responses, recognition of new "hot illnesses",[1] various ethical considerations, the lack of accreditation and case management standards and poorly understood methods for program evaluation.

---

[1] Many illnesses, which in the past were not compensable, have now become recognized as being compensable under employee benefit plan coverage. The result is that employees can be off work with illnesses that are ill defined and poorly understood in terms of case management

This book is a product of the encouragement received from occupational health professionals. They felt the frustration experienced by clients — employers, employees, union leaders, insurers and human resource personnel — regarding what disability management is and how it can be effectively implemented. People also wanted to know what the current best practices are in this area.

INTENDED AUDIENCE

My intention in writing this book is to create a resource for the various players in the workplace disability management field. The readers who may find this book relevant to their practice or areas of work are:

- Occupational health nurses and physicians;
- Human Resource professionals;
- Occupational therapists;
- Safety practitioners;
- Employee Assistance Program counsellors;
- Return-to-work Coordinators;
- Claims administrators;
- Case managers;
- Rehabilitation specialists;
- Union leaders;
- Management personnel; and
- Insurance carrier staff.

In Canada, few books have been written on this topic. The books that do exist tend to focus on the reasons for disability management initiatives, the related costs and some of the relevant principles. However, little has been done to describe how to implement disability management, who should be involved, what each player should do, the legalities involved, how to market such a program, the relationship with Occupational Health & Safety and Wellness Programs and how success or failure can be measured.

As a result, care has been taken to craft the contents of the third edition of this book so that it can be widely understood and applied. As with any rapidly changing field, what is written today may quickly become dated.

---

techniques. Some examples are chronic fatigue syndrome, fibromyalgia, multiple chemical sensitivities and Epstein-Barr syndrome.

FORMAT

Chapter 1 provides an overview of disability management. It describes what disability management is, why it is important, the current models in place and the value that a Disability Management Program can offer various stakeholders. As with any business program, a Disability Management Program must add value to an organization. Chapter 1 discusses how to demonstrate that value to senior management and union leaders to garner their support and endorsement.

Chapter 2 addresses the importance of joint labour-management support and involvement in a Disability Management Program, the reasons this level of support and involvement is essential, what is involved and how successful results can be achieved. Some potential pitfalls that can be encountered are also discussed.

Chapter 3 describes the need for a supportive infrastructure for a Disability Management Program. Successful Disability Management Programs need three components: structure, process and recognizable outcomes. The type of infrastructure required is fully described in this chapter. As well, some examples of the recommended elements are included. To make this chapter even more useful to readers, an industry example of some aspects of a Disability Management Program policy and procedure manual has been crafted. The intent is to assist the reader in exploring some of the areas that should be addressed by a Disability Management Program manual.

Chapter 4 defines the roles and responsibilities of the various stakeholders in a Disability Management Program. As people become involved in disability management, role confusion occurs. Questions like: "Who does what?"; "Where do my responsibilities start and stop?"; "How can we work successfully together to deal with all the relevant issues involved?"; "Who should take charge of co-ordinating the disability?"; and many more loom. Chapter 4 attempts to deal with many of these questions. However, one *caveat* is that each organization has different stakeholders and players. Their exact roles and responsibilities in a Disability Management Program will vary depending on the available organization resources and internal/external expertise. These variations are to be expected — the key is to clarify in each situation who will be doing what, when and how.

Chapter 5 uses an illustration of a Disability Management Program that was industry developed and successfully implemented to explain the requisite principles and elements involved. Questions like: "What is a Disability Management Program?"; "Why is it important; who benefits?"; "What is the purpose?"; "How can it be implemented?"; and "How to measure program outcomes?" are addressed.

Although Chapter 5 addresses outcome measures for a Disability Management Program, Chapter 6 deals with some other measurement techniques that can be used to quantify and present the benefits of a Disability Management Program. The importance of program evaluation, data collection and program evaluation techniques are described.

Over the years, there has been increased interest in the current best practices in the field of disability management, which are summarized in Chapter 7. Concepts such as using an integrated approach to disability management, centralizing responsibility for the program, providing disability management education and training, implementing disability data management processes, recognizing the need for good communication strategies, establishing functional linkages with other organizational programs, standardizing case and claims management practices, protecting any collected employee medical data from inappropriate disclosure, using measurement to monitor and improve the program, developing a supportive infrastructure, having a Graduated Return-to-Work Program, and ensuring that early intervention is one of the cornerstones for the program are discussed. Best practices for each topic are provided.

Chapter 8, The Role of Employee Assistance Programs in Disability Management is presented because the service linkage to assistance programs is so critical. For a Disability Management Program to be successful, ill or injured employees and their families need support. As well, by facilitating a successful re-entry into the workplace, the duration of workplace absence can be reduced. The Employee Assistance Program can also help organizations to be pro-active in management style, and prevent disabilities before they occur.

Chapter 9 is a case study of how employees experiencing a "hot illness", like chronic fatigue syndrome, can be assisted through the recovery process and brought back into the workplace. This case study defines chronic fatigue syndrome, identifies challenges in diagnosing it, outlines its prevalence, and how to manage employees experiencing the syndrome. The secret is to use a multi-disciplinary approach. Although this clinical research was done in 1995, the approach remains relevant today.

In any successful Disability Management Program, a critical element is an Attendance Support and Assistance Program. The best way to prevent disability situations is to be pro-active and deal with a potential employee absence before it happens. Chapter 10 presents the various aspects of employee absenteeism, the costs and the importance of supporting employee work attendance — also called "presenteeism". A model for an Attendance Support and Assistance Program is described and presented for reader use.

Chapter 11 outlines what disability management standards of practice should contain. Four topics, claims management, case management, confidentiality and documentation, are addressed as separate practice standards.

The prevention of employee illness and injury is addressed in Chapters 12 and 13. By examining the potential roles between the Disability Management Program and other company programs such as the Occupational Health and Safety Programs, Employee Assistance Programs, Workplace Wellness Programs, and human resources management practices, opportunities for prevention are identified. Examples of possible synergies are provided, along with a sample workplace wellness model.

Chapter 13 examines the impact that management practices can have on employee health and wellness. The term "toxic workplace" is used to depict those workplaces in which a high number of organizational stressors exist — a place where employee performance is compromised. The outcome is poor employee morale, increased employee absenteeism, high staff turnover and reduced productivity. This chapter was co-authored with Tony Roithmayr, President, Performance by Design and specialist in helping organizations to develop high performance cultures (<http://www.performance–bydesign.com>).

Once a disability management program is developed, it is important to "tell and sell" stakeholders about and on the program. Chapter 14 addresses program marketing techniques.

Chapter 15 offers information on outsourcing disability management services and how this approach to disability management servicing can be achieved. It explores issues like: reasons for outsourcing; what internal preparation is required; conducting a market search; establishing performance measures and contract development; and vendor management. This is a more recent aspect of disability management programming and an area that remains poorly understood.

Disability management is based on relationships and trust. Inevitably when dealing with people and organizational issues, ethical considerations need to be addressed. In Chapter 16, Dr. Bonnie Rogers, Dr PH, BN, MSc, FAAN begins by discussing the key ethical theories and their implications for disability management. Jane Hall, RN, MPA, CCM then addresses ethics and case management. The topics of ethical decision-making and conflicting goals in disability management are also presented.

All stakeholders in the disability management process must be aware of the relevant legislation that may impact on the disability management processes. Chapter 17 addresses the legal aspects of disability management, including the duty to accommodate and privacy legislation. As well, Sharon Chadwick, RN, BScN, COHN(C), COHN-S and Kristine Robidoux, LL.B. look at the impact of changing legislation on the field of disability management.

The last chapter, Chapter 18, provides a discussion on some of the challenges in disability management, namely client confusion regarding disability management; the impact of rising health care costs; the impact of four generations in the workplace; cultural considerations when managing a disability; and the need for effective case management of mental health claims. Appreciation is extended to Heidi Börner, BN, COHN(C), and Sharon Blaney, RN, COHN(C) for their contributions to this chapter. The intent of this chapter is to foster thought about the future of disability management in Canada, and how to effectively address these critical issues.

SUMMARY

This disability management resource has been designed for front-line use. The author's hope is that its readers will find the information useful and readily applicable to their practice areas. As well, if this book can, in any way, clarify the cloudy topic of disability management, then this author's chief aim has been achieved.

Chapter 1

Disability Management: Overview

WHAT IS DISABILITY MANAGEMENT?

The term disability management means different things to different people. For the purposes of this text, disability management is *a systematic, goal-oriented process of actively minimizing the impact of impairment on the individual's capacity to participate competitively in the work environment, and maximizing the health of employees to prevent disability, or further deterioration when a disability exists.*[1]

A Disability Management Program is *a workplace program designed to facilitate the employment of persons with a disability through a coordinated effort that addresses individual needs, workplace conditions and legal responsibilities.*[2]

Ideally, Disability Management Programs are pro-active in nature and incorporate stakeholder involvement and accountability. Most are designed to control the personal and economic costs of employee injury or illness, convey a message that employees are valued and demonstrate compliance with the relevant legislation.

Operationally, disability management includes eight key elements (Figure 1.1):

1. MANAGEMENT-LABOUR COMMITMENT AND SUPPORTIVE POLICIES:

* Be sensitive to the impact of disability on employees, families, work units and the organization;
* Be aware of the relevant legislation and their due diligence to comply;
* Develop supportive policies;
* Create management-labour agreements that protect worker employability;
* Design benefit plans that reward a safe and timely return to work;
* Be cognizant of the potential effect of management practices on worker well-being;
* Develop flexible and creative return-to-work options; and
* Work together towards reducing employee absenteeism.

---

[1] Tate, Habeck & Schwartz, "Disability Management: Origins, Concepts and Principles for Practice" (1986) Journal of Applied Rehabilitation Counselling at 5-11.

[2] NIDMAR, *Code of Practice for Disability Management* (Port Alberni, B.C.: NIDMAR, 2000) at 5.

Figure 1.1: The Umbrella of a Disability Management Program

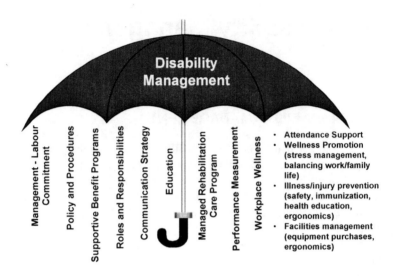

2. STAKEHOLDER EDUCATION AND INVOLVEMENT:

- Establish common goals;
- Develop a Disability Management Program;
- Define stakeholder roles and responsibilities;
- Provide stakeholder education;
- Promote stakeholder sensitivity to the psychological/social/vocational consequences of disability;
- Reward stakeholder participation; and
- Promote employee/supervisor accountability to reduce employee absenteeism.

3. SUPPORTIVE BENEFIT PROGRAMS:

- Provide Employee Assistance Program (EAP) support that includes employee and family counselling;
- Develop benefit plans that encourage a safe and timely return to work by the recovering employee; and
- Implement plans that promote and accommodate workplace rehabilitation.

4. A COORDINATED APPROACH TO INJURY/ILLNESS MANAGEMENT:

- Implement claims management processes;
- Implement case management practices;

- Undertake early intervention;
- Provide employee guidance towards responsible health care services (case management);
- Facilitate medical/vocational fitness-to-work evaluations (*i.e.*, medical forms, job demands analyses, functional capacity assessment referrals, *etc.*);
- Implement multi-disciplinary interventions into the disability management process;
- Develop alliances/linkages with external resources (*i.e.*, health care providers, Employee Assistance Programs (EAPs), vocational rehabilitation, insurers, *etc.*);
- Promote early rehabilitation/retraining for the recovering employee;
- Gather injury/illness data using disability management information systems; and
- Regularly evaluate the claims and case management processes with a view to continuous improvement.

5. A COMMUNICATION STRATEGY:

- Identify the needs of all the key stakeholders;
- Determine the benefits that a Disability Management Program should offer to stakeholders;
- Develop a communication plan for the program that includes a marketing component;
- Ensure that the marketing program clearly identifies the benefits the program can offer to stakeholders;
- Use the available communication vehicles that will reach all stakeholders;
- Build a communication plan that encourages a free-flow of information to and from stakeholders; and
- Evaluate the effectiveness of the implemented communication and marketing plans.

6. A GRADUATED RETURN-TO-WORK PROGRAM:

- Develop flexible and creative return-to-work options;
- Elicit employee/union/line identification of modified/alternate work options;
- Promote and facilitate workplace accommodations;
- Manage safe and timely return-to-work practices;
- Nurture co-worker understanding and support for the program; and
- Enlist insurer support and participation.

7. PERFORMANCE MEASUREMENT:

- Determine suitable performance measures for the program;
- Develop strategies for measuring the desired performances/outcomes;

- Establish a plan of action for performance measurement;
- Evaluate as planned; and
- Determine the return on investment afforded by the Disability Management Program.

8. WORKPLACE WELLNESS:

- Analyze the disability data;
- Recognize the patterns of injury/illness;
- Analyze the jobs/positions that experience an increased incidence of injuries/illness;
- Develop prevention strategies (*i.e.*, workplace safety, ergonomic, positive employee-employer relationships, cultural, *etc.*);
- Actively promote accident prevention practices;
- Reward employee wellness; and
- Promote/support employee/union involvement in the workplace to increase employee job satisfaction.

WHY EARLY INTERVENTION?

Research and industry experiences support the importance of early intervention in any employee work absence. The longer the employee is away from work, the less likely he or she will ever return. The window of opportunity for successfully bringing the employee back into the workplace appears to be within the first 30 days following the absence. By facilitating appropriate and timely treatments and rehabilitation, employers can assist employees in regaining health and returning to work in a shortened time frame. This approach benefits the employee, family and organization.

Informally, many organizations report more success with returning the recovering employee to the workplace if the intervention begins at, or soon after, the time of illness or injury. Typically, early intervention involves contacting the ill or injured employee within five days from the onset of a medical absence, and initiating case management if warranted. Companies demonstrating the best results in disability management begin intervention by day four or five of a non-occupational medical absence, and by day one of an occupational-related medical absence.

Early intervention can:

- decrease/prevent feelings of loneliness and abandonment that reduce the employee's motivation to get well;

- prevent a break in the *occupational bond* — the mutually beneficial relationship between the employee and the employer.[3]
- avoid delays in the employee obtaining appropriate health/rehabilitation services;
- avoid a "run-around" for the employee from health care professional to health care professional;
- help prevent the development of psychological problems, such as the adoption of the "sick role"[4] and related secondary gains;
- help with the physical, psychological, vocational, social and financial implications of a disability situation;[5]
- assist the employee and family in re-establishing a sense of control;
- encourage family members to provide positive reinforcement and support to the recovering employee;
- reduce the negative effects of physical and psychological de-conditioning;
- ease the process of coping and adjustment for the employee/family;
- increase the likelihood of a successful rehabilitation outcome; and
- prove to be cost-effective. Research has shown a 47% return to work rate among workers referred for rehabilitation services within three months post-injury. This led to a 71% cost savings.[6] In contrast, only 33% of those referred for rehabilitation services later at the four to six month post-injury period returned to work, and the cost savings dropped to 61%.[7]

Ill/injured employees tend to fall into one of the following three categories:

1. Those with strong resilience who respond well to treatment;
2. Those who are more vulnerable and prone to emotional reactions in response to an illness/injury or to being away from work; or
3. Those who are physically and/or emotionally fragile and become disabled as a result of the illness/injury or workplace stressors.[8]

For Disability Management Case Managers, the challenge is to identify which category the employee falls into to, and then contact the treating physician to gain

---

[3] D. Shrey, *Principles and Practices of Disability Management in Industry* (Winter Park, Florida: GR Press Inc., 1995).

[4] The "sick role" is a societally-sanctioned role that an ill or injured person assumes once they become ill or injured.

[5] T. Riggar, D. Maki & A. Wolf, *Applied Rehabilitation Counselling* (New York: Springer Publishing Co., 1986).

[6] R. Rundle, "Move Fast if You Want to Rehabilitate the Worker" (1983) May 2 Business Insurance at 10-12.

[7] C. Pati, "Economics of Rehabilitation in the Workplace" (1985) Oct./Nov./Dec. Journal of Rehabilitation at 22-30.

[8] J. Regan, cited in D. Thompson, "In Support of STD", *Benefits Canada* (2001), available online at <http://www.benefitscanada.com/content/legacy/Content/2001/11-1/std.html>.

support for the development and implementation of a treatment plan focused on a safe and timely return to work.

DISABILITY MANAGEMENT MODELS

There are a number of models or paradigms for disability management in today's work and marketplaces. Four examples are:

1. *Traditional Model* — This is a model in which the care plan, authorized leave and return-to-work process are medically directed. The employer relies on the treating practitioners (primarily the physician) to substantiate the validity of the illness and to help the employee to return to work. This is often the starting point for many organizations, as well as insurer disability management models.

2. *Job Matching Approach* — This is a model which involves a fitness assessment of the injured or ill employee and an analysis of the physical/psychological demands of the employee's job. The intent is to determine if there is a "match" or "mismatch" in terms of a safe return to work for the employee.

3. *Managed Care Model* — In a managed care model, the employee's diagnosis is referenced against standardized care plans, procedures and diagnostic testing guidelines to determine if treatment and the physician's suggested leave duration are appropriate. This model, like the traditional model, tends to be medically driven.

4. *Direct Case Management Model* — This employee-employer approach to dealing with the employee's reduced work capacity and the employer's business needs/resources uses some of the elements of the first three models. However, it is the employee and employer who decide the terms of the medical absence and the return-to-work plan.[9]

Although each of these four models was created in response to different needs, they all have valuable contributions to make towards the disability management process. The fact that most Disability Management Programs today use some elements of each model attests to this. Typically, the traditional model is the starting point for a Disability Management Program,[10] and elements of the other models are then added as required.

From experience as a disability management practitioner, and from auditing existing Disability Management Programs within various organizations, I have learned that the best approach to disability management is one that focuses on

---

[9]   A. Clarke, "Disability Case Management Models" (Presented at the Disability Case Management Forum, Vancouver, March 24-26 1997) [unpublished].

[10]   *Ibid.*

maintaining a strong employee-employer relationship. Effective programs, such as the one depicted in the model developed by the National Institute for Disability Management and Research (Figure 1.2), maintain the employee-employer relationship, focus on the employee's capabilities versus disabilities and are supported by a variety of technical specialists and case management approaches.

Supporting the employee and family through an illness or injury period usually promotes a "win-win" situation for all parties and related stakeholders. It also reduces the resistance to claims and case interventions and encourages a successful return to work.

Figure 1.2: Employee-Employer Disability Management Model[11]

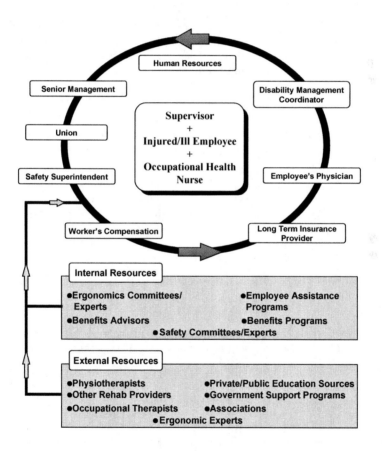

---

[11] Adapted from: National Institute of Disability Management and Research (NIDMAR), *Disability Management in the Workplace: A Guide to Establishing a Joint Workplace Program* (Port Alberni, B.C.: NIDMAR, 1995).

VALUE OF DISABILITY MANAGEMENT TO STAKEHOLDERS

To sell the merits of a Disability Management Program, one must consider the interests and values of the key stakeholders.

For the Corporation

In 2004, Canadian workers missed 9.2 workdays for approximately 102 million lost workdays due to illness/disability and personal or family responsibilities.[12] This cost the Canadian economy about $16.2 billion[13] and absorbed 14.9% of company payrolls.[14] This represents a dramatic increase in employee lost time due to illness since 1998, when workers missed 7.8 workdays for a total of 72 million lost work hours.[15]

In the United States, absences take a hefty toll on the corporate bottom line as well. An estimated 69 million workers reported missing workdays due to illness in 2003, for a total of 407 million lost workdays and $48 billion in lost economic output.[16] This can translate to an overall average cost of $610 per employee per year.[17] The annual worker absence costs can range from $60,000 for small employers to over a million dollars for large organizations.[18]

Employee absence costs are escalating. New illnesses, an aging workforce, increased medical costs, decreased government support, and lack of understanding of the costs related to disabilities, all contribute to the financial burden borne by employers.

Through a Disability Management Program, employers can identify injury or illness causes, prevent injuries, promote employee well-being and contain the disability-related costs. The estimated saving is a 30-50% reduction in lost time and related costs.[19] The net result can be a healthier workforce, reduced

---

[12]   Statistics Canada, *Work Absence Rates, 2004*, Cat. No. 71-211-X1E (Ottawa: Statistics Canada, 2005) at 101.

[13]   Statistics Canada, *Work Absence Rates, 2004*, Cat. No. 71-211-X1E (Ottawa: Statistics Canada, 2005).

[14]   Marsh Risk Consulting, *Workforce Risk: Fourth Annual Marsh Mercer Survey of Employers' Time-Off and Disability Programs* (2003), available online at: <http://www.marshriskconsulting.com/st/PDEv_C_371_SC_228135_NR_306_PI_347745.htm>.

[15]   E. Akyeampong, *Work Absence Rates, 1987 to 1998*, Cat. No. 71-535-MPB, No. 10 (Ottawa: Statistics Canada, 1999).

[16]   M. Mahon, "Lost Labor Time Costs U.S. $260 Billion Each Year" in *Newsroom, The Commonwealth Fund* (31 August 2005), available online at: <http://www.cmwf.org/newsroom/newsroom_ show.htm?.doc_id=294188>.

[17]   CCH Incorporated, *2004 CCH Unscheduled Absence Survey* (Riverwoods, Ill.: CCH Incorporated, 2004).

[18]   CCH Incorporated, "Unscheduled Employee Absenteeism Rises to Five Year High" in *2004 CCH Unscheduled Absence Survey* (Riverwoods, Ill.: CCH Incorporated, 2004), available online at: <http://www.cch.com/press/news/2004/20041007h.asp>.

[19]   NIDMAR, *Occupational Standards in Disability Management: Executive Summary* (Port Alberni, B.C.: NIDMAR, 2000) at 2.

absenteeism, good productivity, lowered disability costs, lower insurance premiums and rates and Workers' Compensation rebates. As well, the employer retains a valuable employee, while decreasing disability costs and meeting legislative obligations.

For the Union

Unions, like management and employees, have a legal responsibility to help ill or injured employees return to work.[20] Through support and participation in a Disability Management Program, unions can demonstrate their level of commitment and compliance to Canadian human rights legislation. As well, a Disability Management Program affords unions the opportunity to:

- promote employee well-being;
- maintain labour rights and principles;
- demonstrate value of the program to union members by protecting the employability of its members;
- interact and build relationships;
- problem-solve in addressing areas of mutual interest and concern; and
- contribute to the company's profitability and competitiveness.

For the Employee

The benefits of a Disability Management Program to the employee and family during a vulnerable period in their lives are numerous and invaluable. Some benefits include:

- the promotion of a speedy rehabilitation;
- the ability to maintain self-identity and respect;
- the opportunity to stay in contact with, and to gain support from, co-workers;
- the ability to remain current in their field; and
- less disruption in their normal family and workplace relationships.

A graduated early Return-to-Work Program allows employees to:

- concentrate on recovery;
- keep a regular routine;
- maintain a sense of self-worth;
- make a contribution to the company;
- work at regular duties for as many hours as possible;

---

[20] B. Armstrong & S. Greckol, "Accommodation Guidelines" in *Illness and Disability Claims in the Unionized Workplace* (Winnipeg: Centre for Labour-Management Development, 1999).

- keep work contacts;
- remain current with the changing work skill sets, duties and responsibilities;
- remain current with changing technology;
- gradually adjust to full-time work; and
- return to work without upgrading.

In summary, a Disability Management Program can be a "win-win" situation for everyone involved. It can promote human savings as well as financial ones. For example, the reported effects of disability on British Columbia's economy were $3.6 billion per year, or eight cents on every dollar earned in the province. This translates to 35% of the disability costs being borne by employers, and 27% borne by disabled individuals and families, and the rest (38%) through government programs.[21] By reducing disabilities, all parties win.

DISABILITY MANAGEMENT: HYPE OR GOOD BUSINESS PRACTICE[22]

A Disability Management Program is like any other business endeavour. For it to survive, it must make good business sense, and a financial return on the resources invested must be demonstrated. Knowing that the effect a Disability Management Program can have on the organization's "bottom-line" must be demonstrated, you need to first determine the required disability costs and resources.

Secondly, determine the outcomes realized by other existing Disability Management Programs, better known as bench-marking. Fortunately, many companies are now reporting their program results at conferences and in print. For example:

- The City of Winnipeg realized a $2.7 million saving since introducing their disability management program;[23]
- Weyerhaeuser was able to reduce their Workers' Compensation Board costs by 51% over six years through disability management efforts. They also noted an average reduction in cost per claim of 18%;[24]
- Petro-Canada, through the Managed Rehabilitation Care Program saved $1.33 million in 1996. They reduced their long-term disability premium

---

[21]   Editor, "Disabilities Draining the B.C. Economy" (1997) 1:7 Back to Work at 1.

[22]   D. Dyck. Excerpts reprinted with permission from *Stating Your Case* (Ottawa: Benefits Canada, 1998) at 55-59.

[23]   *Supra*, note 11.

[24]   Weyerhaeuser, "Transitional Return-to-Work at Weyerhaeuser Company" (Presented at the National Conference on Disability and Work: Solutions for Canadians, Sheraton Centre, Toronto, Ontario, 7-9 October 1996) [unpublished].

rates to 4.8/1,000 (1996), and enjoyed long-term disability plan premium holidays[25] each year since 1991;[26]

- Canada Post saved $54.6 million per year by introducing early return-to-work initiatives. They also experienced a drop in employee absenteeism from 20 to 9.93 days per employee per year;[27]

- The University of Calgary had 71% of employees indicate satisfaction with the Attendance Support Program that the University of Calgary has in place. This is an integrated program that combines occupational health nursing and Employee Assistance Program counselling services to promote an early re-turn to work. The University's annual report indicated that 73.1% of the cases that were closed in 1996 resulted in a return to work by employees;[28]

- The Toronto Transit Commission, through management of soft tissue inju-ries, reduced the length of their Workers' Compensation claims by 17%, their Workers' Compensation medical aid costs by 27%, the length of the short-term disability claims by 19%, and the number of employees on long-term disability by 11%;[29]

- MacMillian Bloedel Ltd., Port Alberni, British Columbia, saved $1.25 mil-lion in disability costs in one year; reduced the number of long-term dis-ability claims by 37% from 1995 to 1996; and decreased the number of lost time days due to occupational illness or injury from 20 days to 4 days through the establishment of a Disability Management Program; and

- BC Hydro (1994) introduced a Disability Management Program that low-ered the employee sick days from 2,732 in 1995, to 2,573 in 1996 (5.8% de-crease). The days off for long-term disability decreased from 1,083 to 934 for that same period. As well, Workers' Compensation premiums were re-duced by $700,000, and the number of employee absences of 10 or more days duration were lowered from 83 to 51 cases.[30]

- A major Airline implemented a total absence management program for a net saving of more than 14% of the total costs over five years.[31]

---

[25] A premium holiday is the period of time that a client or employee is not required to pay insur-ance plan premiums because the plan is over-funded.

[26] Petro-Canada, "Managed Rehabilitation Care Program" (Presented at the CPBI Conference, Calgary, Alberta, 1996) [unpublished].

[27] Canada Post, "Building a Business Case for Disability Management: Proving the Value of a Return to Work Program at Canada Post" (Presented at the National Conference on Disability and Work: Solutions for Canadians, Sheraton Centre, Toronto, Ontario, 7-9 October 1996) [un-published].

[28] University of Calgary, *Annual Report* (Calgary: University of Calgary, 1996).

[29] L. Stellini, "Preferred Provider Network for Integrated Management of Soft Tissue Injuries" (Presented at the conference on Developing Effective Return-to-Work Programs, Toronto, Ontario, 24-25 October 1996) [unpublished].

[30] S. Lebrun, "Employers Take Notice of Disability Costs: Management of Injury and Illness Can Save Millions" (1997) 29 December C.H.R.R.

[31] Aon Consulting, "The Case for Absence Management", *Aon Workforce Strategies, 2003*, avail-able online at: <http://www.aon.com/about/publications/issues/2003_absence_management.jsp>.

Further support for the added value of Disability Management Programs comes from studies done on early intervention following an illness or injury. For example, the American International Group (AIG) claim survey to 300 companies reported that by implementing case management procedures immediately after the occurrence of a Workers' Compensation claim, costs were reduced by as much as 40%.[32]

According to the 2005 Watson Wyatt Staying @ Work Survey, 81% of the 94 participating companies reported that they perceived documented return-to-work plans to be a key factor for managing disability-related costs, and improving employee health, employee satisfaction and productivity.[33]

The Alberta Workers' Compensation Board (2005) reported that employers who instituted post-injury reduction services lowered their 2004 injury claim costs by 20% as compared to non-participants.[34] This is a 3% increase in savings over 10 years ago when the saving was 17%.[35] In short, managing occupational injuries makes good business sense for many Alberta companies.

Lastly, your challenge will be to present the merits of the Disability Management Program in business language. A critical part of that language includes a cost/benefit analysis of launching such a program, the potential influence on the company's bottom-line, and the anticipated return on investment. Research that can support your endeavour includes:

* Since 1996, the number of companies that have implemented integrated disability management programs has increased from 25% to 51% (2004). The reason is simple: it is a cost-effective approach to managing worker absence and mitigating the associated costs. According to a recent Watson Wyatt Worldwide survey, savings of 0.25-1% of payroll can be realized.[36]
* The direct costs of work absence and the related costs equates to 5-6% of payroll. Taking steps to address and lower worker absence just makes good business sense.

---

[32]   AIG Claims Services Inc., "Early Intervention Cuts Workers' Compensation Costs" (Aon Commentary, 17 June 1996).

[33]   Watson Wyatt Worldwide, *Staying @ Work Report 2005* (2005), available online at <http://www.watsonwyatt.com/research/resrender.asp?id=w-860& page=1>.

[34]   Workers' Compensation Board Alberta *2004 Annual Report* (Edmonton: Workers' Compensation Board Alberta, 2005) at 18, online: <http://www.wcb.ab.ca/pdfs/05-ar.pdf>.

[35]   J. Cowell, "Serving Albertans Through Effective Injury Prevention and Disability Management" (Presented at the National Conference on Disability and Work: Solutions for Canadians, Sheraton Centre, Toronto, Ontario, 7-9 October 1996).

[36]   Watson Wyatt Worldwide, *Managing Health Care Costs in a New Era: 10th Annual National Business Group on Health/Watson Wyatt Survey Report 2005*, available online at: <http://www.watsonwyatt.com/research/resrender.asp?id=w-821&page=1>.

- Employers who implement at least three disability and absence management techniques have 74% lower worker absence rates.[37]

HOW TO SELL A DISABILITY MANAGEMENT PROGRAM TO SENIOR MANAGEMENT

Many human resource professionals and occupational health practitioners attend seminars, conferences and work groups on the topic of disability management. They leave these educational sessions convinced that disability management could be of value to their company or organization — however, they are unsure of how they can sell their ideas to senior management.

Perceived Barriers

One of the perceived barriers around initiating a Disability Management Program is the myth that workplace accommodations are expensive. Workplace accommodation includes changes in, or reassignment of, parts of a job so that the recovering employee can return to work. This could translate into modifying existing job duties, offering transitional work, arranging for a training opportunity, providing an alternate job placement, or any combination of these.

A study by Alan Cantor[38] demonstrated that the majority of the workplace accommodations cost under $500, with 31% of the workplace accommodations occurring at no added cost to the employer. In fact, Cantor reported that only 5% of the workplace accommodations cost the company more than $5,000.

A second perceived barrier is that there are limited modified work positions available within an organization for the recovering employee. This perception needs to be challenged. If all stakeholders are committed to making disability management work, modified work opportunities seem to materialize. From past experience, this author has come to appreciate that the employee population, and union members, are very resourceful at unearthing modified work positions. For example, work groups can band together to alter their jobs so that a recovering work-mate can do tasks within his or her reduced work capabilities. In one instance, a company without truck driving positions was able to call on its partner company to provide the modified duties for a recovering employee. The point is that, "where there is a will, there is a way".

---

[37] Washington Business Group on Health, *Fifth Annual Washington Business Group on Health/Watson Wyatt Worldwide Survey on Disability Management* (Watson Wyatt Worldwide, 2004), available online at <http://www.watsonwyatt.com>.

[38] A. Cantor, "The Future of Workplace Accommodations: Containing Costs and Maximizing Effectiveness" (Presented at the National Conference on Disability and Work: Solutions for Canadians, Sheraton Centre, Toronto, Ontario, 7-9 October 1996) [unpublished.]

A third perceived barrier is that the existing benefit plans may be unsupportive of modified work. For example, plans that promote absence with pay, or that allow the employee to earn more staying at home than doing modified work, lack incentives for the employee to return to the workplace. This barrier may be real. For this reason, companies should examine their benefit plans and determine the impact that each has on employee return-to-work outcomes.

A fourth barrier is disability policies and procedures that focus on employee disability rather than capabilities. This approach promotes a "disability mindset", not an "ability mindset" for managers, human resource professionals, unions and employees. This is one area that can negatively impact the corporate culture and that warrants serious introspection by a company.

The fifth barrier centres around the belief of some human resource managers that disability management has become so complex that the practice should be abandoned. This type of mindset tends to be reactive and akin to "throwing in the towel". Although the recent privacy legislation has made it difficult to get medical information, it has not removed the obligation of the employee to provide the workplace with the nature of the absence (work-related or non-work-related); the expected duration of absence; work limitation, if any; and a realistic return-to-work date. By providing human resources and operations relevant information on the employee's fitness to work in a timely manner, disability management coordinators can overcome this barrier.

How to Move Forward

STEP 1: ANALYZE YOUR SITUATION

One way to analyze your situation is to identify the barriers and the drivers for disability management. Using a tool like Lewin's Force Field Analysis (Figure 1.3),[39] you can determine various ways to decrease the barriers for implementing a Disability Management Program, while increasing the drivers for the program.

The force field model helps individuals select the targets for change. By focusing on the restraining forces and looking for ways to reduce their effect, or ways to change them into driving forces, one can identify the real underlying factors preventing the implementation of a Disability Management Program and the potential solution.

STEP 2: GATHER SUPPORTIVE DISABILITY DATA

By using research outcome findings, you can project the potential savings for your company. This includes using recent survey data and the identified trends in disability costs. It also means the inclusion of any hidden costs of disability such as:

---

[39]   M. Brassard & D. Ritter, *The Memory Jogger: Tools for Continuous Improvement and Effective Planning* (Methuen, MA: GOAL/PC, 1994).

- the overtime paid for the remaining workers who assume a heavier work-load while the ill or injured employee is absent;
- hiring replacement workers;
- training costs for replacement workers;
- lowered productivity due to the work-flow disruption;
- customer service disruptions;
- customer dissatisfaction; and
- costs of benefits provided during the disability.

Also, the potential costs of "doing nothing" to manage illness or injury costs should be considered and taken into account.

Figure 1.3: Lewin's Force Field for Disability Management

Driving Forces	Restraining Forces (Barriers)
Rising costs of disability →	← Lack of company/union awareness and buy-in
Disability management reduces costs →	← No early intervention
Available internal resources →	← Non-supportive disability benefit plans
Employees requesting to return to work from a disability →	← Lack of disability-related data
Employee Assistance Program available →	← Fear of workplace accommodation costs
Some supportive policies available →	← Lack of rehabilitation resources
Claims management →	← Lack of formal accountability for employee absence
Attendance Support and Assistance Program in place →	← Mismanagement of medical claims

STEP 3: DEMONSTRATE THE VALUE

Lastly, demonstrate the outcomes of whatever disability management efforts are in place, or are planned. This can be achieved by using the following principles:

- Consider the structure, process and outcomes of the Disability Management Program as per the established performance measures.
- Address the value that the program offers to the organization. Is the program justified from a business standpoint? What is the potential return on investment?

- Consider whether some performance measures should be valued higher than others. That is, is the impact on severity more important than the frequency of occurrence?
- Measure data such as the frequency of claims, number of long-term disability claims avoided, return-to-work statistics, cost of interventions, the cost of replacement workers, degree of cost-avoidance through the return-to-work program, Workers' Compensation Board costs, and any identified trends.

SUMMARY

Employee illness or injury is costly to everyone involved. In Canada, employer and union efforts to manage disability and return employees have advanced to the point where 82% of employers report that they have, at a minimum, return-to-work practices.[40] This is encouraging as in 1999, only 23.1% of Canadian employers had disability management services.[41]

Going forward, employers and unions need to continue to proactively manage employee disabilities. As occupational health or human resource professionals, you can assist with this effort by demonstrating that disability management is good business practice, with immense possibilities for significant returns on the investment made. The remaining chapters of this book are dedicated to helping the reader appreciate this premise.

CHAPTER REFERENCES

AIG Claims Services Inc., "Early Intervention Cuts Workers' Compensation Costs" (Aon Commentary, 17 June 1996).

E. Akyeampong, *Work Absence Rates, 1987 to 1998*, Cat. No. 71-535-MPB, No. 10 (Ottawa: Statistics Canada, 1999).

Aon Consulting, "The Case for Absence Management", *Aon Workforce Strategies, 2003*, online: <http://www.aon.com/about/publications/issues/2003_absence_management.jsp>.

B. Armstrong & S. Greckol, "Accommodation Guidelines" in *Illness and Disability Claims in the Unionized Workplace* (Winnipeg: Centre for Labour-Management Development, 1999).

---

[40]   *Supra*, note 33.
[41]   Conference Board of Canada, *Supporting Workplace Health: An Exploratory Study of Stakeholder Groups* (Ottawa: Conference Board of Canada, 1999). Unpublished study reported in K. Bachmann's *More Than Just Hard Hats and Safety Boots* (Ottawa: Conference Board of Canada, 2000) at 33.

M. Brassard & D. Ritter, *The Memory Jogger: Tools for Continuous Improvement and Effective Planning* (Methuen, MA: GOAL/PC, 1994).

Canada Post, "Building a Business Case for Disability Management: Proving the Value of a Return to Work Program at Canada Post" (Presented at the National Conference on Disability and Work: Solutions for Canadians, Sheraton Centre, Toronto, Ontario, 7-9 October 1996) [unpublished].

A. Cantor, "The Future of Workplace Accommodations: Containing Costs and Maximizing Effectiveness" (Presented at the National Conference on Disability and Work: Solutions for Canadians, Sheraton Centre, Toronto, Ontario, 7-9 October 1996) [unpublished].

CCH Incorporated, *2004 CCH Unscheduled Absence Survey* (Riverwoods, Ill.: CCH Incorporated, 2004).

CCH Incorporated, "Unscheduled Employee Absenteeism Rises to Five Year High", in *2004 CCH Unscheduled Absence Survey* (Riverwoods, Ill.: CCH Incorporated, 2004), online: <http://www.cch.com/press/news/2004/20041007h.asp>.

A. Clarke, "Disability Case Management Models" (Presented at the Disability Case Management Forum, Vancouver, British Columbia, 24-26 March 1997) [unpublished].

Conference Board of Canada, *Supporting Workplace Health: An Exploratory Study of Stakeholder Groups* (Ottawa, ON: Conference Board of Canada, 1999). Unpublished study reported in K. Bachmann's *More Than Just Hard Hats and Safety Boots* (Ottawa: Conference Board of Canada, 2000) at 33.

J. Cowell, "Serving Albertans Through Effective Injury Prevention and Disability Management" (Presented at the National Conference on Disability and Work: Solutions for Canadians, Sheraton Centre, Toronto, Ontario, 7-9 October 1996).

D. Dyck, *Stating Your Case* (Ottawa: Benefits Canada, 1998) at 55-59.

Editor, "Disabilities Draining the B.C. Economy" (1997), Vol. 1:7 Back to Work at 1.

S. Lebrun, "Employers Take Notice of Disability Costs: Management of Injury and Illness Can Save Millions" (1997) 29 December C.H.R.R.

M. Mahon, "Lost Labor Time Costs U.S. $260 Billion Each Year" in *Newsroom, The Commonwealth Fund*, (31 August 2005), available online at: <http://www.cmwf.org/newsroom/newsroom_show.htm?doc-id=294188>.

Marsh Risk Consulting, *Workforce Risk: Fourth Annual Marsh Mercer Survey of Employers' Time-Off and Disability Programs* (2003), available online at: <http://www.marshriskconsulting.com/st/PDEv_C_371_SC_228135_NR_3 06_PI_347745.htm>.

National Institute of Disability Management and Research (NIDMAR), *Disability Management in the Workplace: A Guide to Establishing a Joint Workplace Program* (Port Alberni, B.C.: NIDMAR, 1995).

NIDMAR, *Code of Practice for Disability Management* (Port Alberni, B.C.: NIDMAR, 2000) at 5.

NIDMAR, *Occupational Standards in Disability Management: Executive Summary* (Port Alberni, B.C.: NIDMAR, 2000) at 2.

C. Pati, "Economics of Rehabilitation in the Workplace" (1985) Oct./Nov./Dec. Journal of Rehabilitation at 22-30.

Petro-Canada, "Managed Rehabilitation Care Program" (Presented at the CPBI Conference, Calgary, Alberta, 1996) [unpublished].

J. Regan, reported in D. Thompson, "In Support of STD", *Benefits Canada*, (2001) online: <http://www.benefitscanada.com>.

T. Riggar, D. Maki & A. Wolf, *Applied Rehabilitation Counselling* (New York: Springer Publishing Co., 1986).

R. Rundle, "Move Fast if you Want to Rehabilitate the Worker" (1983) May 2 Business Insurance at 10-12.

D. Shrey, *Principles and Practices of Disability Management in Industry* (Winter Park, Florida: GR Press Inc., 1995).

Statistics Canada, *Work Absence Rates, 2004*, Cat. No. 71-211-X1E (Ottawa: Statistics Canada, 2005).

L. Stellini, "Preferred Provider Network for Integrated Management of Soft Tissue Injuries" (Presented at the Conference on Developing Effective Return-to-Work Programs, Toronto, Ontario, 24-25 October 1996) [unpublished].

Tate, Habeck & Schwartz, "Disability Management: Origins, Concepts and Principles for Practice" (1986) 17 Journal of Applied Rehabilitation Counselling at 5-11.

University of Calgary, *Annual Report* (Calgary: University of Calgary, 1996).

Washington Business Group on Health, *Fifth Annual Washington Business Group Health/Watson Wyatt Worldwide Survey on Disability Management,* (Watson Wyatt Worldwide, 2004), available online at <http://www.watsonwyatt.com>.

Watson Wyatt Worldwide, *Managing Health Care Costs in a New Era: 10th Annual National Business Group on Health/Watson Wyatt Survey Report, 2005*, available online at: <http://www.watsonwyatt.com/research/resrender. asp?id=w-821&page=1>.

Watson Wyatt Worldwide, *Staying @ Work, 2005* (2005), available online at <http://www.watsonwyatt.com/research/resrender.asp?id=w-860&page=1> at 5.

Weyerhaeuser, "Transitional Return-to-Work at Weyerhaeuser Company" (Presented at the National Conference on Disability and Work: Solutions for Canadians, Sheraton Centre, Toronto, Ontario, 7-9 October 1996) [unpublished].

Workers' Compensation Board Alberta, (Edmonton: Workers' Compensation Board Alberta, 2005), *2004 Annual Report* online: <http://www.wcb.ab.ca/pdfs/05-ar.pdf>.

Chapter 2

Joint Labour-Management Support and Involvement

IMPORTANCE

For a Disability Management Program to be successful, joint labour-management endorsement, support and involvement is required. This belief, although widely upheld by researchers in the field,[1] is less likely to be explored or implemented by industry. This chapter is dedicated to a discussion on the rationale for joint-labour involvement, what that entails, what is required from each player and how this partnership can be achieved.

CANADIAN LABOUR UNIONS: HISTORY AND ROLE

History

The history of the trade union movement in Canada started in Montreal with the registration of a union among boot and shoe workers in 1827.[2] However, given the lack of legal support for unions in Canada at the time, it wasn't until 1872 when the John A. Macdonald government introduced the *Trade Unions Act*, that workers had the right to band together to seek better working conditions. In 1907, the enactment of the *Industrial Disputes Investigation Act* introduced the principle of compulsory delay in work stoppages. This Act also made provisions for the investigation and conciliation of labour disputes by a tripartite board — a board with the legal power to investigate the situation, to compel testimony, to determine the root causes of the issues at hand and to recommend labour settlements.

Prior to 1919, the Canadian labour movement appeared to have a bright future. They had played a significant role in improving the working conditions and benefits for Canadian workers. However, the years between 1919 and 1949 became a time of upheaval and change. Unions were "beset by crisis after crisis,

---

[1] National Institute of Disability Management and Research (NIDMAR), *Disability Management in the Workplace: A Guide to Establishing a Joint Workplace Program* (Port Alberni, B.C.: NIDMAR, 1995).

[2] S. Applebaum, M.D. Beckman, L. Boone & D. Kurz, *Contemporary Canadian Business,* 3d ed. (Toronto: Holt, Rinehart & Winston of Canada, Ltd. 1987) at 257.

catastrophe upon catastrophe".[3] Abella recounts that Canadian unions were attacked on all fronts — by business, by governments and by their own respective memberships. There were times during those years when the very survival of an organized labour movement in Canada seemed in jeopardy. Yet by the 1950s, trade unions emerged triumphant and successful as a powerful political and economic force.

Role

Trade unions are organizations of employees who have joined together to obtain a stronger voice in decisions affecting their wages, benefits, working conditions and other aspects of employment. Through the process of collective bargaining, union leaders negotiate collective agreements that spell out the terms and conditions of employment with management. These collective agreements provide structure, process and expected outcomes that help to define the nature of the working relationship between labour and management.

The formation of a union is "an attempt to adjust a power imbalance, and to make the employee as strong as the employer by acting as a single united group".[4] The right to strike remains the union's basic weapon. However, a strike is only successful if production can be shut down, and if the employer is willing to concede due to the withdrawal of services and related costs.

Today, the Canadian labour movement is strong. Over the years, labour demands for improving inhumane working conditions have been met. The more recent focus is on job security and employee benefits. In fact, many unions have become actively involved in employee benefit programs such as Employee Assistance Programs, Disability Management Programs and gradual return-to-work activities.

For example, the labour movement played an instrumental role in assisting the British Columbia Workers' Compensation Board to undertake research and program development in the area of disability management. The National Institute for Disability Management and Research (NIDMAR), in Port Alberni, B.C., is but one example of their efforts.

Since 1994, NIDMAR has been recognized as an organization committed to reducing the human, social and economic costs of disability in Canada. The Institute has developed a recognized educational program for Canadian disability managers, offered educational sessions, produced resource materials, undertaken valuable research on disability management in Canada, promoted workplace solutions to reducing disability rates and costs and supported companies, unions and others in their efforts to develop Disability Management Programs. Some of NIDMAR's notable contributions are:

---

[3]   I. Abella, *On Strike: Six Key Labour Struggles in Canada 1919-1949* (Toronto: James Lorimer & Company, 1975).

[4]   *Ibid.*

- Development of a recognized disability management educational curriculum offered in British Columbia, Alberta, Ontario, New Brunswick and Nova Scotia;
- Presentation and sponsorship of numerous seminars on disability management;
- Research on the cost of disability in British Columbia and published in *The Effects of Disability in B.C.'s Economy*;[5]
- Development of a disability database — REHADAT, which provides data on the relevant legislation, best practice case studies, and other available resources for successful disability management;
- Publishing of numerous resource materials such as *Industrial Disability Management: An Effective Economic and Human Resource Strategy*,[6] *Disability Management in the Workplace*,[7] *Strategies for Success: Disability Management in the Workplace*;[8]
- Producing videos such as *Disability in the Workplace, The Final Step: The Case for Getting Disabled Workers Back on the Job*, and *Every 12 Seconds*; and
- Development of Canada's occupational standards for certified return-to-work coordinators and certified disability management professionals.[9]

Through efforts like these, Canadian trade unions continue to demonstrate their concern about the needs and well-being of their members — particularly those members with disabilities. As well, in industry settings, they have provided their sponsorship and support for employee benefit programs such as Employee Assistance and Disability Management Programs.

MANAGEMENT: BACKGROUND AND ROLE

Management is defined as the achievement of organizational objectives through people and other resources. The challenge is to combine human and technical resources in the best possible way to attain the desired objectives.

Various levels of management within an organization make up a management pyramid. Senior management, the highest level of management on the pyramid,

---

[5] National Institute of Disability Management and Research (NIDMAR), *The Effects of Disability on B.C.'s Economy* (Port Alberni, B.C.: NIDMAR 1995).

[6] National Institute of Disability Management and Research (NIDMAR), *Industrial Disability Management: An Effective Economic and Human Resource Strategy* (Port Alberni, B.C.: NIDMAR, 1992).

[7] *Supra*, note 1.

[8] National Institute of Disability Management and Research (NIDMAR), *Strategies for Success: Disability Management in the Workplace* (Port Alberni, B.C.: NIDMAR, 1997).

[9] C. Moser, "Canada's Occupational Standards Outline Two Certification Possibilities" (1999) 3:7 Back to Work at 1-2.

is composed of the president and senior executives or vice-presidents. Middle management, which includes a level of executives such as plant managers, department heads and assistant vice-presidents, is involved in developing detailed operational plans and procedures to implement the business strategies developed by senior management. Line management, the pyramid base, are the individuals who are directly responsible for assigning workers to specific jobs and evaluating their daily work performances.[10]

To be successful at any level, managers need technical, business and relationship skills. The technical skills involve the ability to understand and use the techniques, knowledge and tools specific to the industry. Business skills include planning, organizing, directing and controlling the business aspects of the organization. This includes the ability to conceptualize — better known as being able to "see the big picture".

Relationship skills are commonly termed the "people skills". They involve the ability to work with and through people to get the work done. The ability for a manager to be able to communicate, lead and motivate people is crucial. So is the ability to listen, empathize, care for and support a troubled employee in a constructive manner. As well, attention to the development of a work environment conducive to top performance by employees is key.

The term *labour relations* describes, "all the interactions between labour and management in which employees are represented by a trade union".[11] In non-unionized settings, this relationship is termed as *employee relations*.

Many managers believe that an organization is less flexible and effective when a union represents all or some of their employees. This belief stems from the perception that wages are above competitive levels, inefficient work practices rule and lower work output occurs due to strikes in unionized workplaces. However, research has shown that unions can increase organizational effectiveness by reducing staff turnover and by inducing management to adopt more efficient policies and practices.[12] Another study found evidence of productivity gains in unionized firms.[13]

The effects of unionization on organizational effectiveness depend both on the development of an effective working relationship between labour and management and on management's ability to make efficient use of labour, capital and technology. "According to an old saying, 'Management usually gets the union it deserves'".[14]

With many Canadian employers interested in managing employee medical absences and disabilities, illness and disability claims and case management in

---

[10]   *Supra*, note 2.
[11]   T. Stone & N. Meltz, *Human Resources Management in Canada,* 2nd edition (Toronto: Holt, Rinehart & Winston of Canada Ltd. 1988) at 540.
[12]   R.B. Freeman & J.L. Medoff, *What Do Unions Do?* (New York: Basic Books, 1984) at 166.
[13]   K.B. Clark, "The Impact of Unionized Productivity: A Case Study" (1980) 33:4 Industrial Labour Relations Review at 451-69.
[14]   *Supra*, note 11, at 547.

the unionized workplace has become a topic of interest. The remainder of this chapter deals specifically with this topic.

DISABILITY MANAGEMENT: JOINT LABOUR-MANAGEMENT SUPPORT

Disability management is based on relationships, and is founded on trust and mutual respect by and for all stakeholders. For a Disability Management Program to be successful, the trust and commitment of all stakeholders must be attained. These programs also depend on stakeholders taking ownership for their problems, and working together to develop workable solutions. As well, the strategies adopted for disability management must fully address stakeholder interests, needs and goals in a way that benefits all parties. For these and numerous other reasons, joint labour-management support and involvement is required.

- *In order to understand the negative impacts of employee absenteeism and disability and the positive aspects afforded through a Disability Management Program in terms of support to the employee, family and work group, joint labour-management support is required.*

Disability brings with it sizable human and financial costs to the employee, family, work group, organization and society in general. One widely-received estimate is that disability-related costs are 1% to 3% of payroll for the direct costs of short-term disability, and 0.5% to 1.5% for the direct costs of long-term disability. The indirect costs are estimated to be one to five times that amount.[15]

Apart from the dollar aspects, disability brings with it a plethora of negative impacts for the employee, family and work group that range from economic hardships, to biological, psychological, social and vocational suffering. The bottom line is that the true cost of disability in Canada remains unknown. Suffice it to say that it is far more than what people "guesstimate" it to be.

By working together, labour and management can identify the true impact and costs for their own organization. This can create a joint awareness of the magnitude of the problem, and the degree of investment required by both parties to own and address the situation.

Successful Disability Management Programs have shown that employees, families and work groups can be supported through periods of illness or injury; that effective return-to-work outcomes can be achieved; that illness or injury

---

[15]   See K. Nagel, "Total Organizational Health Costs: What Are They? What Can Organizations Do About Them?" (Presented at the Strategic Leadership Forum '99, Toronto, Ontario, 20 October 1999) [unpublished]; and B. Anderson, "Disability Management" (Seminar presented in Calgary, Alberta, 1990) [unpublished].

prevention can be accomplished; and that cost-avoidance in terms of disability costs can be realized.

- *Joint labour-management involvement and support is required in order to promote a broad understanding of the Disability Management Program, including the barriers and drivers for a successful return to work by the recovering employee.*

According to the Honourable Lawrence MacAulay, former Minister of Labour for Canada:

> Employers, employees and unions must work together in order to ensure that policies and programs that effectively address the situation of persons with disabilities are introduced into the workplace. Consultation and collaboration are important in addressing questions of accommodation and in raising awareness generally.[16]

Part of this process is to identify the specific barriers and drivers for successful disability management and return-to-work processes within the organization. By working together, employers and unions (if unionized) or employers and employees (if not unionized) can make a significant contribution toward getting a true picture of the issues at hand and toward finding workable solutions.

- *Labour and management must work together to address the corporate cultural issues that impact employee attendance and attitudes towards a Disability Management Program and helping employees to successfully return to work.*

Corporate culture is a major influence on employee work attendance and attitude towards disability management processes. Organizations that send a clear message that work attendance is important, that employees are valued, and that the contribution made by each stakeholder is vital to company success are more likely to have employees that are receptive to regular work attendance, and are also receptive to helping fellow employees get back to work following illness or injury. To develop a positive corporate culture, joint labour-management support and involvement are required. All parties must believe that they are involved, and that they are a part of an exciting and vibrant place to work.

- *Joint labour-management support and involvement will result in a trusting and positive environment in which disability management practices can successfully function.*

---

[16] *Supra*, note 8, at 13.

Trust, as already mentioned, is key to a functional relationship. Disability management is highly dependent on good working relationships. To build a trusting and positive environment in which disability management practices can successfully function, labour and management have to constantly work at relationship building and maintenance. They also need to serve as role models to demonstrate how these positive working relationships should function within their organization.

• *For decision making regarding employee welfare, group benefits and vocational future, joint labour-management support and involvement is required.*

In a disability situation, issues tend to emerge regarding the employee's welfare, vocational future and available group benefits. In the unionized workplace, these are the issues that labour and management address as part of labour relations. Therefore, it is imperative for both parties to play a role in the disability management of the ill or injured employee.

In terms of legalities, management is obliged to work with union leaders to offer effective disability management and rehabilitation services. The rationale behind this arrangement is that the union is the certified bargaining agent for the employee. The premise is based on the fact that the individual gives up his or her individual bargaining position on behalf of a stronger voice with the union. In return, the union has a legal obligation to review decisions made between the employer and employee. If they fail to do so, the union can be sued by the employee.[17]

The union, on the other hand, has the responsibility to fairly represent its member when a complaint comes forward about the employee's work capacity, or likelihood of risk due to health conditions. The employer and the union have the duty to accommodate the ill or injured worker, and that worker has the duty to be accommodated unless there is a Bona Fide Occupational Requirement, or the accommodation is to the point of undue hardship on the employer and union's part.

Thus, in dealing with employee welfare and vocational issues, all parties need to be involved.

• *Labour and management can build creative solutions for supporting employee medical absence, vocational challenges, workplace accommodations and return-to-work practices.*

"For a unionized Canadian employer with reasonable working relationship with the union, a joint disability management initiative is more likely to produce

---

[17] D.B. Mercer, "Roles and Responsibilities in Job Modification and Accommodation" (Seminars in Occupational Health and Medicine, Faculty of Medicine, Continuing Education, University of Calgary, 3 February 1999) [unpublished].

practical and innovative solutions".[18] By all stakeholders taking ownership for the problems and challenges, and by working together, they can develop workable solutions that benefit all.

* *Labour and management must be in compliance with the applicable legislation: Occupational Health and Safety Acts, Human Rights and Duty to Accommodate legislation, and Freedom of Information Acts.*

The various provincial *Occupational Health and Safety Acts* in Canada address the issue of employee personal health data collection. Employee personal health information is not to be collected indiscriminately. Only the personal health information relevant to disability management and relevant to the purposes for which it is to be used should be collected. This means that knowledge and consent of the employee are required for the collection and disclosure of personal health data relevant to disability management. Both labour and management require an appreciation of this regulation and respect the parameters involved. In Chapter 7, this topic is discussed in more detail.

According to the *Canadian Human Rights Act*, disabled employees must be accommodated within the workplace up to the point of "undue hardship" on the person accommodating the disabled employee's needs. This is a tripartite responsibility:

1. The employer must accommodate up to the point of undue hardship;
2. The union must support the employee's return to work and the accommodation process up to the point of undue hardship; and
3. The employee must seek and sustain a workable solution to accommodate his or her disability, and the employee must also provide the necessary information from the physician, and advise the employer of the effectiveness of the modified work measures.[19]

To achieve these legal obligations, all three stakeholders have to work together.

The *Model Code for the Protection of Personal Information* defines "consent" as "the voluntary agreement with what is being done or proposed".[20] While consent may be expressed or implied, organizations should seek express consent where information is of a sensitive nature. Implicit in this act, is that the person providing consent is doing so in an informed manner. Consent of the individual must be obtained unless legal, medical, security or other reasons make it

---

[18] *Supra*, note 8, at 100.
[19] Centre for Labour-Management Development, "Accommodation Guidelines" (Presented at the Illness and Disability Claims in the Unionized Workplace Seminar, 10-11 February 1999) [unpublished].
[20] Canadian Standards Association (CSA), *Model Code for the Protection of Personal Information* (Can/C.S.A. — Q830-96) (Ottawa: CSA, 1996).

impossible or impractical. Obtaining consent for the release of personal health information is a common practice in disability management. It therefore behooves labour and management to adopt a consistent approach for the consent forms and the practices used.

As for the various *Freedom of Information Acts*, which are discussed further in Chapter 17, employers and unions are advised to be aware of the issues around seeking personal health information from employees and maintaining the collected information in a confidential manner.

By working together, labour and management can develop disability management policies, procedures and processes that are in compliance with the relevant Canadian legislation.

- *It is important to be familiar with collective agreements and their impact on disability management initiatives.*

Many unions have included provisions for disability management within their collective agreements. These documents provide the governance for workplace labour practices and impact disability management initiatives within an organization. Thus, both parties need to ensure that the organization and union's disability management practices are in alignment with the applicable collective agreements.

- *Labour and management should work together on health and management issues that tend to co-exist in disability management situations and are difficult to resolve.*

Employee disability brings with it a myriad of issues and situations. Some issues are clearly health related, while other issues are a mixture of health, workplace and performance situations. Difficult disability cases tend to involve performance problems, labour relations issues and workplace discord. Each of these situations can be challenging in their own right. They become even more challenging when health problems exist and information is kept confidential.

In successful Disability Management Programs, labour and management work together with the disability case manager, often an occupational health nurse, to tease apart the health and management issues. Once identified, each issue can be addressed accordingly.

Without working together, labour and management will experience problems when the recovered employee is deemed fit to return to work in some capacity, but the non-medical reasons associated with the disability bar a return to work. By working together, non-medical issues can be addressed in combination with the medical issues so that, hopefully, all issues will be at the same state of preparedness for the person to return to work in a safe and timely manner.

- *Labour and management need to participate in developing prevention strategies required to lower the incidence of employee illness or injury.*

Illness or injury prevention strategies, which are part of a comprehensive Disability Management Program, are highly dependent on stakeholder support and involvement. In order to develop prevention strategies, all parties must understand the importance of pro-activity and prevention as means to reduce employee illness or injury, and must be willing to participate fully in the process. To garner such support from the organization, labour and management leaders need to serve as role models, and demonstrate their commitment and involvement for illness or injury prevention.

- *Labour and management involvement and support can enhance the Disability Management Program's communication capabilities of the organization.*

Open communication is vital to any successful Disability Management Program. For stakeholders to support the program, they need to know what the program is about, how it works and what the expected and actual outcomes are. They also need to know what is in it for them and why they should even care to support such an initiative within their workplace.

In terms of disability case management, good information flow among the parties involved is essential to keep everyone "on track" and focused on the goal at hand — a safe and timely return to work for the employee, or rehabilitation to an optimal level of functioning.

By working together to develop a communication strategy, labour and management can set the stage for good communication around disability management. They can also prepare for a Disability Management Program marketing plan.

- *Labour and management promote the marketing of the Disability Management Program.*

For any Disability Management Program to be recognized, a marketing plan is required. However, joint labour-management involvement and support is required to develop, implement and evaluate the marketing plan. To successfully market a program, all the relevant stakeholders must be identified along with their interests and issues concerning the proposed program. As well, a joint effort is required to determine suitable marketing strategies, messages, communication vehicles and evaluation processes. By working together, labour and management can better undertake this important process.

HOW IS JOINT LABOUR-MANAGEMENT SUPPORT AND INVOLVEMENT ACHIEVED?

To achieve joint labour-management support and involvement, the key element is to develop a positive working relationship based on mutual respect, trust and confidence in each other's integrity and willingness to work together to develop a functional Disability Management Program.

This is not an easy task, especially in settings where labour-management relations are strained. However, successful relations can be achieved by:

* identifying program champions from both labour and management to spearhead the movement towards program development;
* ensuring that the key decision-makers are at the table;
* having equal representation from both parties;
* providing disability management education to all participants so that everyone has the same level of knowledge in the area;
* identifying the current and desired state of disability management initiatives within the organization and the gaps between the two (gap analysis);
* determining which strategies for reducing/eliminating those gaps will be used and in what time frames;
* deciding on the proposed program vision, goals, objectives and desired outcomes;
* identifying and clarifying stakeholder roles and responsibilities within the proposed Disability Management Program;
* deciding how the disability management process will be managed within the organization;
* identifying individual roles within the proposed Disability Management Program through the use of an organizational chart;
* developing supportive linkages between the Disability Management Programs and other employee resources such as Occupational Health and Safety Programs, human resource services, Employee Assistance Programs, employee benefit plans and Workplace Wellness Programs;
* deciding how dispute resolution will be handled within the organization;
* developing evaluation criteria and success indicators for the proposed Disability Management Program;
* establishing evaluation measurement techniques and schedules;
* building a business case for the Disability Management Program;
* developing a communication strategy and marketing plan for the Disability Management Program;
* seeking funding and resources for the proposed Disability Management Program;
* working together to adopt and implement the Disability Management Program as designed; and
* establishing an ongoing forum for dealing with disability management issues.

The development of a joint labour-management steering committee for the Disability Management Program allows for joint involvement in the program design, infrastructure development, implementation (*i.e.*, marketing, training, communication, dispute resolution, *etc.*) and evaluation.

The functions that a joint labour-management steering committee assume are:

- establishing a program vision and philosophy;
- setting the program objectives;
- developing a program design/model;
- mapping out the process flow for the disability management process;
- developing policies and procedures;
- determining the skills required for a central figure such as a Disability Management Coordinator;
- articulating the roles and responsibilities of the stakeholders;
- identifying available return-to-work options;
- educating workers;
- exploring the needs of the various stakeholders;
- increasing the general awareness of the Disability Management Program's goals, benefits and outcomes throughout the organization;
- overseeing the implementation of the program;
- providing a dispute resolution forum;
- participating in the program evaluation process;
- recommending to the senior management/board/executive leadership team the support systems and any program needs identified; and
- encouraging preventative strategies such as an attendance support and assistance program, Employee Assistance Program intervention, occupational health and safety actions and workplace wellness initiatives.[21]

This steering committee advises and consults with all levels of stakeholders and receives advice and suggestions for the Disability Management Program. The committee also receives reports regarding the usage of the Disability Management Program to assist in assessing its overall effectiveness. The information provided to the committee and to the commissioners is population, or aggregate, data so individual employees are not identified.

The resources available to this steering committee could include Disability Management Coordinators (possibly an occupational health nurse), occupational safety personnel, human resource personnel, employee assistance professionals or liaison and internal/external consultants as required.

---

[21]   *Supra*, note 1.

INDUSTRY APPLICATION

One Canadian organization developed a joint labour-management steering committee to address the issue of enhancing employee attendance and disability management practices within their organization. Their first step was to establish a working relationship for the new team. By developing an operating charter, the members established a vision, mission, purpose, values, goals and objectives, roles and ground rules for the steering committee. This approach set the parameters for a functional working relationship, and provided an opportunity for labour and management to work together on a project and earn each other's trust.

Step two involved providing educational sessions on attendance and disability management and program strategy preparation to all the committee members. The educational sessions were intended to provide all players with similar information, and enable them to apply attendance support and disability management theories to their particular workplace setting and issues.

Step three involved the development of a customized disability management strategy for the organization. The process for strategy development that had been discussed in the educational sessions was followed. The outcome was a vision, goal, program objective, and a series of proposed actions for a disability management plan. In essence, the strategy development moved from a preparation model to an actual plan for action.

This step took considerable time to complete. Although a generic template for a Disability Management Program plan was used, adapting it to suit the organization's specific needs was challenging. Revisiting the various aspects of the plan design as new issues came to light was time-consuming. For example, with multiple collective agreements in place, the organization identified a number of conflicts between the proposed disability management plan document and the wording of some of the governing collective agreements. These issues had to be addressed and resolved.

Another test that the committee used for the proposed Disability Management Program plan design was to assess its functionality in terms of how well it would have worked in dealing with past disability situations. By going through some of the known disability management scenarios that the organization had faced in the past, other issues warranting review were identified.

The biggest challenge for the committee was to develop a plan that could address issues such as:

* defining terms such as "modified work" and "alternate work";
* dealing with cross-jurisdictional return-to-work placements;
* budgeting — global versus departmental budgeting;
* worker replacement costs — who assumes the cost;
* re-training costs for permanent placements (alternate work situations); and
* dispute resolution.

Step four resulted in the development of illness or injury prevention strategies. Through a joint approach, the committee identified opportunities for linking the proposed Disability Management Program with the Occupational Health and Safety Program, Employee Assistance Program and Attendance Support and Assistance Program. The intent was to integrate all these programs into a comprehensive approach to managing illness or injury.

Step five involved the development of a business case for the Disability Management Program. Baseline data was used to establish the current and desired states for the organization's disability costs. Targets were set for years one and two of the program.

Step six was to develop a communication strategy. Labour and management worked together to decide who the relevant stakeholders were, what information they would need to have, how best to deliver the information, and when and who should conduct the sessions. The strength of this process came from joint participation. By working together, they were able to identify all the relevant stakeholders, the messages each group would hear, and how to conduct educational and marketing activities. Their plan was to roll out the program using joint labour-management presenters wherever possible.

The last step was to devise a marketing strategy. Here again the benefits of a joint labour-management approach were evident. The organization had a number of communication vehicles, from newsletters to cheque inserts, e-mail, bulletin boards, departmental or union meetings and employee orientation sessions. The intent was to use all these available means to market the Disability Management Program.

This organization moved from a situation in which labour and management were at odds with each other, to one where they were working together towards a cause that both believed could be successfully addressed. The program was successfully developed, but even more importantly, labour-management relations were improved.

POTENTIAL PITFALLS

Not all joint labour-management relationships prove to be as effective as the one described above. Why not, you may ask? There can be a great number of reasons for ineffective labour-management relationships. The list that follows is not meant to be inclusive, but rather a smattering of the more common problems involving joint labour-management working relationships.

Union-Management Culture Mismatch

Unions, like organizations, have their own culture. Depending on the nature of that culture, the union may or may not be amenable to collaborating with management to develop a Disability Management Program. This is particularly evident with a union culture that perceives its role as always defending their members against management. Likewise, some management cultures are innately suspicious of union involvement.

Of the labour-management cultures that have been able to mesh and to form a collaborative approach to disability management, unions and management both have demonstrated a willingness to assist ill or injured workers in returning to work.

Hidden Agendas

When players come together for reasons other than to work together towards a common good, their ulterior motives can erode the trust that is needed to allow successful program development to occur.

Loss of Respect

If, during the course of program development, committee members lose respect for each other, the success of the project can be jeopardized. Loss of respect tends to primarily come from a violation of trust developed between the members. Some common causes are irregular attendance to meetings, failing to take responsibility for assigned duties, divulging information meant to be kept within the committee setting, usurping another member's authority, failing to meet scheduled activities or plans, or blaming others for one's own shortcomings.

Introduction of New Committee Members

The introduction of new players who are not adequately oriented to the joint labour-management approach and the project at hand can undermine the progress made by the committee. Any change in committee members should be handled carefully. Prospective committee members need to be fully briefed on the project, the relevant background materials and all the elements involved in the program development if they are to successfully integrate into the group.

Change in Labour Relations

A decay in the labour relations within an organization can put project development on hold. This is especially true in the development of a Disability Management Program, the basic ingredient for which is *trust*.

Breakdown in Communication

As already mentioned, open, honest communication is key to successful project management and program development. If a communication breakdown occurs, the project can be jeopardized. Likewise, communication should be timely and tailored to the informational needs of the stakeholders group.

INDUSTRY EXAMPLES

Industry examples of joint labour-management support and involvement in disability management have been reported at conferences and in print. Some notable examples are:

MacMillian Bloedel Limited and its unions (CEP/IWA) developed a workplace-based Disability Management Program, one of the first in Canada, that modelled the NIDMAR approach to disability management. The outcome was a long-standing program in which injured or ill employees were able to return to work. The outcome produced significant human and financial savings.[22]

Bowater Pulp and Paper Mill set up its Disability Management Program in 1992 through the joint efforts of labour and management. This Return-to-Work Program was built on a collaborative model: "The multi-stakeholder team fosters a strong sense of co-operation among union and management representatives".[23] The outcome was a program based on good communication and stakeholder education about available return-to-work options, and a financial success. Today, this program is still operational and seeking ways to continually improve its processes.[24]

Weyerhaeuser (1996) reported the development of a Return-to-Work Program sponsored jointly by labour and management. They used a partnership approach, and they were able to put in a Return-to-Work Program that saved them considerable money and demonstrated that Weyerhaeuser valued its people. The results have already been reported in Chapter 1 of this book.[25]

In 1996, the City of Sault Ste. Marie reported that it built a Disability Management Program founded on labour and management ownership. Their program focused on early intervention, rehabilitation and return-to-work opportunities. They have enjoyed success and openly promote the continuation of the program through stakeholder education.[26]

These are but a few examples of many successful Disability Management Programs that have been based on labour-management involvement and support.

FUTURE DISABILITY MANAGEMENT PROGRAMS: UNION IMPACT

At the 2002 Canadian Labour Congress Convention, a national co-ordinated bargaining strategy that focuses on providing workers with disabilities and

---

[22]   *Ibid.*, at iii.

[23]   Editor, "Avenor's Unions Part of Day-to-day RTW Options" (1997) 1:6 Back to Work at 4-5.

[24]   Editor, "Disability Reviews: How Bowater Keeps Getting Better" (1999) 3:7 Back to Work at 4-5.

[25]   Weyerhaeuser, "Transitional Return-to-Work at Weyerhaeuser Company" (Presented at the National Conference on Disability and Work: Solutions for Canadians, Sheraton Centre, Toronto, Ontario, 7-9 October 1996) [unpublished].

[26]   Sault Ste. Marie (City of), "Introduction to E.R.P." (Presented at the National Conference on Disability and Work, October 1996) [unpublished].

disability-related issues with a higher profile during collective bargaining, union organizing, workplace committee work and government lobbying was proposed. Operationalized in *Building a Stronger Movement at the Workplace*, the intent is to push for better wording around disability rights and work accommodation.

Going forward, bargaining objectives should include:

- Anti-discrimination, anti-harassment, pay equity and employment equity for disabled workers;
- The right to transfer or train the worker for another job regardless of whether or not the disability injury/illness was work-related;
- A move to increase employer payment and benefit coverage for LTD plans;
- Employee extended health benefits that include employer-paid prescription drug coverage;
- Obtaining employee counselling services, health services, fitness facilities, job rotation, and workplace health and safety committees;
- A return-to-work policy that covers all types of injuries/illness, and defines the available resources and supports;
- Paid sick leave;
- Provisions by the employer to maintain personal health information confidentiality; and
- The existence of ergonomic programs.[27]

The Canadian Auto Workers (CAW) has been equally proactive towards returning ill or injured employees back into the workplace. At the 2002 Collective Bargaining Convention, CAW proposed to ensure that injured and disabled workers would be accommodated in the workplace, and that jobs are changed so that the potential for re-injury is eliminated.[28]

In essence, we are witnessing a more proactive approach by Canadian unions to promote disability management and set into motion a return-to-work effort that can support their ill or injured members.

SUMMARY

The purpose of this chapter was to demonstrate the importance of joint labour-management involvement in the development and operation of a Disability Management Program. This concept is continually reinforced in upcoming chapters.

---

[27] Canadian Labour Congress, *Building a Stronger Movement at the Workplace* (Presented at the 23rd Constitutional Convention, June 10-14, 2002) [unpublished].

[28] Canadian Auto Workers, "Report on the 2002 Collective Bargaining Convention" *CAW Health, Safety and Environment Newsletter* 10:3 (May/June 2002), online: <http://www.caw.ca/whatwedo/ health&safety/pdf/hse0506.pdf>.

CHAPTER REFERENCES

I. Abella, *On Strike: Six Key Labour Struggles in Canada 1919-1949* (Toronto: James Lorimer & Company, 1975).

B. Anderson, "Disability Management" (Seminar Presented in Calgary, Alberta, 1990).

S. Applebaum, M.D. Beckman, L. Boone & D. Kurz, *Contemporary Canadian Business*, 3d edition (Toronto: Holt, Rinehart & Winston of Canada Ltd., 1987) at 257.

Canadian Auto Workers, "Report on the 2002 Collective Bargaining Convention" *CAW Health, Safety and Environment Newsletter* 10:3 (May/June 2002), online: <http://www.caw.ca/whatwedo/health&safety/pdf/hse0506.pdf>.

Canadian Labour Congress, *Building a Stronger Movement at the Workplace* (Presented at the 23rd Constitutional Convention, June 10-14, 2002) [unpublished].

Canadian Standards Association (CSA), *Model Code for the Protection of Personal Information* (Can/C.S.A. — Q830-96) (Ottawa: CSA, 1996).

Centre for Labour-Management Development, "Accommodation Guidelines" (Presented at the Illness and Disability Claims in the Unionized Workplace Seminar, Edmonton, Alberta, 10-11 February 1999) [unpublished].

K.B. Clark, "The Impact of Unionized Productivity: A Case Study" (1980) 33:4 Industrial Labour Relations Review at 451-69.

Editor, "Avenor's Unions Part of Day-to-Day RTW Options" (1997) 1:6 Back to Work at 4-5.

Editor, "Disability Reviews: How Bowater Keeps Getting Better" (1999) 3:7 Back to Work at 4-5.

R.B. Freeman & J.L. Medoff, *What do Unions Do?* (New York: Basic Books, 1984) at 166.

D.B. Mercer, "Roles and Responsibilities in Job Modification and Accommodation" (Seminars in Occupational Health and Medicine, Faculty of Medicine, Continuing Education, University of Calgary, 3 February 1999) [unpublished].

C. Moser, "Canada's Occupational Standards Outline Two Certification Possibilities", (1999) 3:7 Back to Work at 1-2.

K. Nagel, "Total Organizational Health Costs: What Are They? What Can Organizations Do About Them?" (Presented at the Strategic Leadership Forum '99, Toronto, Ontario, 20 October 1999) [unpublished].

National Institute of Disability Management and Research (NIDMAR), *Industrial Disability Management: An Effective Economic and Human Resource Strategy* (Port Alberni, B.C.: NIDMAR, 1992).

National Institute of Disability Management and Research (NIDMAR), *Strategies for Success: Disability Management in the Workplace* (Port Alberni, B.C.: NIDMAR, 1997).

National Institute of Disability Management and Research (NIDMAR), *Disability Management in the Workplace: A Guide to Establishing a Joint Workplace Program* (Port Alberni, B.C.: NIDMAR, 1995).

National Institute of Disability Management and Research (NIDMAR), *The Effects of Disability on B.C.'s Economy* (Port Alberni, B.C.: NIDMAR, 1995).

Sault Ste. Marie (City of), "Introduction to E.R.P." (Presented at the National Conference on Disability and Work, Sault Ste. Marie, October 1996) [unpublished].

T. Stone & N. Meltz, *Human Resources Management in Canada*, 2nd edition (Toronto: Holt, Rinehart & Winston of Canada Ltd.) at 540.

Weyerhaeuser, "Transitional Return to work at Weyerhaeuser Company" (Presented at the National Conference on Disability and Work: Solutions for Canadians, Sheraton Centre, Toronto, Ontario, 7-9 October 1996) [unpublished].

Chapter 3

The Supportive Infrastructure for a Disability Management Program

WHAT IS A DISABILITY MANAGEMENT INFRASTRUCTURE?

The Disability Management Program infrastructure is the system and environment within which a Disability Management Program can operate. It encompasses the corporate culture, the disability-related policies and procedures, the benefit plans, and the linkages between the Disability Management Program and other company resources. This chapter deals with these four infrastructure components and offers an industry example of how to develop a Disability Management Program manual.

Corporate Culture

The corporate culture embodies the learned values, assumptions and behaviours that convey a sense of identity for employees and management.[1] It acts to encourage employee commitment and organizational stability as desired behaviours.[2]

Depending on the nature of the corporate culture, employees, unions and management may or may not be receptive to:

- helping each other to find innovative ways to accommodate recovering employees back into the workplace;
- taking risks on certain workplace rehabilitation approaches; and
- implementing employee benefit plans that encourage a return to employability for the ill/injured employee.

As well, the corporate culture dictates what type of disability management model will be adopted. For instance, a paternalistic culture tends to adopt a model that is more company-operated and directed. Here, the onus is on the company for the person's successful return to work. This is typical of the more traditional models of disability management that were described in Chapter 1. On the other hand, a democratic culture tends to encourage employee

[1]   V. McNeil, & M.A. Garcia, "Enhancing Program Management Through Cultural Organizational Assessment" (1991) 4:6 AAOHN Update Series at 1-8.
[2]   L. Smircich, "Concepts of Culture and Organizational Analysis" (1983) 28 Administrative Science Quarterly at 339-358.

responsibility for absence and successful return to work. In this model, the company works with the employee to affect a successful rehabilitation plan leaving the employee ultimately in control of his or her situation. The direct case management model for disability management discussed in Chapter 1 exemplifies this.

In a more subtle fashion, the corporate culture affects employer-employee occupational bonding. Occupational bonding is a mutually beneficial relationship between the employee and the employer.[3] When companies have a corporate culture that promotes pride in belonging to the organization and adheres to a strong work ethic, employees are more likely to see personal value in belonging to the social group and in working for the company. They are less likely to be absent except for valid reasons, and they are more likely to return to work as soon as possible. The successful occupational bond is difficult to break.

However, the reverse can also be true. When employees do not experience corporate pride, a sense of belonging, or feel that they add value to the corporation, the occupational bond is easy to break and remaining off work on disability is more likely.

For a Disability Management Program to be successful, the corporate culture should value the employee and convey the message that all employees are valuable contributors, and that absence from the workplace is a matter of great concern.

Disability Management Policies and Procedures

Corporate policies and procedures reflect management's attitude regarding disability management, establish the parameters for the disability management practice and promote equal treatment of all employees. They are designed to facilitate the achievement of established program goals.

Management develops policies as guides for employees in the course of their employment activities. Ideally, they are consistent with the company's goals and business strategies. One of their purposes is to prevent, or help to resolve problems. For that reason, policies should be comprehensive in scope, clear in intent, fair to all, documented and readily available.

Procedures are defined actions that serve to standardize the Disability Management Program. They provide a basis for stakeholder education, clarify the process and facilitate smooth functioning of a program.

Disability management policies and procedures need to be current and appropriate for the organization. For this reason, a periodic review of their applicability is critical to any Disability Management Program's success.

Many aspects of disability management tend to be open to interpretation. Employer-employee trust and relationship issues can often cloud actions that are taken during the management of a disability situation. For this reason, the existence of clear disability management policies and procedures is critical.

---

3   D. Shrey, *Principles and Practices of Disability Management in Industry* (Winter Park, Florida: GR Press Inc., 1995).

The following sections of this chapter address the various components of a typical Disability Management Program policy and procedure manual. Illustrations are provided in an attempt to clarify the concepts presented.

Policy and Procedure Manual Components

MISSION STATEMENT

A mission statement on disability management describes the labour-management commitment to the Disability Management Program. It presents the high-level program objectives and describes the values and beliefs of the workplace towards minimizing the impact of illness or injury on the stakeholders. The commitment to allocate resources to the Disability Management Program's design and implementation is stated.

A well-composed mission statement emphasizes a collaborative approach to returning recovering employees to work. This means that all the stakeholders have a responsibility in the early return-to-work process and that they are held accountable for their respective roles.

Lastly, the mission statement acknowledges and explains the impact of the Disability Management Program on the collective agreements, grievance procedures or other internal programs such as the Occupational Health and Safety Program and the Employee Assistance Program.

An example of a mission statement is as follows:

> Company XYZ's Disability Management Program is designed to attain the best performance in both human and financial terms regarding disability management and workplace health. The program includes case management for sick leave, short-term, long-term disability and workers' compensation illness and injury; fitness to work assessments; health surveillance; emergency response; education and data management. The aim is to ensure the employee's health through active health and workplace management resulting in increased productivity and profitability and decreased absenteeism.
>
> The Disability Management Program will:
> - ensure employees have access to the best available health care services;
> - manage absences and intervene at the onset of illness or injury;
> - facilitate the rehabilitation of employees and expedite an early return to work or modified work;
> - follow confidentiality guidelines;

- respond to the corporate vision of providing employees with a safe and healthy workplace; and convey the message that employees are valued;
- contribute to employee and community morale by conveying the message that employees are valued; and
- demonstrate compliance with legislation and regulations (*e.g.*, workers' compensation and accommodation for disabled workers).

PROGRAM GOALS AND OBJECTIVES

Program goals are the broad statements central to the disability management process. Objectives are the specific aims for the Disability Management Program. They state the desired outcomes in a manner that is meaningful, relevant, realistic, actionable, sustainable, useful, measurable and result-oriented.

Each objective should be written so that it:

- is measurable;
- measures only one thing;
- is attainable, but challenging;
- is time-oriented; and
- addresses an observable behaviour.

For the successful functioning of the Disability Management Program, the program objectives should be mutually agreed upon by management and labour. By accepting these objectives, both parties agree to follow the same path.

An example of a program goal is as follows:

- *To develop an integrated and comprehensive Disability Management Program.*

Examples of program objectives are:

- *To obtain management support for Disability Management Program.*
- *To determine current corporate and employee views on disability management.*
- *To increase stakeholder knowledge and use of disability management concepts, programs and services.*

DISPUTE RESOLUTION POLICY

An inevitable part of any collaborative process is a disagreement between the parties involved. To facilitate effective conflict resolution, it is advisable to have a dispute resolution policy in place to assist with the process.

An example of a dispute resolution policy is as follows:

The Company XYZ maintains an open door policy. All employees will be treated fairly, justly and equitably. Company XYZ will act immediately should problems occur. All employees are encouraged to bring forward to management any complaints or recommendations dealing with the Disability Management Program without fear of reprisal. Any disputes, controversies, or suggestions must first be handled between the employee and supervisor.

An employee who has not obtained a solution within five business days of the circumstances has the right to bring the situation to the attention of the supervisor's immediate superior or human resources representative. That person will review the circumstances within five business days. Complaints should be documented and include all the relevant facts. The employee and supervisor will receive a response within five more business days.

If the employee remains dissatisfied with the outcome, he or she has the right to discuss the problem with senior management. If the problem cannot be resolved at this level, then the matter can be submitted in writing to the board of directors. Their decision will be final.

ADMINISTRATION OF THE DISABILITY MANAGEMENT PROGRAM

This section includes the formal duties of the people (committee members or individuals) responsible for the administration of the Disability Management Program. It includes the by-laws (rules) and the lines of responsibility and accountability. The frequency and purpose of the Disability Management Program committee meetings are also defined.

The specific policies and procedures related to disability management are also presented. Relevant policies and procedures form the standards for case management, confidentiality, documentation of personal health information, retention and storage of personal health information, and access to confidential information. These are described at length in Chapter 11.

STAKEHOLDER ROLES AND RESPONSIBILITIES

The policy and procedures manual identifies the primary stakeholders in the Disability Management Program. These include management, supervisors, employees, unions, occupational health nurses, attending physicians and human resource professionals.

The roles for each stakeholder are described, as well as specific lines of communication and reporting. An effective method of describing roles and lines of communication involves using a simple organization chart, like Figure 3.1, or a more complex flow diagram, like Figure 3.2.

**Figure 3.1: Organizational Structure for
Disability Management Unit within an Organization**

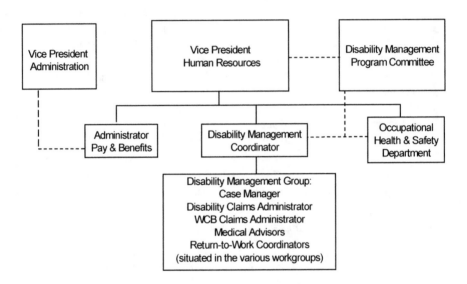

ELIGIBILITY CRITERIA

This section defines who is to be assisted by the Disability Management Program. The general exit requirements and re-entry points are also described. Figure 3.3 provides a simple decision tree that indicates when and how an employee may return to work.

Figure 3.2: Disability Management Program Process

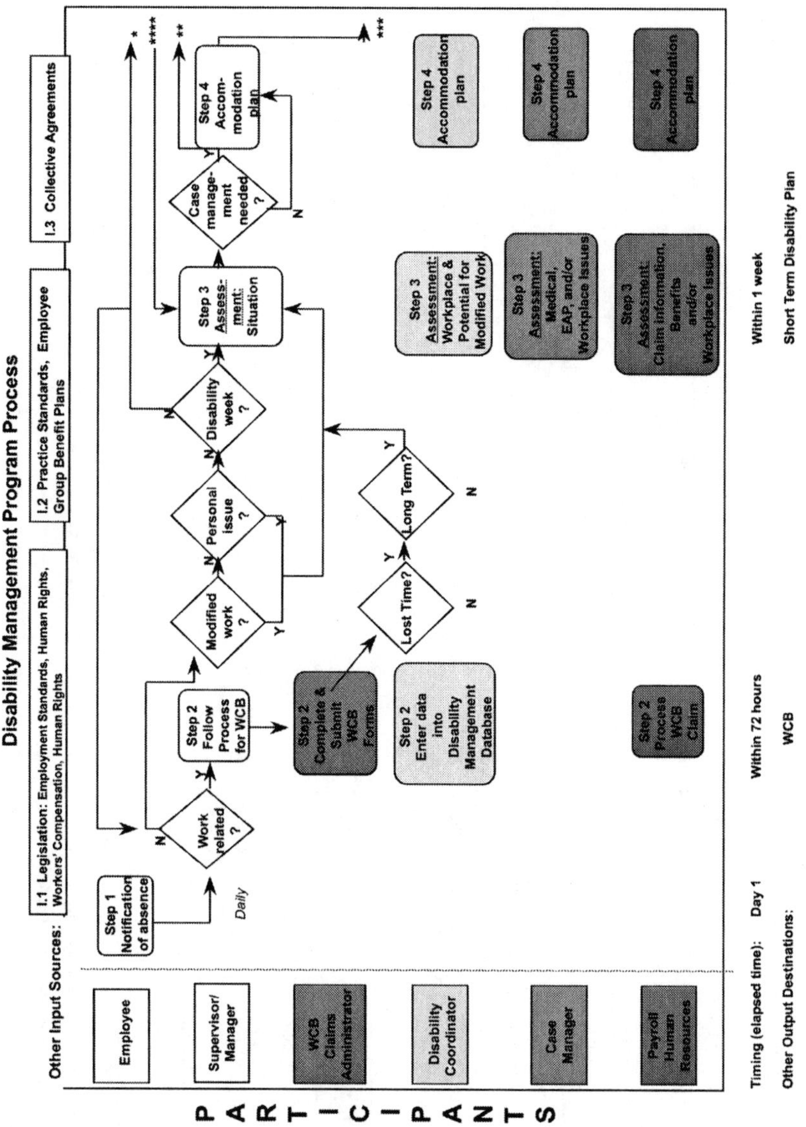

Figure 3.2: Disability Management Program Process (cont'd.)

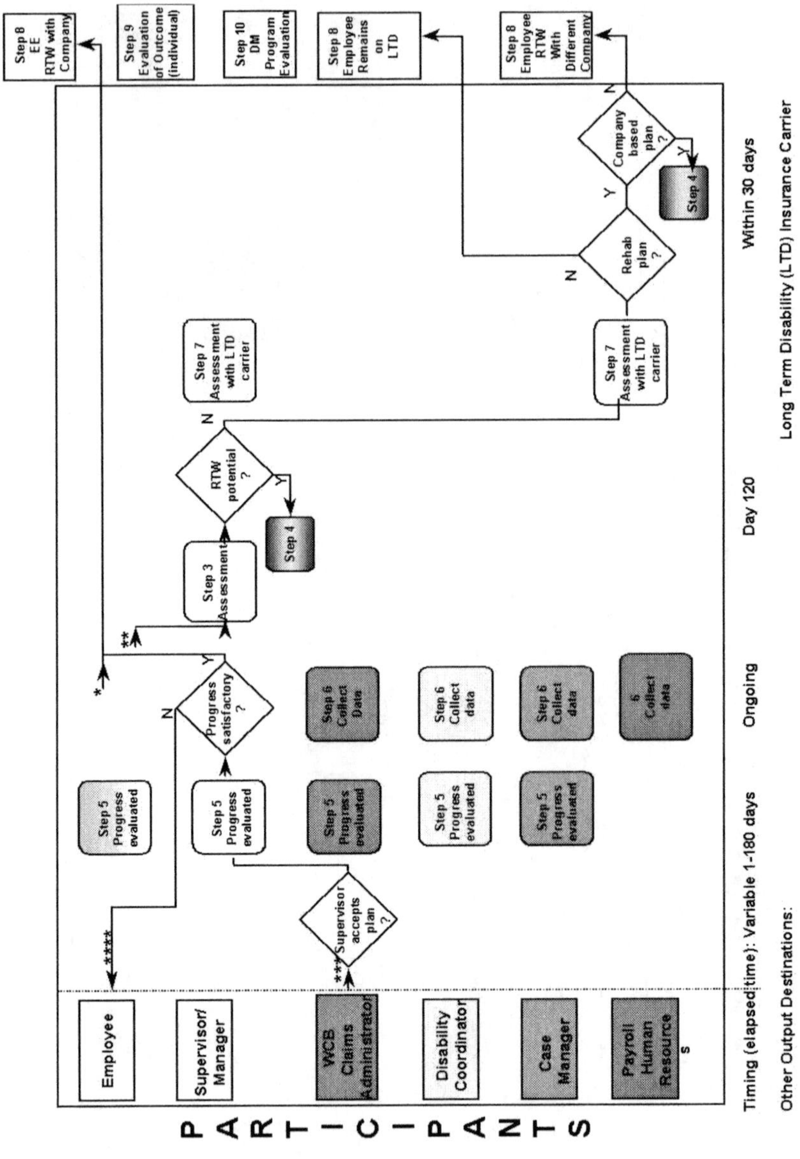

IMPLEMENTATION STRATEGIES

Implementation strategies define methods of assessment, referral points, intervention options, potential job accommodations and alternative jobs.

In Chapter 5, the assessment phase of the managed rehabilitative care program is presented as an example of an implementation strategy. It includes an assessment model that examines the personal, vocational, medical, psychological, performance, physical, educational and financial factors that impact a disability (Figure 5.2). As well, the nature of the employee's job is determined (Figures 5.3 and 5.4). The assessment phase is intended to examine the current and proposed person-job fit.

Figure 3.3: Disability Case Management Flow Chart Decision Tree

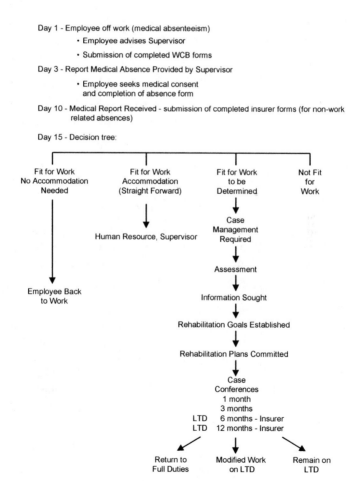

Referral points occur during the case management for a disability management case when the employee is referred for various forms of rehabilitation or vocational assistance. Graphic presentations can be very useful in depicting referral points. For example, Figure 3.4 depicts the management of the employee with a health concern, and Figure 3.5 depicts the management of the employee with a personal issue or problem. Each denotes the appropriate times for initiating referrals.

Implementation strategies also involve gathering information about the various services and resources available to support the Disability Management Program. These include Employee Assistance Programs, Occupational Health and Safety Programs, human resource services, union services, local caregivers (*i.e.*, physicians, hospitals, rehabilitation specialists, *etc.*), government or municipal agencies, insurer (government and private) benefits, in-house training programs, *etc.*

Re-entry for the ill or injured employee back into the workplace often involves accommodating the employee or developing alternative jobs. The usual sequence is:

1.   returning the employee to his or her own job with job modifications;
2.   returning the employee to his or her own job with reduced hours;
3.   undertaking alternate duties full or reduced time;
4.   working with another agency/company.

Job modifications can include adjustments or a redesign of the employee's workstation, use of adaptive devices (*e.g.*, ergonomically designed tools), use of work aids (*e.g.*, enlarged font on the computer for visually impaired employees), and/or telecommuting. The techniques used depend on the nature of the work done by the company and the resources available to facilitate job modifications.

Job modification also involves a job-demands analysis and the development of a job inventory. A job demands analysis (also known as physical demands analysis) is an examination of the various components of a job. For example, what are the sitting, standing, lifting, carrying, pushing, pulling, climbing, finger dexterity, vision, hearing, writing, speech, and/or problem solving requirements for the job? What are the stress factors and travelling demands? Each element should be quantified and qualified whenever possible. A sample Job Demands Analysis form is provided in Chapter 5 (Figure 5.4).

A job inventory is a listing of the available jobs for employees on an early return to work or modified work program. The key element is that these jobs are meaningful ones: that is, if recovering employees were not available to complete the work, then it would have to be contracted out or assigned to in-house employees. Having gainful employment available to the recovering worker is a key element for any Disability Management Program.

Figure 3.4: Management of Employees with Health Problems

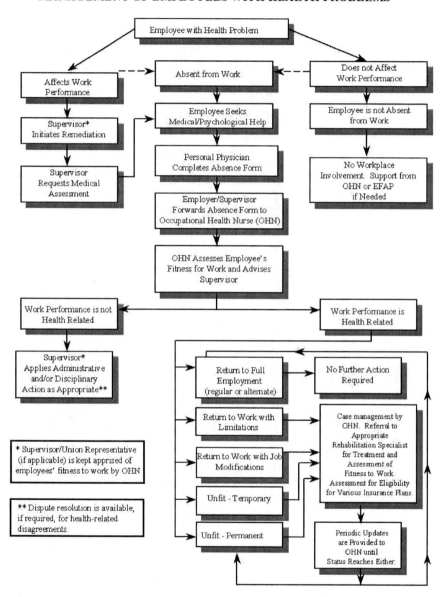

MANAGEMENT OF EMPLOYEES WITH HEALTH PROBLEMS

Figure 3.5: Employee and Family Assistance Program

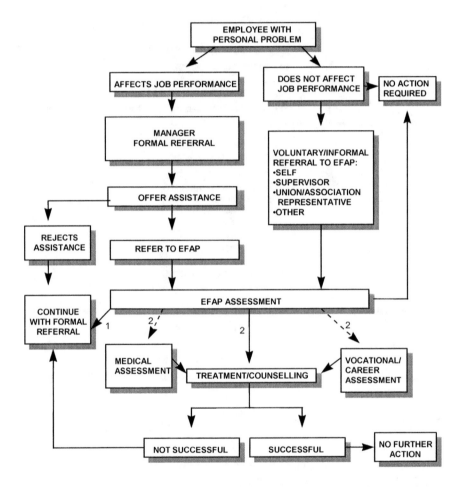

EMPLOYEE AND FAMILY ASSISTANCE PROGRAM
FLOWCHART

NOTE: 1) REJECTS EFAP RECOMMENDATIONS, CONTINUE WITH FORMAL REFERRAL STEPS
        2) SUPERVISOR KEPT INFORMED OF APPROPRIATE INFORMATION (E.G., EMPLOYEE
           FOLLOWING PROGRAM) BUT NOT GIVEN DIAGNOSTIC OR PERSONAL INFORMATION

Job finding is the process of finding suitable alternate employment for the disabled employee. This action is taken as a last resort as it usually involves work external to the company.

Lastly, the establishment of a database to collect information on the Disability Management Program is required. This database can be manual or electronic. The key aspect is that the data on employee medical absence are maintained.

The nature of the data and the types of analyses that can be executed are described in Chapters 6 and 7.

PROGRAM EVALUATION

Many people question the value of evaluating a program. Program evaluation is critical because you cannot manage what has not been measured. This section of the manual should define methods of measuring performance, and the expected outcomes of the Disability Management Program. Chapter 6 discusses program evaluation in detail.

PROGRAM PROMOTION

In the policy and procedures manual, it is important to describe the lines of communication for the Disability Management Program. The "who, what, when, how and where" of promotion should be described in the manual. For example:

Policy
The Disability Management Program should be accessible and make it easy for employees to identify their need for assistance, or for supervisors to refer employees when required.

Procedures
i.   The Disability Management Program should be promoted no less than three times per year at all worksites. Promotion may be accomplished through the distribution of promotional materials, information sessions, e-mail announcements and/or posters.
ii. There should be some form of targeted promotional material made available to eligible employees at least every twelve months.
iii. All employees who go on to disability benefits are to receive an informational package that outlines their responsibilities, provides them with the required forms and articulates their return-to-work options.
iv. Educational sessions on the Disability Management Program are to be presented as a component of the standard employee orientation and supervisory training packages.
v.   Key disability management education/training is to be provided to human resources professionals, occupational health and safety personnel, joint health and safety committee members, union representatives and similar personnel.

This section also explains the strategies that have been developed to inform the internal and external stakeholders of the Disability Management Program and of any changes that may develop.

Lastly, the policy section creates and maintains an awareness of the benefits of the workplace disability management model. This can involve regular feedback on nature of disabilities, modified work initiatives used, program outcomes, and goals of the future Disability Management Program. For example, the use of graphic representations of the Disability Management Program outcomes can be very effective (Figure 3.6). For more details on program marketing, please refer to Chapter 14.

Figure 3.6: Reasons for Medical Absence: 2006

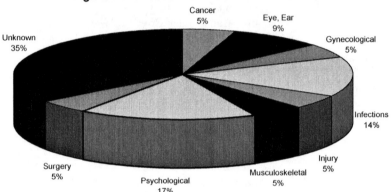

Disability Benefit Plans

A third infrastructure component is the various employee benefit plans that provide income continuance to the ill or injured employee during the disability period. It is important for all stakeholders to understand the terms and lengths of coverage for each plan, and how these plans interrelate. For example, a Disability Case Manager needs to understand the nuances of each type of plan and how they can impact a graduated return-to-work option. Although the principles of the graduated return-to-work process remain the same, the operation of these principles can be different. The following is a brief description of the typical disability benefit plans found in the workplace.

SHORT-TERM DISABILITY PLANS

Short-term disability coverage can take on a variety of forms from weekly indemnity (or accumulated sick leave plan), to short-term disability coverage. The various plans are all designed to provide income replacement for the employee during a period of non-occupationally related injury or illness. The following is a brief description of each type of disability coverage.

Weekly Indemnity

Weekly indemnity is an insurance arrangement that usually begins payments on the first day of a non-occupational accident or absence requiring hospitalization, and on the fourth or eighth day for other illnesses. The percentage of salary continuance paid depends on issues such as the taxation of benefits and corporate philosophy.

Accumulated Sick Leave Plan

For this type of benefit plan, the eligibility of sick leave coverage is directly tied to the employee's length of service. For example, for every month of service, the employee is entitled to a set number of sick leave days. These sick days are "banked" and are used for medical absences during the long-term disability qualifying period.

This type of plan is popular with public sector organizations. In some instances, employees are able to accumulate sick leave days without a ceiling, or maximum number. In others, employees not only accumulate an unlimited number of sick leave days, but also are entitled to a "payout" for the unused portion at the time of retirement.

Short-term Disability

Typically, this type of disability coverage provides the employee with a percentage of salary, usually 75% to 100% depending on years of service, for a set period of time (17 to 26 weeks, or longer). Eligibility can vary, but typically an employee is disabled if they cannot do either 100%, or the essential duties of their job. This type of plan has traditionally been implemented for salaried personnel or management staff.

LONG-TERM DISABILITY

Long-term disability plans provide benefits to employees who are disabled and have exhausted their short-term benefit supports. These plans vary greatly in the following ways:

- *Insurance Arrangement* — Is the employer self-insuring the disability period, or is a third party insurance arrangement in place?
- *Length of Time for the Qualifying Period* — The initial period of time when the employee receives short-term coverage.
- *Definition of "Disability"* — Is the employee disabled because they cannot do 60% of their pre-disability job, or essential duties of their regular position?

- *Replacement Ratios* — The proportion of the employee's net earnings that will be paid out if the employee meets the disability definition. For some plans it is 65% of the pre-disability earnings. For others, the plan may pay 66 2/3% of the first $2,500 of monthly earnings and then a lower percentage for the remaining amount to a monthly maximum benefit.
- *Tax Arrangement* — Is the benefit taxable or non-taxable? Employer-paid plans are taxable, whereas the employee-paid ones tend to be non-taxable.

WORKERS' COMPENSATION

Workers' Compensation is the government or state operated "no fault" insurance agreement between employers and workers that requires employers to be responsible for occupational injuries and/or illness. Under this legislated insurance arrangement, employers pay all the premiums and compensation in exchange for the legally binding agreement that workers who make Workers' Compensation benefit claims forfeit their right to take legal action against the employer.

The types of benefits provided under Workers' Compensation are:

- *Cash Benefits* — This includes both impairment and disability benefits relative to the impairment and the wage loss.
- *Medical Benefits* — Workers' Compensation pays for the medical assessments and treatments, along with the related prescription drug costs and prosthetic devices.
- *Rehabilitation Benefits* — This includes both medical and vocational rehabilitation. Retraining costs may be part of this benefit.
- *Job Searches* — For workers with permanent work restrictions who are ready to re-enter the job market, job search services may be provided to help them find employment or gain job search skills that will help them be competitive in the job market. According to the Alberta Workers' Compensation Board, these services may include help with resume writing, employment leads, and job search and employment skills counselling (employment search techniques, interview skills, presenting a business-like appearance, *etc.*).

Linkages Between the Disability Management Program and Other Company Resources

A Disability Management Program is part of the business system functioning within a company. It operates with, and is affected by, other system components such as employee pension and compensation, employee benefits, Workers' Compensation Board claims management, human resource support, labour union/association support, business operations, Employee Assistance Program, employee fitness facilities, Occupational Health and Safety Programs, corporate counsel support, *etc.* The Disability Management Program needs to be aligned with these business systems and operate according to the general system rules in place within the organization.

In many companies, however, the Disability Management Program works in isolation from the other business activities and from the other employee supports. At times, this isolation can result in programs that work in opposition to each other, rather than in a synergistic fashion. One way to deal with this is to use a flow chart to map out the disability management processes and to identify all the players involved and their optimal time of involvement (Figures 3.2 or 3.3).

One natural linkage is the Disability Management Program with the Employee Assistance Program. Chapter 8 emphasizes the importance of a linkage between a Disability Management Program and the Employee Assistance Program. By aligning the efforts of both programs, employees and employers are served in the most effective and efficient manner.

DISABILITY MANAGEMENT PROGRAM MANUAL DEVELOPMENT: AN INDUSTRY EXAMPLE

For a Disability Management Program to be successfully operated, it requires a number of policies and procedures. As already mentioned, they function to treat employees fairly and equitably, to communicate the rules and regulations that are in place, and to facilitate the functioning of the disability management process. The pages that follow provide some examples of the issues and concerns that a company, like Company XYZ, needs to consider when developing its disability management policies and procedures. Appendix 1 contains an actual example for the reader to observe. The format used is that of a typical policy and procedure manual.

Preliminary Concerns

The following policies are only useful to a company if they are accepted, endorsed and supported by senior management, union leaders and all employees. To create acceptance, we recommend that a company:

- have a committee review and modify the policies to meet stakeholder needs;
- communicate the policies to all employees;
- implement the policies in a unified manner to all employees;
- evaluate their impact; and
- modify and readjust the policies as required.

Development and Maintenance of the Policy Manual

Senior management, human resource practitioners and union leaders, if applicable, must be directly involved in the development of company policies and their presentation to employees. This is one way to get "buying" on the success of the total process. Management, human resources and union involvement ensure greater understanding of the policy by those required to interpret and to administer it, provides insight into employee concerns, and promotes employer-employee communication.

Where practical, a committee should be selected from employees, union representatives, and from middle to senior management. The size of the committee varies depending on management's willingness to broaden the process. Broader representation brings different viewpoints and perspectives to the discussions and helps to develop a better set of policies. The involvement of senior management ensures that the corporate philosophies regarding business, production and employee satisfaction are found within the manual. Chapter 4 contains specifics on the role of a Disability Management Program Committee.

Some suggestions that the Disability Management Program Committee may choose to consider when developing the policy manual are:

- Meet with senior management and union leaders to delineate what is to be accomplished by the guidelines.
- Select a person on the committee to coordinate the development of the disability management program manual.
- Determine which of the company's current policies are to be included in the manual and whether or not they need to be revised.
- Have supervisors/managers and union representatives respond to a checklist of tentative policies and an outline of instructions for implementing policies.
- Set deadlines for completion of the manual.

Another important responsibility of the committee is a training session to introduce the policy disability management program manual to all employees. One option is to consider an employee-orientation meeting during which:

- management and union comment on the importance of the manual and its purposes;
- one or more of the committee members involved in developing the manual presents a brief discussion of its organization, each of its policies and the reasons for including them in the manual; and
- time is allotted for questions and comments from the employees.

If the company has made revisions to any of its current policies, or is adding a few new policies, a more informal meeting may be appropriate.

- *An important part of the process, prior to introducing the manual to employees, is to have a lawyer specializing in human resources, labour and employment law review the contents.*

The manual's publication does not complete the project. As the company grows and its workforce becomes larger and more diverse, new issues need to be faced and new policies developed to address them. Similarly, changes in laws, regulations, employee benefits and other areas necessitate revisions. Plans for periodic reviews of the developed policy and procedure manual should be made and documented for due diligence purposes.

Formatting the Manual

There are several formats available for organizing a Disability Management Program policy and procedure manual. When customizing the guidelines, the following questions should be considered:

- What image does the company want to portray to employees?
- Will the manual be presented in hardcopy or electronic format?
- How often are major revisions to the manual anticipated?
- What will be the maintenance method for the manual? Will manuals be returned to one location for updating, or distributed to employees who will be expected to maintain their own manuals, or will it be electronically updated?

Here are some general points to consider when developing the content of the manual policies and procedures:

- Keep in mind who the policies are written for;
- Organize each policy in a logical operational sequence;
- Stay on the subject;
- Make the sentences and paragraphs brief and succinct;
- Avoid rigid formality unless that degree of strictness is desired;
- Check for user understanding. Try to be flexible and to avoid vague, unclear or indirect statements; and
- Establish the terminology for key words such as gender, organization, location, department, division and positions. These should be used consistently throughout the manual.

If you choose the loose-leaf binder format for the manual, the company name or logo should be prominently presented on each page. The section name and policy title on each page helps in organizing and referencing the manual. The use of "page ___ of ___ pages" makes it easy for everyone to determine if he or she has the complete policy in their version of the manual. The use of "issue effective date" and "revision date" assists in researching the history and changes to each policy. The inclusion of "Approved by" legitimizes the policy and signifies that senior management has reviewed the manual.

SUMMARY

Having a functional infrastructure for a Disability Management Program ensures that the program continues to operate despite changes in personnel responsible for the program, that all employees are treated fairly and equitably, that outcome measures are identified and that the program's success can be measured and reported.

Appendix 1

Disability Management Program Policy and Procedure Manual: An Example

The remainder of this chapter has been used to illustrate a Disability Management Program manual template.

Disability Management Program Manual
Company XYZ[4]
May 1, 2006

Table of Contents

---

[4]   Adapted from: *Policies and Procedures Manual* (Toronto: Aon Consulting, 1990).

INTRODUCTION

This policy and procedure manual is designed to clearly state the policies and procedures that balance employee and employer rights and expectations at Company XYZ (XYZ).

COMPANY XYZ
DISABILITY MANAGEMENT PROGRAM POLICY

Company XYZ will make every effort to promote workplace safety and employee well-being through various practices including the Health & Safety and Attendance Support and Assistance Policies. However in the event that illness/injury occurs, the Disability Management Program provides a forum for:

- managing absences due to illness or injury;
- conveying the message that employees are valued;
- intervening early at the onset of an illness/injury;
- facilitating the rehabilitation of employees while expediting a safe return to work through an early return-to-work plan;
- following confidentiality guidelines;
- responding to the corporate/union vision of providing employees with a safe and healthy workplace;
- focusing on illness/injury prevention;
- promoting the image of a caring and responsible employer/union while contributing to employee and community morale; and
- demonstrating compliance with legislation and regulations (*e.g.*, *Workers' Compensation Act*, Duty to Accommodate, and Collective Agreements).

The Disability Management Program is designed to attain the best performance in managing employee medical absences in both human and financial terms. The aim is to promote employee health and recovery through active claims and case management, and safe return-to-work opportunities.

President
XYZ Company

CONFIDENTIALITY OF EMPLOYEE MEDICAL INFORMATION

Applicable to: **All Employees**

Issue Date: **MAY 1, 2006**

Revision Date:

Approved by:

Company XYZ has established a policy for the confidential management of employee medical information.

Background Information

Employees have a legal right to privacy in relation to personal health information collected by the Company or designates.

Definitions

Confidentiality is the maintenance of trust expressed by an individual verbally, or in writing, and the avoidance of an invasion of privacy through accurate reporting and authorized communication.

Health Information is an accumulation of data relevant to the past, present and future health status of an individual that includes all that Occupational Health Services staff learn while exercising their responsibilities.

Privacy is the claim of individuals, groups or institutions to determine for themselves when, how, and to what extent information about them is communicated to others.

Designated Representative is any individual (or organization) to whom an employee gives written authorization to exercise a right to access.

Policy

Company XYZ requires that all persons who collect, maintain, handle and use health information protect the confidentiality of the information related to employees.

Procedure

- Personal health information is to be treated as confidential and distributed only on a "need-to-know" basis;
- Personal health information is restricted to Occupational Health Services staff who sign a Pledge of Confidentiality and are subject to a recognized professional code of ethics;
- Personal health information related to the management of an occupational illness/injury and a disability claim can be shared **in privacy** between the Occupational Health & Safety and Disability Management professionals and caregivers employed by Company XYZ to enhance the continuity of care and a coordinated injury management approach.
- Documented health information is the property of Company XYZ entrusted to Occupational Health Services staff for safeguarding and protection of confidentiality;
- Information will not be released without the written consent of the employee.
- Employees have the right to access all information regarding his/her health and fitness;
- Disclosure of all other employee personal health information will be considered a breach of confidentiality and will be reported to the Director, Human Resources, and may result in disciplinary action including immediate termination of employment **with cause**.
- All health information is to be stored separately from other employee information.
- All computerized health information is to be secured using passwords and access codes.
- Management Disclosure is having health information released to management and is limited to the following:
  - report of employee fitness to work;
  - determination that a medical condition exists and that the employee is under medical care;
  - time that the employee has been or is expected to be off work;
  - medical limitation/restrictions, if any, to carry out work in a safe and timely manner;
- Should disclosure be necessary because of a clear danger to the employee, the co-workers, the workplace or the public and:
  - The employee concerned consistently refuses to give consent, and
  - A second opinion is obtained from the employee's personal physician when the concern is for the health of the employee or to fellow employees, or from the Medical Officer of Health when the risk is to the public, the Occupational Health Services may make the disclosure to the appropriate manager after giving notice in writing to the employee, indicating that confidential information will be disclosed.
- Destruction of records will render them completely and permanently unidentifiable through destruction by burning, shredding, or automated erasure.

- The Director, Human Resources is responsible for ensuring that the Company XYZ staff involved in Disability Management are aware of and have signed the Pledge of Confidentiality.

INDEPENDENT MEDICAL EXAMINATION

Applicable to: **All Employees**

Issue Date: **MAY 1, 2006**

Revision Date:

Approved by:

Company XYZ has established a step-by-step process for requesting a secondary medical assessment of an employee for an absence due to illness or disability.

Background Information

Company XYZ, as the employer, has the right to ensure that its short-term disability plan is being well run. Part of that process is to ensure that the adjudication of disability claims proceeds so that only those employees who match the pre-defined criteria are eligible for benefits. IMEs can be an integral part of the adjudication process.

Definition

IMEs are third party medical examinations of employees who are presently receiving or have applied for disability benefits. Their purpose is to determine the employee's level of disability, length of disability, and to make recommendations regarding possible rehabilitation and modified work programs.

Policy

An employee may be required to attend a medical assessment under the following circumstances:

(i)   to determine the employee's medical status;
(ii)   to obtain a second medical opinion;
(iii)   to determine the employee's fitness for work;

(iv) to determine the length of time the employee may be absent from work in order to allow for adequate replacement resources;

(v) to determine the employee's restrictions and/or limitations;

(vi) to develop a rehabilitation strategy, if necessary;

(vii) to ensure that the employee can return to work safely and productively fit;

(viii) if the disabling condition claimed for is not usually totally disabling;

(ix) if the actual or estimated period of disability is longer than usual for the identified disabling condition;

(x) if the physician's diagnosis or symptoms are vague rather than a firm diagnosis;

(xi) if the return-to-work date cannot be provided by the physician or is shown as unknown or indefinite; and

(xii) if benefits are applied for when it is convenient not to be at work (lay-offs, strikes, holidays).

Upon receipt of the completed medical assessment, the case manager for disability will advise the supervisor if the employee is fit to return to work and the date of the return.

Costs associated with this type of assessment will be paid by Company XYZ. This does not include the cost of medicals required for insurance purposes.

GRADUATED RETURN-TO-WORK POLICY

Applicable to: **All Employees**

Issue Date: **MAY 1, 2006**

Revision Date:

Approved by:

Company XYZ is committed to helping its disabled employees return to productive work in a safe and timely manner. Company XYZ strives to assist its disabled employees to return to work as soon as they are physically capable. Company XYZ adheres to the general duty to accommodate disabled employees up to the point of undue hardship. Company XYZ has created its modified return-to-work policy to help employees with the transition from being disabled to being fully employed.

Background Information

The goal of a Graduated Return-to-Work Program is to return the injured employee back to work in a safe and timely manner which is cost-effective and accommodates the employee's identified work limitations whenever possible. Rehabilitation following an illness/injury encompasses many things including: social, physical, and psychological well-being. Ideally, a Graduated Return-to-Work Program is considered as part of an overall rehabilitation plan.

Some of the benefits of a Graduated Return-to-Work Program are:

1. increased productivity, as skilled workers stay at work or return to work more quickly after their injury;
2. financial independence for the employee and enhanced feelings of self-worth;
3. greater commitment to health and safety issues from both the employer and the employee;
4. decreased lost time per Workers' Compensation claim and a corresponding decrease in Workers' Compensation costs; and
5. a decrease in Short-term Disability and Long-term Disability costs.

The organizations with successful Graduated Return-to-Work Programs:

• recognize the potential of the injured employee;
• recognize that it is good business practice to have modified work (MW) and alternate work (AW) options available; and
• seek and receive support from all areas of management, union, and employee representation.

Program Manager

Critical for the success of a Graduated Return-to-Work Program, is for the company to choose one person to manage the process — a program champion. This person should have the following characteristics:

• be accepted by both management, union/bargaining group, and employees;
• be knowledgeable about the various jobs available within the company; and
• be able to speak to groups of employers and managers to convince them of the importance of a Graduated Return-to-Work Program; and
• be able to liaise with managers, union representatives, physicians, and rehabilitation specialists.

Policy

To provide a fair and consistent policy for recovering employees who have been ill/injured, Company XYZ recognizes the benefits of a Graduated Return-to-Work Program.

Company XYZ therefore undertakes to provide meaningful employment for both permanently and temporarily disabled employees, thereby returning valuable Human Resources benefits, and productivity into Company XYZ.

Steps

1. DEVELOP AN ACCIDENT HISTORY

This includes:

a) the annual number of accidents over the past five years;
b) trends in the number of reported accidents or in the type of work done by accident victims;
c) statistics on repeat accidents; and
d) the nature of reported injuries and the circumstances under which they occur.

This information is used to improve Company XYZ's Occupational Safety record, and to determine the most common types of physical restrictions that the Graduated Return-to-Work Program will have to accommodate.

2. IDENTIFY JOBS SUITABLE FOR A GRADUATED RETURN-TO-WORK PROGRAM

After determining the most common types of physical restrictions faced by injured employees, the process of identifying jobs that can accommodate common workplace restrictions begins.

A list of potential suitable jobs or tasks from each department or line supervisor is requested. These can be jobs or tasks that are done regularly, on a full-time or part-time basis. The work should be both meaningful and productive. In other words, contributes to Company operations and provides the employee with a goal-oriented job and rehabilitation opportunity.

Although it is easiest and most preferable to have an injured employee return to his/her own department for modified work, this is not always possible. Therefore, a cross-reference to other possible modified/alternate jobs by physical demands needs to be made.

3. COMPLETE A PHYSICAL DEMANDS ANALYSIS

A basic physical and psychological demands analysis on each job will be done so that person/job matching can be done.

The results of the Physical Demands Analysis can then be compared to the relevant data on reported injuries in the Company XYZ's work site accident profile. From this comparison, the jobs that can best accommodate the most common types of physical restriction faced by injured employees are identified.

4. DEVELOP AN INDIVIDUAL PROGRAM FOR THE EMPLOYEE

Since every injured employee has different requirements for modified/alternate work, individual programs have to be developed. This is the responsibility of the supervisor, union representative and employee with input from the Occupational Health Nurse, third party Claims Manager, Human Resources, and Program Manager.

A)   establish the physical capabilities of the employee;
B)   determine the duration of the program;
C)   select appropriate work;
D)   decide what workplace modifications/accommodations are needed; and
E)   create a new job, if necessary.

A) Establish physical capabilities of the employee

In consultation with the employee, the Occupational Health Nurse, the third party claims manager, and supervisor must establish what physical restrictions the returning employee will face.

B) Determine the duration of the program

On the basis of discussions with the employee and relevant personnel, the supervisor should determine whether short or long-term accommodation is required. Generally, a program of 90 days or less is considered short-term.

C) Select appropriate work

Once the duration of the program has been decided, appropriate work must be found. The best solution is to return the employee to his/her pre-accident job, with whatever modifications are needed. This option is preferable so that the employee can perform the job safely and without risk of re-injury or danger to others.

If the employee cannot be accommodated in his/her original job, the supervisor and employee, with help from the Occupational Health Nurse, should select from the list of available jobs, a position best suited to his/her capabilities.

D) Decide what modifications are needed

After a job has been selected, the supervisor and employee, with help from the Occupational Health Nurse, must determine what, if any, workplace modifications are required. Modifications may be administrative; for example, changes in work-rest periods, short scheduling or work sequencing. Modifications may be physical; for example, the addition of specialized equipment, such as reaching assists or moving controls or changes made to the layout of the workplace. Modifications may be psychological; for example, movement to a less mentally demanding position with greater emphasis on routine and manual tasks.

E) Create an alternate position, if necessary

If there is no suitable position in Company XYZ for the returning employee, a third solution is the creation of an alternate position. This requires a sound understanding of the employee's abilities and vocational aptitudes. The Occupational Health Nurse and/or third party insurer claims manager may, therefore, ask the employee to undergo vocational testing.

It is important that the alternate work position be productive, and, if possible, in the employee's pre-accident work department so that he or she can be in a familiar environment, among familiar people.

An alternate work position can be created by combining the duties of various part-time jobs that already exist. Alternatively, a new job may be created on the advice of management to cover residual tasks from other jobs. Again, a Physical Demands Analysis should be done on each task to ensure that it is suitable for the employee. If the employee cannot eventually return to a regular job, Company XYZ will decide if the newly created position should be maintained; that is, the creation of a permanent alternate work position.

5. SET GRADUATED RETURN-TO-WORK PROGRAM GOALS

As soon as suitable work is found, the supervisor and employee should meet to:

- discuss the job duties;
- set a date for the start of modified/alternate work arrangement;
- decide how long the employee will require the modified job; and
- establish the ultimate goal of the program; in most cases, a return to the pre-accident job.

6. MONITOR THE GRADUATED RETURN-TO-WORK OPPORTUNITY

The supervisor should monitor the employee's progress closely to evaluate the program's success and to make additional modifications (if required) to the job. Through the monitoring process, the supervisor can also help the employee adapt to the new job.

7. ESTABLISH PLAN FOR THE EMPLOYEE WHO CANNOT RETURN TO WORK

The injured employee may not be able to return to employment with Company XYZ. If so, Company XYZ should still take an active role in the individual's rehabilitation, particularly since it may be bearing the cost until the employee is financially self-sufficient. Usually an Occupational Health Nurse will be invited to case manage the disability.

The Program Manager should ensure that the employee's entitlement to a Workers' Compensation temporary partial disability pension, or long-term disability insurance through a private carrier is in place. The Program Manager should also ensure that a rehabilitation professional is available to the employee and should meet with both parties to establish a course of action including a program of evaluation, training and/or education, and job placement.

REHABILITATION POLICY

Applicable to:	**All Employees**
Issue Date:	**MAY 1, 2006**
Revision Date:	
Approved by:	

Company XYZ supports the rehabilitation of disabled employees. Disabled employees are actively encouraged to return to work as soon as they are medically fit. Company XYZ will support all reasonable efforts to return an employee to work that meets the guidelines listed below.

Background Information

Rehabilitation may be defined as the restoration of an employee who has been disabled by an injury, disease, or congenital abnormality to an optional level of vocational, medical, social, and psychological functioning. The ultimate goal of rehabilitation is the return of the disabled employee to the workplace with the maximal use of his or her capacities.

Rehabilitation, to be successful, has to be a managed process with mutual understanding and commitment between the supervisor, the employee and the rehabilitation specialists. In practical terms, this means a written rehabilitation plan agreed upon by all parties. The plan must identify a job goal and the therapy, training and job modification needed to achieve this goal. As well, a reasonable schedule against which to measure progress must be established.

Policy

The Company recognizes that rehabilitation:

1. is a cost effective way of supporting disability management;
2. improves employee productivity because experienced workers are returned to work more quickly;
3. reduces absenteeism and lost time frequency; and
4. may improve employee morale because the organization is demonstrating to its employees that it is concerned with their welfare and their prompt return to work.

Note: *Management might want to consider that in the short-term, a supervisor's main goal is productivity and a disabled employee's is income maintenance. Management has to examine the current initiative systems, such as the employee's pay while absent and the supervisor's need for fully productive employees, to ensure that both parties are encouraged to work within the policy.*

Some common disincentives to implementing rehabilitation are:

1. *Benefits under sick leave are usually paid from a corporate account. Savings from returning an employee to work are credited to the corporate account. Rehabilitation and workstation modification are often paid from department cost, effectively making the supervisor pay for rehabilitation.*
2. *Often restraints are put on staffing levels. Therefore, an employee who can only work half days, but who is counted as a full employee, reduces the supervisor's incentive to return the employee to work.*
3. *In many instances, employees are unaware that they are expected to return to work if they can perform some aspects of their duties. All employees should understand that Company XYZ offers rehabilitation programs. Then, if the employees become injured, they know they will be supported in their efforts to return to the job.*

WORKPLACE WELLNESS POLICY

Applicable to:	**All Employees**
Issue Date:	**MAY 1, 2006**
Revision Date:	
Approved by:	

Company XYZ is committed to maintaining a comprehensive Workplace Wellness policy encompassing the physical, emotional and social needs of employees.

Background Information

Wellness in the workplace means that employees are educated and the organization is empowered to manage the challenges facing them. For employees, this workplace support translates to managing both the psychological and physical issues in response to environmental stress. For the organization, it is managing both business functioning and employee well-being in a manner that allows the organization to be more resistant to environmental pressures. It is a valuable adjunct to maintaining employee "fitness to work".

The benefits of a Workplace Wellness program are:

1. It encourages employees to take more responsibility for their health and well-being;
2. It focuses attention on "high risk" workers through health risk assessments that measure such things as blood pressure, cholesterol level, and fitness levels. Thus, the organization can help employees take preventive measures to minimize the risk of disability of these workers;
3. It improves employee productivity because workers feel physically stronger, are better able to handle stress, and are less tired at work; and
4. It helps make Company XYZ an attractive company to work for.

The purpose of a Workplace Wellness policy is to minimize medical and disability costs to the organization while maximizing the physical, social, and emotional well-being of employees. The benefits of individual wellness should be communicated to employees and they should be encouraged to participate in the program regardless of whether they are considered high health risks or not.

Policy

Company XYZ believes that the health and well-being of its employees is key to its process as a company.

HOW TO ESTABLISH A WORKPLACE WELLNESS POLICY

1.   The goals of a Workplace Wellness program are:

- healthier employees,
- increased productivity,
- reduced employee absenteeism, and
- sound control of health care costs.

2.   Seek employee input

- Ask employees what they want from a Workplace Wellness program.

3.   Address problems

- Tailor the Workplace Wellness policy to address the health needs of the workforce.

4.   Utilize Employee Assistance Program resources

- If the organization has an Employee Assistance Program, it can be used to provide organizational and employee wellness support. For employees, this can include education on change management, stress management, smoking cessation, nutrition, and other wellness issues.

5.   Reinforce efforts

- Create incentives for the employee to participate in the various Workplace Wellness program offerings.

6.   Monitor the program's progress

- Evaluate the effectiveness of the policy both quantitatively and qualitatively (*i.e.*, changes in the number of disability claims, absentee rates, safety records, and program participation rates). This will help to determine if the policy is meeting its objectives.

7.   Communicate the program to the workforce.

The long-term success of the Workplace Wellness policy requires wellness to become part of the organization's culture and fabric. It must be a stated priority. The promotion of a healthy workforce has the potential to provide the organization with considerable medical and disability cost savings.

CHAPTER REFERENCES

Aon Consulting, *Policies and Procedures Manual* (Toronto: Aon Consulting, 1990).

V. McNeil & M.A. Garcia, "Enhancing Program Management Through Cultural Organizational Assessment" (1991) 4:6 AAOHN Update Series at 1-8.

L. Smircich, "Concepts of Culture and Organizational Analysis" (1983) 28 Administrative Science Quarterly at 339-358.

D. Shrey, *Principles and Practices of Disability Management in Industry* (Winter Park, Florida: GR Press Inc., 1995).

Chapter 4

Disability Management Program: Stakeholder Roles

WHY STAKEHOLDERS NEED TO BE KNOWLEDGEABLE ABOUT THE DISABILITY MANAGEMENT PROGRAM

The Disability Management Program involves all employees at various levels of the organization. To give their endorsement and support, these stakeholders need to understand the Disability Management Program goals, objectives, benefits and desired outcomes. Only by understanding the magnitude of the issues within their workplace can stakeholders provide their support and input towards a common solution.

Clarity of stakeholder roles is an essential element towards garnering stakeholder support and to ensuring a successful Disability Management Program. This chapter focuses on the roles of the specific personnel involved in the disability management process. In Chapter 4, the roles of senior management, supervisors, employees, unions and family physicians are discussed within the context of an industry graduated return-to-work application.

ROLES OF THE DISABILITY MANAGEMENT PERSONNEL

Role of the Disability Management Program Committee

The Disability Management Program Committee is a joint labour-management committee that acts as a steering committee for a Disability Management Program. The Disability Management Program Committee is the foundation of the Disability Management Program and provides support for the Disability Management Coordinator and the program.

RESPONSIBILITIES

The Disability Management Program Committee is responsible for:

- understanding the business, people and legislative drivers for having a disability management program in place;
- being cognizant of their legal responsibilities related to returning ill/injured employees to work;

- establishing the Disability Management Program vision and philosophy;
- setting the program objectives;
- developing a program design/model, perhaps like the NIDMAR model for disability management (Chapter 1, Figure 1.2);
- mapping-out the process flow for the disability management process like the example provided in Chapter 3, Figures 3.2 and 3.3;
- developing policies and procedures;
- developing and approving the skill sets required for a Disability Management Coordinator position;
- communicating the roles and responsibilities of the various corporate stakeholders;
- supporting the efforts to identify return-to-work options;
- exploring the needs of the various corporate stakeholders;
- increasing the general awareness of the Disability Management Program goals, benefits and outcomes throughout the company;
- overseeing the implementation of the Disability Management Program;
- providing a dispute resolution forum;
- participating with the Disability Management Coordinator to monitor and evaluate the program's effectiveness;
- recommending to management the support systems and any identified program needs; and
- considering preventative strategies such as an Attendance Support and Assistance Program.

This steering committee advises and consults with management, and receives concerns, advice and suggestions for the Disability Management Program from the various stakeholders. The committee also receives reports regarding the usage of the Disability Management Program to assist in assessing its overall effectiveness. The information provided to the committee and to management is population, or aggregate, data. Individual clients are not identified.

The Disability Management Program Committee membership has representatives from labour and management. The chairperson is elected by the committee for a set term. The resources that could be available to this steering committee are the Disability Management Coordinator, the Employee Assistance Program Administrator or Representative, and internal or external consultants as required.

Role of the Disability Management Coordinator

The Disability Management Coordinator is accountable for the overall management of all disabilities. This includes acting as a liaison with all stakeholders, including the third party insurers, being an active supporter of the ill or injured employee and family members, and functioning as a catalyst for facilitating the reintegration of the disabled worker back into the workplace.

RESPONSIBILITIES

The Disability Management Coordinator oversees the coordination of employee medical absences from the onset of illness or injury to the return to full-time work. This involves the overall management of the illness or injuries in the short-term and long-term disability periods. This means that the Disability Management Coordinator is ultimately responsible for overseeing both the claims and case management, and the vocational rehabilitation activities.

Working with management, unions, employee groups, human resources professionals, insurers and internal/external health care service providers, the Disability Management Coordinator leads the disability management team, which:

- assists managers/supervisors in communicating with the employee on the first day of illness/injury;
- manages the claims administration processes;
- assists supervisors in identifying the potential candidates for early intervention;
- works with employee, supervisor and union to establish recovery and rehabilitation goals and objectives;
- oversees the support provided to the employee and family members if required;
- determines if and when outside professional help is needed;
- establishes a liaison with outside professionals, insurers and Workers' Compensation Board, on behalf of employers and employees;
- helps supervisors to establish individual early return-to-work plans;
- maintains confidentiality of medical information;
- works with supervisors and the union leaders to determine modified work opportunities;
- respects the terms of the governing collective agreements in relation to early return-to-work initiatives;
- arranges for workplace modifications or job restructuring when needed, facilitates regular, open communication between stakeholders to ensure a smooth, seamless transition from short-term disability to long-term disability, when required;
- develops strategic alliances with community and internal groups;
- collects and evaluates the disability management data;
- reports the disability management outcomes to the appropriate stakeholders; and
- educates management, supervisors and employees with respect to disability management.

SCOPE AND DIMENSIONS

The scope of this position includes the management of people, functions and disability costs. The Disability Management Coordinator:

- is accountable for the Disability Management Program function and the disability management services (Figure 3.1);
- establishes communication plans regarding the Disability Management Program;
- provides focus to cost-avoidance goals and objectives by evaluating injury and illness statistics and trends, identifying opportunities to prevent disabilities and absences, developing approaches and strategies to minimize the impact of employee absence due to disability, and facilitating or negotiating modified work opportunities;
- assists in the monitoring of employee disability benefits and conducts cost-benefit analysis on the impact of disability management on employee benefit costs;
- partners externally with insurers and third party service providers, and internally with management, human resource department (*i.e.*, benefits, payroll, labour relations), occupational health and safety, unions and the Disability Management Program Committee to continually improve policies and procedures, to contain absenteeism costs and to meet legislative requirements;
- works with people and groups in crisis situations serving as a facilitator and offering innovative approaches towards resolutions that best serve the company and employees;
- develops and conducts an evaluation process of the program that considers client satisfaction, processes, outcomes and cost-effectiveness;
- is accountable for all disability management services, program communications, programs and prevention;
- safeguards confidentiality of employee personal health and disability information and records;
- identifies researchable problems with a view to disability prevention; and
- assumes accountability for personal and staff professional development and continuing education.

GENERAL DIRECTION

Program direction is generally provided to the Disability Management Coordinator through the Disability Management Program Committee, whereas the general and functional direction may come from a set department such as the occupational health or human resources department. Figure 3.1 provides a graphic example of how this could be organized. For the Disability Management Coordinator, authority should be delegated within established limits for programming, financial, personnel and material management matters.

INFORMATION ACCESS

The Disability Management Coordinator has access to confidential medical information, and is consulted in advance on employee terminations, performance issues and grievances that involve disability-related issues.

REQUIRED SKILLS AND ABILITIES

The Disability Management Coordinator must have the requisite skills and abilities to do the job. Typically the eligible candidate possesses:

- A university degree with additional certification in occupational health, and/or disability management.
- Experience of eight to 10 years in occupational health and/or disability management with evidence of progressive scope and responsibility. If this role is to include the management of the occupational health function, then a strong background in occupational health is essential.
- Knowledge of human resource functions. A certificate, degree or experience in human resource management would be a definite asset.

A full description of the skills required for this senior professional position is provided in Appendix 1. In summary, the key skills include:

- high-level technical skills;
- leadership;
- high-level communication skills;
- strong interpersonal skills;
- networking skills;
- negotiating skills;
- process facilitation;
- crisis management;
- coaching skills;
- consulting skills;
- project management;
- risk management; and
- change management.

CHALLENGES

This position involves many challenges, including:

- Managing disability costs and ensuring a quality Disability Management Program by balancing cost-containment within the company and escalating external health care costs.

- Ensuring a consistent high quality Disability Management Program and service delivery. This involves achieving the expected results, identifying problems and issues, recommending corrective actions and monitoring solutions.
- Minimizing the illness/injury costs and the disruptions for the employees and company operations through effective disability management.
- Balancing the conflicting needs of the company to meet its service and "due diligence" requirements, and of the employees' health concerns.
- Consulting with management, supervisors, employees, health professionals, and human resource professionals on fitness-to-work and workplace accommodation when there are complicating medical, psychological and personnel or labour relation issues.
- Influencing and co-managing issues with insurance organizations (private insurers and Workers' Compensation Board), medical professionals and industry organizations to best serve the company and its employees.
- Being an effective risk manager regarding disability issues.
- Coordinating disability management efforts with the company's strategic business plan.
- Working across organizational boundaries anticipating and proactively planning for major changes that would impact the company's operations, the employees and the Disability Management Program. The intent is to continually improve the disability management process and methods used.
- Planning, designing, implementing and evaluating information systems so that disability management data can be collected and analyzed, and the composite findings interpreted to management in an accurate, timely and meaningful manner.
- Scanning the rapidly changing external environment for provincial and federal legislation on disability management and human rights. The purpose is to identify trends and issues, to assess the potential impact, and to design appropriate strategies of response that "best fit" the company's culture and commitment to employee health and well-being.

Role of the Disability Case Manager

Many organizations confuse the roles of the Disability Claims Manager and Disability Case Manager. The two functions are entirely different. Disability case management *is a collaborative process for assessing, planning, implementing, coordinating, monitoring and evaluating the options and services available to meet an individual's health needs through communication and accessible resources.*[1] *The intent is to promote high-quality, cost-effective outcomes to disability management.*

---

[1]   Case Management Society of America (CMSA), *Standards for Practice of Case Management* (Little Rock, Arkansas: CMSA, 1995).

Disability claims management *is the service provided in administering income loss claims through employee benefit plans such as short-term disability, Workers' Compensation, and long-term disability.* This activity includes the determination of eligibility to receive benefits according to the definition of eligibility contained in the plan contract, the facilitation of income loss replacement and the processing of the claim towards a resolution or termination.

The Disability Case Manager is an occupational health professional who practices within an occupational setting to assist ill and injured workers in reaching maximum health and productivity. The Disability Case Manager is also responsible for the coordination of employee health care services across multiple environmental systems from the onset of injury or illness to a safe return to work or an optimal alternative. The Disability Case Manager is determined to achieve quality care delivered in a cost-effective manner. Using a unique knowledge of employees, their families and the work environment, the Disability Case Manager assesses, plans, implements, coordinates, monitors and evaluates care for clients in the Disability Management Program.

FUNCTION

The Disability Case Manager:

- assesses the broad spectrum of client needs, including physical and psycho-social factors, using data from employees and families, other health care providers, health records, *etc.*;
- identifies client (employee and employer) goals, objectives and actions in a comprehensive case management plan to achieve desired outcomes within designated time frames;
- identifies the need for vocational rehabilitation when appropriate;
- is accountable for the progression of a disability claim/case;
- establishes communication plans involving internal and external parties, as appropriate;
- implements interventions to achieve client goals and objectives;
- identifies qualifications and expectations for, and monitors and evaluates outcomes and quality of services delivered by, health care providers and vendors in the treatment outcomes;
- identifies needed community resources and coordinates referrals as appropriate;
- assists with the Disability Management Program evaluation process regarding client satisfaction, processes, outcomes and cost effectiveness;
- supports claims processing with insurance and third party representatives;
- generates consistent documentation of the case management aspects of the program;
- contributes to the assessment of Disability Management Program using company, insurance and other health data;

- acts as a professional occupational health resource for the company's management in planning and maintaining the Disability Management Program;
- assists with the development of primary, secondary and tertiary prevention and health promotion strategies to optimize employee health and prevent injuries/illness;
- assists with the establishment of criteria to identify employees for inclusion in the Disability Management Program;
- assists with the development of processes for identifying situations that require early intervention to maximize the desired outcomes;
- supports the vocational rehabilitation efforts implemented by the Vocational Rehabilitation Specialist;
- maintains and safeguards confidentiality of employee personal health, and disability information and records;
- develops and conducts educational programs to enhance case management for health care providers, management and employees;
- identifies researchable problems and participates in studies and projects according to research skills; and
- assumes responsibility for his or her own professional development and continuing education.

QUALIFICATIONS

The qualifications for the Disability Case Manager depend on the breadth and scope of the position. Typically, a Disability Case Manager should possess:

- a current licence to practise as an occupational health professional;
- five or more years of occupational health nursing experience or equivalency;
- experience in occupational health nursing, case management, disability management and rehabilitation services;
- experience in coordinating services, working with multiple organizational groups and acting as a team member to make practice judgments;
- current knowledge of laws and regulations governing worker and occupational safety and health;
- the ability to organize work and manage time effectively;
- the ability to express ideas clearly in oral and written forms; and
- a university degree in nursing, or a related health discipline, and certification in occupational health.

Role of the Disability Claims Administrator

Keeping the definition of claims management in mind, the Disability Claims Administrator is responsible for the administration of the claims adjudication process for medical absences, including follow-up procedures for the various employee benefit plans such as short-term disability and long-term disability.

In smaller companies, the Disability Claims Administrator also processes all Workers' Compensation claims. For the purpose of clarity, the roles of Disability Claims Administrator and Workers' Compensation Claims Administrator have been described separately.

FUNCTION

The Disability Claims Administrator:

- acts as resource and contact person with respect to the claims management for non-occupationally-related medical absences;
- coordinates all the related medical absence claims;
- calculates benefits payable under the long-term disability plan with consideration for any offsets, if applicable;
- prepares cheque requisitions, long-term disability cheques and employee information forms, if required;
- assists in the administration (oral and written) and interpretation of company policies to staff and supervisors;
- consults with the Disability Case Manager, Vocational Rehabilitation Specialist, medical advisor, attending physicians, human resources, claimants and departments to establish and coordinate claims follow-up;
- maintains liaison with claimants, departments, insurance agencies and legal representatives regarding claims management;
- maintains a computerized database of non-occupational medical absences;
- participates in claim appeals;
- acts as secretary to committee meetings in preparation of agenda, minutes and follow-up action as required;
- provides clerical support for the Disability Management Coordinator, Medical Advisor, Case Manager and Vocational Rehabilitation Specialist, and composes non-routine correspondence;
- assists in special projects assigned by the Disability Management Coordinator;
- prepares monthly long-term disability claims reports for budget and planning purposes;
- performs related duties as assigned; and
- supports the Workers' Compensation Claims Administrator when required.

QUALIFICATIONS

To function effectively as a Disability Claims Administrator, the candidate should possess:

- two to three years claims management experience;
- claims management training;

- experience in coordinating activities, working with professionals, and acting as a team member to make claims process judgments;
- current knowledge of the related disability benefit plans and policies, along with other related employee benefits;
- strong computer skills in word processing, database management, report generation and systems;
- the ability to organize work and time effectively; and
- the ability to express ideas clearly in oral and written forms.

Role of the Workers' Compensation Claims Administrator

The Workers' Compensation Claims Administrator is responsible for the administration and implementation of the Workers' Compensation Claims. The Workers' Compensation Claims Administrator advises the company of the appropriate process and procedure relating to Workers' Compensation; provides interpretation, advice and guidance to employees on how to proceed with Workers' Compensation claims; and is the contact and liaison for Workers' Compensation matters for the employees and departments.

FUNCTION

The Workers' Compensation Claims Administrator:

- processes any Workers' Compensation claims generated by employees;
- assists with the completion of forms and explains the claims submission process;
- advises employees as to what are their responsibilities and benefits;
- monitors progress of claims;
- keeps the departments, employees and Workers' Compensation updated on any changes to a claim;
- identifies trends (*e.g.*, repetitive injuries, needle punctures, *etc.*) in specific areas or by specific individuals;
- processes Workers' Compensation payments through payroll, making sure that dates and amounts are correct;
- verifies monthly statement of cost for the company;
- assesses the validity of all claims;
- handles the required internal processes for Workers' Compensation benefit payments;
- initiates appeals when warranted. This involves evaluating Workers' Compensation's acceptance or denial, investigating and assembling information to protest a Workers' Compensation decision;
- follows up on the claimant's recovery by:
    1. confirming that proper treatment plans are complied with until the claimant returns to work;

    2.   recommending modified work to departments and Workers' Compensation, if applicable;

    3.   advising the disability management team of any candidates that may need assistance in securing rehabilitation employment so that they may coordinate with Workers' Compensation rehabilitation; and

    4.   ensuring the proper financial arrangements are met.

- maintains a computerized database on Workers' Compensation claims and status;
- represents the company in meetings with the Workers' Compensation Board;
- makes presentations to departments and employees regarding the current Workers' Compensation regulations and benefits; and
- supports the position of Disability Claims Administrator as required.

QUALIFICATIONS

- Minimum of a post-secondary diploma in business, health sciences or social sciences with three to five years in a Workers' Compensation-related position;
- Thorough knowledge of the applicable Workers' Compensation regulations, and of the company's long-term disability plan regulations and policies; and
- Workers' Compensation claims cost-avoidance training.

Role of the Vocational Rehabilitation Specialist

Some organizations employ or contract internal rehabilitation specialists. In the model proposed in this chapter, the Vocational Rehabilitation Specialist is responsible for the coordination of the vocational rehabilitation of ill or injured employees. The Vocational Rehabilitation Specialist coordinates rehabilitation efforts across multiple environmental systems as part of the disability management team and facilitates a return to employability.

Rehabilitation is coordinated with a focus on achieving quality service in a cost-effective manner. Drawing from vocational rehabilitation knowledge, research and experience, the Vocational Rehabilitation Specialist assesses, plans, implements, coordinates, monitors and evaluates the rehabilitation care for clients in the Disability Management Program.

FUNCTION

The Vocational Rehabilitation Specialist:

- assists ill/injured employees in reaching their optimal level of vocational functioning;

- as part of a disability management team, assesses the barriers to a successful return to work, including physical and psychosocial factors, using data from clients and families, other health care providers, health records, *etc.*;
- assists the client in addressing the barriers to returning to work;
- identifies client goals, objectives and actions in a comprehensive vocational rehabilitation plan to achieve desired outcomes within designated time frames;
- maintains open communication involving internal and external parties, as appropriate;
- assists with the development of processes for identifying situations that require early vocational rehabilitation interventions to maximize the desired rehabilitation outcomes;
- facilitates the development of an on-campus network that works toward placing disabled employees back to work and toward developing a supportive network for employee assessment;
- implements interventions to achieve client goals and objectives;
- identifies qualifications and expectations for, and monitors and evaluates outcomes and quality of services delivered by, rehabilitation care service providers and vendors in the treatment and rehabilitation outcomes;
- identifies needed community resources and coordinates referrals as appropriate;
- contributes to the assessment of the rehabilitation aspects of the Disability Management Program using company, insurance and other rehabilitation outcome data;
- acts as a professional rehabilitation resource for the company's management in planning and maintaining the Disability Management Program;
- assists with the establishment of criteria to identify employees for vocational rehabilitation under the company's Disability Management Program;
- assists supervisors and employees with return-to-work issues including modified scheduling and job accommodations;
- conducts job demands analyses of company positions as appropriate;
- contributes to the prevention of workplace injuries through the appropriate implementation of ergonomic measures;
- maintains and safeguards confidentiality of employee rehabilitation information and records;
- identifies researchable rehabilitation problems and participates in studies and projects according to research skills; and
- assumes the responsibility for his or her own professional development and continuing education.

QUALIFICATIONS

The requisite qualifications for the Vocational Rehabilitation Specialist typically include:

- current registration in a vocational rehabilitation association;
- five or more years vocational rehabilitation experience;
- experience in coordinating services, working with various organizational groups and acting as a team member to make practice judgments;
- the ability to counsel and facilitate conflict resolution;
- the ability to organize work and manage time effectively;
- the ability to express ideas clearly in oral and written forms; and
- a university degree in a vocational rehabilitation discipline.

Role of the Return-to-Work Coordinator

The Return-to-Work Coordinator is accountable for working with the other team members to facilitate the safe and timely return to work by the recovering employee. This includes acting as a liaison between the Disability Management Program team and the workgroups, employee groups and unions.

FUNCTION

The Return-to-Work Coordinator:

- identifies the available return-to-work opportunities (modified work, or alternate work);
- works with the Disability Management Program team to evaluate the person-job fit for the potential placement;
- coaches the returning employee, as required;
- monitors the return-to-work placement;
- collects, analyzes and interprets data on various return-to-work placements; and
- prepares reports on the return-to-work placement outcomes.

QUALIFICATIONS

- In-depth Disability Management Program training and knowledge, ideally certified as a Return-to-Work Coordinator (Certification available through NIDMAR, Port Alberni, British Columbia);
- Knowledge of the workplace; and
- Respect and trust of the stakeholders.

SUMMARY

Each stakeholder has a role to play in the disability management process. The Disability Management Program Committee, Disability Management Coordinator, Disability Case Manager, Disability Claims Manager, Workers' Compensation

Administrator, Vocational Rehabilitation Specialist and Return-to-Work Coordinator have been described in this chapter. These are the Disability Management Program players. Their roles will vary with the size of the organization, the industry and geographic location. The roles of the employee, management, union and other key stakeholders are described in Chapter 5.

The communication of these roles to all involved is of prime importance. How this is accomplished will vary. Some organizations choose to design, or have designed, their own educational sessions, and to deliver them to all stakeholders. Others will use community educational programs to transmit the required information. Others will rely on case-by-case experience to explain disability management to the organization.

In general, the best approach is to clearly articulate what the Disability Management Program is, who is involved, what their role is and how those roles will be enacted. Without that information, the program will be misinterpreted and will not succeed as designed.

Appendix 1

Required Skills for the Disability Management Coordinator

The Disability Management Coordinator requires the following skill sets:

1.   Core Management/Business Skills;
2.   Relationship Skills; and
3.   Technical/Specialist Skills.

Core Management/Business Skills are the skills required to effectively manage people and business functions. They include planning and organization, decision-making, problem-solving, leadership, financial/business perspective, negotiating, information systems, internal consulting, process facilitation, performance management, employee development, training, change management, presentation making and risk communications.

Relationship Skills are otherwise known as "people skills" and include communication, interpersonal skills, team-building/team-work, mentoring, negotiating and reputation management.

Technical/Specialist Skills are the skills required for disability management and encompass counselling, health promotion, professional networking, fitness-to-work evaluation, human factor analysis, worksite evaluation, risk assessment, quality assurance, regulatory compliance, technical communication, case management, auditing, program evaluation, social marketing and strategic issues management.

The remainder of this appendix fully defines each of these skills.

1. CORE MANAGEMENT/BUSINESS SKILLS

Planning and Organization

The ability to set appropriate goals and objectives, to predetermine a realistic course of action, and to negotiate correctly and allocate the resources required to complete a project.

WHAT IS INVOLVED? THE ABILITY TO:

*   consider the potential problems and opportunities that may arise from the implementation of actions to prevent problems and maximize opportunities;

- formulate a desired outcome and assign resources to effectively achieve that outcome;
- visualize goals and objectives, implement activities directed toward goal-attainment while regularly monitoring and managing the process;
- evaluate the project goals, objectives and outcomes; and
- implement necessary changes.

Decision-making

The ability to objectively analyze a range of possible alternatives and to apply judgment in selecting the most appropriate course of action.

WHAT IS INVOLVED? THE ABILITY TO:

- establish requirements for the decision;
- create a range of possible alternatives;
- assess and compare alternatives based on requirements; and
- assess and minimize the risk factors.

Problem-solving

The ability to apply rational and creative approaches for analyzing and solving problems.

WHAT IS INVOLVED? THE ABILITY TO:

- identify the problem;
- determine true cause(s);
- consider possible solutions;
- isolate the solution which effectively addresses the cause of the problem; and
- implement the solution.

Leadership

The ability to influence the activity of another individual, or a group, in an effort to accomplish desired goals and objectives.

WHAT IS INVOLVED? THE ABILITY TO:

- formulate a vision and direction and translate it into goals and objectives;
- use the appropriate style of leadership considering the people involved, the task at hand, and the results to be achieved;
- lead and motivate others toward the desired results when one has formal authority to do so through position; and

- influence and motivate others toward the desired results when one has no formal authority to direct them.

Financial/Business Perspective

The ability to understand and to apply basic financial concepts (*i.e.*, profit/loss, loss control, variance, *etc.*) to the management and stewardship of the company's operations, and to understand the relevance of a specific job activity or function to the company operations and objectives as a whole.

WHAT IS INVOLVED? THE ABILITY TO:

- assess any implications, problems, decisions, plans and results from a financial viewpoint through a basic understanding and application of financial principles;
- understand the relevance of jobs, activities or functions, both internally and externally (*i.e.*, to the industry, economy and political environment), in which operations take place;
- develop priorities and work plans based on the company objectives; and
- participate in interdepartmental task forces or committees working on loss control/risk management concerns.

Negotiating

The ability to interact with internal and external parties, with a view to making joint decisions when the involved parties have different preferences.

WHAT IS INVOLVED? THE ABILITY TO:

- negotiate wisely on the issues, and diplomatically with the people involved. The discussions are two-way and designed to reach an agreement where both parties have some interests that are shared, and others that are opposed; and
- quickly understand and/or calculate the implications of proposed actions and decisions prior to agreements, and utilize this technique to improve the company's position.

Information Systems

The ability to access basic computer systems for daily activities and familiarity with the application of computer technology to disability management functioning.

WHAT IS INVOLVED? THE ABILITY TO:

- use existing computer technology (*e.g.*, electronic mail, employee health monitoring systems, loss control management systems, electronic spread sheets, *etc.*) in daily work situations; and
- apply the understanding of computer technology to develop or enhance the current disability management functioning.

Consulting

The ability to provide temporary professional help to assist a client in addressing current or potential problems or opportunities.

WHAT IS INVOLVED? THE ABILITY TO:

- help the client discover problems and to facilitate the assessment of the client's needs and willingness to change;
- ensure clarity of roles, responsibilities and resources through formal, and/or informal, contracting with the client;
- gather and present facts, observations, opinions and feelings that assist the client to define problems;
- coordinate the implementation of one or more interventions (*i.e.*, resource, expert or process) which successfully and productively addresses the defined problems in a manner that is fully supported by the client;
- evaluate the effectiveness of the intervention and identify any further actions required;
- develop self-sufficiency in the client-system in order to minimize dependence on the consultant, and to ensure a minimum of stress during disengagement; and
- assume any of the varying roles of a consultant as an advocate, technical specialist, trainer or educator, collaborator in problem-solving, identifier of alternatives, fact-finder, process specialist or reflector.

Process Facilitation

The ability to introduce and steward a process to assist a client or group to achieve the desired results in an effective, collaborative manner.

WHAT IS INVOLVED? THE ABILITY TO:

- develop methods for groups to use to examine, discuss, problem-solve, evaluate and/or come to agreements within time constraints and with available resources;

- use techniques (*e.g.*, brainstorming) that will encourage involvement of group members, yielding more information, ideas and better solutions to problems;
- create a climate in which group members feel free to express their opinions and beliefs, and will respect the opinions and beliefs of others;
- build a sense of team-work among group members which can carry over to other work situations; and
- manage conflict so that a "win-win" resolution occurs.

Performance Management

The ability to plan, monitor and evaluate the individual performance and development of the employees reporting to the position of Disability Management Coordinator.

WHAT IS INVOLVED? THE ABILITY TO:

- plan the work to be accomplished and set performance standards jointly with employees;
- provide ongoing coaching and feedback to improve performance; and
- objectively review accomplishments.

Employee Development

The ability to define the developmental experiences required to enhance an employee's job performance, and to prepare the employee for future responsibilities.

WHAT IS INVOLVED? THE ABILITY TO:

- assist employees to examine personal career interests;
- identify and initiate with employees the appropriate developmental activities (*e.g.*, special assignments, projects, on-the-job coaching) to achieve their personal developmental goals; and
- establish with employees a plan to achieve developmental goals based on realistic opportunities for development within the company.

Training

The ability to provide clients with the skills and attitudes required to accomplish a task and to keep current regarding changes.

WHAT IS INVOLVED? THE ABILITY TO:

- analyze and define the client's needs so that the training is relevant and useful;
- design training that will suit the client's needs, to know existing training tools and modify them accordingly;
- apply appropriate training techniques to ensure that participants gain the required competency and/or knowledge levels;
- evaluate the training objectives; and
- institute changes if warranted.

Change Management

The ability to anticipate and to proactively plan for major changes impacting the company's operations.

WHAT IS INVOLVED? THE ABILITY TO:

- redirect goals and objectives with flexibility and with minimal disruption to ongoing company operations; and
- provide the appropriate leadership to those affected by major changes so that performance and productivity are maintained or enhanced.

Presentations

The ability to orally convey facts, concepts and reasoning to a group, and to receive feedback from that group.

WHAT IS INVOLVED? THE ABILITY TO:

- communicate orally in a clear and concise manner in order to generate understanding by others;
- use various audio-visual aids (*i.e.*, slides, overheads, video programs, *etc.*) to enhance the communication process; and
- listen effectively to facts, feelings and intentions generated by the group, and coherently summarize group reactions.

Risk Communications

The exchange of information among interested parties about the nature, magnitude, significance or control of a risk. Interested parties include individual citizens or communities, unions, scientists, government or industry associations.

WHAT IS INVOLVED? THE ABILITY TO:

- have an in-depth knowledge of risk communication research;
- have an in-depth understanding of the knowledge, attitudes and perceptions of the target audience;
- develop trust and credibility with audience;
- organize content meaningfully and interpret risks;
- present facts and figures effectively, and organize comprehensible arguments to be acted upon; and
- respond effectively to difficult health, safety or environmental questions.

2. RELATIONSHIP SKILLS

Communication

The ability to convey facts, concepts or reasoning clearly to others, and to receive and understand the communication of others.

WHAT IS INVOLVED? THE ABILITY TO:

- communicate in a clear and concise manner to facilitate comprehension of the message;
- understand communication of others through careful listening for facts, feelings and intentions; and
- apply communication skills effectively in meetings, presentations, discussions and in writing.

Interpersonal

The ability to form and to maintain effective working relationships with individuals or groups.

WHAT IS INVOLVED? THE ABILITY TO:

- resolve situations effectively where the feelings and attitudes of others may threaten individual or group performance;
- demonstrate an awareness and understanding of people and their feelings;
- apply a practical and effective method of coping with interpersonal differences; and
- listen effectively and be willing to consider other points of view.

Team-building

The ability to plan steps designed to gather and analyze data on group functioning and to implement changes to increase group effectiveness.

WHAT IS INVOLVED? THE ABILITY TO:

- identify whether a problem exists;
- gather information on the level of group functioning in regards to task and relationship behaviours;
- analyze and interpret the data;
- decide on a plan of action;
- implement plans to move the group towards a mature stage of decision-making and performance; and
- evaluate the results.

Team-work

Team-work involves a group of people working together to pool their skills, talents and knowledge to address specific problems and arrive at solutions.

WHAT IS INVOLVED? THE ABILITY TO:

- develop a foundation of mutual respect, cooperation, open communication and flexible ties in an employee group; and
- collectively use this foundation to problem-solve, make decisions and achieve quality results and continuous improvement.

Mentoring

The process of coaching employees to learn a new role.

WHAT IS INVOLVED? THE ABILITY TO:

- guide employees towards career development both within and outside the organizational group;
- provide a supportive work experience and challenging perspectives; and
- empower employees to achieve their career goals.

Reputation Management

The process of establishing and maintaining the esteem of the internal and external publics regarding the company's disability management responsibility.

WHAT IS INVOLVED? THE ABILITY TO:

- maintain high standards for the Disability Management Program;
- support internal and external groups in their endeavours to safely function in business;

- be an active member of corporate, community and professional groups involved in disability management and occupational health and safety practices/issues; and
- support Canadian research and other efforts towards improving disability management practices.

3. TECHNICAL/SPECIALIST SKILLS

Counselling

The process of helping employees (clients) manage health and psychosocial problems.

WHAT IS INVOLVED? THE ABILITY TO:

- develop a healthy client relationship based on mutual trust and respect;
- assist the client in exploring and clarifying problem situations or opportunities for involvement;
- help the client to interpret and understand experiences, behaviour and feelings; explore consequences of behaviour; and move to action;
- contract with the client to commit to specific goals;
- provide challenging and supportive feedback to the client; and
- identify and refer the client to appropriate professional experts to enhance skill and knowledge development.

Health Promotion

The process of enabling individuals and groups to control and to improve their health.

WHAT IS INVOLVED? THE ABILITY TO:

- effectively counsel individuals to make decisions and take actions in the interest of their own health;
- motivate behavioural changes and elicit social support through effective group presentations;
- network and negotiate with external resources, as well as to analyze health and research findings in an effort to identify healthy approaches to behavioural and organizational change;
- plan, develop, implement and evaluate programs so that they become effective, efficient and quality-assured; and
- create an organizational climate which effectively responds to major health challenges through consultations, partnerships and healthy public policy development.

Professional Networking

The process of establishing relationships with community professionals to best serve the needs of employees and the organization.

WHAT IS INVOLVED? THE ABILITY TO:

- identify and maintain health-related resource lists which include agencies, organizations, professionals, self-help groups, and the ability to appropriately refer employees;
- develop working relationships with the employees' physicians to ensure that fitness-for-work standards are met;
- select and designate through agreement, or contract, specialists and specialist functions (*i.e.*, service providers, rehabilitation units, treatment centres, clinics, *etc.*) to serve the needs of the company; and
- assess the quality of services provided to the company, and to monitor the fee-for-service costs.

Fitness-to-Work Evaluation

The ability to determine suitability of an individual or group's health in relation to the job and work environment.

WHAT IS INVOLVED? THE ABILITY TO:

- evaluate physical and psychosocial health of individuals or groups;
- understand the physical, chemical, biological and psychological impact of a job on individuals and groups;
- network with internal and external resources to communicate and resolve issues;
- effectively advise individuals and managers by providing expert information, defining limitations and producing alternative approaches; and
- maintain privacy and confidentiality of medical information.

Human Factor Analysis

The process of analyzing the relationship between people, technology and organizational systems to optimize organizational goals and human health.

WHAT IS INVOLVED? THE ABILITY TO:

- assess the impact of psychological and psychosocial stressors, technology and organizational systems on human health;

- recognize the health needs of a diverse employee population, and to utilize this information when adapting workplace technology and systems to optimize human performance;
- identify individual and group health concerns, and to recommend appropriate ergonomic, organizational and system changes; and
- communicate and teach about the relationship between humans and work systems and the potential related health impacts.

Worksite Evaluation

The ability to assess worksites for physical, chemical, biological, safety and psychosocial hazards, and to recommend corrective activities.

WHAT IS INVOLVED? THE ABILITY TO:

- analyze worksites effectively for the purpose of identification and evaluation of places, processes and products potentially detrimental to health;
- understand legal, political and organizational parameters which can impact health, safety and environmental issues and solutions; and
- consult and negotiate with internal and external resources to ensure corrective actions.

Risk Assessment

The ability to evaluate environment, health and safety risks to employees and the public that may arise from company operations.

WHAT IS INVOLVED? THE ABILITY TO:

- identify and characterize risk;
- assess the risk of current or potential operations quantitatively by evaluating research and by using risk-management models;
- critically evaluate risk assessment done by regulators and other outside parties, and to determine whether appropriate theories and models have been used in their assessment of risk; and
- communicate risks and uncertainties to management, government and the public in a manner that the audience understands, and that allows for informed decision-making.

Quality Assurance

The ability to assure a high level of excellence in Disability Management Programs and servicing.

WHAT IS INVOLVED? THE ABILITY TO:

- set standards for programs and professional practices;
- monitor/audit programs, practices and results;
- interpret and evaluate data collected;
- recommend and ensure corrective action; and
- recommend and communicate positive practices.

Regulatory Compliance

The process of managing the company's statutory obligations regarding disability management.

WHAT IS INVOLVED? THE ABILITY TO:

- assess and forecast areas of regulatory concerns and their potential impact;
- negotiate with government agencies directly, or through industry associations, to address regulatory issues; and
- recommend specific actions in environmental, health and safety areas for addressing present and future operational compliance.

Technical Communication

The ability to research, analyze, transform and present technical data into a format understandable by targeted groups.

WHAT IS INVOLVED? THE ABILITY TO:

- research and analyze technical data from numerous sources;
- recognize the characteristics of risk perception to identify concerns and account for typical reactions of client groups;
- transform technical information accurately into the appropriate communication format (*i.e.*, oral or written forums); and
- communicate the data in a format understandable to targeted sub-groups (*i.e.*, unions, employees, management, community and government) and to address their questions, concerns and issues.

Case Management

The planned coordination of activities to maintain, or rehabilitate, an employee to an optimal level of functioning and gainful employment without risk to the health of the employee or fellow workers.

WHAT IS INVOLVED? THE ABILITY TO:

- identify at an early stage the employees who may require a managed, coordinated return-to-work rehabilitation effort;
- assess physical, medical, psychological and job factors, and to develop a proactive intervention approach;
- assist employees and managers with re-entry to the workplace and with accommodation strategies while monitoring the impact on their health;
- coordinate activities with community and human resource systems to effectively manage re-employment with minimal organizational disruptions; and
- collect and to provide population data reports on incidence rates and trends while identifying system issues and providing recommended solutions.

Auditing

The process to systematically examine the Disability Management Unit performance for the purposes of evaluating and reporting on company operations and of being compliant with company standards and regulatory requirements.

WHAT IS INVOLVED? THE ABILITY TO:

- evaluate management systems and processes objectively in order to determine the level of risk that exists for the company;
- compare analytical results with standard requirements;
- anticipate potential risks and to recommend proactive plans to address them; and
- communicate the audit results to appropriate parties effectively, and to take effective action on audit feedback.

Program Evaluation

The examination of whether a program has met its objectives, of other consequences that have occurred because of the program, and of whether the program's structure and activities are relevant and appropriate in terms of the program, company and government goals and changing conditions.

WHAT IS INVOLVED? THE ABILITY TO:

- use research-based examination techniques to demonstrate program accountability;
- analyze findings to improve, amend, replace or dispense with an element of the program;
- estimate the consequences of program changes;
- allocate, or reallocate resources; and
- monitor the program costs.

Social Marketing

The process of applying organizational analysis, planning and control to problems associated with social change in order to persuade different groups to accept the recommended ideas, concepts and actions.

WHAT IS INVOLVED? THE ABILITY TO:

- analyze situations through the use of quantitative research (*i.e.*, survey, polls, *etc.*) and qualitative research (*i.e.*, in-depth interviews, focus groups, *etc.*) to assess the competition and to review the current situation;
- develop communication strategies for target groups. This requires consideration of the group's psychological, demographic and health characteristics;
- position information, through the use of marketing tools (*i.e.*, public relations, promotions, distribution and response channels, *etc.*), so that it is heard; and
- measure the effectiveness of the implemented strategies on health and social change within the population groups.

Strategic Issues Management

Disability Management Strategic Issues Management links major health and safety issues to the corporate strategic business plans.

WHAT IS INVOLVED? THE ABILITY TO:

- understand the complex state of health issues and their potential opportunities and risks for the corporation;
- use an array of relationship skills (*i.e.*, consult, negotiate, interact, *etc.*) to incorporate a strategy that addresses the environmental, health and safety issues into the corporation's business direction; and
- report systematically the company's progress on the implementation of recommended programs.

CHAPTER REFERENCES

Case Management Society of America, *Standards for Practice of Case Management* (Little Rock, Arkansas: CMSA, 1995).

Chapter 5

A Disability Management Program: The Managed Rehabilitative Care Program[1]

This chapter describes the functioning of a Disability Management Program. In 1989, Marilyn Walker, BScN, coined the phrase "Managed Rehabilitative Care". "Managed" indicates that the process is monitored and controlled. The word "Rehabilitative" denotes the nature and the intent of the program. "Care" symbolizes the overall sentiment and objective for the program.

WHAT IS MANAGED REHABILITATIVE CARE?

Managed Rehabilitative Care is a comprehensive approach towards accommodating ill or injured employees back into the workplace as soon as they are medically fit to function without harm to themselves or others. Goal-oriented and gainful work is offered to eligible employees in the form of modified/alternate work on a temporary basis, or alternate work on a permanent basis.

WHY IS IT IMPORTANT?

There are many warning signs that may alert a company to problems associated with the management of short-term disability, long-term disability and Workers' Compensation Board programs, such as:

*   significant numbers of employees taking advantage of the short-term disability plan with minimal or non-existent use of rehabilitation;
*   unquestioned acceptance of report of absence claims signed by personal physicians and submitted by employees as proof of qualification for short-term disability;
*   rising short-term disability and long-term disability costs;

---

[1]   Excerpts taken from: D. Dyck, "Managed Rehabilitative Care: Overview for Occupational Health Nurses" (1996) 44:1 AAOHN Journal at 18-27. Reprinted with permission from the AAOHN Journal.

- a shift in the employee absence reasons to include an increasing number of stress claims;
- concern that there is minimal integration, or monitoring, between the short-term disability and long-term disability programs; and
- receipt of employee personal health information without a mechanism for confidential data management.

Organizations should be prepared to provide rehabilitative care to ill or injured employees in an effective, efficient and managed way.

WHO DOES MANAGED REHABILITATIVE CARE BENEFIT?

A Managed Rehabilitative Care Program benefits the employee, the company, the union, the third party insurance companies and both the provincial Workers' Compensation Boards and private carriers. In Chapter 1, the value of Disability Management to stakeholders was discussed. As was indicated, both employer and employee benefit from getting employees back to work in a safe and timely fashion. Insurers recognize this, and over the past five years they have been actively endorsing early intervention and graduated return-to-work programs.

BACKGROUND HISTORY

Thirty-three per cent of the working population will become disabled and unable to work for six months at some point in their lives.[2] Disability costs in Canada were approximately $1,112 per employee per annum in 1991 dollars.[3] Today, based on an eight-hour day and the average hourly earning of $19.86,[4] the average direct disability costs for the Canadian workforce are approximately $1,462 per full time worker.[5] In American dollars, United States employers paid $4,581 per employee as total disability costs and $2,685 in medical costs.[6]

In 1991, 63% of the Canadian workforce was between the ages of 20 and 62 years.[7] By 2001, Canada's working-age population was made up of a higher number of older workers. The number of workers aged 45-64 years of age had

---

[2] B. Anderson, "Disability Claims Management" (Seminar presented by M. Mercier at Westin Hotel, Calgary, Alberta, February 1992) [unpublished].

[3] Peat, Marwick, Stevenson & Kellog, *Data Produced on 1991 Employee Benefit Costs in Canada*, (1993) [unpublished].

[4] Statistics Canada, *Average Hourly Wages of Employees by Selected Characteristics*, online: <http://www40.statcan.ca/l01/cst01/labr69a.htm>.

[5] Statistics Canada, *Work Absence Rates, 2004* (Ottawa: Statistics Canada, 2005).

[6] Work Loss Data Institute, *Disability Benchmarks by Major Diagnostic Category* (Corpus Christi, Tex: Work Loss Data Institute, 2002).

[7] *Supra*, note 3.

increased by 35.8% and the median age of Canadian workers reached an all-time high of 37.6 years.[8]

Not surprisingly the number of lost time workdays increased as well, with older workers experiencing more lost days due to illness than did their younger co-workers. In 2001, older workers missed more workdays than did workers in any other age category.[9] This phenomenon continues today. Workers aged 55-64 years missed an average of 11.1 days, while younger workers (15-19 years) missed an average of 5.2 days.[10]

To provide a picture of what absence costs could look like, Nagel[11] estimated the indirect financial or productivity costs for employee absences per full time employee. Using 2004 worker absence data and Nagel's model, the cost of absence for companies of various sizes would be as follows:

Figure 5.1: Productivity Costs for Employee Absence

Number of employees	Days Absent (Average/ employee[12])	Wage/Day (8 hr) (Two ranges**)	Estimated Lost Time Cost (Two ranges***)
1 - 99	9.2 days	$160 – $240	$145,728 – $218,592
100 - 199	9.2 days	$160 – $240	$292,928 – $439,392
500 – 1,999	9.2 days	$160 – $240	$2,942,528 – $4,413,792
2,000 – 4,999	9.2 days	$160 – $240	$7,358,528 – $11,037,792
5,000 – 10,000	9.2 days	$160 – $240	$14,720,000 – $22,080,000

** Based on an earnings range of $20.00 – $30.00 per hour
*** Based on an end point for the range

Clearly worker absence is expensive and the reality is that short-term disability, long-term disability and Workers' Compensation Board costs are expected to continue to escalate primarily due to the aging population and the increased cost of health care.

The number of long-term disability claims has been increasing due to the impact of an aging workforce and the following six factors:

1. *Difficult economic conditions* — Experience has shown that, with a down turn in the economy, more employees opt for long-term disability. Employees with disabilities, who have been balancing work and health issues, tend

---

[8]   Statistics Canada, *2001 Census, Release 2 — July 16, 2003* (Ottawa: Statistics Canada 2003), online: <http://www12.statcan.ca/english/census01/release/age_sex.cfm>.

[9]   *Supra*, note 3.

[10] *Supra*, note 5.

[11] K. Nagel, "Total Organizational Health Costs: What Are They? What Can Organizations Do About Them?" (Presented at the Strategic Leadership Forum '99, Toronto, Ontario, 20 October 1999) [unpublished].

[12] *Supra*, note 5.

to apply for long-term disability as opposed to continuing to struggle to work.

2. *Dual income families* — Some families can manage on long-term disability benefits if at least one steady full-time income continues.

3. *Changing disabilities* — New categories of disability, "hot illnesses", have been accepted as valid reasons for long-term disability. These "hot illnesses" include conditions such as stress, sick building syndrome, chronic fatigue syndrome and repetitive strain injuries.

4. *Change in work ethics* — Long-term disability is now more socially acceptable than it used to be. [13]

5. *Changing worker demographics in the workplace* – Having four generations in the workplace for the first time brings with it increased worker medical absences and disabilities. The impact of this phenomenon is discussed in more depth in Chapter 18.

6. *Increased work demands and pressures* — Employees who could return to work doing a "basic" level of work are challenged to work at a higher level and greater work pace. In some instances, cross-functional activities are required. For these reasons, employees are unable to remain in the changing world of work.

In a time of shrinking profits and tough market competition, the rising costs of disability and Workers' Compensation rates tend to tax company budgets to the maximum. In Ontario, hardest hit by Workers' Compensation assessments and costs in 1991, the employers' average annual Workers' Compensation Board assessment had more than tripled since 1980, to $2.5 billion dollars. [14] To add to the insult, the disability dollars were "after tax dollars", which meant that organizations had to make a certain amount of product, or provide a certain amount of services, to pay for their disability costs. In short, illness and accidents were, and still are, costly.

The costs associated with illness or injury-related absences may arise from:

*   paid employee sick leave, weekly indemnity and/or short-term disability;
*   salary for replacement workers;
*   recruitment and training of replacement workers;
*   health care benefits;
*   extended supplementary health care benefits;
*   rising provincial Workers' Compensation rates;
*   long-term disability premium rates and costs; and
*   lowered productivity.

---

[13]   Great West Life, "Coordinated Disability Care" (Presentation to Petro-Canada, Calgary, Alberta, 1993) [unpublished].

[14]   R. Maynard, "The Pain Threshold" *Canadian Business* (February 1993) at 18.

In this day and age, the issues of early intervention and effective rehabilitation of injured or ill employees should be of concern to all companies. The degree of commitment that a company has in managing employee absence can, and does, directly affect the company's disability costs and Workers' Compensation Board rates. The good news is that companies can be proactive in managing employee absenteeism and can realize significant cost savings. The alternative to proactive management is a cycle of steadily increasing absence and disability costs that can erode company profits.

PURPOSE

A Disability Management Program, like the Managed Rehabilitative Care Program, is designed to maintain the health of employees and the integrity of corporate short-term disability, long-term disability and Workers' Compensation Board plans. The Managed Rehabilitative Care Program can prove to be an effective method of returning healthy employees to work while contributing to cost-containment.

The development, introduction and implementation of a Managed Rehabilitative Care framework for the organization have broader and possibly more significant implications for companies. It can:

- institute an effective administrative process for managing absences due to illness/injury;
- facilitate the rehabilitation of employees to an optimal level of health and capability through modified/alternate work and a process of work hardening thereby expediting a graduated return to work;
- convey a sense of concern for employees, and ultimately convey the message that employees are valued;
- promote the image of a caring and responsible employer while contributing to employee and community morale; and
- respond to the corporate vision of providing employees with a safe and healthy workplace, and uphold a company's social and moral obligations.

More specifically, Managed Rehabilitative Care can help demonstrate compliance with the "duty to accommodate" legislation which is law in all Canadian provinces.[15] As well, with the recent changes in the Canadian Workers' Compensation Board and human rights legislation, new pressures for workplace accommodation of the disabled worker are being placed on organizations.

---

[15] Ontario Human Rights Commission, *Guidelines for Assessing Accommodation Requirements for Persons with Disabilities* (Toronto: Ontario Human Rights Commission, 1990).

Accommodation to the point of "undue hardship" can mean workplace, and/or work-duty modifications, or even necessitate the creation of alternate positions.[16]

GENERAL FACTS

An overwhelming majority (80% to 85%) of injured, ill or disabled employees return to work without any difficulty.[17] However, for approximately 15% to 20% of employees on short-term disability, long-term disability or Workers' Compensation, their disability provokes a constellation of personal, emotional and work-related issues that may delay their return to work.[18] The existence of person-job mismatch, workplace discord and performance problems are the best indicators of a prolonged absence from work due to illness or injury.

Some of the factors associated with a delay in an employee's return to work are:

- the absence of a graduated return-to-work program;
- time lags in obtaining medical care or other forms of therapy;
- lack of knowledge on the part of the community practitioner about the workplace and what accommodations can be made for the disabled employee;
- disability insurance plans that promote a "reward" for being disabled;[19]
- unreliable methods for tracking the ill or injured worker;
- employee fear of losing disability income if he or she attempts an unsuccessful return to work;[20]
- physical pain;
- employee fear of relapse or re-injury;[21]
- employee anxiety concerning poor job performance due to disability;
- decreased self-confidence;[22]
- a work situation perceived as intolerable by the employee;
- a negative industrial relations climate;
- layoffs due to "downsizing";
- cultural differences in illness/injury response;

---

[16] L. Steeves & R. Smithies, "Foresight is Your Best Defence" (1996) 4:2 Group Health Care Management at 29-32.

[17] Petro-Canada Inc., *Managed Rehabilitative Care Program, Occupational Health* (Calgary: Petro-Canada, 1990).

[18] *Ibid.*

[19] P. Booth, *Employee Absenteeism: Strategies for Promoting an Attendance-Oriented Corporate Culture* (Ottawa: The Conference Board of Canada, 1993) at 2.

[20] L. Gross, "Managing Your Escalating Health and Safety Costs" (Presented to the Petroleum Industry's Annual Safety Seminar, Alberta, May 1993) [unpublished].

[21] *Ibid.*

[22] *Ibid.*

- a breakdown in communication between the employee and employer; and
- lack of understanding by all stakeholders of the real costs associated with disability.

Since there are many reasons for the existence of these barriers to returning to work, it takes a concerted effort by employers, unions, employees and health care professionals to overcome them.

In comparison, the factors associated with a timely return to work are:

- job satisfaction;
- mutual respect for the employee/supervisor;
- open communication between the supervisor and employee;
- existence of a Graduated Return-to-Work Program; and
- the use of a team approach (*i.e.*, employee, supervisor, union, insurance company, human resource professionals, personal physician, occupational health professionals, *etc.*) towards a graduated return to work with the employee being the key player.

The objective of a Managed Rehabilitative Care Program is to promote a safe and timely return to work. The challenge is to reinforce the drivers to return to work, and to mitigate barriers standing in their way.

Occupational health professionals have the expertise and, with management/union approval, can be given the responsibility to provide a planned approach to minimize barriers so that employees can return to work in a timely fashion without risk to their health, or to the health of others.

TERMINOLOGY

Disability is the loss or reduction of functional ability and activity consequent to impairment.[23] This is the reduction of the ability to "do things" such as performing movements or tasks.

Managed rehabilitative care is an approach towards accommodating ill or injured employees back into the workplace. Goal-oriented and gainful work is offered to eligible employees in the form of modified or alternate work. The aspects of the Managed Rehabilitative Care Program include:

- liaison between the workplace, management, union, employees, community, health care services and third party insurance carriers;
- client advocacy;
- provision of graduated return-to-work opportunities; and

---

[23] World Health Organization, *International Classification of Impairment, Disabilities and Handicaps* (Geneva: World Health Organization, 1980).

- claims management and case management.

Early Intervention is an employer-initiated response to a worker's medical absence that occurs within three to five days from the onset of the illness/injury. The intent is to facilitate appropriate and timely treatment, rehabilitation and return to work. In Chapter 1, the rationale for early intervention was discussed.

Liaison is the position, or responsibility, within an organization for maintaining communication links with external individuals, agencies or organizations.

Client advocacy is the activity associated with pleading or representing an employee's cause to management, or to external individuals or agencies.[24]

Accommodation is the process and implementation of changes to a job which enable a disabled person to perform the job productively and/or to the environment in which the job is accomplished.[25]

Modified/alternate work is the change of work duties or time to accommodate the individual currently off because of illness or injury. It is any job, task or function, or combination of functions that a worker who suffers from a diminished capacity may safely perform without risk to self or to others, which would not normally be done by that worker. The key ingredient is that the work be gainful with rehabilitation as the ultimate goal.

Modified work is interim work offered to recovering employees, or those experiencing a diminished capacity when it is medically foreseen that the employee will return to their own occupation. It includes:

- changing the existing "own" occupation conditions (*i.e.*, hours, duties, responsibilities, *etc.*);
- accommodating workplace restrictions (*i.e.*, lifting, sitting, bending, climbing, driving, *etc.*);
- providing transitional work;
- providing different duties within another occupation/worksite;
- providing a training opportunity;
- all, or any combination of the above.[26]

Alternate work is a permanent placement offered to recovering employees, or those with diminished capacity, when it is medically determined that the employee will not return to their own occupation. It includes:

- changing existing "own" occupation conditions (hours/duties/responsibilities);

---

[24] J. White, "The Evolving Role of Nursing in Patient Advocacy" *Canadian Nursing Management* (May 1992) at 6-8.

[25] NIDMAR, *Code of Practice for Disability Management* (Port Alberni, B.C.: NIDMAR, 2000), at 4.

[26] Term defined by City of Medicine Hat Disability Management Program Steering Committee, April 1999.

- providing different duties within another occupation/worksite; and/or
- providing retraining or job search assistance for movement to a new occupation.[27]

Case management is a collaborative process for assessing, planning, implementing, coordinating, monitoring and evaluating the options and services available to meet an individual's health needs through communication and accessible resources. The intent is to promote quality, cost-effective outcomes to disability management.[28] To rehabilitate an employee to the optimal level of functioning without risk to personal or fellow workers' health, involves specific goals, case coordination and evaluation.

Case management has been used in social work to coordinate and develop the use of resources and services. The same process applies to coordinating employment issues for disabled employees. Case management promotes return-to-work efforts, early identification of disability claims for services, and coordination of services, such as: early intervention, maintaining contact with disabled employees, developing modified/alternate work opportunities, monitoring modified/alternate work, coordinating issues with the insurer, and establishing vocational rehabilitation if required.

Claims management is the service provided in administering income loss claims through employee benefit plans such as short-term disability, Workers' Compensation and long-term disability. This activity includes the determination of eligibility to receive a benefit according to the definition of eligibility contained in the plan contract, the facilitation of income loss replacement and the processing of the claim towards a resolution or termination.

Rehabilitation is the process of assisting medically disabled employees to adjust to their disabled condition, and to recognize and maximize their financial, occupational and social goals.[29]

MANAGED REHABILITATIVE CARE IMPLEMENTATION

Key Stakeholders and Their Roles

A Managed Rehabilitative Care program is a company-wide effort that involves cooperation by employees, supervisors, human resource personnel and occupational health professionals. Support of the program by senior management and union leaders is essential if program credibility and acceptance is to be established.

---

[27] *Ibid.*
[28] Case Management Society of America (CMSA), *Standards for Practice of Case Management* (Little Rock, AR: CMSA, 1995).
[29] *Supra*, note 2.

SENIOR MANAGEMENT

Management's role in establishing a Managed Rehabilitative Care Program is to endorse the initiative. Once the decision has been made to develop a Managed Rehabilitative Care Program, the following key steps should be taken:

- involve the workforce in the development of the Managed Rehabilitative Care Program and obtain its commitment to the program;
- develop a company policy on Managed Rehabilitative Care and modified/alternate work;
- determine the operational relationship of modified/alternate work with short-term disability, long-term disability and Workers' Compensation insurance plans;
- reach a formal understanding with unions;
- publicize the program;
- promote the identification of jobs within the organization that would be suitable for modified/alternate work;
- support the development of Managed Rehabilitative Care protocols; and
- insist on the establishment of rehabilitation plans for employees unable to return to their own jobs.

Broad-based support for the program is important. Experience has shown that the most successful companies have taken the following measures to:

- recognize the capabilities and potential contributions that the injured employee can make to the company;
- recognize that it is good business to have a Graduated Return-to-Work Program like the Managed Rehabilitative Care Program;
- involve the employee in his or her rehabilitation process from the onset of illness or injury;
- enlist the cooperation of their unions as early as possible; and/or
- obtain endorsement, support and involvement from all stakeholders.

THE UNION

Union support of a Managed Rehabilitative Care Program is crucial. Meetings between senior management and union representatives should occur early so that an understanding about the program objectives and requirements can be reached by both parties. Issues like modified/alternate work and employee benefits while employees are on modified/alternate work are of concern to unions.

THE EMPLOYEE

The injured or ill employee plays a key role in a successful Managed Rehabilitative Care Program with the chief responsibilities being:

- advise the supervisor of an injury or illness as soon as possible;
- have a report of absence form of some kind completed by his or her treating physician;
- maintain regular contact with the occupational health nurse or company liaison working with the external insurer;
- communicate medical, social and psychological concerns that may impact the timely and safe return to work;
- take an active role in initiating and developing a modified/alternate work opportunity with the supervisor;
- obtain medical clearance for modified/alternate work;
- communicate any concerns about the functionality of the modified/alternate work experience so that potential problems can be quickly resolved; and
- when possible, schedule other activities (*i.e.*, physiotherapy, doctor's appointments, *etc.*) so they do not interfere with the modified/alternate work experience.

MIDDLE MANAGEMENT AND SUPERVISORS

The full support of middle management and supervisors is paramount if a Managed Rehabilitative Care Program is to be successful. In essence, this level of management will have the greatest impact on the timely and safe return to work by the employee. For this reason, they need to be well informed about disability management principles, graduated return-to-work practices, the economic benefits of a Managed Rehabilitative Care Program and its positive impacts on employee morale and productivity.

The key roles and responsibilities of middle management and supervisors are:

- generating a formal report of absence form when an employee is absent. This form should indicate the nature of the disability (*i.e.*, illness or injury, occupational/non-occupational); prognosis (anticipated return-to-work date and workplace limitations, if any); treatment plan (if the employee is under an appropriate treatment and compliant); and suggested workplace support (*i.e.*, accommodation needs). Sample of forms that could be used for this purpose are provided in Chapter 11, Appendix 3, Form 2a and Form 2b. Form 2a is designed to be submitted to occupational health services, because it requests confidential medical information. On the other hand, Form 2b is applicable to work settings that are without occupational health support and are limited to specific pieces of information as outlined above;
- participating to provide modified/alternate work opportunities when required;
- supporting employees working modified/alternate work;
- helping the occupational health nurse, or company liaison for an external insurer, to monitor the progress of workers on modified/alternate work; and

- providing feedback on the Managed Rehabilitative Care Program's processes and outcomes.

OCCUPATIONAL HEALTH NURSES

Ideally, one person is responsible for the overall program management and the daily operations of a Managed Rehabilitative Care Program.[30] Continuity and consistency are the keys to success of such a program.

In many companies, this role is assumed by an occupational health nurse. The occupational health nurse becomes the first-line contact with the ill or injured employee. Liaison with the employee, workplace and external professionals, client advocacy, case management and program evaluation are roles that occupational health nurses regularly assume.

The occupational health nurse's responsibilities in programs like the Managed Rehabilitative Care include:

- communicating with the employee as soon as possible after the injury or illness onset;
- working with the employee and supervisor to establish recovery and rehabilitation goals and objectives;
- determining what outside professional help is needed, if any;
- liaisons with outside professionals and the Workers' Compensation Board, if applicable, on the employee's behalf;
- establishing individual programs for workers with help from other professionals;
- advising the supervisor of an employee's expected return-to-work date, physical capabilities and work restrictions that may apply;
- if applicable, working with supervisor or management to determine if modified/alternate work opportunities are available;
- respecting the terms of an existent collective agreement in relation to modified/alternate work, if they apply;
- monitoring the progress of employees on modified/alternate work;
- collecting and evaluating Managed Rehabilitative Care Program data; and
- reporting the Managed Rehabilitative Care Program outcomes to management.

Companies that do not have an occupational health nurse employed can purchase similar disability management services from the marketplace. However, these companies still require an internal Disability Management Program and a graduated return-to-work process for the contracted services to be successfully implemented.

---

[30] R. Berresford, J. Farmery & D. Mitchell, *Modified/Alternate Work Guidelines* (Toronto: Aon Consulting Inc., 1993) at 4.

HUMAN RESOURCE PROFESSIONALS

Developing the Managed Rehabilitative Care Program policy and procedures, and employee benefit plans are typically the responsibility of the human resource professionals. However, the depth and breadth of their role is much greater than that. Ideally, it includes:

- advertising the intent and goals of the Managed Rehabilitative Care Program;
- communicating the roles and responsibilities of all the key players;
- developing the protocols required to implement the program;
- coaching middle management and supervisors on modified/alternate work possibilities and opportunities;
- developing contractual agreements associated with modified/alternate work; and
- helping with the management of returning workers when performance issues and other workplace issues impede a graduated return to work.

ATTENDING PHYSICIAN

The attending physician is an important link between the employee, the company and the Workers' Compensation Board, if involved. This professional can provide the necessary information regarding the employee's expected return-to-work date, the limitations that may apply and the prognosis of the illness or injury. Ongoing communication between the treating physician and the occupational health nurse, disability management service provider or external insurer is essential. This helps to prevent misunderstandings among the stakeholders and prolonged employee absences.

Management of Health Care and Personal Problems

A collaborative approach between the employee, manager/supervisor, union representative (where applicable), and occupational health nurse is required to successfully manage employee health problems.

When job performance appears to be affected by employee health or personal problems, the manager/supervisor can address them by:

- identifying corporate expectations for the employee's level of performance;
- reviewing the employee's actual performance or conduct;
- explaining the consequences of performance deficiencies and attempting to identify any personal or job barriers to corrective action;
- referring the employee for help if a health problem is suspected or admitted (see Chapter 3, Figure 3.4); and

• referring the employee for Employee Assistance Program help if a personal or work-related problem is suspected or admitted (see Chapter 3, Figure 3.5).

The *supervisor or union representative*, if applicable, should not attempt to diagnose the problem. They do not have the right to know the details of the employee's medical and/or personal problems. However, the supervisor or union representative needs to know:

• if the illness/injury is work-related;
• the expected return-to-work date;
• the employee's capabilities and work limitations; and
• the expected duration of any work limitations following the employee's return to work.

The *employee* is obliged to:

• provide the employer with a reasonable explanation for absence from work;
• provide the required information from a physician or other health care provider;
• seek and sustain a workable return-to-work opportunity; and
• advise the supervisor or union representative and/or occupational health nurse of the effectiveness of the return-to-work opportunity.

> *In accordance with the Canadian human rights legislation (duty to accommodate) an employee is obliged to maintain open communication with the workplace, to provide adequate medical documentation supporting the absence and to participate in safe and timely return-to-work opportunities.*

The *occupational health nurse* is the health advisor specializing in providing information to managers/supervisors on employee fitness to work, disability case management and suitable return-to-work accommodations.

Managed Rehabilitative Care Guidelines

The Managed Rehabilitative Care guidelines were designed to be applied to the case management of the 15% to 20% of employees having difficulty returning to work from medical disability, whether on short-term disability, long-term disability or Workers' Compensation. The occupational health nurse, in accordance with recognized professional practice standards, evaluates illness or injury situations with a view to a safe and timely return to work. This includes assessments of the employee and workplace situation, development of a rehabilitation plan, goal setting, and coordination of the case and return-to-work opportunities.

EARLY IDENTIFICATION OF CASES

The criteria for the early identification of employees who require case management coordination include:

- expected duration of disability exceeding one month;
- hospitalization greater than one week;
- Workers' Compensation Board claims that go on longer than one week;
- employee 50 years of age or older;
- stress as the medical diagnosis;
- diagnoses of cardiovascular, cancer, digestive, neurological, skeletal or psychological conditions;
- multiple diagnoses;
- cases which fail just before the expected return-to-work date;
- presence of labour relations problems;
- presence of pending litigation associated with the illness or injury;
- an injured or ill employee with a high rate of absenteeism; and
- any multiple of the above.

ASSESSMENT

An early initial contact with the employee is carried out to determine the potential for the illness or injury to become chronic, and to establish whether help is necessary. Some of the factors to be assessed include:

Physical factors, such as:

- physical capabilities;
- job demands;
- potential for job modification;
- potential for use of adaptive devices; and
- potential for worksite/environmental modifications.

Personal factors, such as:

- changes in the family since the onset of the illness or injury;
- the presence of a personal crisis compounding the disability (*i.e.*, legal, domestic problems, job insecurity, *etc.*);
- the health status of other family members; and
- how the family dynamics impact the current disability situation.

Vocational factors, such as:

- degree of job satisfaction
- the occurrence of recent changes at work (*i.e.*, hours, assignment, performance, availability of work, *etc.*);
- any previous work activities and other marketable skills;
- the employee's vocational interests and aptitudes; and
- the supervisor's and human resource professional's promotion of a graduated return to work.

Medical factors, such as:

- diagnosis;
- prognosis;
- treatment plan;
- expected return-to-work date;
- employee confidence and satisfaction with medical treatment;
- potential residual limitations;
- presence of pain and coping skills;
- presence of other health problems; and
- independent practitioner, nutritional guidance, adaptive devices, aids to daily living, home help, and/or home care services, *etc.*

Psychological factors, such as:

- the employee's reaction to illness/injury;
- the employee's thoughts and feelings, level of self-esteem, outlook, locus of control and degree of personal power;
- cultural factors;
- the employee's interests and attitude about work and the illness or injury;
- reliance on alcohol and/or drugs;
- stress management needs; and
- the employee's willingness to try modified work/alternate work duties.

Performance issues, such as:

- the quality of the relationship between the employee and his/her supervisor;
- the quality of relationships with co-workers;
- employee's past and recent work performance; and
- past history of absenteeism.

Educational factors, such as:

- formal education; and
- specialized training.

Financial factors, such as:

- available employee benefits;
- income;
- financial assets/liabilities; and
- treatment/rehabilitation expenses.

Organizational factors, such as:

- willingness to host case management conferences to expedite a successful graduated return-to-work plan; and
- resources to meet the employee's rehabilitation needs.

A Rehabilitation Assessment can be done for each short-term disability and Workers' Compensation Board case and recorded on a form such as the one provided in Figure 5.2.

DEVELOPMENT OF REHABILITATION PLAN

Once the rehabilitation assessment is complete, the occupational health nurse develops a specific rehabilitation plan with the assistance of the employee, supervisor, union representative (if applicable) and human resource personnel (if required), for each employee who can benefit from proactive case management. A variety of tools, as described below, are used in this process.

Job Analysis

Using a standard Job Analysis Form (Figure 5.3),[31] the physical demands for the job can be used to identify the employee's capabilities, as well as his or her limitations. Comparisons are then made between the job demands and the employee's capabilities and limitations, to determine fitness to work and appropriate early return-to-work options.

The "Physical Abilities" section examines the physical demands of the job. For each area, bending, walking, sitting, lifting, standing and hand-eye coordination, the user notes whether or not the activity occurs and records the data indicating how often, for how long, or how much, each activity is done. Using the guidelines provided, a value from one to four is assigned to each activity.

---

[31] *Ibid.*

The "Language Skills" section also converts data to numerical values. These forms can be adapted to meet the needs of many industries.

Another option is to have Job Demands Analysis for each position within a company (Figure 5.4), dealing with both the physical and psychological demands of a job.

Linkage with the Attending Physician or Health Care Provider

The purpose of the Managed Rehabilitative Care Program is to work as a team to benefit the employee. The occupational health nurse liaises with the attending health care providers to explain the benefits and supports available to employees. Examples of the types of assistance offered by some companies are:

- occupational health services that offers ergonomic assistance, and manages the confidentiality of employee health information;
- job or worksite modifications, such as a temporarily reduced work schedule, change of work duties, physical changes to the worksite, and/or use of specialized tools, or adaptive devices;
- availability of an Employee Assistance Program to help with work stress, personal issues and any mental health component of the existent medical condition(s);
- coordination with a specialist, when warranted, to obtain a timely appointment for the employee; and
- third party functional capacity assessment with reports going to the family physician if the employee consents to the communication.

Job Modifications

Job changes, or the reassignment of parts of a job, are considered so that the employee can return to work in a safe and timely manner. Once the employee's capabilities have been identified by an occupational health professional, the supervisor, union representative, Return-to-Work Coordinator and human resource personnel are usually the leaders of a modified/alternate work opportunity.

Adaptive Devices

Special clothing, devices or equipment that allows adaptation of the work to the employee's limitations are considered where possible. From the beginning, the disabled employee and supervisor are involved in selecting and learning how to use any device that assists in the workplace accommodation of the returning employee. This is one area where occupational hygiene professionals can be an excellent team resource.

Figure 5.2: Rehabilitation Assessment Form

EMPLOYEE: _____	EMPLOYEE #: _____
WORK LOCATION: _____	TEL #: _____
OCCUPATION: _____	
DIAGNOSIS: _____	PHYSICIAN: _____

FACTOR	(Check if appropriate)	COMMENTS
A. PHYSICAL	Physical capabilities	_____
	Job demands	_____
	Job modification potential	_____
	Need for adaptive devices	_____
	Worksite modification	_____
B. PERSONAL	Change in family dynamics	_____
	Personal crisis	_____
	Health of family members	_____
	Impact of disability on family	_____
C. VOCATIONAL	Level of Job satisfaction	_____
	Work changes	_____
	General employment skills	_____
	Vocational interests/aptitudes	_____
	Supervisory support for MW	_____
D. MEDICAL	Diagnosis	_____
	Prognosis	_____
	Treatment plan	_____
	Expected RTW date	_____
	Employee's confidence/ satisfaction with treatment	_____
	Potential residual limitations	_____
	Pain and coping skills	_____
	Other Health Problems	_____
	Other Health care supports	_____
E. PSYCHOLOGICAL	Employee's reaction	_____
	Employee outlook/self-esteem	_____
	Cultural factors	_____
	Employee treatment goals	_____
	Use of alcohol, drugs	_____
	Stress management needs	_____
	Willingness to work MW	_____
F. PERFORMANCE	Relationship with supervisor	_____
	Relations with co-workers	_____
	Work performance	_____
	Past absenteeism rate	_____
G. EDUCATIONAL	Formal education	_____
	Specialized training	_____
H. FINANCIAL	Available group benefits	_____
	Income	_____
	Financial assets/liabilities	_____
	Treatment costs	_____
H. ORGANIZATIONAL	Use of case conferences	_____
	Available rehabilitation resources	_____

GOAL – Return to Work Date _____

OWN JOB ☐   OTHER JOB ☐

Figure 5.3: Standard Job Analysis Form

Worker's Name: _____Job: _____

Date of Evaluation: _____Completed by: _____

Address:_____Phone: _____

Physical Abilities

Comments

Bending	At waist	1	2	3	4	_____
	Stooping	1	2	3	4	_____
	Kneeling	1	2	3	4	_____
	Crouching	1	2	3	4	_____
	Crawling	1	2	3	4	_____
Walking	Level Surface	1	2	3	4	_____
	Rough Ground	1	2	3	4	_____
	Stairs	1	2	3	4	_____
	Ladders	1	2	3	4	_____
Sitting	Chair	1	2	3	4	_____
	Stool	1	2	3	4	_____
	Vehicle Seat	1	2	3	4	_____
Lifting	From Ground	1	2	3	4	_____
	From Bench	1	2	3	4	_____
	From Shoulder	1	2	3	4	_____
	Over Head	1	2	3	4	_____
	Carrying	1	2	3	4	_____
	Pushing	1	2	3	4	_____
	Pulling	1	2	3	4	_____
Standing	Inside	1	2	3	4	_____
	Outside	1	2	3	4	_____
Hand-Eye Coordination		1	2	3	4	_____

Language Skills

		Yes	No=1	Minimal=2	Average=3	Fluent=4
English	Spoken	❑	❑	❑	❑	❑
	Written	❑	❑	❑	❑	❑
French	Spoken	❑	❑	❑	❑	❑
	Written	❑	❑	❑	❑	❑
Other	Spoken	❑	❑	❑	❑	❑
	Written	❑	❑	❑	❑	❑

Clerical Skills

Required: Yes ❑ No ❑   Specify: _____

Figure 5.4: Job Demands Analysis

Company XYZ **Job Demands Analysis**

Date:		Hours in Shift:		Business Unit:	
Job Title:		Occupation:		Location:	

	Job Demands	Category	Frequency 0	1	2	3	Essential Duty Yes / No		Description
S T R E N G T H	Lifts:	Usual weight							
		Max. weight							
	Lifting:	Floor to waist							
		Waist & higher							
	Carrying:	Usual weight							
		Max. weight							
	Carrying:	Single arm							
		Double arm							
	Handling:	Right							
		Left							
	Reaching: Shoulder height	Above							
		Below							
	Gripping:	Minimum							
		Moderate							
		Maximum							
	Finger Movements:	Right							
		Left							
M O B I L I T Y	Sitting								
	Standing								
	Walking								
	Climbing								
	Stooping								
	Crouching								
	Kneeling								
	Crawling								
	Twisting								
P E R C E P T I O N	Hearing:	Conversation							
		Other Sounds							
	Smelling:								
	Vision:	Far							
		Near							
		Colour							
		Depth							
	Reading/Writing								
	Speech								
W O R K E N V I R O N M E N T	Inside Work (% of time)								
	Outside Work (% of time)								
	Noise Exposed Worker								
	Exposure to Extreme Heat (≥26°C)								
	Exposure to Extreme Cold (≤-7°C)								
	Exposure to Vibration Sources								
	Exposure to Chemicals								
	Exposure to Hazardous Materials								
	Exposure to Radiation								
	Exposure to Biological Hazards								
	Exposure to Electrical Hazards								
	Exposure to Dust								
	Exposure to Welding Fumes								
	Works With Moving Objects								
	Operates a Vehicle or Mobile equipment								
	Operates Hazardous Machines/Equipment								
	Works With Sharp Tools								
	Works on Uneven/Slippery Terrain/Surfaces								
	Exposed to Confined Spaces								
	Use of Respiratory Equipment								
	Works at Heights (> 2.4 meters high)								
	Repetitive Motion								
	Video Display Terminal Use								
G E N E R A L	Air Travel								
	Vehicle Travel								
	Interaction With Public								
	Overtime								
	On-call Responsibilities								
	Emergency Response Duties								
P S Y C H O L O G I C A L	Work Demands/Pressures								
	Work Pace								
	Supervisory/ Managerial Duties								
	Control of Work								
	Span of Control								
	Irregular Hours/Fatigue								

Job Specific Comments:

Independent Medical Examination

Independent, "third party" medical examinations can be used to determine the employee's level of disability, the length of duration of disability and possible recommendations for rehabilitation and successful return to work. The independent medical examination is not disciplinary in nature, nor is it intended to determine the employee's eligibility for benefit plan coverage.

An independent medical examination may be arranged for one or more of the following circumstances:

1. To determine the employee's medical status and fitness for work.
2. To determine the length of time the employee may be absent from work in order to allow for adequate replacement resources.
3. To determine the employee's work restrictions and/or limitations.
4. To assist with the development of a rehabilitation strategy, if necessary.
5. To ensure that the employee can return to work safely and productively.
6. If the disabling condition is not usually "totally disabling".
7. If the actual or estimated period of disability is longer than usual for the disabling condition.
8. If there is no definitive diagnosis.
9. If the return-to-work date cannot be provided by the physician, or is shown as "unknown" or "indefinite".
10. To obtain a second medical opinion and/or case management guidance.

Job Finding

Whenever there is the likelihood that the employee will not be able to return to his or her own job, the human resource professionals are advised. Then, the challenge of finding the employee an alternate job suitable to his or her capabilities begins. By early placement of a permanently disabled employee into a suitable job, long-term disability can be avoided.

Employee Education

Resources can be used to help the employee understand and cope with his or her disability. Education is important when trying to encourage a positive attitude towards illness or injury management. The employee needs to feel a sense of control over his or her life to cope successfully with the situation.

GOAL SETTING

Specific goals with time frames are developed and communicated to the team of which the employee is the key player. A Rehabilitation Action Plan, which can be used to document rehabilitation goals, is provided in Figure 5.5.

Figure 5.5: Rehabilitation Action Plan

Health	Date	Completed

Vocational (human resources, supervisor)	Date	Completed

Benefit/Insurance	Date	Completed

Key Decision-makers (telephone numbers)

1._____   4._____
2._____   5._____
3._____   6._____

Other Comments   Date

_____
_____

_____   _____
Signature   Date

CASE COORDINATION

Occupational health professionals advocate and negotiate on the company and employee's behalf with all the professionals involved. Employees become better consumers of health care and are provided with support to enhance compliance with treatment regimens.

The Managed Rehabilitative Care process chart (Chapter 3, Figure 3.3) is used by all members of the team.

GRADUATED RETURN TO WORK

Graduated return-to-work opportunities are intended to assist recovering employees in safely returning to the workplace and, ultimately, to regular full-time employment. Often, a Return-to-Work Coordinator is involved to facilitate the process. However, regardless of who is involved, a successful graduated return-to-work outcome depends on a cooperative and collaborative approach between the employee, union representative and management.

Objectives of the Graduated Return-to-Work Plan

A return-to-work plan is designed to achieve the following objectives:

1. ensure fair and consistent treatment for all employees who are returning to work;
2. promote shared responsibility for effective return-to-work plans and placements among supervisors, union representatives, ill/injured employees, occupational health nurses and the Disability Management Coordinator, if applicable;
3. provide coordinated claims and case management services for the ill/injured employee; and
4. mitigate medical absence costs associated with disability claims.

Graduated return-to-work opportunities are intended to assist recovering employees in safely returning to the workplace and, ultimately, to regular full-time employment. Often, a Return-to-Work Coordinator is involved to facilitate the process. However, regardless of who is involved, a successful graduated return-to-work outcome depends on a cooperative and collaborative approach between the employee, union representative and management.

Principles of a Graduated Return-to-Work Plan

A Graduated Return-to-Work Plan is based on a number of principles. Some examples are as follows:

1. *A safe and timely return to work is in the best interest of the ill or injured employee and the organization.* The employee benefits from having meaningful employment, gradual work conditioning and the social supports associated with being at work, when deemed appropriate. The organization is able to mitigate the costs associated with lost production, hiring and training replacement workers, and rescheduling of other workers. Supporting the recovering employee to return to productive work minimizes the direct and indirect costs associated with disability.

2. *Early intervention is critical to achieving a positive return-to-work experience.* It can:

    *   help the employee to receive appropriate and timely care;
    *   help with the physical, social, psychological, vocational and financial implications of illness/injury;
    *   increase the likelihood of successful rehabilitation;
    *   facilitate the process of coping and adjustment for the employee, family and work group;
    *   promote a safe, timely and successful return to work; and
    *   be cost-effective for the employee, family and employer.

3. *A positive approach to disability is advantageous.* This means focusing on the person's capabilities and the contributions that he or she can make to the workplace. By bringing ill or injured employees back into the work-place, the organization and unions can demonstrate the belief that each employee, regardless of disability, has abilities that can be valuable. This approach can enhance employee morale.

4. *Return-to-work plans should include meaningful, goal-oriented work that matches the employee's capabilities.* Modifications consider the type of work to be performed and the hours to be worked.

5. *Employees should be compensated in accordance with the work per-formed.*

6. *Crossing union jurisdictional issues must be addressed and resolved for a Graduated Return-to-Work Program to function successfully.*

7. *A return-to-work plan must recognize the employee's diminished capabil-ity and not compromise the employee's recovery or safety.*

8. *A return-to-work plan must ensure that the general workplace safety is not compromised.*

9. *The return-to-work plan is not a disciplinary tool.* Performance issues are to be resolved through the appropriate administrative processes and col-lective agreements.

10. *A return-to-work plan may include a return to*:
    - the employee's own job with reduced hours;
    - a portion of the employee's own job duties with full-time or part-time hours;
    - a different job within the employee's department on a full-time or part-time basis;
    - an unrelated job in another department on a full-time or part-time basis; and/or
    - a new job outside of the organization on a full-time, or part-time, basis.
    (The Hierarchy of Return-to-Work Options is provided in Figure 5.6.)

In essence, a Disability Management Program like the Managed Rehabilita-tive Care Program can help companies cope with rising disability costs, the challenges of an aging and changing workforce, the effects of uncertain eco-nomic times on disability costs, the intricacies of a complex health care system, and the administration of disability cases.

Figure 5.6: Hierarchy of Return-to-Work Options

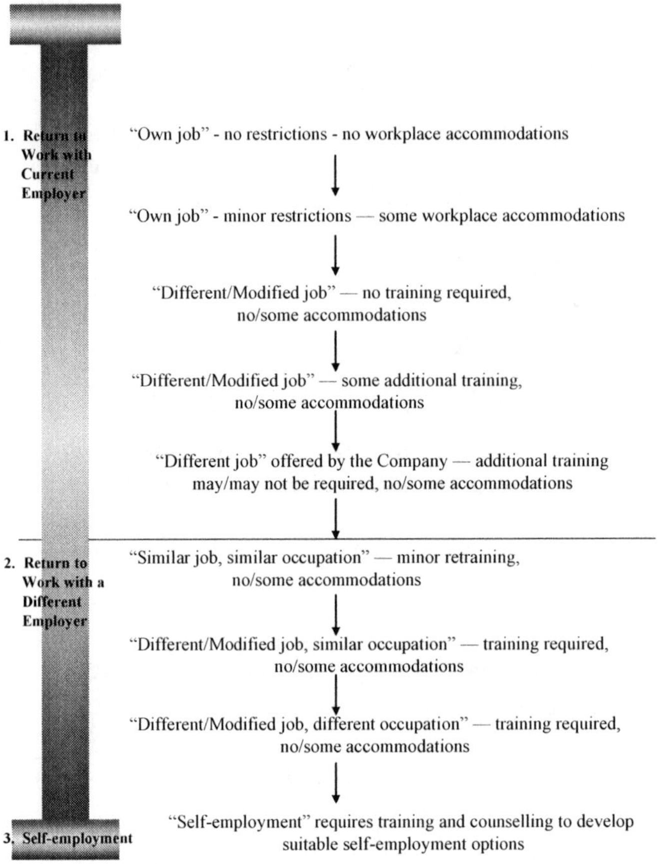

1. **Return to Work with Current Employer**

"Own job" - no restrictions - no workplace accommodations

↓

"Own job" - minor restrictions — some workplace accommodations

↓

"Different/Modified job" — no training required, no/some accommodations

↓

"Different/Modified job" — some additional training, no/some accommodations

↓

"Different job" offered by the Company — additional training may/may not be required, no/some accommodations

↓

2. **Return to Work with a Different Employer**

"Similar job, similar occupation" — minor retraining, no/some accommodations

↓

"Different/Modified job, similar occupation" — training required, no/some accommodations

↓

"Different/Modified job, different occupation" — training required, no/some accommodations

↓

3. **Self-employment**

"Self-employment" requires training and counselling to develop suitable self-employment options

Managed Rehabilitative Care Outcome Measures

What benefits can be realized through the implementation of a Managed Rehabilitative Care Program? Realistically, one can expect a decline in short-term disability and Workers' Compensation Board costs, a reduction in lost-time hours and fewer long-term disability claims. Additionally, the information gathered from a reduction in lost-time hours and fewer long-term disability claims. Additionally, the information gathered from a Managed Rehabilitative Care program can help identify emerging problems, or the development of trends that warrant further investigation.

MEASURING SUCCESS

The evaluation process can occur at many levels. At the individual case level, the process and results are continually reviewed throughout the course of the disability and improvements are sought. At the program level, program results, costs, system concerns and recommendations are analyzed and reported periodically to local management. Confidentiality of individual information is maintained in accordance with medical or nursing confidentiality codes of practice. At the process level, auditing of the Managed Rehabilitative Care Program is recommended.

An example of a spreadsheet for setting up a Managed Rehabilitative Care Program database is provided in Figure 5.7.

Figure 5.7: Managed Rehabilitative Care Spreadsheet

Name	STD Start	STD End	STD Length	Cause	MWP	Days Saved
X	05.08.06	05.09.20	32 days	Cancer	N	0 days
A	05.08.12	05.10.01	35	N.O.A	N	0
C	05.08.26	06.01.10	92	N.O.I	Y	41
B	05.09.03	06.03.03	124	N.O.I.	Y	66
D	05.09.03	06.03.03	124	R.S.I.	N	0
I	05.07.02	05.11.13	90	R.S.I.	Y	52
Y	05.09.16	05.10.25	29	Stress	Y	10
M	05.09.09	06.02.03	119	Stress	Y	72
J	05.08.01	05.08.23	15	N.O.I.	N	0
N	05.09.12	05.09.20	7	Flu	N	0
T	05.09.03	05.10.15	30	Surgery	Y	15
U	05.09.03	05.09.13	9	N.O.I.	N	0
W	05.09.24	05.11.22	42	E.T.O.H.	N	0
O	05.09.18	05.09.25	6	Surgery	N	0
P	05.09.19	05.10.07	11	Surgery	Y	5
L	05.09.12	05.11.01	36	Surgery	Y	5
V	05.10.22	06.04.20	124	Deg. C.	Y	38
E	05.10.22	05.12.02	29	Back	Y	19
F	05.10.07	06.04.07	125	Back	Y	78
H	05.10.15	05.10.25	9	Flu	N	0
K	05.10.16	06.03.11	100	Stress	Y	97
Q	05.10.30	05.11.22	17	Surgery	Y	5
R	05.11.05	05.11.15	8	Cardiac	N	0
S	05.10.28	06.01.02	43	Stress	N	0
G	05.11.10	05.11.18	8	Surgery	N	0
25 Employees			**1264 Days**		**13 Employees**	**503 Days**

Legend:
N.O.A. = Non-occupational Accident; N.O.I. = Non-occupational Injury; E.T.O.H. = Alcohol Abuse; R.S.I. = Repetitive Strain Injury; Deg. C. = Degenerative Condition; MWP = Modified Work Program.

This table indicates that 25 employees were on short-term disability for a total of 1264 days at an average of 50.5 workdays per case. At a rate of $233 per day, this totals $294,512 and averages $11,766.50 per case. As well, 13 (52%) of the employees returned to modified/alternate work for a total of 503 workdays. The dollar saving by the modified/alternate work initiative is $117,199. By subtracting the "days saved" from the total short-term disability days, the "time lost" is calculated. In this scenario, that is 761 days at a cost of $117,313.

Using Managed Rehabilitative Care data, many types of reports can be generated. Figure 5.8 is an example of an annual report.

Figure 5.8: Annual Results of the Managed Rehabilitative Care Program

Summary Statistics: Short-term Disability

Results for 1 year		
Number on STD	103 employees	
Total STD days	3309 days	$ 770,997*
Average total STD time	32 days	$ 7,456
% on M.W.P.**	44%	
Days saved	1382 days	$ 322,006
Actual STD time	2124 days away	$ 494,892
Average STD time	21 days away	$ 4,893

* Sick-Leave Cost = $770,997
** MWP = Modified/alternate work program

The cost to have 103 employees on short-term disability was $770,997 for the year. The average time off was 32 days. This meant an average of $7,456 per case. By placing 44% of the recovering employees on modified/alternate work, 1382 days were saved — a saving of $322,006.

There are other ways to evaluate success. The following are a few techniques that may be employed.

1. Determine the "difference" that a Managed Rehabilitative Care Program has made:
    *   Calculate the total number of employees on each of the disability programs before the program began and after it had been operational for one year. Compare the differences.
    *   Quarterly and annual comparisons can also be made as shown in the example in Figure 5.9.

Figure 5.9: Comparison of Results for Four Quarters, 2005

Measures	1st Q	2nd Q	3rd Q	4th Q
Number on STD	30	31	50	41
Total STD days	882	823	955	960
Average STD time (days)	29.4	26.5	19.1	23.6
% on MWP	20%	48%	64%	58%
Days saved	204	318	414	429

2.   Calculate the cost of the total sick-time:
   •   Establish the total number of days on short-term disability and then multiply that number by the average, or actual employee salary including the burden factor. Some companies use a set cost, such as an average salary of $233 per day as the "sick leave cost" (Figure 5.10). This is increased to $633 per day if a replacement worker is required for that period of time. In this scenario, the "replacement cost" is $400 per day.

Figure 5.10: Quarterly Report on Managed Rehabilitative Care Program

2005.07.01 – 2005.09.30

Number of employees on STD**	30
Total STD days	882 days
Average STD time per employee	29.4 days
Total STD costs	$205,506*
Average STD cost per employee	$ 6,850.20
STD costs per month	$ 68,502

* Total short-term disability costs = Sick-Leave Cost ($233 per day) x Total short-term disability days
** Absences of 5 or more days

3.   Calculate the total "days-saved":
   •   This can be done two ways, or by combining both:
      a)   determine the difference between the predicted and actual return-to-work time, or,
      b)   determine the number of days each employee is on modified/alternate work.
      Either of these methods yields the "days saved" by the Managed Rehabilitative Care Program.
   •   To place a dollar-savings on this figure, multiply the number of "days saved" by the "sick-leave cost", with or without the "replacement cost", as the actual case might be.

4.   Calculate the causes of the claims:
   •   Determine the cause for each claim, short-term disability, long-term disability or Workers' Compensation, whichever is of interest. Broad categories like occupational illness, occupational injury, non-occupational illness or non-occupational injury could be used. Other possible classifications include surgery, stress, degenerative conditions, infections, *etc.* (Figure 5.11).

Figure 5.11: Causes of Short-term Disability

n = 99 S.T.D. cases

Cause of STD	Percent
Surgery	37%
Infections	17%
Non-occupational injuries	10%
Stress	9%
Pregnancy disorders	5%
Degenerative conditions	5%
Back disorders	3%
Cardiac conditions	3%
Immune disorders	3%
Neurological disorders	2%
Cancer	2%
Others	3%

5.   Calculate the cost of each cause to the company:
   •   This involves determining the "time-lost" for each category of causes and assigning a dollar figure to the cause (Figure 5.12).

Figure 5.12: Causes of Short-term Disability,
Percent of Total Short-term Disability Days (3208 days)

Cause of STD	STD Days	Percent of Total STD
Surgery	1050	33%
Non-occupational injuries	603	19%
Degenerative conditions	320	10%
Infections	252	8%
Stress	232	7%
Back disorders	177	6%
Cancer	168	5%
Immune disorders	146	4%
Pregnancy disorders	127	4%
Cardiac conditions	61	2%
Neurological disorders	10	0.3%
Others	62	2%

6. Calculate the success of modified/alternate work initiatives:
   - Examine the data on all the short-term disability cases that went into modified/alternate work. Subdivide the group by the disability causes. Total the number of "days saved" for each case in each disability subgroup and then, add a dollar figure to the "days saved" for each. This will indicate where the biggest differences were made by modified/alternate work (Figure 5.13).

Figure 5.13: Savings Realized by Modified/Alternate Work Initiatives

n = 48 modified/alternate work opportunities

Condition	Employees Returned to Work	Average Days Saved	Savings per Case
Back	3/3	51	$ 11,883
Non-Occupational Injuries	7/11	46	$ 10,718
Pregnancy Disorders	3/5	28	$ 6,524
Degenerative Conditions	2/5	24	$ 5,592
Infections	8/16	21	$ 4,893
Stress	6/9	20.5	$ 4,777
Surgery	16/37	10	$ 2,330
Immune Disorders	1/3	93	$ 21,669
Others	1/3	43	$ 10,019
Cancer	1/2	24	$ 5,592

- Figure 5.13 shows that all the employees with back disabilities went to modified/alternate work and an average of 51 days were saved for each case. This translates to a savings of $11,883 per case. In comparison, only 16 out of 37 of the surgery cases returned early to modified/alternate work. An average of 10 days per case was saved, $2,330 per case.
- This type of data helps occupational health professionals to decide where and how they can make the biggest difference to the company's "bottom line".

7. Determine the workplace accommodations made:
    - List each worker who received any type of workplace accommodation by occupation, nature of disability and type of accommodation made. This stands as a record of a company's "duty to accommodate" (Figure 5.14).

Figure 5.14: Workplace Accommodations (2005-2006)

Occupation	Disability	Accommodation
Driver	Wrist dysfunction: inability to drive safely	Computer work within the distribution terminal
Office worker	Heart disease	Given a rest area to use at noon hour so work can be tolerated
Computer Operator	Repetitive strain injury	Bilateral articulating arms for computer work station
Computer Operator	Eye disease	Job modified to half day, optic shield on computer screen to reduce glare
Computer Operator	Eye degeneration	Optic shield on computer
Field Operator Maintenance	Heart disease	Alternate work on eight-hour days
Maintenance Supervisor	Deteriorating spine	Permanent office work organizing maintenance
Millwright	Heart disease	Permanent position in tool crib

The final way of evaluating a Managed Rehabilitative Care Program is to audit the program. This can be done in many ways as well: the aim is to determine whether the program is meeting its objectives or not, and the degree to which this is being done. Examples of some auditing questions are provided on Figure 5.15.

Figure 5.15: Managed Rehabilitative Care Audit Questions

Audit Questions	Comments
Does the employee receive the right service at the right time?	
How often is the Case Manager notified of an absence by day five?	
Is the standardized case management approach used in all cases?	
Who are the usual members of the Managed Rehabilitative Care management team?	
How often is modified/alternate work usually available?	
Is the modified/alternate work "gainful employment"?	
Are supervisors proactive in the Managed Rehabilitative Care Program?	
How does senior management demonstrate support for the Managed Rehabilitative Care Program?	
How do union leaders demonstrate support for the Managed Rehabilitative Care Program?	
What percentage of employees return to work within one month? Within three months? Within six months?	
How many short-term disability claims move to long-term disability?	
How many Workers' Compensation claims move to long-term disability?	
What types of workplace accommodations are made?	

OTHER OUTCOME MEASURES

Much operational information can be obtained through review and analysis of the Managed Rehabilitative Care data. For instance:

- By knowing the causes of disability claims, a proactive approach to prevent injury or illness occurrence can be recommended for implementation by the company. For example, if the main cause of disability is "non-occupational injuries", an Off-the-Job Safety Program may be warranted. Or, if the major reason for disability is associated with back injuries, a back-care program or a fitness program may prove cost-effective. If degenerative diseases are top on the list of disability causes, proactive lifestyle practices could be promoted.
- By comparing the disability claims of the company's various divisions, a standard for performance can be set. A comparison of the business, health and safety practices between the "best" and "worst" performers may provide insight into ways to lower the company's disability claims.

SUMMARY

The incentives for instituting a Disability Management Program, like the Managed Rehabilitative Care Program are:

- rising disability costs;
- past experience of companies using Managed Rehabilitative Care to make a difference in their claims experience;
- pressures to recognize the "human element" in the workplace;
- pending legislation forcing employers to accommodate disabled employees in the workplace; and
- a depressed economy.

Disability Management Programs can help companies cope with the rising disability costs, the challenges of an aging and changing workforce, the effects of uncertain economic times on disability costs, the intricacies of a complex health care system, and the administration of disability cases.

By working with employees, their medical practitioners, employee assistance professionals, human resource professionals and community agencies, occupational health professionals can help to rehabilitate employees thereby getting them back to work earlier. In short, a Disability Management Program can be a very effective means of maintaining the integrity of disability programs.

CHAPTER REFERENCES

B. Anderson, "Disability Claims Management" (Seminar presented by M. Mercier at Westin Hotel, Calgary, Alberta, February 1992) [unpublished].

R. Berresford, J. Farmery & D. Mitchell, *Modified/alternate Work Guidelines* (Toronto: Aon Consulting Inc., 1993).

P. Booth, *Employee Absenteeism: Strategies for Promoting an Attendance-Oriented Corporate Culture* (Ottawa: The Conference Board of Canada, 1993) at 2.

Case Management Society of America (CMSA), *Standards for Practice of Case Management* (Little Rock, AR: CMSA, 1995).

City of Medicine Hat Disability Management Program Steering Committee, April 1999.

D. Dyck, "Managed Rehabilitative Care: Overview for Occupational Health Nurses" (1996) 44:1 AAOHN Journal at 18-27.

Great West Life, "Coordinated Disability Care" (Presentation to Petro-Canada. Calgary, Alberta, 1993) [unpublished].

L. Gross, "Managing Your Escalating Health and Safety Costs" (Presented to the Petroleum Industry's Annual Safety Seminar, Alberta, May 1993) [unpublished].

T. Hoverstad & S. Kjolstad, "Use of Focus Groups to Study Absenteeism Due to Illness" (1991), American College of Occupational Medicine at 1046-1050.

R. Maynard, "The Pain Threshold" *Canadian Business* (February 1993) at 18.

K.A. Melnyk, "Barriers, a Critical Review of Recent Literature" (1988), Vol. 37(4) Nursing Research.

K. Nagel, "Total Organizational Health Costs: What Are They? What Can Organizations Do About Them?" (Presented at the Strategic Leadership Forum '99, Toronto, Ontario, 20 October 1999) [unpublished].

NIDMAR, *Code of Practice for Disability Management* (Port Alberni, B.C.: NIDMAR, 2000), at 4.

Ontario Human Rights Commission, *Guidelines for Assessing Accommodation Requirements for Persons with Disabilities* (Toronto: Ontario Human Rights Commission, 1990).

Peat, Marwick, Stevenson & Kellog, *Statistical Data on 1991 Employee Benefit Costs in Canada* (1993) [unpublished].

Petro-Canada Inc., *Managed Rehabilitative Care Program Occupational Health* (Calgary: Petro-Canada, 1990).

L. Steeves & R. Smithies, "Foresight is Your Best Defence" (1996) 4:2 Group Healthcare Management at 29-32.

Statistics Canada, *2001 Census, Release 2 – July 16, 2003* (Ottawa: Statistics Canada 2003), online: <http://www12.statcan.ca/english/census01/release/age_sex.cfm>.

Statistics Canada, *Work Absences, 2004* (Ottawa: Statistics Canada, 2005).

Statistics Canada, *Average Hourly Wages of Employees by Selected Characteristics*, online: <http://www40.statcan.ca/l01/cst01/labr69a.htm>.

J. White, "The Evolving Role of Nursing in Patient Advocacy" *Canadian Nursing Management* (May 1992) at 6-8.

World Health Organization, *International Classification of Impairment, Disabilities and Handicaps* (Geneva: World Health Organization, 1980).

Work Loss Data Institute, *Disability Benchmarks by Major Diagnostic Category* (Corpus Christi, Tex: Work Loss Data Institute, 2002).

Chapter 6

Disability Management Program: Outcome Measurements

WHY MEASURE PROGRAM OUTCOMES?

To measure the productivity and effectiveness of a Disability Management Program, data must be collected and documented. Canadian and American employers recognize that the costs associated with employee absence are significant. The current estimate in that the direct disability-related absences cost Canadian employers between $1,462[1] to $1,756 per employee per year.[2] For a company of 1000 employees, this cost would be between $1.4 to $1.8 million. This number would double or even triple if the indirect costs of employee absence were to be included. However, despite evidence of increasing employee absenteeism rates and costs, most employers are not measuring absence and disability rates and outcomes.

Disability Management experts believe that, "You can't manage what you can't measure." The process of data collection reveals the hidden costs of disability, and the added costs of lost productivity, staff replacement and retraining to management. Analyzing the data provides a measure of the Disability Management Program's cost-effectiveness, which in turn directly impacts the company bottom-line. Data collection and analysis also provides reports demonstrating compliance with Canadian duty to accommodate legislation, and supports the legal concept of due diligence.

Data Collection Techniques

There are many data collection techniques available, from manual to electronic. The main issue is to identify the relevant variables on which to collect disability management data. In Chapter 5, a number of data collection techniques were described. However, these techniques are by no means all-encompassing. As more data on disability is being collected and linked with other databases, more ways to evaluate Disability Management Programs emerge.

---

[1] Statistics Canada, *Average Hourly Wages of Employees by Selected Characteristics*, online: <http://www40.statcan.ca/l01/cst01/labr69a.htm>.

[2] Hewitt Associates, Press Release, "Ignoring Employee Absences May Prove Costly for Canadian Organizations, According to Hewitt" (15 June 2005), online: <http://was4.hewitt.com/hewitt/ resource/newsroom/pressrel/2005/06-15-05eng.htm>.

Typically, Disability Management Program evaluation involves:

- determining the differences made by the Disability Management Program;
- calculating the causes and costs of disability claims;
- calculating the number of employees who work modified/alternate work and the resulting cost-avoidance;
- documenting the number and nature of workplace accommodations;
- noting trends in the disability experience; and
- auditing the program outcomes against the expectations for the Disability Management Program.

The types of variables collected often include the:

- nature of the disability (*i.e.*, severity, functional impairments, prognosis, *etc.*);
- course of medical management used (*i.e.*, treatments, therapies, independent medical examinations, *etc.*);
- number and cost of "lost time" hours;
- age of the ill/injured employee;
- length of service with the company;
- type of disability benefit coverage;
- history of employee's disability claims;
- presence/absence of labour relations issues;
- employee's performance ratings;
- level of employee job satisfaction;
- level of employer satisfaction with the employee;
- psychological aspects of the disability;
- marital/family status;
- presence/absence of secondary health problems or conditions; and
- type of return-to-work option used.

Using these data, along with information from other databases, disability patterns can be identified. These patterns may include seasonal variations, off-the-job injuries versus workplace injuries, psychological illnesses associated with specific work units, increased injuries in high-risk occupations, disabilities due to lifestyle versus workplace injuries, and so on.

The information required to determine disability patterns are:

- rates of disability by job (high and low risk jobs);
- lost time hours/days by work unit;
- age group patterns;
- ergonomic job modification needs;
- types of injuries/illness by age, gender, work units and jobs;
- body parts affected;

- causes of injury;
- rate of recurrent claims; and
- other absenteeism or lost time patterns such as seasonal differences, affect of job insecurity or labour relation problems.

Computerized Data Management

Computerized disability data management software programs tend to collect the employee demographic data such as employee name, home address, date of birth, marital status, work details, job details, hours of work, salary and relevant medical history or work restrictions. This information is then used to assist with the data analysis and interpretation for all Disability Management Program data.

In terms of individual medical absence, information on the nature of the absence (*i.e.*, illness or injury, occupational or non-occupational, *etc.*), date and time of the absence, expected length of absence, modified/alternate work activity and the actual return to work should be collected. Using this data, most software programs are able to determine the hours lost and the cost; the hours and the cost avoided on modified/alternate work; and the costs associated with the nature of absence. This data is usually available by work location, department and supervisor. In this way, the Disability Management Program manager/coordinator can establish the costs, and cost-avoidance opportunities, associated with the disability management activities. This is one way to demonstrate the value of the Disability Management Program to the company.

Some software programs deal with strictly Workers' Compensation Board absences while others address all employee absences. Some programs use a linear approach to data analysis, while others use an integrated approach. The linear approach deals with the absence data only. However, the integrated approach allows the user to examine absence data in relation to demographic data, workplace descriptors, industrial hygiene data, Employee Assistance Program information and occupational or non-occupational absence data.

This latter approach is by far the more powerful of the two options because many disabilities are the end result of other factors such as management styles, labour disputes, organizational change, an economic downturn and/or changing societal beliefs and values. By linking the variables and outcomes from a number of occupational areas or databases, trends and associations can be established.

Program Evaluation Techniques

There are a number of ways to measure program success. By auditing a program, one can measure the program procedures and outcomes against the established program objectives and/or standards. This measurement technique allows for the identification of the gaps between the current and ideal state of the program. Typically, the process includes recommendations for reaching the ideal state.

NIDMAR has recently developed a Consensus Based Disability Management Audit (CBDMA) that can be used for benchmarking purposes. The CBDMA is designed to set the minimum acceptable criteria for disability management programs, identify improvement opportunities and promote the use of "best practices" in disability management.[3]

A second approach to measuring program success is to undertake a cost-benefit analysis projection. This involves establishing the causal relationships between the Disability Management Program and the benefits realized (Figure 6.1); categorizing the costs and benefits as short-term versus long-term, and fixed versus variable; quantifying the benefits and costs through direct or indirect projections; and comparing the benefits and costs (Figure 6.2).

One formula that can be used for determining the cost-benefit of a return-to-work program is:

$$\text{Program Cost/Benefit Analysis} = \frac{\text{Potential Cost}}{\text{Actual Cost}} = \frac{(\text{Potential hours off work} \times \text{hourly salary}) + \text{Average LTD debt/case}}{(\text{Actual hours off work on STD}) + (\text{Program Costs per case})}$$

This formula can be applied to calculate the cost per benefit of individual cases, and a mean value can be derived for the entire program.

A third approach is to measure the return on investment (ROI) for the Disability Management Program. This can be done at an individual, group or program level. Basically, the process involves determining the costs, benefits and savings realized by the disability management services and/or activities. The return on investment is calculated by dividing the savings by the costs required by a company to realize those savings.

A formula that can be used to determine the return on investment for a particular case is as follows:

$$\text{ROI} = \frac{\text{Savings realized through modified/alternate work} + \text{Program intervention savings} + \text{Unused LTD reserve}}{\text{Total costs for the case}}$$

In this formula,

Total Costs for the Case = (STD/LTD Costs) + (Assessment, treatment, rehabilitation and accommodation costs)

A model, like the one presented in Figure 6.3, can be used to determine both the cost/benefits of a Disability Management Program and the return on investment. The model operates by determining the company costs with and without a Disability Management Program. The model calculates the saving realized by having a Disability Management Program in place. To determine the return on

---

[3]   NIDMAR, *Consensus Based Disability Management Audit* (Port Alberni, B.C.: NIDMAR, 2004).

investment, the established saving value is divided by the amount invested to realize this saving. Models like this function with the use of assumptions, the key factor is to ensure that the assumptions used are valid.

Figure 6.1: Causal Relationships Between Programs and Benefits

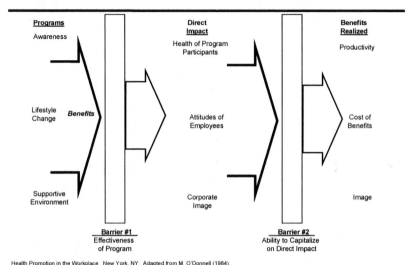

Health Promotion in the Workplace. New York, NY: Adapted from M. O'Donnell (1984).

Figure 6.2: Framework For Cost-Benefit Analysis Projection

Establish Causal Relationships Between Program and Benefit		

Categorize Benefits and Costs		
Short-term vs. Long-term		Fixed vs. Variable

Quantify Benefits and Costs	
Direct Projections	Comparison with Other Projects

Compare Benefits and Costs	
Breakeven Analysis	Net Present Value Analysis

Health Promotion in the Workplace. New York, NY: Adapted from M. O'Donnell (1984).

Benchmarking program data against that of external parties is a fourth approach. Benchmarking is a continual and collaborative discipline that involves measuring and comparing the results of the key process with "best performers" or with one's own previous achievements. Internally, benchmarking can be used to compare against previous program outcomes, processes, practices and performance. Externally, benchmarking involves comparing your company's programs, processes and/or results against another company.

Typically, benchmarking is undertaken to improve the quality of the service or product, address an identified problem, learn "best practices" or in response to increased pressures to improve performance. It is not an exact science, but rather a methodology designed to determine the best way to do things.

In terms of benchmarking Disability Management Programs, the process would be to:

1. plan what and who to benchmark;
2. collect and analyze relevant data;
3. integrate the findings into your frame of reference; and
4. develop an action plan that would implement, monitor and evaluate the changes made.

The benefit of benchmarking is that the methodology provides a rational and objective framework for observing what others are doing, how they are doing it, and what you can do to improve the process even more. In essence, it is a quality improvement tool because the decision-making is based on facts and learning from the actions of others.

A fifth approach is a client satisfaction survey regarding the disability management services offered. The typical approach is to ask those employees who participated in the Disability Management Program their impressions of the service, caregivers and outcomes. The questions that are usually asked are designed to measure specific elements of the program such as timeliness, accessibility, appropriateness and universality of the program. The last section of this chapter describes in detail a client satisfaction survey technique that not only elicits responses about the service, but also identifies the techniques for dealing with any gaps in service that are identified.

Figure 6.3: Estimated Return on Investment for Company XYZ'S DMP

ASSUMES
- 15% reduction in Sick Leave through DMP;
- Company XYZ employs 800 employees at an average salary of $45,000;
- 14.23% WCB discount (rebate);
- 7% incidence rate for LTD each year; and
- LTD reserve per claimant to be $95,000.

	COSTS WITHOUT DMP	
A	Cost of Sick Leave	$800,000
B	Cost of WCB Assessment	$277,200
C	WCB Rebates (Discounts)	14.23%
D	PIR Incentive Discount (5%)	$13,860
E	Net WCB Costs (B – D)	$263,340
F	LTD Rates (Assumes a 7% LTD rate or 2-3 LTD cases per year)	$2,391,025
G	Total Costs (A + E + F)	$3,454,365

	COSTS WITH DMP	
H	Cost of Sick Leave (assumes a 15% reduction)	$680,000
I	Cost of WCB Assessment (assumes a 5% improvement)	$262,800
J	WCB Rebate (Discount) – 5% increase	19.23%
K	PIR Incentive Discount (5 + 5%)	$26,280
L	Net WCB Costs (B-D)	$236,520
M	LTD Rates (assumes a reduction of 5 claims and lowered reserves – 5 x $95,000 = $475,000 reduction)	$1,916,025
N	Total Costs with the DMP (H + L + M)	$2,832,545
O	Total Price for the DMP	$80,000

	SAVINGS WITH DMP	
P	(G-N)	$3,454,365-$2,832,545	$621,820

	RETURN ON INVESTMENT	
Q	(P ÷ O)	$621,820 + $80,000	7.77

GAP ANALYSIS OF A MANAGED REHABILITATIVE CARE PROGRAM[4]

The first part of this section explains the Gap Analysis process and the SERVQUAL instrument, which is a survey tool used to measure client satisfaction in regards to a service.[5] The last part demonstrates how the instrument can be used to measure client satisfaction with an entire Disability Management Program, or its parts, like the Managed Rehabilitative Care Program or Graduated Return-to-Work Program.

Introduction

There is an oriental saying "The customer is God".[6] However, few occupational health services focus on client satisfaction. Traditionally, the emphasis has been on evaluating the quality of care given believing that the client's knowledge of expert care is limited. However, with the increased level of client knowledge about health care and the rise in consumerism, occupational health services should pay attention to client satisfaction. Client satisfaction can be defined as the client being aware of receiving care in a timely fashion and of the many variables in the environment that contribute to recovery.[7]

Successful companies know that concentrating on client satisfaction is essential and, by knowing their clients' expectations, they are able to formulate their fundamental business structure. As well, client-focused companies recognize that client perceptions are formed as a result of every contact with the company. For this reason, it is important to determine the degree of harmony between client expectations and the service quality that service providers believe they are delivering.

This section defines service quality, identifies the causes of service quality problems, and outlines what occupational health services can do to solve these problems.

Service Quality

Service quality can be defined as the extent of discrepancy between client expectations, or desires, and their perceptions (Figure 6.4). The key to good service quality is meeting or exceeding what clients expect from the service.[8]

---

[4] D. Dyck, "Gap Analysis of Health Services: Client Satisfaction Surveys" (1996) 44:1 AOHNA Journal at 541-549.

[5] V. Zeithaml, A. Parasuraman & L. Berry, *Delivering Quality Service* (Toronto: The Free Press, 1990).

[6] M. Youngblood, *Eating the Chocolate Elephant: Take Charge of Change Through Total Process Management* (Richardson, Texas: Micrografx Inc., 1994).

[7] E. Sullivan & P. Decker, *Effective Management in Nursing*, 2d ed. (Menlo Park, California: Addison-Wesley Publishing Company, 1988).

[8] *Supra*, note 5.

Service quality is important because we live in a highly competitive service economy. Efficient servicing can be a source of superiority for an agency. "Excellent service pays off because it creates true customers" and "true customers are like annuities".[9]

Excellent service also differentiates service providers from otherwise similar competitors. Companies that provide excellent service perform better on the bottom-line because they perform better for their clients. Clients respond to these companies because they perceive more value. Value is the client's "overall assessment of the utility of a product based on perceptions of what is received and what is given".[10] The concept of value helps to explain why companies with strong service reputations are able to charge higher prices than their competitors. Clients are willing to pay more to have confidence in the service and product.

Figure 6.4: Components of Service Quality

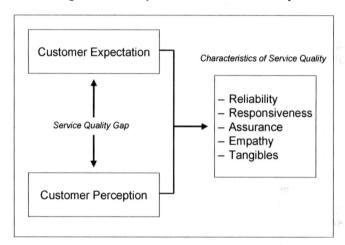

Services are more difficult to evaluate than products. First, services are intangible, "when what is being sold is purely performance, the criteria customers use to evaluate it may be complex and difficult to capture precisely".[11] Second, services are heterogeneous — performance often varies from provider to provider, from client to client and from day to day.[12] Third, the production and consumption of many services are inseparable: "quality in services often occurs during the service delivery, usually in an interaction between the client and the

---

[9] *Ibid.*

[10] V. Zeithaml, "Consumer Perceptions of Price, Quality and Value: A Means-end Model and Synthesis of Evidence" *Journal of Marketing* (July 1988).

[11] *Supra*, note 5.

[12] *Ibid.*

provider, rather than being engineered at the manufacturing plant and delivered intact to the client".[13]

The factors that influence client expectations are word of mouth communications, personal needs of the clients, past experience with a service, and external communications from service providers about the service.[14] Their relationship to expected service is depicted in Figure 6.5.

Clients judge service quality by the following criteria:

Figure 6.5: Dimensions of Service Quality

Dimension of Service Quality	Definition	Examples
Tangibles	Appearance of physical facilities, equipment, personnel and communication materials.	Are the OHS facilities attractive? Are the EAP Advisors dressed appropriately? Is communication to clients easy to understand (*i.e.*, correspondence letters, memos, presentations, *etc.*)?
Reliability	Ability to perform the promised service dependably and accurately.	Are the service records free of error? Is a client's concern addressed properly the first time?
Responsiveness	Willingness to help clients and provide prompt service.	Do we give clients a specific time when we will see them? How long do clients have to wait for an appointment?
Assurance	<u>Competence</u> Possession of required skills and knowledge to perform the service.	Can we process client needs without fumbling around? Are we able to answer client questions upon request?
	<u>Courtesy</u> Politeness, respect, consideration and friendliness.	Do we have a friendly attitude? Do we act like clients are interrupting us when they ask a question?
	<u>Credibility</u> Trustworthiness, believability, honesty of the service provider.	Does the department have a good reputation? Are our service costs consistent with the services provided?
	<u>Security</u> Freedom from danger, risk or doubt.	Is client confidentiality trusted? Can clients be confident that the prescribed treatment/modification is safe for use?

---

[13] *Ibid.*
[14] *Ibid.*

Dimension of Service Quality	Definition	Examples
Empathy	Access Approachability and ease of contact.	How easy is it for clients to talk to a caregiver when they have a problem? Is the service open at hours that a client can get help?
	Communication Keeping clients informed and listening to them.	When clients call the department, are we willing to listen to them? Can we explain clearly all the various details of the client's circumstance?
	Understand the client Making the effort to know clients and their needs.	Do we recognize clients after their initial visit? Are we willing to be flexible enough to accommodate the client's schedule?

Gap Analysis

The service gap analysis methodology integrates the concepts, ideas and findings that emerged from a study of service quality which started in 1983. Research sponsored by the Marketing Science Institute in Cambridge, Massachusetts[15] resulted in the conceptual models of service quality discussed below and a methodology for measuring client perceptions of service quality — the Gap Analysis.

If the key to ensuring good service is meeting or exceeding what clients expect from the service, judgements of high and low service quality depend on how clients perceive the actual service performance in the context of what they expected (Figure 6.4).

The client's perception of service quality is altered when there are gaps between:

- the client's expectations and the service provider's perception of those expectations (Gap 1);
- the service provider's perception of client expectations and the specifications of service quality under which the services are governed (Gap 2);
- the specifications of service quality and the actual service that is delivered (Gap 3);
- the actual service that is delivered and what the service organization communicates to the clients about what it will deliver (Gap 4); or
- the client's expected level of service quality and their perception of what level of service quality they actually received (Gap 5).

---

[15] A. Parasuraman, V. Zeithaml & L. Berry, "SERVQUAL: A Multiple-item Scale for Measuring Consumer Perceptions of Service Quality" *Journal of Retailing* (Spring 1988) at 12-40.

The nature of these gaps is explained further below.

GAP 1 — GAP BETWEEN THE CLIENT'S EXPECTATIONS AND THE SERVICE PROVIDER'S PERCEPTION OF THOSE EXPECTATIONS

Knowing what clients expect is the first and most critical step in delivering quality service. This gap sometimes occurs because companies miss the mark by thinking "inside-out". That is, they operate based on what they believe clients should want and deliver it accordingly. When this happens, services do not match clients' expectations, important features are left out and the levels of performance on features that are provided are inadequate.

The contributing factors that account for this gap include insufficient market research, inadequate use of market research findings and insufficient communication between client and service provider.

The first step in improving the quality of service is for service providers to acquire accurate information about client expectations.

GAP 2 — GAP BETWEEN THE SERVICE PROVIDER'S PERCEPTION OF CLIENT EXPECTATIONS AND THE SPECIFICATIONS OF SERVICE QUALITY UNDER WHICH THE SERVICES ARE GOVERNED

Correct perceptions of client expectations are necessary. Once service providers accurately understand what clients expect, they face a second critical challenge: using this knowledge to set appropriate service quality standards.

The contributing factors that may account for this gap include inadequate commitment to service quality, perception of unfeasibility, inadequate standardization of tasks and absence of goal setting.

Another prerequisite for providing high service quality is the presence of performance standards.

GAP 3 — GAP BETWEEN THE SPECIFICATIONS OF SERVICE QUALITY AND THE ACTUAL SERVICE THAT IS DELIVERED

In some cases, although service providers may understand client expectations and set appropriate specifications (either formally or informally), the service delivered by the organization still falls short of the expectations of the client or clients.

The primary factor in the cause of a service-performance gap is the possibility that employees are unable and/or unwilling to perform the service at the desired level. This may be a result of an inadequate understanding of his or her role; role conflict; poor employee-job fit; poor employee-technology fit; inappropriate measurement/reward systems; lack of empowerment; and/or lack of team-work.

Gap 4 — Gap Between the Actual Service that is Delivered and What the Service Organization Communicates to the Clients About What it Will Deliver

Promises made by a service group serve as the standard against which clients assess service quality. A discrepancy between actual service and promised service may have an adverse effect on client perceptions of service quality if the service has been over-promised.

Gap 5 — Gap Between the Client's Expected Level of Service Quality and Their Perception of What Level of Service Quality They Actually Received

A gap in any one of the four areas listed above will cause a gap between what clients expect to receive and their perception of the level of service quality actually received. The key to closing this last gap is to close Gaps 1 through 4 and to keep them closed. Figure 6.6 is a summary of the reasons these gaps exist and the areas to investigate when closing the gaps.

Gaps 1 and 2 are managerial gaps. Gap 1 stems from a manager's lack of understanding of customer expectations while Gap 2 represents a manager's failure to set appropriate service qualifications.

Gaps 3 and 4 are front-line gaps. Front-line employees' service-delivery performance may fall short of service specifications (Gap 3) and fail to fulfil promises made through external communications (Gap 4).

Figure 6.6: Reasons for Gaps and Areas to Investigate

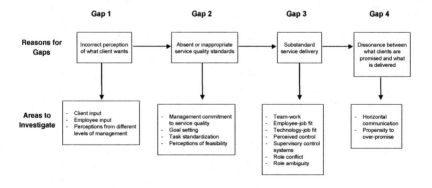

Addressing Service Quality Gaps

The major benefit of the SERVQUAL tool is that it not only identifies the gaps that exist, but also offers recommendations for addressing the problems. Figure 6.7 provides an overview of the potential causes of service quality gaps. The following discussion on each gap provides suggestions for narrowing or eliminating the gaps.

Figure 6.7: Potential Causes of Service Quality Shortfalls

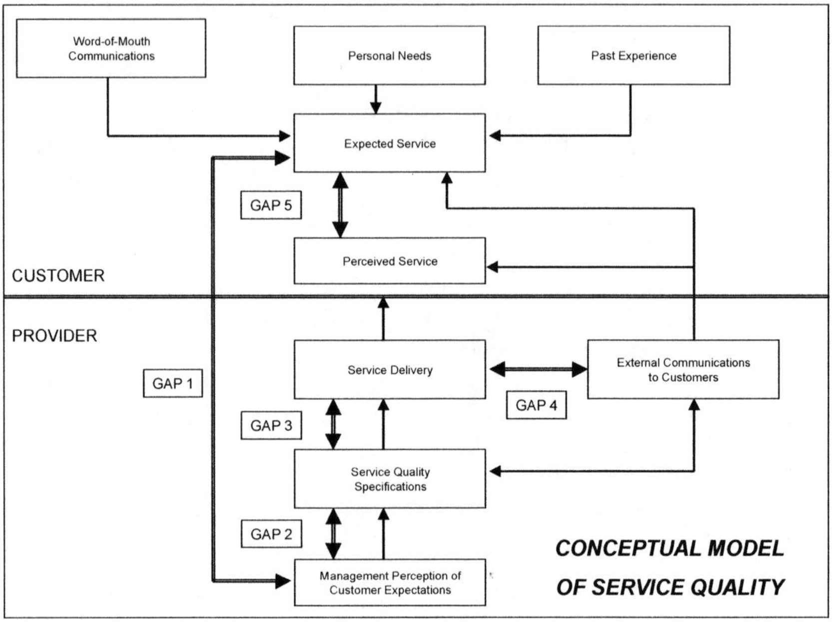

GAP 1 — CLIENT EXPECTATIONS AND MANAGEMENT PERCEPTIONS

Management may be unaware of the characteristics or service features that are valued by clients. When this happens, companies provide services that do not match client expectations. Thus, they may make decisions and resource allocations resulting in client perceptions of poor service quality. The necessary first step in improving service quality is for management to obtain accurate information about client expectations. The key contributing factors that make up Gap 1, as well as ways to close Gap 1 are provided in Figure 6.8.

Figure 6.8: Factors Contributing to Gap 1

Problem	Ways to Close Gap 1
Insufficient market research	Research client expectations Use complaints strategically

Problem	Ways to Close Gap 1
	Research clients' expectations of similar services
	Research intermediate clients such as contact professionals/staff
	Conduct key client studies
	Track client satisfaction with individual servicing
	Engage in comprehensive client expectation studies
Inadequate use of market research findings	Use market research findings effectively
Lack of interaction between management and clients	Increase management-client interaction
Insufficient upward communication from contact personnel to management	Improve upward communication from contact professionals/staff
Too many levels between contact personnel/staff and management	Flatten the organizational structure

GAP 2 — MANAGEMENT PERCEPTION AND SERVICE QUALITY SPECIFICATIONS

Once management understands client expectations, the next challenge is using this knowledge to set service quality standards. However, management may not be willing or able to meet these expectations or the actual specifications established for service delivery. The causes of Gap 2 are provided in Figure 6.9.

Figure 6.9: Factors Contributing to Gap 2

Problem	Ways to Close Gap 2
Inadequate management commitment to service quality	Commit to quality and ensure middle management commitment to service quality
	Develop performance standards that mirror management's perception of client expectations
Perception of unfeasibility	Create possibilities

Problem	Ways to Close Gap 2
Inadequate standardization of tasks	Standardize tasks with hard technology (*i.e.*, databases, systems) and with soft technology (*i.e.*, policies, procedures, changed work processes, *etc.*)
Lack of goal setting	Set service quality goals

GAP 3 — SERVICE QUALITY SPECIFICATIONS AND SERVICE DELIVERY

Both clients and providers experience and respond to each other's mannerisms, attitudes, competencies, moods and language. Maintaining service quality depends on maintaining a workforce willing and able to perform at specified levels.

The factors contributing to Gap 3 are included in Figure 6.10.

Figure 6.10: Factors Contributing to Gap 3

Problem	Ways to Close Gap 3
Employee-job fit Technology-job fit	Improve employee/technology-job fit
Employee role ambiguity	Provide role clarity
Role conflict	Eliminate role conflict
Lack of perceived control	Empower service providers
Inappropriate supervisory control systems	Measure and reward service performance
Lack of team-work	Nurture team-work Actively build team-work

GAP 4 — SERVICE DELIVERY AND EXTERNAL COMMUNICATIONS TO CLIENTS

A discrepancy between actual and promised service reflects an underlying breakdown in coordination between those responsible for delivering the service and those charged with describing or promising the service.

Marketing can influence client expectations by informing clients of all the behind-the-scenes activities performed in order to protect them. By making clients aware of the commitment to quality service, improvements in client service perceptions are realized. Service perceptions can be enhanced by educating clients to be better consumers and service users. The factors contributing to Gap 4 are provided in Figure 6.11. By closing Gaps 1 through 4, Gap 5 is eliminated.

Figure 6.11: Factors Contributing to Gap 4

Problem	Ways to Close Gap 4
Inadequate horizontal communication	Open channels of communication between those marketing the service and those providing the service
Avoid over-promising	Develop appropriate and effective communications about the service
Differing policies and procedures	Provide consistent servicing throughout the agency/company

Instrument Reliability and Validity

The SERVQUAL instrument[16] was designed to help companies better understand service expectations and perceptions of their clients. It is a multi-item scale with good reliability and validity. A complete discussion of the instrument's reliability and validity can be found in the research sponsored by the Marketing Science Institute.[17]

This instrument can be used in a number of companies or services and the developers acknowledge that it can be adapted to meet the individual needs of a company.[18]

In addition to computing service quality gaps, SERVQUAL can also be used to:

- identify trends in client expectations and perceptions over time;
- compare a company's or service's SERVQUAL scores against those of competitors;
- examine client segments with differing quality perceptions; and
- assess quality perceptions of internal customers.

Industry Application

At one large Canadian company, as part of total quality management, client satisfaction surveys were conducted by many service departments in an effort to continually improve service quality and delivery. Occupational health services joined this effort and chose the Gap Analysis method to evaluate its early Return-to-Work Program and Managed Rehabilitative Care program.

---

[16] *Supra*, note 5.
[17] *Supra*, note 15.
[18] *Supra*, note 15.

Since SERVQUAL was designed to evaluate business servicing, changes had to be made to adapt the questions for a disability management service. Care was taken to ensure that the service qualities continued to be measured as originally developed. Also, all the questions were left in their order of presentation. Comment sections were included to augment the standardized questions and to elicit responses not dealt with by the questions. The result was two survey tools designed for this type of service evaluation using the Gap Analysis technique.

SURVEY METHODOLOGY

The Managed Rehabilitation Care surveys were distributed to all employees on modified/alternate work plans while on short-term disability or long-term disability between January 1, 1994 and September 30, 1994. For each client on a modified/alternate work plan, a corresponding manager was included. These client-participant and client-manager survey numbers are distinguished with the suffixes P and M, respectively. In addition, all relevant disability management professionals involved with the Managed Rehabilitation Care program were surveyed.

The assessment of gaps in service quality was performed through the use of two questionnaires: one questionnaire was sent to the clients of the service (Appendix 1); the other to caregivers, management and staff (Appendix 2).

The client questionnaire focused on priorities, expectations for service quality and perceptions of the quality of service clients are receiving. The caregiver questionnaire focused on measuring:

- the caregiver's understanding of client expectations;
- whether service quality standards are formalized within the service group;
- whether the actual service delivery meets service quality standards; and
- the degree to which the service delivers what is promised to clients.

It was recognized that problems would occur in attempting to use a business tool to evaluate health services. Some issues encountered were:

- awkwardly worded questions which were difficult for clients to interpret and understand;
- redundant or leading questions;
- respondents who reported that they were too inexperienced with the service to answer the questions posed;
- too much focus on quantitative measures, as opposed to qualitative measures; and
- the dimensions of service quality (*i.e.*, tangibles, reliability, responsiveness, assurance, empathy, *etc.*) were measured at a macro-level, which proved difficult for clients to understand. This resulted in a very general

questionnaire, which did not deal with why individual cases were successes or failures.

If these services are to be surveyed again, the questionnaires used would have to focus more on human concerns than on business concerns.

MANAGED REHABILITATION CARE SERVICE SURVEY RESULTS

Out of the 67 surveys sent out to Managed Rehabilitation Care service clients, 51 responded (76%), 48 (72%) were used for analysis and three were incomplete and could not be used.

Figure 6.12: MRC Client Expectations versus Perceptions — Gap 5

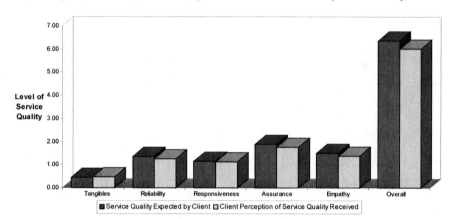

FINDINGS

1. Managed Rehabilitation Care caregivers do not have a clear understanding of what service qualities are most important to clients. Client-participants indicate that the most important service quality is assurance. Client-managers indicate that the most important service quality is reliability. Caregivers think that the most important service qualities are reliability and empathy.

    Result: More attention could be given to assurance.

2. Managed Rehabilitation Care caregivers may understand that reliability is important to client-managers, however they do not seem to understand how important other service qualities are to clients. Client-participants rate assurance much higher in importance than caregivers do. Client-managers rate reliability much higher in importance than caregivers do.

    Result: More attention could be given to assurance and reliability.

3. Managed Rehabilitation Care caregivers generally understand and meet both client groups' expectations, however the client-participant group has a higher expectation of Managed Rehabilitation Care assurance than they perceive they get. The client-manager group has a higher expectation of Managed Rehabilitation Care reliability than they perceive they get.

4. If Managed Rehabilitation Care service desires to increase the understanding of the service qualities important to clients, suggested improvement activities would include:

    (a) Increase market research (*i.e.*, track satisfaction with individual transactions, use complaints strategically, *etc.*).
    (b) Assess performance measurement/reward systems to ensure caregivers are rewarded for quality service provided.

OVERALL RESULTS

Service quality assessments indicated that the clients perceive the service quality as relatively high, and that only small gaps were revealed in the survey. However, there were opportunities for improvement and this information came from the client commentaries.

Positive Client Feedback

*   Reliable and quick responses are appreciated by employees.
*   Security is vital: confidentiality of employee health information remains paramount and constant vigilance is required to uphold this confidentiality.
*   Professional competence is important.
*   Courtesy is important.
*   Empathy is essential.
*   Credible counselling and care is valued.

Issues to Address

*   Market the available services better.
*   Educate managers/supervisors on the use of Managed Rehabilitation Care as supports for employees.
*   Educate stakeholders about their roles and responsibilities concerning Managed Rehabilitation Care.
*   Increase communication with all involved in Managed Rehabilitation Care to ensure efficient business functioning and effective employee participation occurs.
*   Pay more attention to the case management of employees off on Workers' Compensation.

- Be proactive regarding ergonomics, indoor air quality, employee wellness, mental/social health and balancing work and family life.

RESEARCH CONCLUSION

To remain competitive in this economic market, client satisfaction is key to successful servicing. Gap analysis can be a powerful method for evaluating client satisfaction. The strengths of the SERVQUAL instrument are that it identifies service quality gaps, provides suggestions for closing those gaps and allows for service quality analysis. It has been well researched, clinically tested and demonstrates reliability and validity. Its limitations are that it does not provide opportunity for client commentary and tends to focus more on the business aspects and less on the human aspects of servicing. However, by adding in comment sections, as was done in the above industry application, the elicited client responses proved valuable in understanding the nature of the gaps identified.

SUMMARY

Outcome measurements are vital to any program, especially one in which the participation of a number of stakeholders is critical for program success and longevity. For stakeholders to continue to support a program, they must have data to demonstrate the value that the program adds to the organization as a whole, and to specific individuals. The bottom-line is "What is in it for me and how can I recognize the benefits that the program is offering?"

Appendix 1

Client Survey Tool Managed Rehabilitation Care Service Client Service Quality Survey

Client Name: _____

Department: _____

Directions — Part 1

Based on your experiences as a consumer of a Managed Rehabilitation Care service, please think about the kind of Managed Rehabilitation Care services that would deliver excellent quality of service and with which you would be pleased to work. Please show the extent to which you think such a Managed Rehabilitation Care service would possess the feature described by each statement.

If you feel a feature is *not at all essential* for excellent Managed Rehabilitation Care services, circle the number 1. If you feel a feature is *absolutely essential*, circle 7. If your feelings are less strong, circle one of the numbers in the middle. There are no right or wrong answers — all we are interested in is a number that truly reflects your feelings regarding services that would deliver excellent quality of service.

		Strongly Disagree						**Strongly Agree**
1.	An excellent Managed Rehabilitation Care service will be housed in modern looking facilities.	1	2	3	4	5	6	7
2.	The physical facilities will be visually appealing.	1	2	3	4	5	6	7

		Strongly Disagree						Strongly Agree

3. Employees involved with an excellent Managed Rehabilitation Care service will be professional in their appearance.

    1   2   3   4   5   6   7

4. The materials associated with the service (*i.e.*, notices, memos, forms, educational materials, *etc.*) will have a professional appearance in an excellent Managed Rehabilitation Care service.

    1   2   3   4   5   6   7

5. When an excellent Managed Rehabilitation Care service promises to do something by a certain time, it does so.

    1   2   3   4   5   6   7

6. When a client has a problem, an excellent Managed Rehabilitation Care service will show a sincere interest in dealing with it.

    1   2   3   4   5   6   7

7. An excellent Managed Rehabilitation Care service will perform the service right the first time.

    1   2   3   4   5   6   7

8. An excellent Managed Rehabilitation Care service will provide services at the promised time.

    1   2   3   4   5   6   7

9. An excellent Managed Rehabilitation Care service will insist on error-free records.

    1   2   3   4   5   6   7

10. Employees involved with an excellent Managed Rehabilitation Care service will tell clients when the services will be performed.

    1   2   3   4   5   6   7

	Strongly Disagree						**Strongly Agree**
11. Employees involved with an excellent Managed Rehabilitation Care service will give prompt service to clients.	1	2	3	4	5	6	7
12. Employees involved with an excellent Managed Rehabilitation Care service will always be willing to help clients.	1	2	3	4	5	6	7
13. Employees involved with an excellent Managed Rehabilitation Care service will never be too busy to respond to client requests.	1	2	3	4	5	6	7
14. The behaviour of employees involved with an excellent Managed Rehabilitation Care service will instil confidence in clients.	1	2	3	4	5	6	7
15. Clients of an excellent Managed Rehabilitation Care service will feel safe in their interactions.	1	2	3	4	5	6	7
16. Employees involved with an excellent Managed Rehabilitation Care service will be consistently courteous to clients.	1	2	3	4	5	6	7
17. Employees involved with an excellent Managed Rehabilitation Care service will have the knowledge or resources to answer client questions.	1	2	3	4	5	6	7
18. An excellent Managed Rehabilitation Care service will give clients individual attention.	1	2	3	4	5	6	7

	Strongly Disagree					**Strongly Agree**

19. An excellent Managed Rehabilitation Care service will have operating hours convenient to all clients.

   1 2 3 4 5 6 7

20. An excellent Managed Rehabilitation Care service will have employees who give clients personal attention.

   1 2 3 4 5 6 7

21. An excellent Managed Rehabilitation Care service will have the client's best interests at heart.

   1 2 3 4 5 6 7

22. The employees involved with an excellent Managed Rehabilitation Care service will understand the specific needs of their clients.

   1 2 3 4 5 6 7

Directions — Part 2

Listed below are five features pertaining to Managed Rehabilitation Care services and the services they offer. We would like to know how important each of these features is to you when you evaluate the service quality of Managed Rehabilitation Care services.

Please allocate a total of 100 points among the five features *according to how important each feature is to you* — the more important a feature is to you, the more points you should allocate to it. *Please ensure that the points you allocate to the five features add up to 100.*

1. The appearance of the Managed Rehabilitation Care service's physical facilities, equipment, personnel and communication materials.   _____ points

2. The Managed Rehabilitation Care service's ability to perform the promised service dependably and accurately.   _____ points

3. The Managed Rehabilitation Care service's willingness to help clients and provide prompt service.   _____ points

4. The knowledge and courtesy of the Managed Rehabilitation Care service employees and their ability to convey trust and confidence.   _____ points

5. The caring, individualized attention the Managed Rehabilitation Care service provides clients.   _____ points

       TOTAL points allocated   **100   points**

Which *one* feature among the above five is *most important* to you? (please enter the feature's number)   _____

Which feature is *second most important* to you?   _____

Which feature is *least important* to you?   _____

Directions — Part 3

The following set of statements relate to your feelings about Company XYZ's in-house Managed Rehabilitation Care service. *For each statement, please show the extent to which you believe Company XYZ's Managed Rehabilitation Care service has the feature described by the statement.*

Circling 1 means that you strongly disagree that Company XYZ's Managed Rehabilitation Care service has that feature, and circling 7 means that you strongly agree. You may circle any of the numbers in the middle that show how strong your feelings are. There are no right or wrong answers — all we are interested in is a number that best shows your perceptions about Company XYZ's Managed Rehabilitation Care service.

		Strongly Disagree					Strongly Agree	

1. Company XYZ's Managed Rehabilitation Care service is housed in a modern looking facility.

   1   2   3   4   5   6   7

2. The Company XYZ Managed Rehabilitation Care service's physical facilities are visually appealing.

   1   2   3   4   5   6   7

3. Company XYZ's Managed Rehabilitation Care service employees are professional looking in their appearance.

   1   2   3   4   5   6   7

4. The materials associated with Company XYZ's Managed Rehabilitation Care service (*i.e.*, notices, memos, forms, educational materials, *etc.*) are professional looking.

   1   2   3   4   5   6   7

5. When Company XYZ's Managed Rehabilitation Care service promises to do something by a certain time, it does so.

   1   2   3   4   5   6   7

6. When you have a problem, Company XYZ's Managed Rehabilitation Care service shows a sincere interest in dealing with it.

   1   2   3   4   5   6   7

7. Company XYZ's Managed Rehabilitation Care service performs the service right the first time.

   1   2   3   4   5   6   7

8. Company XYZ's Managed Rehabilitation Care service provides its services at the promised time.

   1   2   3   4   5   6   7

9. Company XYZ's Managed Rehabilitation Care service insists on error-free records.

   1   2   3   4   5   6   7

	Strongly Disagree					**Strongly Agree**	

10. Employees involved with Company XYZ's Managed Rehabilitation Care service tell you exactly when services will be performed.
    1 2 3 4 5 6 7

11. Employees involved with Company XYZ's Managed Rehabilitation Care service give you prompt service.
    1 2 3 4 5 6 7

12. Employees involved with Company XYZ's Managed Rehabilitation Care service are always willing to help you.
    1 2 3 4 5 6 7

13. Employees involved with Company XYZ's Managed Rehabilitation Care service are never too busy to respond to your requests.
    1 2 3 4 5 6 7

14. The behaviour of employees involved with Company XYZ's Managed Rehabilitation Care service instils confidence in you.
    1 2 3 4 5 6 7

15. You feel safe in your interactions with Company XYZ's Managed Rehabilitation Care service (*e.g.*, information is kept confidential).
    1 2 3 4 5 6 7

16. Employees involved with Company XYZ's Managed Rehabilitation Care service are consistently courteous with you.
    1 2 3 4 5 6 7

17. Employees involved with Company XYZ's Managed Rehabilitation Care service have the knowledge to answer your questions.
    1 2 3 4 5 6 7

	Strongly Disagree					Strongly Agree	
18. Company XYZ's Managed Reha- bilitation Care service gives you individual attention.	1	2	3	4	5	6	7
19. Company XYZ's Managed Reha- bilitation Care service is readily accessible.	1	2	3	4	5	6	7
20. Company XYZ's Managed Re- habilitation Care service has em- ployees who give you personal attention.	1	2	3	4	5	6	7
21. Company XYZ's Managed Re- habilitation Care service has your best interests at heart.	1	2	3	4	5	6	7
22. The employees of Company XYZ's Managed Rehabilitation Care service understand your specific needs.	1	2	3	4	5	6	7

Part 4

Your comments and suggestions concerning Company XYZ's Managed Rehabilitation Care Program are helpful to us. Please feel free to address any issue surrounding the health services, modified work, interaction with insurance carriers, *etc.*

_____

_____

_____

_____

_____

_____

_____

Part 5

	Strongly Disagree					Strongly Agree	
Do you believe that this questionnaire is a valid way to assess a Managed Rehabilitation Care service?	1	2	3	4	5	6	7

Comments:

_____
_____
_____
_____
_____
_____
_____
_____
_____
_____
_____
_____
_____
_____
_____
_____
_____

Appendix 2

Caregiver Survey Tool

MANAGED REHABILITATION CARE SERVICES EMPLOYEE SERVICE QUALITY SURVEY

Directions — Part 1

This portion of the survey deals with *how you think your clients feel* about a Managed Rehabilitation Care service, that *in their view*, delivers an excellent quality of service. *Please indicate the extent to which your clients feel that an excellent Managed Rehabilitation Care service would possess the feature described by each statement.*

If *your clients* are likely to feel a feature is *not at all essential* for excellent Managed Rehabilitation Care service, circle 1. If *your clients* are likely to feel a feature is *absolutely essential*, circle 7. If *your clients* are likely to feel less strongly about an issue, circle one of the numbers in the middle. Remember, there are no right or wrong answers — we are interested in what you think your clients' feelings are regarding Managed Rehabilitation Care services that would deliver excellent quality of service.

		Our Clients Would Strongly Disagree						Our Clients Would Strongly Agree
1.	An excellent Managed Rehabilitation Care service will be housed in modern looking facilities.	1	2	3	4	5	6	7
2.	The physical facilities will be visually appealing.	1	2	3	4	5	6	7
3.	Employees involved with an excellent Managed Rehabilitation Care service will present as professionals.	1	2	3	4	5	6	7

	Our Clients Would Strongly Disagree					**Our Clients Would Strongly Agree**	
4. The materials associated with the service (*i.e.*, notices, memos, forms, educational materials, *etc.*) will have a professional appearance in an excellent Managed Rehabilitation Care service.	1	2	3	4	5	6	7
5. When an excellent Managed Rehabilitation Care service promises to do something by a certain time, it does so.	1	2	3	4	5	6	7
6. When a client has a problem, an excellent Managed Rehabilitation Care service will show sincere interest in dealing with it.	1	2	3	4	5	6	7
7. An excellent Managed Rehabilitation Care service will perform the service right the first time.	1	2	3	4	5	6	7
8. An excellent Managed Rehabilitation Care service will provide services at the promised time.	1	2	3	4	5	6	7
9. An excellent Managed Rehabilitation Care service will insist on error-free records.	1	2	3	4	5	6	7

	Our Clients Would Strongly Disagree					Our Clients Would Strongly Agree	
10. Employees involved with an excellent Managed Rehabilitation Care service will give prompt service to clients.	1	2	3	4	5	6	7
11. Employees involved with an excellent Managed Rehabilitation Care service will always be willing to help clients.	1	2	3	4	5	6	7
12. Employees involved with an excellent Managed Rehabilitation Care service will never be too busy to respond to client requests.	1	2	3	4	5	6	7
13. The behaviour of employees involved with an excellent Managed Rehabilitation Care service will instil confidence in clients.	1	2	3	4	5	6	7
14. Clients of an excellent Managed Rehabilitation Care service will feel safe in their interactions.	1	2	3	4	5	6	7
15. Employees involved with an excellent Managed Rehabilitation Care service will be consistently courteous to clients.	1	2	3	4	5	6	7

	Our Clients Would Strongly Disagree					Our Clients Would Strongly Agree	
16. Employees involved with an excellent Managed Rehabilitation Care service will have the knowledge or resources to answer client questions.	1	2	3	4	5	6	7
17. An excellent Managed Rehabilitation Care service will give clients individual attention.	1	2	3	4	5	6	7
18. An excellent Managed Rehabilitation Care service will have operating hours convenient to all their clients.	1	2	3	4	5	6	7
19. An excellent Managed Rehabilitation Care service will have employees who give clients personal attention.	1	2	3	4	5	6	7
20. An excellent Managed Rehabilitation Care service will have the client's best interests at heart.	1	2	3	4	5	6	7
21. The employees involved with an excellent Managed Rehabilitation Care service will understand the specific needs of their clients.	1	2	3	4	5	6	7

Directions — Part 2

Listed below are five features pertaining to Managed Rehabilitation Care services and the services they offer. We would like to know how important each of these features is to *your clients* when they evaluate a Managed Rehabilitation Care service's quality of service.

Please allocate a total of *100 points among the five features according to how important each feature is to your clients* — the more important a feature is likely to be to your clients, the more points you should allocate to it. *Please ensure that the points you allocate to the five features add up to 100.*

1. The appearance of the Managed Rehabilitation Care service's physical facilities, equipment, personnel and communication materials. _____ points

2. The Managed Rehabilitation Care service's ability to perform the promised service dependably and accurately. _____ points

3. The Managed Rehabilitation Care service's willingness to help clients and provide prompt service. _____ points

4. The knowledge and courtesy of the Managed Rehabilitation Care service employees and their ability to convey trust and confidence. _____ points

5. The caring, individualized attention the Managed Rehabilitation Care service provides its clients. _____ points

TOTAL points allocated **100 points**

Which *one* feature among the above five is *most important to your clients*? (please enter the feature's number) _____

Which feature is likely to be *second most important to your clients*? _____

Which feature is likely to be *least important to your clients*? _____

Directions — Part 3

Service quality performance standards in companies can be *formal* — written, explicit, and communicated to employees. They can also be *informal* — oral, implicit, and assumed to be understood by employees.

For each of the following features, circle the number that best describes the extent to which service quality performance standards are formalized in your department. If there are no standards in your department, check the appropriate box.

	Informal Standards				Formal Standards		No Standards Exist	
1. The appearance of the Company XYZ Managed Rehabilitation Care service's physical facilities, equipment, personnel and communication materials.	1	2	3	4	5	6	7	[ ]
2. The ability of the Company XYZ Managed Rehabilitation Care service to perform the promised service dependably and accurately.	1	2	3	4	5	6	7	[ ]
3. The willingness of the Company XYZ Managed Rehabilitation Care service to help clients and provide prompt service.	1	2	3	4	5	6	7	[ ]
4. The knowledge and courtesy of the Company XYZ Managed Rehabilitation Care service employees and their ability to convey trust and confidence.	1	2	3	4	5	6	7	[ ]

		Informal Standards				Formal Standards		No Standards Exist	
5.	The caring, individualized attention the Company XYZ Managed Rehabilitation Care service provides its clients.	1	2	3	4	5	6	7	[ ]

Directions — Part 4

Listed below are the same five features as in Part 3. Employees and units sometimes experience difficulty in achieving the service quality standards established for them.

For each feature below, circle the number that best represents the degree to which your department and its staff are able to meet the formal service quality performance standards established.

Remember, there are no right or wrong answers — we need your candid assessments for this question to be helpful.

		Unable to Meet Standards Consistently				Able to Meet Standards Consistently		No Standards Exist	
1.	The appearance of the Company XYZ Managed Rehabilitation Care service's physical facilities, equipment, personnel and communication materials.	1	2	3	4	5	6	7	[ ]
2.	The ability of Company XYZ's Managed Rehabilitation Care service to perform the promised service dependably and accurately.	1	2	3	4	5	6	7	[ ]

	Unable to Meet Standards Consistently				Able to Meet Standards Consistently		No Standards Exist	
3. The willingness of Company XYZ's Managed Rehabilitation Care service to help clients and provide prompt service.	1	2	3	4	5	6	7	[ ]
4. The knowledge and courtesy of Company XYZ's Managed Rehabilitation Care service employees and their ability to convey trust and confidence.	1	2	3	4	5	6	7	[ ]
5. The caring, individualized attention Company XYZ's Managed Rehabilitation Care service provides its clients.	1	2	3	4	5	6	7	[ ]

Directions — Part 5

Often, promises are made about the level of service a group will deliver. Sometimes, it is not possible to fulfil these promises.

For each feature below, we want to know the extent to which you believe that your department and its staff deliver the level of service promised to clients. Circle the number that best describes your perception.

	Unable to Meet Promises Consistently						Able to Meet Promises Consistently
1. The appearance of the Company XYZ Managed Rehabilitation Care service's physical facilities, equipment, personnel and communication materials.	1	2	3	4	5	6	7
2. The ability of Company XYZ's Managed Rehabilitation Care service to perform the promised service dependably and accurately.	1	2	3	4	5	6	7
3. The willingness of Company XYZ's Managed Rehabilitation Care service to help clients and provide prompt service.	1	2	3	4	5	6	7
4. The knowledge and courtesy of the Company XYZ Managed Rehabilitation Care service employees and their ability to convey trust and confidence.	1	2	3	4	5	6	7
5. The caring, individualized attention Company XYZ's Managed Rehabilitation Care service provides its clients.	1	2	3	4	5	6	7

Directions — Part 6

Listed below are a number of statements intended to measure your perceptions about your department and its operations.

Please indicate the extent to which you disagree or agree with each statement by circling one of the seven numbers next to each statement.

If you strongly disagree, circle 1. If you strongly agree, circle 7. If your feelings are not strong, circle one of the numbers in the middle. There are no right or wrong answers. Please tell us honestly how you feel.

PLEASE READ THE QUESTIONS CAREFULLY

		Strongly Disagree					Strongly Agree	
1.	We regularly collect information about the needs of our Managed Rehabilitation Care clients.	1	2	3	4	5	6	7
2.	We rarely use marketing research information that is collected about our Managed Rehabilitation Care clients.	1	2	3	4	5	6	7
3.	We regularly collect information about the service-quality expectations of our Managed Rehabilitation Care clients.	1	2	3	4	5	6	7
4.	The Director of our Managed Rehabilitation Care service rarely interacts with clients.	1	2	3	4	5	6	7
5.	The front-line employees involved with our Managed Rehabilitation Care service frequently communicate with the Director.	1	2	3	4	5	6	7
6.	The Director in our Managed Rehabilitation Care service rarely seeks suggestions about serving Managed Rehabilitation Care clients from front-line employees.	1	2	3	4	5	6	7

		Strongly Disagree						Strongly Agree
7.	The Director in our Managed Rehabilitation Care service frequently has face-to-face interactions with front-line employees.	1	2	3	4	5	6	7
8.	The primary means of communication in our Managed Rehabilitation Care service between front-line employees and the Director is through memos.	1	2	3	4	5	6	7
9.	Our Managed Rehabilitation Care service has too many levels of management between front-line employees and the Director.	1	2	3	4	5	6	7
10.	Our Managed Rehabilitation Care service does not commit the necessary resources for service quality.	1	2	3	4	5	6	7
11.	Our Managed Rehabilitation Care service has internal programs for improving the quality of service to Managed Rehabilitation Care clients.	1	2	3	4	5	6	7
12.	In the occupational health group, the Advisor who improves service quality is more likely to be rewarded than other Advisors in the company.	1	2	3	4	5	6	7

	Strongly Disagree					Strongly Agree	

13. Our Managed Rehabilitation Care service group emphasizes service marketing as much as, or more, than it emphasizes serving Managed Rehabilitation Care clients.

1   2   3   4   5   6   7

14. Our Managed Rehabilitation Care service group has a formal process for setting service quality goals for employees.

1   2   3   4   5   6   7

15. In our Managed Rehabilitation Care service group, we try to set specific quality of service goals.

1   2   3   4   5   6   7

16. Our Managed Rehabilitation Care service group effectively uses automation to achieve consistency in serving Managed Rehabilitation Care clients.

1   2   3   4   5   6   7

17. Programs are in place in our Managed Rehabilitation Care service group to improve operating procedures so as to provide consistent service.

1   2   3   4   5   6   7

18. Our Managed Rehabilitation Care service has the necessary capabilities to meet client requirements for service.

1   2   3   4   5   6   7

19. If we gave our Managed Rehabilitation Care clients the level of service they really want, Company XYZ would go broke.

1   2   3   4   5   6   7

	Strongly Disagree					**Strongly Agree**	
20. Our Managed Rehabilitation Care service has the operating systems to deliver the level of service that clients demand.	1	2	3	4	5	6	7

Directions — Part 7

Listed below are a number of statements intended to measure your perceptions about your department and its operations.

Please indicate the extent to which you disagree or agree with each statement by circling one of the seven numbers next to each statement.

If you strongly disagree, circle 1. If you strongly agree, circle 7. If your feelings are not strong, circle one of the numbers in the middle. There are no right or wrong answers. Please tell us honestly how you feel.

PLEASE READ THE QUESTIONS CAREFULLY

	Strongly Disagree					**Strongly Agree**	
1. I feel that I am part of a team providing Company XYZ's Managed Rehabilitation Care service.	1	2	3	4	5	6	7
2. Everyone in Company XYZ occupational health service contributes to a team effort in servicing Managed Rehabilitation Care clients.	1	2	3	4	5	6	7
3. I feel a sense of responsibility to help my fellow employees do their jobs well.	1	2	3	4	5	6	7
4. My fellow employees and I cooperate more often than we compete.	1	2	3	4	5	6	7
5. I feel that I am an important member of this Managed Rehabilitation Care service group.	1	2	3	4	5	6	7

	Strongly Disagree						Strongly Agree

6. I feel comfortable in my job in the sense that I am able to perform the job well.

1 2 3 4 5 6 7

7. Company XYZ's occupational health service hires people who are qualified to do Managed Rehabilitation Care as part of their jobs.

1 2 3 4 5 6 7

8. Company XYZ's occupational health services gives me the tools and equipment that I need to perform the Managed Rehabilitation Care portion of my job well.

1 2 3 4 5 6 7

9. I spend a lot of time in my job trying to resolve problems over which I have little control.

1 2 3 4 5 6 7

10. I have the freedom in my job to truly satisfy my Managed Rehabilitation Care clients' needs.

1 2 3 4 5 6 7

11. I sometimes feel a lack of control over my job because too many Managed Rehabilitation Care clients demand service at the same time.

1 2 3 4 5 6 7

12. One of my frustrations on the job is that I sometimes have to depend on other employees involved with serving my Managed Rehabilitation Care clients.

1 2 3 4 5 6 7

	Strongly Disagree						Strongly Agree
13. My supervisor's appraisal of my job performance includes how well I interact with Managed Rehabilitation Care clients.	1	2	3	4	5	6	7
14. At Company XYZ, making a special effort to serve Managed Rehabilitation Care clients well does not result in more pay or in more recognition.	1	2	3	4	5	6	7
15. At Company XYZ, employees who do the best job serving their Managed Rehabilitation Care clients are more likely to be rewarded than other employees.	1	2	3	4	5	6	7
16. The amount of paperwork in my job makes it hard for me to effectively serve my Managed Rehabilitation Care clients.	1	2	3	4	5	6	7
17. The Managed Rehabilitation Care service group places so much emphasis on marketing to clients that it is difficult to serve our clients properly.	1	2	3	4	5	6	7
18. What my Managed Rehabilitation Care clients want me to do and what the Director wants me to do are usually the same thing.	1	2	3	4	5	6	7

	Strongly Disagree						Strongly Agree
19. The Managed Rehabilitation Care service group and I have the same ideas about how the Managed Rehabilitation Care portion of my job should be performed.	1	2	3	4	5	6	7
20. I receive a sufficient amount of information from the Director concerning what I am supposed to do in the Managed Rehabilitation Care portion of my job.	1	2	3	4	5	6	7
21. I often feel that I do not understand the services offered by Company XYZ's Managed Rehabilitation Care service.	1	2	3	4	5	6	7
22. I am able to keep up with changes in the occupational health service group that affect the Managed Rehabilitation Care portion of my job.	1	2	3	4	5	6	7
23. I am not sure which aspects of my job my supervisor will stress most in my evaluation.	1	2	3	4	5	6	7
24. The people who develop our Managed Rehabilitation Care marketing presentations consult employees like me about the realism of promises made in those presentations.	1	2	3	4	5	6	7

		Strongly Disagree					**Strongly Agree**
25. I am often not aware in advance of the promises made in the Managed Rehabilitation Care service marketing presentations.	1	2	3	4	5	6	7
26. Employees like me interact with other operations people to discuss the level of service Company XYZ's Managed Rehabilitation Care services can deliver to clients.	1	2	3	4	5	6	7
27. Our Company XYZ Managed Rehabilitation Care service policies on serving clients are consistent for everyone in the group that services clients.	1	2	3	4	5	6	7
28. Intense competition from external occupational health vendors is creating more pressure inside this group to generate new ideas and ways of managing rehabilitative care.	1	2	3	4	5	6	7
29. Our key occupational health service competitors make promises in Managed Rehabilitation Care they cannot possibly keep in an effort to gain new clients.	1	2	3	4	5	6	7

Part 8

Your comments and suggestions concerning Company XYZ's Managed Rehabilitation Care program are helpful to us. Please feel free to address any issue surrounding the health services, modified work, contact with insurance carriers or Workers' Compensation.

_____
_____
_____
_____
_____
_____
_____

Part 9

	Strongly Disagree						Strongly Agree
Do you believe that this questionnaire is a valid way to assess a Managed Rehabilitation Care service?	1	2	3	4	5	6	7

Comments:

_____
_____
_____
_____
_____
_____
_____
_____
_____
_____

CHAPTER REFERENCES

D. Dyck, "Gap Analysis of Health Services: Client Satisfaction Surveys" (1996) 44:1 AOHNA Journal at 541-549.

Hewitt Associates, Press Release, "Ignoring Employee Absences May Prove Costly for Canadian Organizations, According to Hewitt" (15 June 2005), online: <http://was4.hewitt.com/hewitt/resource/newsroom/pressrel/2005-15-05eng.htm>.

NIDMAR, *Consensus Based Disability Management Audit* (Port Alberni, B.C.: NIDMAR 2004).

M. O'Donnell, *Health Promotion in the Workplace* (New York: John Wiley & Sons, 1984).

A. Parasuraman, V. Zeithaml & L. Berry, "SERVQUAL: A Multiple-item Scale for Measuring Consumer Perceptions of Service Quality" *Journal of Retailing* (Spring 1988) at 12-40.

Statistics Canada, *Average Hourly Wages of Employees by Selected Characteristics*, online: <http://www40.statcan.ca/l01/cst01/labr69a.htm>.

E. Sullivan & P. Decker, *Effective Management in Nursing*, 2d ed. (Menlo Park, California: Addison-Wesley Publishing Company, 1988).

M. Youngblood, *Eating the Chocolate Elephant: Take Charge of Change through Total Process Management* (Richardson, Texas: Micrografx Inc., 1994).

V. Zeithaml, "Consumer Perceptions of Price, Quality and Value: A Means-end Model and Synthesis of Evidence" *Journal of Marketing* (July 1988).

V. Zeithaml, A. Parasuraman & L. Berry, *Delivering Quality Service* (Toronto: The Free Press, 1990).

Chapter 7

Disability Management
Best Practices

DISABILITY MANAGEMENT BEST PRACTICES DEFINED

Disability management, in its entirety, can be defined as the process of preventing and managing absence from work. Operationally, it is an active process directed towards promoting and supporting regular workplace attendance and minimizing the impact of impairment on the ill or injured employee's ability to compete in the workplace.

As noted in Chapter 1, the *key elements* of any Disability Management Program are:

- management-employee commitment and supportive policies;
- stakeholder education and involvement;
- supportive benefit plans;
- a coordinated approach to injury/illness management with a focus on early intervention;
- a communication strategy;
- a Graduated Return-to-Work Program;
- measurement of outcomes; and
- disability prevention, including workplace wellness, attendance support and occupational health and safety initiatives.

Best practices are a form of benchmarking that result from direct observation of clinical practices.[1] They are based on real examples and can be used to gradually promote system improvement. Best practices can serve as guidelines for practice and measurement of outcomes. However, changes in technology, knowledge and practice advancements can alter any best practice. This means that benchmarks and guidelines must undergo frequent reviews and updates to remain current and credible.

---

[1] H. Bruckman & J. Harris, "Occupational Medicine Practice Guidelines" (1998) 13:4 Occupational Medicine: State of the Art Reviews.

Disability Management: Best Practices

The intent of this chapter is to summarize the current best practices in disability management. In this chapter, discussion of the topic will be followed by a presentation of the relevant best practices.

INTEGRATE DISABILITY MANAGEMENT EFFORTS

For effective disability management, a design or model for an integrated Disability Management Program should exist. An integrated Disability Management Program model (Chapter 1, Figure 1.2) contains the following elements:

* joint union-labour-management endorsement, commitment and involvement;
* supportive policies, procedures and systems;
* a system that ensures accountability by all parties;
* absenteeism and disability data collection for analysis and evaluation;
* claims management and adjudication;
* case management and coordination;
* multi-disciplinary interventions — occupational safety, human resource, Employee Assistance Program, medical, vocational or occupational rehabilitation;
* early intervention and a graduated return-to-work program; and
* attendance support and disability prevention strategies.

According to Watson Wyatt Worldwide, employers who have integrated Disability Management Programs experience an average reduction of 19-25% in their total disability costs.[2]

BEST PRACTICES

1. Have a joint labour-management committee act as a steering committee for the Disability Management Program.[3] This committee would be the foundation of the Disability Management Program. Roles assigned to members of the committee have been defined in Chapter 4.

   The steering committee advises and consults with management and union leaders, evaluates concerns and receives advice and suggestions for the Disability Management Program from various stakeholders in the

---

[2] Watson Wyatt Worldwide, News Release, "Employers that Measure Results from Integrated Disability Management Programs Report Big Savings" (15 October 1998), online: <http://www.watsonwyatt.com/news/press.asp?ID=6900>.

[3] National Institute for Disability Management and Research (NIDMAR), *Disability Management in the Workplace: A Guide to Establishing a Joint Workplace Program* (Port Alberni, B.C.: NIDMAR, 1995).

company or organization. The committee also receives reports regarding the usage of the Disability Management Program, which assess the program's overall effectiveness. The information provided to the committee and to management is population, or aggregate, data so that individual clients cannot be identified.

Typically, the steering committee membership has representatives from management and labour, and the chairperson is elected by the members for a set term.

2. Ensure effective functioning by having one central figure oversee the daily operations of a Disability Management Program. This is typically a Disability Management Coordinator.

3. Ensure that resources, such as the Disability Management Coordinator, the administrator and internal/external consultants, are available to the steering committee.

4. Conduct a comprehensive needs-analysis to identify specific organizational needs, and to establish baseline data before implementing an integrated Disability Management Program. This should include an assessment of labour/management attitudes towards disability management practices, the identification of the company or organization's disability profile, an acknowledgment of the types of assistance available to the ill or injured employee and an estimate of the level of disability support required.

5. Examine all related disability policies and procedures in terms of their impact on the Disability Management Program.

6. Review and revise, where necessary, the current disability-related policies and procedures.

7. Identify and communicate the roles and responsibilities of all major stakeholders involved in the Disability Management Program.

8. Define the available return-to-work options to all the stakeholders.

9. Identify the milestones or specific steps to be taken in the return-to-work process.

10. Review and revise, as appropriate, the current return-to-work strategies.

11. Assess, where necessary, the disability claim forms with a view to their functionality and contribution to the effectiveness of the Disability Management Program. Forms should focus on the claimant's capabilities versus disabilities.

12. Develop an absence and disability database for all types of absences — incidental absence, short-term disability, occupational absence, and long-term disability. Link this system with the company or organization's Employee Assistance Program, Occupational Health and Safety Program, employee benefit plans and Workplace Wellness Program outcomes.

13. Use the above outcome data along with other human resource and group benefit plan outcomes to assist in the interpretation of disability management issues.

CENTRALIZE THE RESPONSIBILITY FOR AN INTEGRATED DISABILITY MANAGEMENT PROGRAM

To ensure effective functioning, one central figure should coordinate the daily operations of a Disability Management Program.[4,5] This is typically a Disability Management Coordinator. The functions for this position are discussed in detail in Chapter 4.

BEST PRACTICES

1. Delegate the coordination of the Disability Management Program to one central person. The Disability Management Coordinator is responsible for the overall management (including data organization and analysis) of all employee disabilities; acts as a point of contact for all stakeholders; is an active supporter of the ill or injured employee and family members; and functions as a catalyst for facilitating the reintegration of the disabled worker into the workplace.
2. Coordinate disability management initiatives with the Employee Assistance Program, Occupational Health and Safety Program, Workplace Wellness Program and human resource benefit efforts.
3. Advise the company's occupational health and safety department of the cause and nature of all Workers' Compensation Board claims as part of the overall Disability Management Program. The intent is to seek workable illness and injury prevention strategies.

DISABILITY MANAGEMENT EDUCATION AND TRAINING

The purpose of Disability Management education and training is to create awareness around the need for and value afforded by workplace-based attendance and Disability Management Programs. Recent studies indicate that the response of the supervisor to the worker's medical absence is one of the most important factors in the worker's timely return to work. For example, workers who felt blamed, penalized, mistrusted or belittled by their supervisor when they first reported a work-related injury had a significantly longer work absence.[6]

Supervisors, union leaders and management benefit from specific information on:

*   helping employees attain regular workplace attendance;

---

[4] *Ibid.*
[5] D. Lyons, "Integrated Disability Management: Assessing Its Fit for Your Company", *Ideas at Work* (Winter 2004), online: <http://www.libertymutual.com/omapps/ContentServer?cid=1058290626910&pagename=CMln>.
[6] G. Pransky & W. Shaw, "Injury Response: Optimizing the Role of Supervisors", *Ideas at Work* (Spring 2002) at 11-12, online: <http://www.libertymutual.com/omapps/ContentsServer?cid=1058816266173&pagename=CMln>.

- the values and objectives of attendance support and disability management;
- communicating effectively with the ill/injured employee and family;
- identifying markers that indicate a potential problem situation;
- overcoming barriers to graduated return-to-work efforts;
- tracking of absences and modified/alternate work initiatives;
- the related cost/benefit issues; and
- success and failure indicators for a Disability Management Program.

Ongoing training is required for a Disability Management Coordinator to develop and maintain the specific skills and knowledge necessary to facilitate a safe and timely return to work for ill or injured employees. A Disability Management Coordinator must have a practical knowledge of:

- the various roles and responsibilities of health professionals who affect the return-to-work process (*i.e.*, physicians, occupational health nurses, physiotherapists, occupational therapists, rehabilitation specialists, *etc.*);
- ergonomics;
- principles of occupational health and safety;
- claims management methods;
- case management methods;
- barriers to graduated return-to-work efforts within the organization and how to overcome them; and
- the accepted dispute resolution procedures.

BEST PRACTICE

Specialized training in disability management is required for the Disability Management Coordinator, and generalized training for all supervisors and human resource staff in dealing with ill or injured employees and family members. Disability management education for union and other staff leaders facilitates Disability Management Program implementation.[7] This may be possible through a government or private agency specializing in disability management.

JOINT LABOUR-MANAGEMENT COMMITMENT TO A DISABILITY MANAGEMENT PROGRAM

The most successful workplace models of disability management involve joint labour-management support and participation. In terms of legalities, management is obliged to work with union leaders to offer effective disability services, Employee Assistance Programs and rehabilitation services. The rationale is that the union is the certified bargaining agent for the employee. As noted in Chapter

---

[7] Canadian Centre on Disability Studies, *Best Practices in Contemporary Disability Management: Executive Summary* (1998), online: <http://www.disabilitystudies.ca/cdmes.htm>.

2, the employee gives up his or her individual bargaining position on behalf of a stronger collective voice with the union. In return, the union has a duty to review any employment decisions made between the employer and employee. If the union fails to do so, the employee can sue the union.[8]

The union has a duty to fairly represent its member when a complaint comes forward about the employee's work capacity, or likelihood of risk due to health conditions. The employer and the union have the duty to accommodate the ill or injured worker, and the worker has the right to be accommodated unless there is a Bona Fide Occupational Requirement, or the accommodation is to the point of undue hardship on the employer's part.

BEST PRACTICES

1. Encourage joint labour-management involvement in disability management initiatives and activities.
2. Encourage joint labour-management participation in the Disability Management Program steering committee.
3. Invite and strongly encourage union/employee promotion and participation in graduated return-to-work activities.

DISABILITY DATA MANAGEMENT

Data collection and analysis is the foundation on which the successful development and maintenance of a disability management program is based. Companies which choose not to measure disability-related costs may be missing information that could help them identify health and productivity issues. As well, disability data can play a major role in justifying the need for a disability management program, for demonstrating the value added to the company by the program and for making informed decisions on continuous improvement efforts.

Information regarding workplace absence can be obtained from both internal and external areas and is often accumulated without thought to integration or management. Some examples of information pockets are discussed below:

Short-term Absences

In general, employee absence from work is affected by a number of variables:

- *industry sector* — workers in the public sector tend to miss, on average, 12 workdays per year,[9] while private sector workers miss 8.4 workdays per year;[10]

---

[8]   D.B. Mercer, "Roles and Responsibilities in Job Modification and Accommodation" (Seminars in Occupational Health and Medicine, Faculty of Medicine, Continuing Education, University of Calgary, 3 February 1999) [unpublished].

[9]   Statistics Canada, *Work Absence Rates 2004*, Catalogue No. 71-211-XIE (Ottawa: Statistics Canada, 2005) at 28.

[10]   *Ibid.*, at 29.

- *industry* — health care and social assistance workers (14.4 days), public administration employees — Federal (13.1 days) and transportation and warehousing workers (11.1 days) posted the most absence time in 2004. Those in professional, scientific and technical industries missed the least time (5.6 workdays per year);[11]
- *size of organization* — larger organizations (*i.e.*, more than 500 employees) experience higher absenteeism (12.0 workdays per year) than smaller ones, with less than 20 employees (7.4 workdays per year);[12]
- *work status* — permanent full-time employment is associated with more sick time than part-time employment status. Those with permanent job status miss 9.4 workdays per year versus 7.4 workdays per year for those with non-permanent job status;[13]
- *union status* — union coverage is associated with almost twice the absence rate (13.1 workdays per year) of non-union coverage (7.3 workdays per year);[14]
- *occupation* — employees in more physically demanding, hazardous or stressful occupations lose the most time. For example, labourers lost 15.1 days per year, health care occupations lost 15.0 workdays; while those in managerial occupations experienced the least absence days (5.3 workdays per year). Two occupations topped the list – nursing at 18.7 lost workdays per year and health support staff at 15.6 days;[15]
- *job tenure* — in 2004, workers with the most tenure missed the most time from work. New workers (12 months or less on the job) missed only 6.6 days. Workers who had been on the job for over 14 years missed an average of 11.6 days per year;[16]
- *shift work* — in 1997, shift workers experienced higher absence days (4.3 workdays per year) than non-shift workers (3.6 workdays per year);[17]
- *educational attainment* — the more education attained, the less likely the employee was off work. In 2004, employees with a university degree missed 7.0 days/year, while those with less than grade 9 education missed 12.7 days;[18] and
- *sick leave plan* — those entitled to a sick leave plan are absent more (4.2 workdays per year) than those who are without (3.0 workdays per year).
- *geographic location* — in 1997, Newfoundland, British Columbia and Québec had the highest rates (9.6, 8.7 and 8.4 workdays per year respectively); while Prince Edward Island and Alberta had the lowest (6.5 and 6.9 workdays

---

[11] *Ibid.*, at 32.
[12] *Ibid.*, at 22.
[13] *Ibid.*, at 24.
[14] *Ibid.*, at 29.
[15] *Ibid.*, at 35.
[16] *Ibid.*, at 23.
[17] E. Akyeampong, *Work Absences: New Data, New Insights, Spring 1998 Perspective*, Cat. No. 75-001-XPE (Ottawa: Statistics Canada, 1998) at 16-22.
[18] Statistics Canada, *Work Absence Rates 2004* (Ottawa: Statistics Canada, 2005) at 21.

per year respectively). This is a variable factor as can be seen in the following table:

Figure 7.1: Days Lost per Canadian Worker due to Illness or Disability (I/D) & Personal or Family Responsibility (P/F)[19]

Province	Year															
	1997		1998		1999		2000		2001		2002		2003		2004	
	I/D	P/F	I/D	P/F	I/D	P/F	I/D	P/F	I/D	P/F	I/D	P/F	I/D	P/F	I/D	P/F
Canada	6.2	1.2	6.6	1.2	6.7	1.3	6.7	1.3	7.0	1.5	7.4	1.7	7.5	1.7	7.5	1.7
Newfoundland & Lab.	6.1	1.5	8.1	1.3	7.6	0.7	7.7	1.4	7.4	1.3	6.9	1.7	9.1	1.4	8.8	1.5
Prince Edward Island	6.4	1.3	5.1	1.4	6.7	1.6	5.8	1.1	6.5	1.2	6.9	1.6	6.4	1.3	6.0	1.6
Nova Scotia	6.0	1.0	6.6	1.2	6.9	1.1	8.2	1.3	8.3	1.4	8.8	1.6	8.1	1.7	9.1	1.9
New Brunswick	6.5	0.8	7.0	0.9	6.7	1.1	7.6	1.0	8.8	1.4	8.4	1.3	8.7	1.4	8.0	1.7
Quebec	7.4	1.0	7.4	1.0	7.7	1.0	7.8	1.0	7.9	1.2	8.4	1.4	9.3	1.5	9.4	1.4
Ontario	5.4	1.2	6.0	1.3	5.8	1.3	5.7	1.3	6.0	1.6	6.6	1.9	6.5	1.8	6.7	1.9
Manitoba	6.7	1.3	6.9	1.3	7.0	1.4	7.1	1.6	7.7	1.7	8.4	1.7	7.8	1.6	8.0	1.8
Saskatchewan	5.8	1.6	6.7	1.5	7.0	1.7	7.7	1.6	8.1	1.8	8.4	2.0	8.6	1.8	8.0	2.2
Alberta	5.2	1.3	5.5	1.4	6.2	1.7	6.1	1.5	6.5	1.7	6.7	1.8	6.2	1.8	5.6	1.9
British Columbia	7.2	1.5	7.4	1.2	8.2	1.5	7.4	1.3	8.3	1.4	7.8	1.7	8.1	1.7	7.3	1.5

As of 2004, the provinces with the highest absence rates were Nova Scotia, Quebec, Saskatchewan and Newfoundland & Labrador.

• *gender* — on average, women are absent more days from work per year than are men;[20]

Figure 7.2: Work Absence by Gender

Work Absence by Gender (workdays/year)		
Year	Women	Men
1997	9.0	6.2
1998	9.1	6.8
1999	9.5	7.0
2000	9.4	7.0
2001	9.8	7.6
2002	10.7	8.0
2003	10.7	8.2
2004	10.9	8.0

---

[19] *Ibid.*, at 100-112.
[20] *Ibid.*, at 100.

- *age* — older workers are absent more often than younger workers (55 to 64 years = 12.5 missed workdays per year; and 45 to 54 years = 9.9 workdays per year, versus 20 to 24 year olds = 6.4 workdays per year);[21]
- *child care* — workers with preschoolers miss, on average, 10.4 workdays per year (women – 13.9; men – 8.6). Those without children are absent 8.7 workdays per year (women – 9.8; men – 8.0);[22]
- *eldercare* — workers who care for aging relatives report spending 60 hours per month with those needing care.[23] The impact of providing eldercare can be great. These workers are more likely to report sleep loss, lack of time for personal care and health problems. The result is an increase in employer costs due to more work absenteeism, increased employee benefit costs, lower productivity while at work, and a reluctance to taking on expanded job opportunities or duties.

Thus, there are many factors that impact workplace absence. Astute employers are beginning to recognize this and look for ways to address these issues. On average, the absenteeism and disability costs for Canadian and American employers are approximately 14.9% of payroll.[24]

In 1997, the average time lost to medical absenteeism in Canada was 7.4 workdays, with 6.2 workdays due to medical reasons and 1.2 workdays due to personal or family reasons. In 2000, this number increased to 9.0 workdays (6.7 lost due to illness/disability and 1.3 days lost due to personal/family reasons). By 2004, workers lost 9.2 workdays with 7.5 days away due to illness or disability and 1.7 days due to personal or family reasons. In eight years, Canadian employers have witnessed a 24% increase in absenteeism, and increased costs.

One *caveat*, in terms of comparison, this and the above data is provided by Statistics Canada and is based on a worker-reported survey. Employer data may differ. In fact, the Conference Board of Canada, *2000 Compensation Planning Outlook Report*[25] indicated that employee absenteeism due to illness, disability, or family responsibility, for a period of at least 50% of the day but less than 52 consecutive weeks were as follows:

---

[21] *Ibid.*, at 20.

[22] *Ibid.*, at 22.

[23] Conference Board of Canada, News Release, "Eldercare taking its toll on Canadian Workers" (10 November 1999).

[24] Marsh Risk Consulting, *Workforce Risk: Fourth Annual Marsh Mercer Survey of Employers' Time-Off and Disability Programs* (2003), online: <http://www.marshriskconsulting.com/st/PDEv_C_371_SC_228135_NR_306_Pl_347745.htm>.

[25] Conference Board of Canada, *Compensation Planning Outlook 2000* (Ottawa: Conference Board of Canada, 1999).

Figure 7.3: Absenteeism Rates

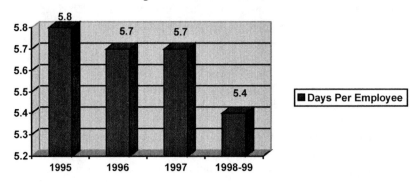

Typically, the main reasons for short-term, non-occupational disabilities are musculoskeletal and psychological disorders. However, this can vary by industry and with the length of the short-term disability absence. For example, the reasons for going on short-term disability and those for remaining on claim are demonstrated on the table below.[26]

Figure 7.4: Reasons for Remaining on Short-term Disability

Reason	Short-term Disability Claim	Remaining on Short-term Disability
Accident	36%	19%
Mental/Nervous Disorder	11%	22%
Musculoskeletal Disorder	11%	15%
Circulatory Disorder	5%	12%

In this example, the non-work accidents are the main reason for a claimant going on short-term disability, but mental disorders are the top reason for a claimant remaining on short-term disability.

Workplace Illness or Injury

The trends in work-related illness and injuries are:

- most injuries tend to occur to workers between the ages of 25 and 44 years;
- young workers, males and inexperienced workers account for a majority of the lost-time claims;
- the primary causes for work-related lost-time claims are strains and sprains, contusions or concussions, cuts and fractures or dislocations;

---

[26] The Mutual Group, *Block of Business: January 01, 1998 to December 31, 1998, STD Claims Management Report — Statistics* (Waterloo: The Mutual Group, 1998).

- the parts of the body most frequently injured are the back, torso and hands;
- the main sources of injury are bodily motion and working surfaces; and
- the duration of disability claims is usually less than 10 days — however, about 15% of these claims last longer than 50 days in length.[27]

Long-term Absences

The incidence rates for long-term disability per 1,000 employees are between 4.5 and 10 for third party insured long-term disability programs with the lower rates experienced by companies who actually case manage their own disability claims. These rates vary depending on the type of work done:[28]

Figure 7.5: Long-term Disability Incidence by Occupation

Occupation	Long-term Disability Incidence
Professionals[29]	4.5/1000
White Collar Workers[30]	5.5/1000
Blue Collar Workers[31]	10.0/1000
Service Providers[32]	8.0/1000

The top six reasons, by cause, for long-term disability are as follows:[33]

Figure 7.6: Long-term Disability Claims by Cause

Cause of Disability	New Long-term Disability Claims	Ongoing Long-term Disability Claims
Mental Disorder	25%	22%
Musculoskeletal System and Connective Tissue Disorder	24%	30%
Cancer	14%	6%
Circulatory System Disease	11%	14%
Non-work Accident	9%	7%

---

[27] Alberta Labour, *Occupational Injury and Disease in Alberta, 1996 Summary: Lost-time Claims and Claim Rates* (Edmonton: Alberta Labour, 1998).

[28] The Mutual Group, *LTD Claims Trends: 1996* (Waterloo, The Mutual Group, 1996).

[29] Professionals include accountants, computer operators, dentists, engineers, physiotherapists, doctors, lawyers, registered nurses.

[30] White Collar Workers include technicians, managers, letter carriers, cashiers, administrators, contractors, clerks and tellers.

[31] Blue Collar Workers include craftsmen, foremen, inspectors, labourers, electricians, mechanics, machine operators, and miners.

[32] Service Workers include hotel staff, police, firefighters, nurses' aides, orderlies, registered nursing assistants, janitors and restaurant staff.

[33] *Supra*, note 28.

Thus, the reasons for going on long-term disability differ from the reasons for continuing on claim. Interestingly, research shows that mental/nervous disorders have now replaced musculoskeletal disorders as causes for LTD, and make up at least 50% of the reasons for going onto STD. This is a 20% increase over the 1990 data.[34]

Likewise, the causes for long-term disability claim coverage differ by occupation, as seen in the next table:[35]

Figure 7.7: Musculoskeletal and Mental Disorders by Occupation

Occupation	Musculoskeletal Disorders	Mental Disorders
Professionals	27%	28%
White Collar Workers	23%	26%
Blue Collar Workers	34%	15%
Service Providers	38%	18%

Data Systems

The types of data that organizations tend to collect include the:

- number and duration of casual illness, short-term disability, Workers' Compensation and long-term disability;
- nature of disability reason (either as illness/injury or actual diagnosis);
- total number of lost time days and costs (in salary);
- number and types of modified/alternate work opportunities;
- duration of modified/alternate work;
- savings (cost-avoidance) realized through modified/alternate work;
- assessment, treatment and rehabilitation costs; and
- outcome measures, such as the number of short-term disability days or the amount of Workers' Compensation that proceed long-term disability cases in which the employee returns to work, dies, terminates or moves to another form of leave.

---

[34] The Insurance Journal, cited in L. Duxbury and C. Higgins, "Wrestling with Workload: Organizational Strategies for Success", *Conference Board of Canada Report* (May 2005) at 2.
[35] *Ibid.*

This data can be tabulated to calculate the exact cost of a Disability Management Program for a company for a given period of time:[36]

Figure 7.8: Company Disability Management Program Costs

Disability Costs Component	Average Cost
Workers' Compensation indemnity payment/case average	$
Average medical costs per day per injured worker (WCB)	$
Salary continuation/average cost per case	$
Average long-term disability costs per day per injured worker	$
Rehabilitation costs per case	$
Average labour replacement wages per day	$
Average supervisor hourly wages × number of hours of orientation	$
Average per day total of overtime payment to other worker(s) to maintain department daily productivity in the absence of the disabled worker	$
Average unit cost of lost productivity with and/or without replacement labour	$
Average lost opportunity cost	$
Average turnover cost	$
Average human resources costs in time to recruit and arrange temporary help, orient to policies, *etc.*	$
Average permanent disability settlements	$
Average legal costs	$
Total	$

---

[36] J. Hall, "State of the Art Case Management" (1998) 13:4, Occupational Medicine: State of the Art Review at 711.

As well, the cost of disability to an employee can be calculated using the following worksheet:[37]

Figure 7.9: Employee Disability Costs

Disability Component Costs	Average Cost/ Employee
Lost wages that are not covered by Workers' Compensation or other wage replacement plan	$
Lost wages from inability to do a second job	$
Lost wages from inability to receive overtime wages	$
Decreased accrual of paid time off	$
Non-reimbursed rehabilitation costs	$
Litigation and grievance costs	$
Total	$
Non-quantifiable Components: • disturbance of work/family routines and roles • spousal impact • loss of self-esteem/pride	

These two spreadsheets can be used to demonstrate the costs of disability to the organization and the employee.

Many companies or organizations have realized the need for a computerized system to facilitate the collection of disability management, Workers' Compensation Board claims and occupational health and safety data; to follow up on case management of claims; to analyze employee benefit programs, Workers' Compensation Board, occupational health and safety programs and Employee Assistance Program data; and to examine linkages between these three areas.

In fact, more proactive organizations are combining the above data with Employee Assistance Program utilization, case mix and costs; Group Benefit Plan experience and costs; and management practices. The intent is to identify all the prevention,[38] detection[39] and failure[40] costs related to employee and organizational well-being.

---

[37]   *Ibid.*, at 714.

[38]   "Prevention" is described as the focus on addressing and/or eliminating the identified concerns or issues so they do not worsen.

[39]   "Detection" is described as the focus on identifying concerns or issues before they become problematic.

[40]   "Failure" is described as the losses an organization incurs due to breakdowns in the system.

BEST PRACTICES

1. Capture all absence and disability data in a format that can be compared with other Canadian industry disability databases.
2. Ensure that the claims and case management data collected includes incidental, short-term and long-term disability absence rates and costs.
3. Monitor the Workers' Compensation Board data, investigate opportunities for cost avoidance and cost savings and seek guidance regarding Workers' Compensation Board claims management techniques. Canadian Workers' Compensation Board legislation and practices are in a state of constant flux.

   Best practice organizations remain current by seeking guidance from the Workers' Compensation Board (*i.e.*, employer services, seminars, *etc.*) and industry safety associations; by verifying the quality of Workers' Compensation Board claims submissions; by monitoring claims cost summaries; by training Workers' Compensation Board claims personnel and supervisors; and by ensuring timely reporting and follow-up.
4. Investigate the potential implementation of an integrated occupational health and safety data management system that can link Disability Management Program outcomes (*i.e.*, short-term disability, Workers' Compensation Board claims, long-term disability, *etc.*) with Occupational Health and Safety Programs, Employee Assistance Programs, employee benefits and Workplace Wellness Programs.
5. Seek opportunities to link employee absence data with human resource information on employees. Some companies do this through a linkage with a Human Resource Information System (HRIS). This allows for a comprehensive picture of employee characteristics, workplace situation and absence nature and outcome.
6. Use the company's available communication systems (*e.g.*, e-mail, internal mail, cheque inserts, newsletters, reports, *etc.*) to encourage the transmission of absence, disability and modified/alternate work data. This allows for the timely receipt of data and dissemination of information about absenteeism and Disability Management Program efforts from various work locations.
7. Ensure that all stakeholders are aware of the reasons for, and costs of, medical absenteeism. This is an essential step towards encouraging ownership of the problem, and disability management solutions.

DISABILITY MANAGEMENT COMMUNICATION STRATEGY

An essential component of any successful Disability Management Program is the widespread understanding and support of stakeholders both within the workplace and in the broader community. This is a dynamic process. Education and open, honest communication about program objectives, successes, failures and future plans are powerful tools that can alter entrenched attitudes and build trust between individuals. The reality is that attendance support and disability management is built on relationships, and these relationships need to be constantly nurtured.

BEST PRACTICES

1. Develop a communication strategy and plan to promote awareness and overcome organizational barriers to implementing a Disability Management Program (Chapter 14 provides more details).
2. Keep all key stakeholders in the information loop and part of the decision-making process.
3. Provide stakeholders with relevant outcome data and benefits realized by the Disability Management Program. This garners continued support for the Disability Management Program.
4. Use the available communication vehicles to spread the word about the Disability Management Program, both internally and externally, to supervisors and managers, union leaders and employees. In this manner, the stakeholders can be part of an ongoing solution for employee attendance support and disability management.

LINK THE DISABILITY MANAGEMENT PROGRAM WITH THE EMPLOYEE ASSISTANCE PROGRAM

External services can play an important role in effective employee attendance support and disability management. Companies that integrate the Employee Assistance Program services with attendance support and Disability Management Programs experience the need for a comprehensive Employee Assistance Program service when dealing with the psychological and physiological aspects of absence. Workplace-focused programs can be designed to assist with the identification and resolution of personal concerns that can impair employee attendance and productivity and lead to increased disability costs. The rationale for such an approach is detailed in Chapter 8.

The most effective formal linkages are the ones in which there is a predetermined working relationship between Case Managers and Employee Assistance Program service providers. Appropriate consents are put in place so that the relevant issues surrounding the employee's fitness to work, treatment plans and workplace accommodations can be discussed. Issues are discussed on a need-to-know basis and pertain to a successful re-entry to the workplace.

BEST PRACTICES

1. Ensure that the proposed Disability Management Program model includes a formal linkage with company or organization's Employee Assistance Program. Effective linkage can be achieved before, during or after the disability occurs.

2.   Ensure that all the service providers attain a mutual understanding of and respect for the individual program goals and objectives, as well as for the overall Disability Management Program goals and objectives.
3.   Promote a partnership approach that allows for multi-disciplinary interventions.
4.   Examine the outcome measures on the cases served jointly by the Employee Assistance Program and Disability Management Program personnel. Knowledge of utilization rates, types of cases served, trend analyses and success or failure rates, and anticipatory guidance for illness and injury prevention can be provided using aggregate data.

The intent is to be able to assess the value of the linkage and its contribution to the overall process. This outcome data can also be compared to those cases that were not co-managed to determine the value of the Disability Management Program-Employee Assistance Program linkage.

CASE MANAGEMENT PRACTICES

As already noted, case management is a collaborative process for assessing, planning, implementing, coordinating, monitoring and evaluating the options and services available to meet individual health needs through communication and accessible resources. Effective case management promotes quality, cost-effective outcomes.

The Case Manager:

- maintains contact with the injured/ill employee, health professionals, long-term disability carrier, the Workers' Compensation Board, supervisor, Employee Assistance Program service providers and others;
- assesses the biological, psychological and social factors involved in the disability;
- reviews the medical or psychological care and the response to treatment;
- facilitates and coordinates information sharing;
- communicates and educates return-to-work guidelines to all involved;
- facilitates return-to-work strategies;
- monitors return-to-work (modified/alternate work and alternate work) activities;
- establishes vocational rehabilitation and monitors the outcomes; and
- collects data to show cost-effectiveness of the intervention and the need for proactive measures.

To assist Case Managers, many organizations and insurers have developed practice standards or codes of practice for illness and injury management. Unlike disability guidelines, which merely advise on expected length of absences for various illnesses or injuries, these standards or codes outline rehabilitation strategies and steps.

Case management standards are a guide to professional practices. They define the practice, goal, role and qualifications of the Case Manager, the case management process, the problem and outcome identification process, the planning process, monitoring and coordination, evaluation techniques, documentation, document handling, confidentiality and administrative responsibilities for the program. An example of a generic version of a case management practice standard is provided in Chapter 11.

The case management approaches that have proven most effective:

- use an established planned and systematic approach;
- use early intervention;
- use direct, face-to-face contact with the employee to promote engagement in the process;
- provide support to the absent employee, workplace and union representative;
- develop written rehabilitation plans with goals, time frames and lines of accountability for action for all cases;[41]
- use a multi-disciplinary approach when indicated (*i.e.*, medical, nursing, psychological, vocational and rehabilitation interventions, *etc.*);
- maintain a regular progress review of all open cases;
- follow up on the employee throughout the absence, modified/alternate work period and return to work for at least until two weeks following the return to full-time duties;
- promote a mechanism for the early identification of cases;
- encourage self-reporting by employees of illness/injury before the absence occurs; and
- maintain on-going process evaluation to ensure quality delivery of services.

There is no conclusive research indicating which specific case management practices result in the best rates of return to work for employees.

BEST PRACTICES

1. Establish case management standards and educate Case Managers on their use.
2. Institute documented rehabilitation plans for all ill or injured employees who are offered case management.
3. Continue to track long-term disability data, plus hours of modified/alternate work, dollars saved with modified/alternate work and types of cases that were the most successful with early return-to-work initiatives.

---

[41] Watson Wyatt Worldwide, *Staying @ Work Report, 2005* (2005), available online at <http://www.watsonwyatt. com/research/resrender.asp?id=w-860&page=1> at 5.

4. Evaluate the case management process through the use of peer, or internal, reviews, or external quality assurance measures (audits).
5. Track occupational health and vocational rehabilitation activities, such as the amount of time required to case manage each claim, administer the service, train supervisors, undertake process development, conduct follow-up activities and pursue professional development. A data management software program can facilitate this process.
6. Evaluate, case-by-case, the return on investment of the case management interventions.
7. Continue to review long-term disability claims outcomes, paying special attention to claims that are closed. Use closed claims as indicators of case management outcomes.
8. Support regular evaluation of the Disability Management Program as part of the improvement process.

THE ADJUDICATION PROCESS

Typically, the adjudication process involves deciding if an individual is eligible to receive an income replacement benefit and the associated services. It involves:

-   determining eligibility to receive a benefit;
-   determining eligibility based on the nature of the medical condition; and
-   the critical match between the person's abilities and the employee's job demands.

Third party insurers adjudicate the Workers' Compensation and long-term disability claims. However, for self-insured short-term disability plans, employers require a documented process for adjudication. This helps to ensure a standardized approach. The exact criteria used to determine eligibility depend on the terms of the benefit plan in place. The typical steps for claims adjudication include:

Step 1: Receipt and coding of claim.
Step 2: Determination of eligibility:
    a) eligibility requirements are reviewed according to the benefit plan or insurance contract; and
    b) determination of acceptance or rejection is made on the basis of eligibility.
Step 3: Determination of any limitations or exclusions:
    a) pre-existing conditions (if applicable);
    b) pregnancy, maternity or parental leave; or
    c) specialized clauses by plan design or contract.
Step 4: Assessment of medical profile:
    a) existing medical information is reviewed (fit or unfit to work);
    b) resources for review of the claim are used, such as:

       i)   medical consultant;
       ii)   independent medical examiner;
       iii)   functional capacity examination; or
       iv)   rehabilitation.

Step 5: Determination of acceptance, rejection or need for more detailed information.

Step 6: Approval for a specific time.

Step 7: Creation of a management strategy.

Step 8: Closing the file:
       a) appeal;
       b) close; and
       c) return to work.[42]

Using these steps, the employee's eligibility for disability plan coverage is determined. However, claim adjudication is not a one time event — rather it is an ongoing process. In general, adjudication should occur at a number of points in the disability management process:

- at the onset of illness/injury;
- during the short-term absence period;
- at the transition point to long-term disability;
- during the long-term disability period; and
- at the transition of the "own occupation" period to the "any occupation" period.

BEST PRACTICES

1. Incorporate critical points for claims adjudication along with the definitive eligibility criteria in the design of the Disability Management Program. In general, special attention should be paid to the onset of illness or injury, the short-term disability period and to the transition from the "own occupation" period to the "any occupation" in the long-term disability period.

2. If human resource policies and procedures are not in place to accommodate the establishment of satisfactory benefit plan eligibility requirements, ensure that they are created and adopted.

MEDICAL CONSENTS AND CERTIFICATES

In regards to the medical consents and certificates obtained for disability management purposes, this area is governed by the following:

---

[42] A. Leckie, *Disability Claims Management* (Toronto: Butterworths, 2002).

- the various provincial Freedom of Information and Protection of Privacy Acts;
- Canadian Life and Health Insurance Association Guidelines; and
- *Model Code for the Protection of Personal Information.*[43]

The *Model Code for the Protection of Personal Information* defines "consent" as "the voluntary agreement with what is being done or proposed". While consent may be expressed or implied, organizations should seek express consent where information is sensitive. The person must provide consent in an informed manner. Consent of the individual must be obtained unless legal, medical, security or other reasons make it impossible or impractical.

The following are the requirements for informed consent:

- There is an obligation to ensure that sufficient information is provided to employees concerning the true nature and consequences of the intended use of information in order to allow the employee to come to a reasoned decision.
- The employee is mentally competent and has the ability to understand and appreciate the nature and consequences of the procedure.
- Consent is freely given.
- Consent is not obtained through misrepresentation or fraud.
- Consent cannot be given to the performance of an illegal procedure.
- Consent is in relation to a specific act contemplated and provided in a timely manner in relation to the information sought.

Personal health information should not be collected indiscriminately. Rather, it must be relevant to the purposes for which it is to be used and restricted to staff that sign a pledge of confidentiality (see Chapter 11, Figure 11.6).

The process of obtaining consent to collect personal health information creates a reasonable expectation of privacy by the employee. This requires the employer to take all reasonable steps to ensure the level of confidentiality promised in the consent form is not compromised. Some reasonable steps include:

- maintaining confidentiality;
- retaining information;
- secure storage of information;
- appropriate disclosure of information internally and externally;
- proper transmittal of information;
- appropriate methods of destruction; and
- identification of the consequences for staff violations, if any should occur.

---

[43] Canadian Standards Association (CSA), *Model Code for the Protection of Personal Information*, (CAN/CSA – Q830-96) (Ottawa: CAN/CSA, 1996).

BEST PRACTICES

1. Ensure the existence of a consent form that is to be signed by the ill or injured worker before any contact is made with the physician.
2. Review disability claim forms, and revise forms that fail to gather the necessary information in a manner that is in compliance with applicable legislation.
3. Establish measures to protect the confidentiality of personal health information.
4. Assess the degree of compliance of the Disability Management Program practices and medical forms with the human rights and protection of personal information legislation and relevant guidelines.

POLICIES AND PROCEDURES TO PROTECT THE CONFIDENTIALITY OF MEDICAL DATA

Medical diagnoses and health-related data are obtained during the course of claims and case management. Policies and procedures are required to deal with confidentiality and access to medical files, as well as with the retention, storage, transfer or disposal of medical data.

BEST PRACTICES

1. Develop a policy that deals with the confidential management of employee medical data. This should comply with applicable legislation (see Chapters 3 and 11 for more details).
2. Develop a protocol for the retention, maintenance, release and disposal of medical documentation (see Chapter 11 for more details).
3. Retain all medical data in a secure and confidential manner with access by authorized personnel and only on a need-to-know basis.
4. Retain all medical documentation for a minimum period of seven years from the last point of activity.
5. Limit the dissemination of medical diagnoses to broad categories or neutral descriptors, such as occupational injury, occupational illness, non-occupational injury or non-occupational illness. When diagnoses are used, limit them to disease classifications or aggregate the data so individual diagnoses cannot be determined.

MEASUREMENT, MONITORING AND IMPROVEMENT OF THE DISABILITY MANAGEMENT PROGRAM

Workplace-based attendance and Disability Management Programs must evolve to meet the changing needs of businesses and employees. Changes in operating or management styles open new avenues for the reintegration of injured or ill employees. As well, technological advancements and changing attitudes create modified/alternate work opportunities not before available.

A successful Disability Management Program includes continuous evaluation and modifications to:

- justify the program;
- improve workplace health and safety practices;
- ensure that the program objectives are met; and
- ensure that employer and employee needs are met.

BEST PRACTICES

1. Develop short-term disability performance measures that include absentee rates, lost time hours, lost time costs, average absentee length, percentage of hours saved on modified/alternate work, dollars saved due to modified/alternate work activities, percentage of employees who returned to work, number and types of interventions used and number of short-term disability claims that were successfully resolved.
2. Review the Workers' Compensation Board data, investigate opportunities for cost avoidance and cost savings, and seek guidance regarding Workers' Compensation Board claims management techniques.
3. Institute program outcome measures in the long-term disability period which include the following: reduced disabled lives liability, reduced long-term disability claims and costs, increased cost avoidance due to early intervention and modified/alternate work initiatives, case-by-case return on investment due to intervention, and return on investment using a formula customized to suit the company or organization's needs (see Chapter 6, Figure 6.3 for sample model).
4. Establish the contributing factors for absenteeism and disability such as employee age, lifestyle, drug or alcohol use, work environment, employee-employer relationships, seasonal issues, legal issues, financial issues and existence of pre-existing health conditions.
5. Measure the effectiveness of the Disability Management Program through interviews, surveys, data analyses, return-on-investment for the services provided and associated benefit costs.
6. Set program management targets for each year and measure success.
7. Use the disability management data to provide insight into opportunities for corporate occupational health and safety initiatives and prevention strategies.
8. Regularly disseminate this information to all the departments along with the related costs.

DISABILITY PROGRAM POLICIES AND PROCEDURES

Policies and procedures for maintaining contact with absent staff members, accessing treatment or rehabilitation and ensuring an expedient return to work can be applied to the entire continuum of absence regardless of cause, including incidental absence, short-term disability, Workers' Compensation Board and long-term disability. The intent of policies and procedures is to ensure that processes are in place and are applied fairly, equally and consistently.[44]

BEST PRACTICES

1.   Develop and implement policies and procedures that deal with:

- disability leaves (*i.e.*, short-term disability, Workers' Compensation Board, long-term disability, *etc.*);
- rehabilitation measures (*i.e.*, case/claims management, vocational rehabilitation, *etc.*);
- case management standards of practice;
- confidentiality standard of practice;
- documentation standard of practice;
- return-to-work program; and
- alcohol and drug policy.

More detail on relevant policies and procedures is provided in Chapter 3.

2.   Regularly review and update these policies to assess their continued applicability.

GRADUATED RETURN-TO-WORK PROGRAMS

Graduated Return-to-Work Programs can be an effective method of systematically returning employees to health and work, and can contribute to cost-containment.[45]

The recommended components of a Graduated Return-to-Work Program are:

- employee and supervisor submission of all the necessary claim forms;
- early intervention;
- communication with the employee and attending physician regarding the availability of modified/alternate work;
- regular follow-up with the employee and physician regarding fitness to work;
- availability of modified/alternate work for the recovering employee;
- the placement of the employee into suitable modified/alternate work;
- the monitoring of the employee's progress and fitness to work;

---

[44] Canadian Centre on Disability Studies, *Best Practices in Contemporary Disability Management: Executive Summary* (1998), online: <http://www.disabilitystudies.ca/cdmes.htm> at 8.

[45] D. Lyons, "Integrated Disability Management: Assessing Its Fit for Your Company", *Ideas at Work* (Winter 2004), online: <http://www.libertymutual.com>.

- a gradual return to full-time duties;
- evaluation of the case; and
- data management.

Companies who have implemented Graduated Return-to-Work Programs have noted significant success at returning employees to work, and at containing their disability rates and costs. As well, they are able to demonstrate compliance with the Canadian "duty to accommodate" legislation.

The Canadian duty to accommodate legislation varies by province. In general, this legislation indicates that the employer, employee and unions have a tripartite responsibility to accommodate the injured or ill employee back into the workplace, up to the point of "undue hardship".[46]

The key practices of a successful Graduated Return-to-Work Program are:

- arranging acceptable practices with unions for modified/alternate work opportunities within the collective agreements;
- ensuring that the modified/alternate work offered is meaningful and gainful employment;
- having set time lines for the modified/alternate work opportunity; and
- clearly defining the differences between modified and alternate work.

This topic of Graduated Return-to-Work Programs is covered in more detail in Chapter 5.

BEST PRACTICES

1. Develop and implement a corporate-wide Graduated Return-to-Work Program that has labour and management support and participation.
2. Communicate the roles, responsibilities and accountabilities of the key stakeholders.
3. Elicit employee, union and line identification of modified/alternate work options.
4. Manage safe and timely return-to-work activities.
5. Develop flexible and creative return-to-work options.
6. Collect and manage modified/alternate work data, and the Graduated Return-to-Work Program outcomes.
7. Evaluate the program regularly.
8. Communicate the benefits, challenges and outcomes to all key stakeholders.

---

[46] L. Steeves & R. Smithies, "Foresight is Your Best Defence" (1996) 4:2 Group Healthcare Management at 29-32.

EARLY INTERVENTION

Research and industry experience has supported the importance of early intervention in any absence.[47,48] Informally, many organizations report more success with returning the recovering employee to the workplace if intervention begins at, or soon after, the time of injury. By maintaining the person in the workplace, the occupational bond, the identity of the employee with the workplace, is not broken.

Early intervention is discussed in detail in Chapters 1 and 5.

BEST PRACTICES

1.   Institute early contact with the ill or injured employee. Ideally, the supervisor should do this on the first day of absence.
2.   If required, implement early case management (within the first three to five days).
3.   Involve the Employee Assistance Program in situations as appropriate.

MANAGEMENT OF MENTAL HEALTH DISABILITIES

The incidence of mental health claims is on the rise. These claims tend to be lengthy, with many non-medical issues and most challenging to successfully resolve. For example, serious depression can result in workplace absences of 40 or more days and include many workplace and performance issues. Partly due to denial and partly due to trying to work through their depression, the person not only has to recover from the illness but also deal with the "burned bridges" and damaged relationships that occurred before they left the workplace.

BEST PRACTICES

1.   Institute early contact with the ill or injured employee. Ideally, the supervisor should do this on the first day of absence.
2.   Implement early case management (within the first three to five days).
3.   Involve the Employee Assistance Program or some other form of counselling as part of the treatment plan.
4.   Use a technique such as the Green Chart (Chapter 18), to keep open the lines of communication between the caregivers and occupational health professionals who represent the workplace interests.
5.   Work with a significant person in the individual's life to ensure that workplace issues/concerns are addressed.
6.   Ensure that support is available to the employee upon a return to work.

---

[47]   *Supra*, note 41 at 6-7.
[48]   M. Creen, "Best Practices for Disability Management", *Journal of the Ontario Occupational Health Nurses Association* (Winter 2002) at 5-8.

SUMMARY

The listing of best practices for disability management in this chapter is not meant to be exhaustive in nature. Rather, this chapter merely presents some examples of currently held beliefs in disability management practices. As noted in the opening of this chapter, these beliefs will change as technology, knowledge and practice advancements occur. The key is to be sensitive to the changes in disability management practices, and to adapt them to your program and practices.

CHAPTER REFERENCES

E. Akyeampong, *Work Absences: New Data, New Insights*, Spring 1998 Perspective, Cat. No. 75-001-XPE (Ottawa: Statistics Canada, 1998) at 16-22.

Alberta Labour, *Occupational Injury and Disease in Alberta, 1996 Summary: Lost-time Claims and Claim Rates* (Edmonton: Alberta Labour, 1998).

H. Bruckman & J. Harris, "Occupational Medicine Practice Guidelines" (1998) 13:4 Occupational Medicine: State of the Art Reviews.

Canadian Centre on Disability Studies, *Best Practices in Contemporary Disability Management: Executive Summary* (1998), online: <http://www.disabilitystudies.ca/cdmes.htm>.

Canadian Standards Association (CSA), *Model Code for the Protection of Personal Information* (CAN/CSA - Q830-96) (Ottawa: CAN/CSA, 1996).

Conference Board of Canada, *Compensation Planning Outlook 2000* (Ottawa: Conference Board of Canada, 1999).

Conference Board of Canada, News Release, "Eldercare taking its toll on Canadian Workers" (10 November 1999).

M. Creen, "Best Practices for Disability Management", *Journal of the Ontario Occupational Health Nurses Association* (Winter 2002) at 5-8.

J. Hall, "State of the Art Case Management" (1998) 13:4 Occupational Medicine: State of the Art Review.

The Insurance Journal, cited in L. Duxbury and C. Higgins, "Wrestling with Workload: Organizational Strategies for Success", *Conference Board of Canada Report* (May 2005) at 2.

A. Leckie, *Disability Claims Management* (Toronto: Butterworths, 2002).

D. Lyons, "Integrated Disability Management: Assessing Its Fit for Your Company", *Ideas at Work* (Winter 2004), online: <http://www.libertymutual.com/omapps/ContentServer?cid=1058290626910&pagename=CMln>.

Marsh Risk Consulting, *Workforce Risk: Fourth Annual Marsh Mercer Survey of Employers' Time-Off and Disability Programs* (2003), online: <http://www.marshriskconsulting.com/st/PDEv_C_371_SC_228135_NR_3 06_Pl_347745.htm>.

D.B. Mercer, "Roles and Responsibilities in Job Modification and Accommodation" (Seminars in Occupational Health and Medicine, Faculty of Medicine, Continuing Education, University of Calgary, 3 February 1999) [unpublished].

The Mutual Group, *LTD Claims Trends: 1996* (Waterloo, The Mutual Group, 1996).

The Mutual Group, *Block of Business: January 01, 1998 to December 31, 1998, STD Claims Management Report — Statistics* (Waterloo: The Mutual Group, 1998).

National Institute for Disability Management and Research (NIDMAR), *Disability Management in the Workplace: A Guide to Establishing a Joint Workplace Program* (Port Alberni, B.C.: NIDMAR, 1995).

G. Pransky & W. Shaw, "Injury Response: Optimizing the Role of Supervisors", *Ideas at Work* (Spring 2002), at 11-12 online: <http:// www.libertymutual. com/omapps/ContentsServer?cid=1058816266A3&pagename=CMln>.

Statistics Canada, *Work Absence Rates 2004* (Ottawa: Statistics Canada, 2005).

L. Steeves & R. Smithies, "Foresight is Your Best Defence" (1996) 4:2 Group Healthcare Management at 29-32.

Watson Wyatt Worldwide, News Release, "Employers that Measure Results from Integrated Disability Management Programs Report Big Savings" (15 October 1998), online: <http://www.watsonwyatt.com/news/press.asp?id=6900>.

Watson Wyatt Worldwide, *Staying @ Work Report, 2005* (2005), online: <http:// www.watsonwyatt.com/research/resrender.asp?id=w-860&page=1> at 5.

Chapter 8

The Role of Employee Assistance Programs in Disability Management[1]

INTRODUCTION

As mentioned in Chapter 7, Canadian employees missed an average of 9.2 workdays in 2004, of which an average of 1.7 days were due to personal or family demands.[2] For this time period, mental health and stress-related disorders are estimated to have cost the Canadian economy about $33 billion in lowered productivity, lost workdays, disability and medical costs.[3] These absences have negatively impacted Canadian employers and the Canadian economy.

In 1995, the direct disability costs were approximately 2% of the employer annual payroll, while the indirect costs equated to about three to five times the direct costs.[4] A current estimate is that Canadian employers are paying close to 14.9% of payroll towards disability-related costs and the operation of disability management programs.[5]

In the United States, the picture is similar. Workers reported stress, family reasons and personal needs as the key reasons for 51% of the unscheduled absences in 2005. This was a three per cent increase over 2004 results and a five per cent increase over the 1995 findings.[6] According to the American Institute of Stress, job stress costs the American industry $300 billion annually in absenteeism, diminished work productivity, staff turnover and direct medical, legal and insurance fees. The problem employee was estimated to cost an average of 25%

[1] Adapted from D. Dyck, "Directions in Disability Management" (1997) 44:2 EAP Digest at 16. Reprinted with permission.

[2] Statistics Canada, *Work Absence Rate, 2004* (Ottawa: Statistics Canada, 2005).

[3] W. Weeks, "Stressing Prevention" *Benefits Canada* (May 2004) at 54, available online at: <http://www.benefitscanada.com/benefits/benefits10.jsp>.

[4] M. Visser, "Opportunities for a Managed Care Approach to Psychological Disabilities" (Presented at the Psychological Disabilities in the Workplace: Prevention, Rehabilitation and Cost Control Conference, Toronto, 10-11 June 1996) [unpublished].

[5] Marsh Risk Consulting, *Workforce Risk: Fourth Annual Marsh Mercer Survey of Employers' Time-Off and Disability Programs* (2003), available online at: <http://www.marshriskconsulting.com/st/PDEv_C_371_SC_228135_NR_306_PI_347745.htm>.

[6] CCH, "Unscheduled Absenteeism Rises to a Five-year High" *Human Resources Management Trends & Ideas* (October 2005, Issue No. 616).

of annual salary per year.[7] In short, mental health issues are steadily rising and remain costly.

Absenteeism costs are often symptomatic of serious workplace problems. The changing dynamics in the modern workplace have been linked with numerous health problems.[8] For example, job insecurity, unequal power distribution, role conflicts and antagonistic labour-management relations have been associated with physiological changes, somatic complaints and psychological distress.[9] Fatigue, chronic infections and digestive disturbances have been linked with the increased pace of work.[10] Increased work demands have been connected with family discord, alcoholism and psychological disturbances.[11] Unreasonable demands and deadlines, withholding important information, lack of recognition for work done and failing to allow employee discretion in conducting their work and work priorities leads to high stress and ill health.[12] In short, economic and workplace restructuring can have damaging effects on employee and family health and well-being (Figure 8.1).

As early as 1993, it was noted that 26% of workplace absenteeism was related to stress.[13] In 1994, the Mercantile and General Claims Survey discovered that mental and nervous claims accounted for 19% of the group long-term disability claims, and 15% of the individual portfolio long-term disability claims.[14] They also noted that mental and nervous claims were alarmingly high for the professional and academic occupations, for those aged 30 to 39 years and for women.

---

7   Concern: EAP, *Cost Effectiveness* (2005), online: <http://www.concern-eap.com/html/bc-cost-effective.htm>.

8   K. Blair, "Probing the Links Between Work and Health" *Canadian Human Resource Reporter* (7 April 1997) at 6; R. Csiernik, "From EAP to Wellness: Program Evolution and Service Provider Selection" (Presented at the Psychological Disabilities in the Workplace: Prevention, Rehabilitation and Cost Control Conference, Toronto, 10-11 June 1996) [unpublished].

9   J. Eakin, "Psychological Aspects of Workplace Health" Canadian Centre for Occupational Health and Safety (April 1992) at 8-10; S. Klitzman, J. House, B. Isreal & R. Mero, "Work Stress, Nonwork Stress and Health" (1990) 13:3 Journal of Behavioural Medicine at 221-243; and R. Karask & T. Theorell, *Healthy Work: Stress, Productivity and Reconstruction of Working Life* (New York: Basic Books, 1990).

10 L. Lewis, "Employers Place More Emphasis on Managing Employee Stress" (1993) 11:2 Business & Health at 46-50. M. Ross, "Psychiatric Disability Management" (Presentation at The Disability Management Conference, Toronto, 27-28 May 1996) [unpublished]; S.T. Maier, L.R. Watkins & M. Fleshner, "Psychoneuroimmunology: The Interface Between Behaviour, Brain and Immunity" (1994) 40 American Psychologist at 771-776.

11 *Supra*, note 9.

12 *Supra*, note 3.

13 Ontario Ministry of Labour, "Counting the Cost of Absenteeism" (1993) 1:1 Group Healthcare Management at 9.

14 H. Minuk, "The Mercantile and General Disability Claims Survey, 1994" (Presented at the Psychological Disabilities in the Workplace: Prevention, Rehabilitation and Cost Control Conference, Toronto, 10-11 June 1996) [unpublished].

The *Ontario Health Survey, Mental Health Supplement, 1994* indicated that 5.7% of the Canadian population 15 years and older reported a major depressive episode within the last 12 months. Of those aged 15 to 24 years, 25% reported one or more mental disorders within the last 12 months.[15]

Figure 8.1: Related Statistics

FACTS

- In any workforce, 15% of the employees are "troubled".[16]
- Stress-related issues account for 20% loss in productivity.[17]
- Stress-related illness cost the Canadian economy approximately $5 billion per year.[18]
- Fifty per cent of disability cases have a psychological component — cases which are considered the most difficult to handle.[19]
- The largest number of psychological claims occurred with women, the teaching profession and people aged 30 to 39 years old.[20]
- Mental and nervous conditions are, respectively, the primary and secondary causes of 55-60% of disability claims.[21]
- Disability and related costs for mental illness have been estimated to cost companies up to 14% of their net annual profits.[22]

The Canadian Insurance Association (CIA) identified that psychological disorders account for 23.8% of long-term disability claims in Canada per year. There are occupational variances in this rate. For example, the teaching or academic occupations experience 44% of all psychological disorders, white collar occupations experience 36%, service workers 28% and blue collar occupations 16%.[23]

---

[15] *Ibid.*

[16] C. Sherman, "Who is the Problem Employee?" *Human Resources Management in Canada* (February 1989) at 70, 507-70, 508.

[17] A. Bierbrier, "Opening Remarks" (Presented at the Psychological Disabilities in the Workplace: Prevention, Rehabilitation and Cost Control Conference, Toronto, 10-11 June 1996) [unpublished].

[18] J. Kranc, "Fact Check" *Benefits Canada* (March 2004) at 70-71.

[19] R.W. Francis, "Medcan Health Management" (Presentation at The Disability Management Conference, Toronto, 27-28 May 1996) [unpublished].

[20] *Supra*, note 14.

[21] *Supra*, note 3.

[22] *Supra*, note 18 at 70.

[23] Canadian Actuaries Institute (CIA), *Long-term Disability Causes* (Ottawa: CIA Group Experience Committee, 1997).

DRIVERS OF STRESS-RELATED CLAIMS

There appear to be three main drivers for an increase in the number of stress-related claims. First, there are the work-related drivers that include:

- increased job uncertainty;
- increased stress at work due to increased performance expectations and limited resources;
- perceived lack of control in the workplace — *i.e.*, unreasonable demands, urgent deadlines, lack of recognition for work performed, lack of discretion on how to do the work, inability to set own work priorities;[24,25]
- increased work hours resulting in problems balancing work and family life[26] and feeling overwhelmed;[27]
- increased workload which contributes to an increased prevalence of the "I can't wait to retire" attitude, the desire to leave the job and a decreased capacity for creativity and innovation;[28]
- the "Do it at any cost" approach to management;
- constant technological advancements mean that employees are in a continuous learning mode, which is tiring;
- limited management response to signs and symptoms of employee distress;
- employees have to expend energy to adapt to stressful workplace situations;
- multi-tasking, for example, talking on the telephone while reading or responding to mail; and
- information overload — the estimate is that the average employee receives and sends 190 messages per day (voice mail, e-mail, fax), and is interrupted on average, six times per hour.[29]

In short, in North America, we are our jobs. We tend to measure our self-esteem by our job and position in an organization. When job issues or pressures loom or the employer-employee relationship is in jeopardy, employees react negatively. In many instances, this can lead to physical or psychological ailments and in some cases a disability claim.

Second, there are societal drivers that contribute to an increase in stress-related disability claims. They include:

---

[24] *Supra*, note 8.

[25] *Supra*, note 3.

[26] *Supra*, note 17. See also L. Duxbury, C. Higgins & K. Johnson, *An Examination of the Implications and Costs of Work-life Conflict in Canada* (Ottawa: Health Canada, 1999).

[27] L. Duxbury & C. Higgins, "Wrestling with Workload: Organizational Strategies for Success" *Conference Board of Canada Report* (May 2005) at 1.

[28] *Ibid.*, at 3.

[29] Conference Board of Canada, News Release, "Workplace Solutions for Stressed Out Workers" (7 September 1999).

- a general increase in the prevalence of depression and anxiety disorders;[30]
- increased perception of entitlement to compensation for psychological disorders;
- greater societal acceptance of mental health problems;
- many dual income families;
- the responsibilities and stressors of the so-called "sandwich generation", those caught between the demands of their children and their parents. Eldercare is on the increase and those responsible for this care report a lack of sleep, decreased personal time and more health problems;[31]
- increased economic and financial pressures;
- a society that is 44% more difficult than 30 years ago according to the Likert Scale for measuring stress to societies.[32] For example, in 1999 twice as many Canadian workers reported moderate to high stress levels due to problems balancing work and family life as opposed to 10 years ago (46.2% in 1999 versus 26.7% in 1989).[33] Those experiencing a high degree of perceived stress also said they missed twice as much work as those reporting lower stress levels;[34] and
- a tendency to adapt to dysfunctional situations, making it impossible to detect the negative effects of stress until it is too late.

The third driver is the medicalization of social and/or employment problems. Our society is poorly prepared to support people with interpersonal difficulties such as marital problems, relationship breakdowns and identity crises. As a result, the troubled employee tends to seek medical advice to deal with such issues. Society expects physicians to identify and cure ailments. Thus, employees tend to end up with a diagnosis of burn-out, anxiety attacks, sleep disorders or migraines for marital, interpersonal and personal crises. This is also true for over-extended lifestyles and traumatic life events such as death, victimization, harassment or grievance. Recently, these diagnoses have become compensable, resulting in new reasons for workplace absences. The outcome has been a steady increase in new types of disability claims.

---

[30] B. Wilkerson, "Perspective on Mental Health in the Workplace," reported in Watson Wyatt Worldwide, *Staying @ Work Report, 2005* (2005), available online at: <http://www.watsonwyatt.com/research/resrender.asp?id=w-860&page=1> at 9.

[31] J. MacBride-King, *Caring about Caregiving: The Eldercare Responsibilities of Canadian Workers and the Impact on Employers* (Ottawa: The Conference Board of Canada, 1999).

[32] B.A. Cryer, "Neutralizing Workplace Stress: The Physiology of Human Performance and Organizational Effectiveness" (Presented at the Psychological Disabilities in the Workplace: Prevention, Rehabilitation and Cost Control Conference, Toronto, 10-11 June 1996) [unpublished].

[33] *Supra*, note 31.

[34] Conference Board of Canada, *Survey of Canadian Workers on Work-Life Balance* (Ottawa: Conference Board of Canada, 1999).

DISABILITY MANAGEMENT

Disability management, as previously described, is a systematic, goal-oriented process of actively minimizing the impact of impairment in the individual's capacity to participate competitively in the work environment, and maximizing the health of employees to prevent disability, or further deterioration when a disability exists.[35] It means being proactive, demonstrating joint responsibility and promoting illness and injury prevention. It involves joint labour-management support, supportive policies and procedures, education, a modified work program and data collection and analysis.

However, just helping an employee get well does not help them overcome their vocational problems, nor regain their vocational capacity. Employees who were poor performers before getting ill or injured do not turn into shining stars after a course of rehabilitation. The acquisition of new life and job skills is required along with the opportunity and the encouragement to practice the new skills in a safe environment.

The good news is that employees who receive disability management support are more likely to achieve vocational success. When these support services are continuous and well coordinated, vocational achievement is even more probable.

EMPLOYEE ASSISTANCE PROGRAM

An Employee Assistance Program provides confidential, professional assistance to employees and their families to help them resolve problems affecting their personal lives and, in some cases, their job performance.

Historically, Employee Assistance Programs were introduced to deal with employee alcohol and drug abuse (Figure 8.2). However over time and with a changing marketplace, most Employee Assistance Programs now provide such services as:

- crisis management;
- financial counselling;
- legal counselling;
- career/vocational counselling;
- stress management counselling/seminars;
- time management counselling/seminars;
- change management counselling/seminars; and
- alternative therapies.

---

[35] D.G. Tate, R.V. Habeck & G. Schwartz, "Disability Management: Origins, Concepts and Principles for Practice" (1986) 17 Journal of Applied Rehabilitation Counselling at 5-11.

Figure 8.2: Scope of Employee Assistance Programs

In Canada, approximately 80% of companies with 500 or more employees have EAPs available for their employees and families.[36] However, EAPs work for employers of any size and the range of savings that can be realized are exciting. For example,

- Ninety per cent of workers benefit from using EAP services.[37]
- At McDonnell Douglas, employees treated for alcohol and drug dependency missed 44 fewer days of work.[38]
- Black & Decker experienced a decrease in behavioural health claims and a 60% decrease in behavioural health benefit costs.
- Abbott Labs realized a $2000 per employee savings on their medical claim costs because of employee use of the EAP.[39]
- Many companies report that EAPs are very effective for improving employee health and satisfaction and moderately effective in contributing to lower absenteeism costs and higher work productivity.[40]
- Research indicates that employers save four to $17 per dollar invested.[41, 42]

---

[36] Conference Board of Canada, *Compensation Planning Outlook* (Ottawa: Conference Board of Canada, 1997).

[37] EAP, *Why Your Company Needs an EAP* (2005), available online at <www.eap4u.com/needeap.aspx>.

[38] McDonnell Douglas, "EAP Dollars and Sense", *Solutions* (2005), available online at: <www.solutionseap.com/ infoforemp /eap_benefit_studies.htm>.

[39] J. Prohofofsky, "Speaking to Your CEO About EAPs: Three Strategies that Can Make EAP Believers Out of CEO Skeptics", *EAP Digest* (May 2005).

[40] Watson Wyatt Worldwide, *Staying @ Work 2005* (2005), available online at: <http://www.watsonwyatt.com/research/resrender.asp?id=w-860&page=1>.

[41] *Supra*, note 34.

[42] *Supra*, note 35.

EMPLOYEE ASSISTANCE PROGRAMS AND DISABILITY MANAGEMENT

Employee Assistance Program counsellors and services have a significant role to play in disability management (Figure 8.3). They can be involved before the disability occurs, during the disability period, in the return-to-work process and as part of the follow-up process.

Figure 8.3: Levels of Prevention for Employee Assistance Program Intervention

Level of Primary Prevention (Before problems exist)	Level of Secondary Prevention (Dealing with identified problems)	Level of Tertiary Prevention (Keeping chronic situations from worsening)
Change Management (group/individual)	Counselling	Counselling
Stress Management (group/individual)	Counselling	Counselling
Crisis Management - policies	Trauma Counselling (group/individual)	Counselling
Career counselling - retirement planning	Counselling	Counselling
Harassment - education	Counselling	Counselling
Substance abuse in workplace - education	Counselling Support for employee & work group	Substance abuse therapy sessions Support for employee & workplace

Primary prevention involves Employee Assistance Program counsellors conducting seminars on change management, stress management, crisis management, career counselling, substance abuse awareness, workplace harassment and balancing work and family life. These seminars address people and work issues before they become serious health conditions. Their effectiveness in reducing employee stress was recently demonstrated in a study on rising health care costs. The indication was that 66% of the employer respondents felt that their EAP reduced employee stress and 50% noted that the EAP helped to lower employee absenteeism.[43]

During the disability and the return-to-work process (secondary prevention), Employee Assistance Program counsellors can assist the disabled employee in

---

[43] K. Bachmann, *Workplace Solutions for Stressed Out Workers* (Ottawa, Ontario: Conference Board of Canada, 1999).

dealing with identified problems. This may involve individual counselling, group therapy, and referrals to self-help groups and/or treatment centres. The idea is to assist employees and families in acquiring the coping skills necessary for successful recovery.

As part of the follow-up process (tertiary prevention), Employee Assistance Program counselling and support can help employees keep chronic disabilities from worsening. Employee Assistance Program support for the employee, family members and the workplace can prevent recurrences and promote optimal functioning.

Case Scenarios

The following case scenarios are some real-life examples of how Employee Assistance Program support can assist Case Managers and employees with disability management:

CASE A

James, a 32-year-old analyst, experienced a recurrent episode of depression and anxiety. He was still working, but he was fearful, indecisive and visibly anxious, had insomnia, and was unable to focus on issues. He had been part of a team that was involved in an intense project, working 70 hours a week for the past eight months.

James had many family and community responsibilities. He also had good family, workplace and peer support. He had a history of three major depressions and was aware of his need for help. As a result, he sought Employee Assistance Program help and was referred to the occupational health centre for disability management.

A multi-disciplinary intervention ensued. The Case Manager worked with the Employee Assistance Program counsellor to:

- coordinate care between James, his wife and his attending physician;
- educate the couple about chronic depression and the need for treatment;
- help James maximize his capabilities;
- assist James in setting personal boundaries and in increasing his coping skills;
- encourage James to set priorities in his life; and
- promote a graduated return to work.

This approach included assessing and preparing the workplace and James' co-workers for his return to work. Without Employee Assistance Program support, this successful return to work could not have occurred, nor would James have been likely to remain healthy.

Depression will affect one in 10 Canadians in any given year.[44] However, people need help to understand the nature of this disorder and the acceptable forms of treatment. Also, people need assistance in realistically setting limits on their capabilities and being comfortable with those limits. Employee Assistance Programs can provide support in both these areas.

CASE B

Sally was absent and produced a medical note stating, "Off for six weeks due to stress". The Case Manager interviewed Sally to assess the biopsychosocial aspects of her disability situation. The real issue was job dissatisfaction, but Sally lacked the insight and skills to deal with her unhappiness.

The Case Manager referred Sally to the Employee Assistance Program counsellor. Using a Stress Map,[45] Sally and the Employee Assistance Program counsellor were able to identify the stressors in her life. As well, they addressed Sally's vocational and personal likes and dislikes.

The outcome was that Sally decided that her job was not meeting growth needs. The Employee Assistance Program counsellor then assisted Sally in identifying some career options to pursue. Sally returned to work within two weeks and then made plans to leave her job and enrol in university.

Many people who have complex life and vocational decisions to make get stuck and are unable to complete the process. They know they are unhappy, but do not know what to do to rectify the situation. In a number of cases, like this one, they become ill and need help to move on. Employee Assistance Program counsellors are well-equipped to assist employees and their dependents in addressing such challenges.

CASE C

Janet, a 30-year-old woman, had been with a company for 17 years. During that time she averaged 27 days off per year. Each absence was for a different medically substantiated reason. Janet's attendance was monitored several times but her high rate of absenteeism continued.

The Case Manager, in reviewing a recent absence, decided to refer Janet to the Employee Assistance Program for a thorough assessment. The assessment revealed that Janet had been suffering from anorexia and bulimia since the age of 15 and the numerous ailments were secondary events to these major health problems.

---

[44] Canadian Mental Health Association, "Canadian Mental Health Association (CMHA): Depression in the Workplace" (Presented at the Psychological Disabilities in the Workplace: Prevention, Rehabilitation and Cost Control Conference, Toronto, 10-11 June 1996) [unpublished].

[45] Essi Systems, *Stress Map: A Personal Exploration* (Collingwood: Essi Systems, 1987).

Janet was then referred to an eating disorder clinic. The treatment focused on an examination of the family, the origin of the issues and the development of self-esteem.

Janet's personal growth was amazing. She began to realize the impact of her illness on her job, her marriage and her family. As well, she recognized the drivers for her behaviour and decided to disclose her secret to her family and work group. She was tired of the secrecy and wanted to enlist support to help her to make the changes she wanted. The Case Manager and Employee Assistance Program counsellor were instrumental in helping Janet with her plan of action. The work group was astounded, and, once they understood the nature of the disorder, they were quick to rally to Janet's side.

Personal growth for the employee and work group was achieved, and the disability that had been a source of work group dissension became the seed of work group unity and support. Janet remains well and after six years of treatment and peer support, she is enjoying a much better quality of life and work.

In summary, the complex disability cases are made up of 10% medical components and 90% other factors. There is no quick approach to rehabilitation of ill or injured workers. People's lives are complicated and illnesses or injuries make things more complex. A multi-faceted, multi-disciplinary approach to rehabilitation is essential.

THE VALUE OF EMPLOYEE ASSISTANCE PROGRAMS IN DISABILITY MANAGEMENT

Much work has been done in determining the cost-benefits of an Employee Assistance Program.[46] The "value-addedness" of an Employee Assistance Program can be measured in the disability management arena. Research has shown that employees were absent fewer short-term disability days when treated by Employee Assistance Program services versus medical practitioners. Also, Employee Assistance Program management of psychiatric short-term disability claims led to a decrease in the average duration of illness.[47] In general, Employee Assistance Programs are reported to yield five dollars of savings and three dollars of productivity gains for every one dollar invested in Employee Assistance Program services to manage and prevent disabilities.[48]

---

[46] R. Csiernik, "From Employee Assistance Program to Wellness: Program Evolution and Service Provider Selection" (Presented at the Psychological Disabilities in the Workplace: Prevention, Rehabilitation and Cost Control Conference, Toronto, 10-11 June 1996) [unpublished].

[47] D.J. Conti, "The Management of Psychiatric Short-term Disability" (Presented at the American Psychiatric Association Annual Meeting, Miami, Florida, 21 May 1996) [unpublished].

[48] R.J. Price, "Absenteeism and Disability" (1995) The ACPM Reporter at 34-37.

Conclusion

The workplace is a powerful determinant of employee wellness. It can also be a strong support to ill or injured employees and to their families. Through disability management, which is integrated with the Employee Assistance Program and other corporate resources (*i.e.*, human resources, occupational safety, industrial hygiene, *etc.*), a multi-faceted, multi-disciplinary approach involving the employee and line management can be achieved. Organizations that have used this approach have been successful at containing both the human and financial costs of disability. In essence, it allows for a holistic approach that is tailored to the employee, the disability and the workplace, so that an optimal level of functioning can be regained.

THE FUTURE CHALLENGES FOR AN EMPLOYEE ASSISTANCE PROGRAM SERVICE PROVIDER

There are a number of future challenges for workplaces that Employee Assistance Program service providers can address. The discussion below will cover five of these future challenges, along with some suggestions for involvement by the Employee Assistance Program service provider.

ISSUE 1

People today seem to be locked into a "fight or flight" mode. Responses to daily pressures and demands tend to be edgy, with a readiness to react. Instead of being a useful reaction, the "fight or flight" response can become dysfunctional. For example, increased heart rate, elevated blood pressure and increased respirations can be helpful when fleeing from an enemy. However, these symptoms can be dysfunctional when they are reactions to stress, and they can cause incapacitating anxiety attacks.

The challenge for the Employee Assistance Program service is to:

• understand the employee's physical responses to events, both functional and dysfunctional;
• teach and encourage coping skills; and
• promote the value and existence of social support (*i.e.*, group or team-work).

ISSUE 2

According to Cryer, individuals tend to experience problems with perception of situations and therefore can have negative reactions. This can lead to distress:

"Unmanaged reactions to stressful events in life create a chain reaction that inhibits our learning ability and clouds our perception on life".[49]

The challenge for the Employee Assistance Program is to help people to recognize their perceptions and reactions. In that way, they can learn and cope with life events successfully.

ISSUE 3

Emotional intelligence (EQ) is the ability to motivate oneself and persist despite frustrations; to control impulse and delay gratification; to regulate one's moods; and to empathize and to hope. It has been identified as the key to a better integration of an individual's physical, mental and emotional resources. People who possess a high EQ tend to be the most successful in their life endeavours. Likewise, companies or organizations that demonstrate a high EQ are the most successful at attaining business goals.[50]

The challenge for the Employee Assistance Program is to help employees and organizations foster and master the skills associated with high EQ for their benefit.

ISSUE 4

Many organizations exhibit the net effect of emotional mismanagement, better known as being under the state of an emotional virus. The symptoms of this emotional virus include caustic humour, defeatism; "us versus them" mentality; judgemental approaches to life; constant complaints; resentment; suspiciousness; and chronic anxiety, fear, intolerance, resignation, antagonism and despair. Many popular cartoons depict this virus well. This virus can be very infectious and deadly to company morale. If left unchecked, it can infect an entire workforce. However, it can be neutralized.

The challenge for the Employee Assistance Program is to assist both individuals and organizations. For employees, the Employee Assistance Program can assist in developing and maintaining credible supports, in the development of insight and self-esteem, and in the development of motivation. For the organization, the Employee Assistance Program can help management and employers identify the emotional virus and neutralize it. This involves applying internal self-management, creating a people-focused culture, applying heart intelligence and providing good communication.

---

[49] *Supra*, note 32.

[50] D. Goldman, *Emotional Intelligence: Why it Can Matter More Than IQ* (New York: Bantam Books, 1995).

Issue 5

Many organizations exhibit maladaptive and dysfunctional behaviour. These can be symptomatic of severe management problems.

The challenge for an Employee Assistance Program is to assist the organization in establishing or regaining balance in its level of functioning. Balance comes from equal value and attention being placed on five areas (Figure 8.4):

- *Intellectual Health* — Focus on employee development, and reward or compensate creativity, knowledge and intuitiveness.
- *Social Health* — Promote a supportive environment and team building activities.
- *Spiritual Health* — Maintain a positive belief in what is right and in the value of work, hope and empathy.
- *Mental Health* — Promote work group support to reduce stress, address problem solving, shape a cultural self-image and demonstrate that employees are valued.
- *Physical Health* — Support employee physical well-being through the promotion of healthy lifestyles.

Figure 8.4: Employee Assistance Program: Organizational Assistance Program

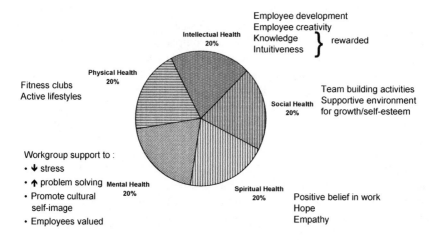

SUMMARY

Employee Assistance Programs have traditionally been involved in reactive approaches to dealing with employee personal and workplace problems. However, by addressing issues at the source, employee and organizational well-being can be enhanced.

CHAPTER REFERENCES

K. Bachmann, *Workplace Solutions for Stressed Out Workers* (Ottawa, Ontario: Conference Board of Canada, 1999).

A. Bierbrier, "Opening Remarks" (Presented at the Psychological Disabilities in the Workplace: Prevention, Rehabilitation and Cost Control Conference, Toronto, 10-11 June 1996) [unpublished].

K. Blair, "Probing the Links Between Work and Health" *Canadian Human Resource Report* (7 April 1997) at 6.

Canadian Actuaries Institute (CIA), *Long-term Disability Causes* (Ottawa: CIA Group Experience Committee, 1997).

Canadian Mental Health Association, "Canadian Mental Health Association (CMHA): Depression in the Workplace" (Presented at the Psychological Disabilities in the Workplace: Prevention, Rehabilitation and Cost Control Conference, Toronto, 10-11 June 1996) [unpublished].

CCH, "Unscheduled Absenteeism Rises to a Five-year High" *Human Resources Management Trends & Ideas* (October 2005, Issue No. 616).

Concern: EAP, *Cost Effectiveness* (2005), available online at www.concern-eap.com/html/bc-cost-effective.htm>.

Conference Board of Canada, *Compensation Planning Outlook* (Ottawa: Conference Board of Canada, 1997).

Conference Board of Canada, *Caring about Caregiving: The Eldercare Responsibilities of Canadian Workers and the Impact on Employers* (Ottawa, Ontario: Conference Board of Canada, 1999).

Conference Board of Canada, *Survey of Canadian Workers on Work-life Balance* (Ottawa: Conference Board of Canada, 1999).

Conference Board of Canada, News Release, "Workplace Solutions for Stressed Out Workers" (7 September 1999).

D.J. Conti, "The Management of Psychiatric Short-term Disability" (Presented at the American Psychiatric Association Annual Meeting, Miami, Florida, 21 May 1996) [unpublished].

B.A. Cryer, "Neutralizing Workplace Stress: The Physiology of Human Performance and Organizational Effectiveness" (Presented at the Psychological Disabilities in the Workplace: Prevention, Rehabilitation and Cost Control Conference, Toronto, 10-11 June 1996) [unpublished].

R. Csiernik, "From Employee Assistance Program to Wellness: Program Evolution and Service Provider Selection" (Presented at the Psychological Disabilities in the Workplace: Prevention, Rehabilitation and Cost Control Conference, Toronto, 10-11 June 1996) [unpublished].

L. Duxbury, C. Higgins & K. Johnson, *An Examination of the Implications and Costs of Work-Life Conflict in Canada* (Ottawa: Health Canada, 1999).

L. Duxbury & C. Higgins, "Wrestling with Workload: Organizational Strategies for Success" (Conference Board of Canada Report May 2005) at 1-3.

D. Dyck, "Directions in Disability Management" (1997) 44:2 EAP Digest at 16-20.

J. Eakin, "Psychological Aspects of Workplace Health" *Canadian Centre for Occupational Health and Safety* (April 1992) at 8-10.

EAP, *Why Your Company Needs an EAP* (2005) available online at: <http://www.eap4u.com/needeap.aspx>.

Essi Systems, *Stress Map: A Personal Exploration* (Collingwood: Essi Systems, 1987).

R.W. Francis, "Medcan Health Management" (Presentation at The Disability Management Conference, Toronto, 27-28 May 1996) [unpublished].

D. Goldman, *Emotional Intelligence: Why it Can Matter More Than IQ* (New York: Bantam Books, 1995).

R. Karask & T. Theorell, *Healthy Work: Stress, Productivity and Reconstruction of Working Life* (New York: Basic Books, 1990).

S. Klitzman, J. House, B. Isreal & R. Mero, "Work Stress, Nonwork Stress and Health" (1990) 13:3 Journal of Behavioural Medicine at 221-243.

J. Kranc, "Fact Check" *Benefits Canada* (March 2004) at 70.

L. Lewis, "Employers Place More Emphasis on Managing Employee Stress" (1993) 11:2 Business & Health at 46-50.

J. MacBride-King, *Caring about Caregiving: The Eldercare Responsibilities of Canadian Workers and the Impact on Employers* (Ottawa: The Conference Board of Canada, 1999).

S.T. Maier, L.R. Watkins & M. Fleshner, "Psychoneuroimmunology: The Interface Between Behaviour, Brain and Immunity" (1994) 40 American Psychologist at 771-776.

Marsh Risk Consulting, *Marsh/Mercer Survey of Employers' Time-Off and Disability Management Programs* (2003), online: <http://www.marshrisk consulting.com/st/PDEv_C_371_SC_2L8135_NR_306_PI_347745.htm>.

McDonnell Douglas, "EAP Dollars and Sense", *Solutions* (2005), online: <http://www.solutions-eap.com/infoforemp/eap_benefit_s.tudies.htm>.

H. Minuk, "The Mercantile and General Disability Claims Survey, 1994" (Presented at the Psychological Disabilities in the Workplace: Prevention, Rehabilitation and Cost Control Conference, Toronto, 10-11 June 1996) [unpublished].

Ontario Ministry of Labour, "Counting the Cost of Absenteeism" (1993) 1:1 Group Healthcare Management at 9.

J. Prohofofsky, "Speaking to Your CEO About EAPs: Three Strategies that Can Make EAP Believers Out of CEO Skeptics", *EAP Digest* (May 2005).

R.J. Price, "Absenteeism and Disability" (1995), The ACPM Reporter at 34-37.

M. Ross, "Psychiatric Disability Management" (Presentation at The Disability Management Conference, Toronto, 27-28 May 1996) [unpublished].

C. Sherman, "Who is the Problem Employee" *Human Resources Management in Canada* (February 1989) at 70, 507-70.

Statistics Canada, *Work Absence Rate*, 2004, (Ottawa: Statistics Canada, 2005).

D.G. Tate, R.V. Habeck & G. Schwartz, "Disability Management: Origins, Concepts and Principles for Practice" (1986) 17 *Journal of Applied Rehabilitation Counselling* at 5-11.

M. Visser, "Opportunities for a Managed Care Approach to Psychological Disabilities" (Presented at the Psychological Disabilities in the Workplace: Prevention, Rehabilitation and Cost Control Conference, Toronto, 10-11 June 1996) [unpublished].

Watson Wyatt Worldwide, *Staying @ Work 2005* (2005), online: <http://www.watsonwyatt.com/research/resrender.asp?id=w-860&page=1>.

W. Weeks, "Stressing Prevention" *Benefits Canada* (May 2004) at 54, available online at: <http://www.benefitscanada.com/benefits/benefits10.jsp>.

B. Wilkerson, "Perspective on Mental Health in the Workplace", reported in Watson Wyatt Worldwide, *Staying @ Work Report, 2005* (2005), online: <http://www.watsonwyatt.com/research/resrender.asp?id=w-860&page=1> at 9.

Chapter 9

Management of Chronic Fatigue Syndrome: Case Study[1]

INTRODUCTION

Some of the most difficult disability management cases to deal with are the ones that are poorly understood, and have primarily subjective symptomatology. This includes illnesses such as chronic fatigue syndrome, fibromyalgia and multiple chemical sensitivities. This chapter has been included to demonstrate an industry practice in dealing with employees absent due to chronic fatigue syndrome.

CHRONIC FATIGUE SYNDROME

Chronic fatigue syndrome is a complex disorder marked by incapacitating fatigue of uncertain etiology which results in at least a 50% reduction in activity and is of at least six months in duration.[2] Although women aged 20 to 50 years are the most susceptible to chronic fatigue syndrome, anyone at any age can be affected.

Chronic fatigue syndrome has been called many things, for example, "Yuppie Flu", 20th Century Disease, chronic Epstein-Barr virus, M.E. (myalgic encephalomyelitis), yet it is not a new disorder. In fact, the same syndrome, or similar ones, can be found in various pieces of medical literature under such names as yeast syndrome, epidemic vegetative neuritis, chronic brucellosis, nervous exhaustion, ads neurasthenia or Iceland disease.[3]

Several different agents have been proposed as the potential causes of chronic fatigue syndrome, ranging from fatigue due to a chronic overachieving or "type A" personality, to viral infections such as Epstein-Barr virus or an unknown retrovirus; to sleep disorders; to psychosomatic disorders; to psychiatric illness; or to deconditioning. Whatever the cause, the person with chronic fatigue syndrome experiences debilitating fatigue that is extremely frustrating and distressing to live with.

[1] D. Dyck, "Management of Chronic Fatigue Syndrome: Case Study" (1996) 44:2 AAOHN Journal at 85-92. Reprinted with permission.

[2] G.P. Holmes, J.E. Kaplan *et al.*, "Chronic Fatigue Syndrome: A Working Definition" (1988) 108 Annals of Internal Medicine at 387-9.

[3] S.E. Abbey & S.D. Shafran, "Chronic Fatigue Syndrome: It's Real, It's Treatable" (1993) March Patient Care at 35-51.

DIAGNOSING CHRONIC FATIGUE

When a person develops chronic fatigue syndrome, getting a definitive diagnosis can be very challenging.[4] There are no markers to objectively identify the presence of chronic fatigue syndrome. Diagnosing depends heavily on the presence of subjective complaints. Unfortunately, many physicians are unfamiliar with chronic fatigue syndrome and have difficulty diagnosing it.[5] Typically, the person with chronic fatigue syndrome travels from physician to physician looking for a cause for their fatigue, only to be subjected to more tests and investigative procedures. This process can reinforce the sick role, or the expression of illness behaviours, and can increase health care costs through repetitive tests and procedures.

This phenomenon partly stems from the U.S. Center for Disease Control's definition of chronic fatigue syndrome (Figure 9.1).

Figure 9.1: Diagnosing Chronic Fatigue Syndrome: Case Definition 2005[6]

Major Criteria

- Incapacitating exhaustion or fatigue of at least six or more consecutive months in duration with over 50% reduction in activity level
- Exclusion of medical and psychiatric causes
- Concurrently have four or more of the following symptoms:

  - Substantial impairment in short-term memory or concentration
  - Sore throat
  - Tender lymph nodes
  - Multi-joint pain without swelling or redness
  - Headaches of a new type, pattern or severity
  - Unrefreshing sleep
  - Post-exertional malaise lasting more than 24 hours

To be diagnosed with chronic fatigue syndrome, the person must experience incapacitating fatigue of longer than six consecutive months in duration and 50% reduction in activity level *to the exclusion* of all other medical and psychiatric conditions. This means ruling out the presence of malignancies, infectious diseases, endocrine disease, autoimmune disease, sleep disorders, neuromuscular or neurological disease, exposure to toxic agents and psychiatric disorders. As well, the definition relies on the presence of four or more other signs and symptoms, which must also not have predated the fatigue.

---

[4] K. Fukuda, S. Straus, I. Hickie, *et al.*, "The Chronic Fatigue Syndrome: A Comprehensive Approach to its Definition and Study" (1994) 121:12 American College of Physicians at 953-59.

[5] *Supra*, note 3.

[6] Centers for Disease Control and Prevention, *Chronic Fatigue Syndrome* (2005), available online at: <http://www.cdc.gov/ncidod/diseases/cfs/index.htm>.

PREVALENCE OF CHRONIC FATIGUE SYNDROME

In primary care settings, the incidence of chronic fatigue syndrome is 0.3% to 2.5% depending on the reporting agency.[7] In the community, the prevalence is reported to be less than 0.01%, or between 3.4/10,000 to 75/10,000. The variance is thought to be due to reporting nuances.[8]

According to Dr. Buchwald, the belief that chronic fatigue syndrome occurs mainly with Caucasians and women, is a myth. Research indicates that there is a one to one ratio for men and women and that all races can contract chronic fatigue syndrome. She believes this myth developed because women and men express the condition differently. Her research demonstrates that women tend to present primarily with painful lymph nodes and fibromyalgia, whereas men complain of painful lymph nodes and exhibit more alcohol abuse.[9] The result is a difference in diagnosing.

PROGNOSIS

People with chronic fatigue syndrome can present with a wide range of physical symptoms ranging from obvious invalidism to looking perfectly well. They can experience any of the physical symptoms outlined in Figure 9.1, with overwhelming fatigue being the major complaint. Since weight gain is common, family and friends often question the legitimacy of the illness.

Recovery can be a very slow process. Symptoms may last six years or more.[10] The best prognosis for recovery occurs if the person experiences a high fever at the onset, and if he or she has a job or occupation to return to after recovery.[11]

MANAGEMENT OF CHRONIC FATIGUE SYNDROME

There are numerous management approaches for helping chronic fatigue syndrome patients cope with their illness. One of the most popular models is based on Butler's Vicious Circle model (Figure 9.2).

According to this model, the patient develops the chronic fatigue syndrome symptoms and avoids activity, which results in deconditioning and a reduced tolerance for activity. This leads to resentment because the person is unable to

---

[7]   D. Buchwald, "Current Concepts in Assessment and Treatment of Chronic Fatigue" (Presented at Understanding Chronic Fatigue Conference Symposium conducted at Health Science Theatre, Medical Sciences, University of Calgary, October 1994) [unpublished].

[8]   *Ibid.*

[9]   *Ibid.*

[10]   *Supra*, note 3.

[11]   *Supra*, note 7.

do the activities of normal daily living. The patient tries to resume his or her familiar activities and is thwarted and left feeling helpless. This produces more symptoms and the circle continues.

Figure 9.2: Vicious Circle Model of Chronic Fatigue Syndrome

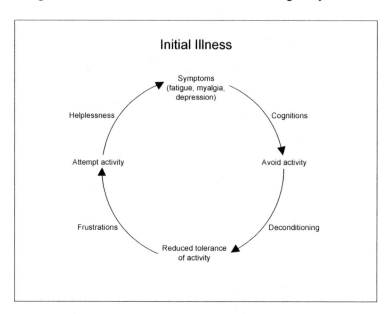

S. Butler *et al.*, "Cognitive Behavior in Chronic Fatigue Syndrome" (1991) 54 Journal of Neurological and Neurosurgical Psychiatry at 153-158.

The current trend in chronic fatigue syndrome management is to use a multi-disciplinary approach incorporating the following rehabilitation goals:

- restore a sense of self-efficacy and control;
- gradually increase physical activity; and
- decrease the restrictions imposed by chronic fatigue syndrome.[12]

The techniques involved to achieve these goals vary. However, the following are some common suggestions for chronic fatigue syndrome rehabilitation:

- validate the condition: acknowledge that chronic fatigue syndrome is a recognizable illness that many people suffer from;
- educate the person regarding chronic fatigue syndrome, the effects of physical deconditioning and the cognitive effects of inactivity;

---

[12] *Supra*, note 3.

- encourage the person to consider a wide range of explanations other than "virus" for an increase in, or return of, symptoms;
- identify dysfunctional thought patterns and demonstrate ways to think more functionally;
- focus on the person's capabilities not disabilities;
- gradually increase activities and monitor tolerance for activities;
- record all activity; and
- help the person recognize progress.

A WORKPLACE APPLICATION

Background

In 1994, a major Canadian oil and gas company faced the challenge of rehabilitating two employees diagnosed with chronic fatigue syndrome. Both employees developed severe flu-like symptoms in the fall of 1993. They experienced an acute onset of fever, sore throat, coughing and swollen glands. Later, they developed unexplained muscle weakness and discomfort, all-encompassing fatigue, arthralgia, forgetfulness, confusion, inability to concentrate, depression and sleep disturbances (*i.e.*, restless legs, snoring, insomnia, and fitful sleep). Both exhibited thyroid dysfunction and hoarse voices to the point of laryngitis.

During the short term disability phase, these employees attempted to return to work in a modified work capacity, but had to withdraw due to increased fatigue and a return of symptoms. After six months of short-term disability, both were transferred to long term disability with the company's third party insurance carrier.

Rehabilitation Program Plan

Active rehabilitation of employees on short-term disability and long-term disability was within the mandate of the company's Managed Rehabilitation Care Program. As a result, a number of health and fitness care practitioners were invited to work on a plan to actively rehabilitate these two employees. They developed the chronic fatigue syndrome rehabilitation program's goals, strategies and plan, which is outlined in Figure 9.3.

Figure 9.3: Chronic Fatigue Syndrome Rehabilitation Program

Goals
- To provide a multi-disciplinary rehabilitation program for people suffering from chronic fatigue syndrome.
- To support the participants in reaching an optimal level of functioning and an improved quality of life.
- To decrease the restrictions associated with the disability and to focus on wellness and moving on with life.
- To restore a sense of self-efficacy and control.
- To promote an early return to work.

Strategies
- To provide a holistic approach towards dealing with disability through the use of the available fitness facilities, Employee Assistance Program services, occupational health services and vocational rehabilitation services.
- To increase activity tolerance through a graduated physical fitness program, relaxation and stretching guidance, nutritional counselling, physiotherapy instruction and massage therapy.
- To increase psychological tolerance through developing strategies for coping with disability and achieving a sense of wellness.
- To increase vocational tolerance through developing strategies for work re-entry.

Plan
- To educate the patient about chronic fatigue syndrome by providing information about:
  1. the nature of chronic fatigue syndrome;
  2. the effects of physical deconditioning on muscle; and
  3. the phenomenon of increased anxiety when a failed activity is re-attempted.
- To identify the dysfunctional thought patterns and to try to change cognition about health status.
- To encourage the participant to consider a range of explanations other than a "virus" for an increase in, or return of symptoms.
- To focus on what the participant can do rather than what they cannot do.
- To gradually increase activity levels.
- To record activity so that progress can be monitored.
- To institute fitness twice a week under the guidance of a personal trainer.
- To provide instruction on relaxation and stretching techniques.
- To provide massage therapy for each participant.

- To provide dietary counselling.
- To provide physiotherapy counselling.
- To provide a forum for exploring strategies for living with a disability.
- To explore vocational issues related to the disability.
- To use peer support to help deal with the effects of chronic disease.

A multi-disciplinary program was designed to operate out of the company's fitness club for two 90-minute sessions per week conducted over a three-month period. Each session was designed to include an educational component lasting 30 minutes, fitness activities with a personal trainer lasting 30 minutes and stretching and relaxation techniques also lasting 30 minutes. The educational component encompassed information about chronic fatigue syndrome, sleep problems, psychological support for living with a disability, dietary counselling, vocational counselling and physiotherapy guidance. The psychological support was provided weekly, while the other topics rotated through the remaining session.

Educational sessions were also offered to the family members, co-workers and the involved work groups. In addition, the participants were provided with weekly massage sessions arranged outside of the set rehabilitation program time. To evaluate the value of the rehabilitation program, individual pre-intervention and post-intervention assessments were made. These will now be described, as a part of the post-intervention results.

Results

PSYCHOLOGICAL TESTS

The participants were asked to complete scales and questionnaires that measure:

- *Attribution* — the individual's perception of disease, in particular physical versus psychological etiologies;
- *Coping* — the ability to deal with illness and life issues;
- *Fatigue Rating* — the characteristics of fatigue;
- *Functional Status* — the ability to function in daily life;
- *General Health History* — the experienced somatic and psychological distress;
- *Locus of Control* — the belief that health is determined by behaviour;
- *Quality of Life* — the perceived satisfaction with daily activities and relationships;
- *Social Supports: Family and Friends* — the emotional, instrumental and problem-solving support obtained from family and friends; and
- *Stress* — the stress factors identified in the areas of environmental pressures and satisfactions, coping responses, cognition and signals of distress.

Figure 9.4: Psychological Test Results

Scale/Questionnaire	Case 1	Case 2
Attribution Scale	Shift in belief that the problem was purely physical to believing that psychological factors were impacting the condition	Shift in belief that the problem was purely physical to believing that psychological factors were impacting the condition
Coping Scale: Problem-based	Increased ability to manage the source of difficulties	Increased ability to manage the source of difficulties
Coping Scale: Emotion-based	Reduced ability to minimize distress	No change in ability to cope
Fatigue Rating	Less interference in daily activities due to fatigue	Less interference in daily activities due to fatigue
Functional Status Questionnaire (Medical Measures)		
Physical function	Improvement	Improvement
Role function	Improvement	Improvement
Social function	Improvement	Improvement
Mental health	Improvement	No change
General health	Improvement	No change
Body pain	Improvement	Improvement
Vitality	Improvement	Improvement
General Health History Questionnaire (Distress Measure)	No distress	Change from being "in distress" to "not being in distress"
Locus of Control Scale	Slight shift to externality	Slight shift to externality
Quality of Life Scale	General improvement	General improvement

Scale/Questionnaire	Case 1	Case 2
Social Support Scale (Family)	High score originally: Unchanged	Increased support
Social Support Scale (Friends)	Moderately high score originally: Unchanged	Moderately high score originally: Unchanged
Stress Map		
Work world	Improvement	Not applicable*
Personal world	Improvement	Improvement
Coping responses	Improvement in self-care, direct action, support seeking, situation mastery and adaptability: negative change in time management	Improvement in self-care, direct action, situation mastery and adaptability: no change in support seeking and time management
Thinking patterns	Improvement in self-esteem and positive outlook: no change in personal power — at the burnout stage	Improvement in self-esteem, support seeking and positive outlook
Feeling patterns	Improvement in connection and compassion: negative change in expression	Improvement in connection: no change in expression and compassion
Symptoms	Improvement in physical symptoms, behavioural symptoms and emotional symptoms: all were at the level of burnout originally	Improvement in physical symptoms, behavioural symptoms and emotional symptoms: at the level of burnout originally

*   At the time of pre-and post-testing, this participant was not working.

The scores from psychological tests were used for pre-intervention and post-intervention comparison purposes.

In general, the participants showed either gradual improvements or no change between the pre-intervention and post-intervention results (Figure 9.4).

FITNESS TESTS

A treadmill test was used to assess cardiovascular fitness. Subjects were asked to maintain heart rates within their Target Heart Rate Zones[13] as the speed and grade of the treadmill was gradually increased. Their tolerance for this activity over three minutes was then measured and recorded.

The fitness consultants were unable to implement other standardized fitness tests as the participants did not possess the necessary grip or upper body strength for even the most elementary level of testing. Consequently, the participants were asked to give maximum effort to the use of the rowing machine and free weights, and measurements of those activities were made and documented.

Improvements were seen in tolerance for activity, level of fitness and strength training as summarized in Figure 9.5.

Figure 9.5: Fitness Results

Assessment	Case 1	Case 2
Treadmill	Increased speed 1.3 miles per hour Increased endurance by 9 minutes Increased grade by 2%	Increased speed 1.5 miles per hour Increased endurance by 14 minutes Increased grade by 5%
Rowing Machine	Rowing 10 minutes at 26 strokes per min.	Rowing 12 minutes at 26 strokes per min.
Weight Training	2 x 10 reps at 3 kg biceps curls 2 x 10 reps at 3 kg bent over row 2 x 10 reps at 2 kg lateral raise 2 x 10 reps at 35 lb. leg curls 2 x 10 reps at 40 lb. leg extensions	2 x 15 reps at 3 kg biceps curls 2 x 15 reps at 3 kg bent over row 2 x 15 reps at 2 kg lateral raise 2 x 15 reps at 35 lb. leg curls 2 x 15 reps at 35 lb. leg extensions 2 x 15 reps at 20 lb. triceps press downs

---

[13] Canadian Society for Exercise Physiology (CSEP), *Physical Fitness Testing: Certified Fitness Appraiser, Resource Manual* (Gloucester, Ontario: CSEP, 1993).

PAIN TESTING

At the first massage session, the participants were administered the following series of massage tests:

- *Resisted Active Test*
  Therapist immobilizes the joint and provides resistance against client's muscular contraction (about 20% to 39% of maximum strength). This test determines muscular strains and trigger points.

- *Relaxed Passive Test*
  The therapist manually moves the client's limb through a full range of motion while the client relaxes the surrounding joint muscles. This test helps to determine joint pathologies.

- *Free Active Test*
  The client moves the limb through a full range of motion. This allows for assessment of the presence or absence of pain and abnormalities in the movement mechanics.

- *Trigger Point Test*
  A trigger point is pain in a muscle that, when pressed, allocates pain locally and/or refers pain to other areas of the body. They can be latent (pain present only upon application of stimulus), or active (pain present without the application of pressure).

During the baseline massage assessment, both participants indicated pain when simple techniques were administered. Their pain and sensitivity was more intense on the left side of the body. Both reported having muscle cramps associated with movement, and, at times, these cramps were present without movement.

Trigger point testing was done on the shoulder, cervical and lumbar joints. Initially, pain was indicated on resisted active and passive tests. There was an absence of pain with free active testing indicating the lack of joint pathology. Trigger points were active and referring pain in the following muscles:

1. *Levator scapula* (left) causing pain into the cervical, suboccipital and shoulder area;
2. *Quadrutus lumborum* (left) causing pain in the lumbar, hip and gluteals; and
3. Tricep, lateral head (left) being localized and extremely sensitive to the touch.

The initial massage treatment was extremely painful and the body was hypersensitive to touch. Using a pain scale of 1 to 10, 1 being ticklish and 10 being intolerable, the weight of the hand on their bodies registered 9-10. It took two to three sessions before the pain and discomfort was reduced enough (to a 5-6 level) to allow the implementation of therapeutic techniques. By the sixth session, massage was reportedly enjoyable and beneficial.

Likewise, relaxation was initially difficult for both participants to achieve. This was probably associated with the pain experienced during massage treatments. By the sixth treatment, both were able to relax enough to allow the masseur to incorporate joint mobilizations.

Figure 9.6: Massage Results

Assessment	**Case 1**	**Case 2**
Trigger Points	Referred trigger point pain was lessened. Local trigger point pain was reduced in intensity.	Referred trigger point pain reduced in all initial trigger points. Therapeutic pressure was reached by the third session.
Relaxation	Remarkable improvement in relaxation state. Developed ability to trust and relax enough to allow joint mobilizations after fifth session.	Relaxation easily achieved by third session.

DIETARY ASSESSMENT

The participants were asked to complete a dietary history, which includes a physical symptom history, weight history, brief family history, lifestyle history, height, weight, age and a three-day food record. The three-day food record was then computer-analyzed using the Nuts 3.7 nutrient assessment program for nutritional adequacy.[14]

The Nomogram[15] (Mayo Clinic, 1994) was used to calculate the caloric recommendations. The only subjective information used in this equation was the activity factor, which was estimated at a low level for both participants. Weights were monitored throughout the study using a Gold Brand beam scale. Gastrointestinal symptoms were obtained by self-report.

---

[14] Quichena Consulting Limited, *Nuts Version 3.7* (Victoria: Quichena Consulting Ltd., 1992).
[15] J. K. Nelson *et al.*, *Mayo Clinic Diet Manual: A Handbook of Nutritional Practices*, 7th ed. (St. Louis: The C.V. Mosby Company, 1994).

Prior to the program, both participants were consuming calories well below their basal caloric requirements. This finding was consistent with nutritional literature on chronic fatigue syndrome.[16] The basal metabolic rate decreases primarily due to muscle tissue breakdown common to starvation states, and, combined with decreased activity due to fatigue, the person gains weight even on a low caloric intake.

Post-intervention, both participants reported a greater awareness of the gap between their dietary deficits and the recommended daily nutritional requirements.[17] One participant was able to attain the recommended daily caloric intake, while the other came close to doing likewise. Food sensitivities were identified and addressed by one participant. This resulted in a reduction of gastrointestinal symptoms. The other participant reported an increase in the number of "positive feeling" days, improved appetite, less insomnia and fewer episodes of laryngitis and swollen glands. However, both participants gained significant weight from the onset of the illness, and, even now, remain unable to lose the extra weight.

FUNCTIONAL ASSESSMENT

Daily activity logs (Figure 9.7) were kept by the two participants for the duration of the program. The intent was to track sleep patterns, activity levels and tolerance, fatigue levels and mood. As well, health status was regularly monitored through the company's occupational health centre.

The daily activity logs that each participant completed showed a gradual increase in activities and an increased tolerance for those activities. Not only did the participants look and feel better, but also they were able to begin a gradual re-entry process back into the workplace.

VOCATIONAL ASSESSMENT

Standardized vocational tests were not conducted, however, a number of observations were made. Prior to the program, one participant was attempting modified work for one to two hours a day, the other was unable to work. Both participants expressed fears that their jobs would be abolished and that they would be unable to secure employment when they were well enough to return to work. Lack of confidence in their ability to market themselves to potential employers was a noted source of anxiety.

---

[16] I.J. Russell, "Neurohormonal Dysfunction in Chronic Fatigue and Fibromyalgia" (7th International Symposium of Physical Medicine Research Foundation on Repetitive Strain Injuries, Fibromyalgia, and Chronic Fatigue Syndrome, June 1994) [unpublished]; M. Winther, "Essential Fatty Acid Therapy for Myalgic Encephalomyelitis" in *The Clinical and Scientific Basis of Myalgic Encephalomyelitis — Chronic Fatigue Syndrome* (Ottawa: Nightingale Research Foundation, 1992) at 628-633.

[17] Canadian Diabetic Association (CDA), *Good Healthy Eating Guide, Resource Manual* (Edmonton: CDA, 1994).

Figure 9.7: Daily Activity Log

Date: _____

Hour of Awakening: _____ Sedation Used: Yes _____ No _____

No. of Sleep Disturbances: _____ Dream Activity: Low ____ Medium ____

High ____

	Exhausted								Totally Refreshed	
Refreshed:	1	2	3	4	5	6	7	8	9	10

Comments:_____

_____

_____

Calendar of Activities

6:00 a.m.	
7:00 a.m.	
8:00 a.m.	
9:00 a.m.	
10:00 a.m.	
11:00 a.m.	
12:00 noon	
1:00 p.m.	
2:00 p.m.	
3:00 p.m.	
4:00 p.m.	
5:00 p.m.	
6:00 p.m.	
7:00 p.m.	
8:00 p.m.	
9:00 p.m.	
10:00 p.m.	
11:00 p.m.	

Appraisal of the Day

	Low								High	
Activity Level	1	2	3	4	5	6	7	8	9	10
Fatigue Level	1	2	3	4	5	6	7	8	9	10
Mood Level	1	2	3	4	5	6	7	8	9	10

Comments:_____

Both participants demonstrated an increased awareness of their marketable skills, particularly in the areas of personal and transferable skills. The initial reluctance to take ownership of their strengths and skills was gradually reduced.

There was an increased willingness to accept that a broad range of vocational options exists in the labour market, and that these options are obtainable through a strategic job search.

Discussion

Chronic fatigue syndrome is a multifaceted condition and requires a team approach to produce positive recovery results. The following is a discussion of how the Chronic Fatigue Syndrome Rehabilitation Program strategies were met and the findings that emerged:

Strategy 1: Provide a holistic approach towards dealing with disability through the use of available company resources: the fitness centre, Employee Assistance Program, occupational health services and vocational rehabilitation services.

The program operated as planned, however the original design of the program failed to include a transitional period from dependency on the program providers, to self-sufficiency by the participant. During the course of the program, the designers recognized that this aspect was important if the demonstrated recovery behaviours were to be sustained. Thus, the program was extended by a month.

Strategy 2: Support the participant in attaining an optimal level of functioning and an improved quality of life.

The functional status questionnaire (medical measures), Figure 9.4, indicated improvements in physical function, role function, social function, mental health, general health and vitality. As well, there was an improvement in quality of life and a reduction in chronic fatigue syndrome symptomatology (stress map).

In the pre-intervention test, both participants scored high on the social support scale (friends) (Figure 9.4). As a result, change was not expected nor seen. As for family support, one participant indicated an increase in family support at the post-intervention test. This was probably associated with the psychological counselling, which encouraged the participants to control perfectionist tendencies, lower expectations and accept help from family members.

As for the cognitive and behavioural coping strategies for dealing with internal and external demands in stressful situations, both participants increased their ability to manage problems, but neither demonstrated an improvement in coping with the associated emotional issues. In fact, one participant demonstrated a reduced ability to cope with emotional problems on the stress map and emotion-based coping scale (Figure 9.4). When this was examined further, it was noted that at the time of the post-intervention test, this person was reacting to the deaths of a number of family members. Interestingly, the grieving process lasted a normal period of time without a setback in the recovery process. Some credit for this degree of coping may be attributable to the psychological support provided by the Chronic Fatigue Syndrome Rehabilitation Program.

Although there were some improvements in the participants' feeling patterns, Figure 9.4, more help may have been warranted in some areas. For example, the test results indicated negative, or no change, in expression and compassion. Expression is sharing what one thinks and how one feels with others through direct and indirect communication.[18] Compassion is the capacity to empathize with another person, understanding another point of view and recognizing other peoples' strengths and limits.[19] In discussion with the program designers, it was believed to be unrealistic to expect change in these areas as a result of a three-month program. Healthy people can function adequately at lower levels of both these values.

One area where no change was noted was time management. Given the fact that both participants had been absent for many months and were returned to a scheduled program and into a modified work program, the designers of the program should have anticipated that time management would be a challenge. If a similar program were repeated, inclusion of a time management session, as well as help with balancing home and work life pressures, would be recommended.

Strategy 3: Decrease the restrictions associated with the disability and focus on wellness and "moving on with life".

An increase in activity tolerance was illustrated by the fitness test results, massage results, activity logs and gradual return-to-work initiatives. Now, three months after the end of the program, both participants have sustained their activity levels, and, in fact, they are increasing their hours of work.

The fatigue rating results indicated less interference in daily activities due to fatigue. Part of this finding appears to be due to the physical reconditioning; part may be due to the psychological counselling which encouraged a gradual increase in activity and also encouraged the participants not to be frustrated by trying to "do it all at once". In this way, the vicious circle of chronic fatigue syndrome was interrupted.

The results of the related psychological tests appear to indicate that the counselling around living with a chronic disability helped both participants. Prior to the program, they believed that chronic fatigue syndrome was strictly physical in nature. Attempts to explore any associated emotional factors in the earlier stages of the recovery process proved unsuccessful. By the end of the Chronic Fatigue Syndrome Rehabilitation Program, there was a shift in belief that some psychological factors were impacting the conditions. In short, psychological tolerance was increased.

---

[18] Essi Systems, *Stress Map: A Personal Exploration* (Collingwood: The Centre for High Performance, 1987).
[19] *Ibid.*

A reduction in some of the physical symptoms of chronic fatigue syndrome may also have been due to dietary changes. For example, an improved nutrient intake can increase blood sugar and glycogen stores and aid in greater tissue anabolism instead of tissue catabolism. Tissue catabolism from inadequate caloric and nutrient intake can result in ketosis and the resulting elevated uric acid levels. These can promote a "gouty condition" creating joint pain, weakness, fatigue, poor exercise tolerance, *etc.*, paralleling the symptoms seen with chronic fatigue syndrome.

One month into the program, it became apparent that sleep disturbances remained a barrier to the participants' successful recovery. Dr. Adam Moscovitz, of the University of Calgary Sleep Disorder Clinic, was consulted. He recommended that sleep logs be kept by each participant for screening purposes. He also agreed to conduct an educational session on the abnormalities of sleep in persons with chronic fatigue syndrome. Both participants tested positively for the presence of sleep disturbances and were referred for extensive investigations. Sleep disturbances often co-exist with chronic fatigue syndrome and are potentially treatable.[20] For this reason, the participants attended a sleep clinic.

Strategy 4: Restore a sense of self-efficacy and control.

Both participants reported a heightened sense of control over their recovery process and their lives. When the Chronic Fatigue Syndrome Rehabilitation Program ended, both employees chose to continue their rehabilitation efforts by continuing their fitness programs, psychological counselling, dietary counselling and massage therapy. Their goal was to sustain and build on the gains that they had already made.

Strategy 5: Promote an early return to work.

In association with the program, both participants worked modified work duties. However, due to a changing work environment, guarantees of a return to a permanent job are uncertain. For this reason, a referral for focused job search assistance was made to a private career-coaching program that has a philosophy consistent with the goals of the Chronic Fatigue Syndrome Rehabilitation Program. The outcome was that one participant chose to do a thorough career evaluation, while the other decided to do on-the-job training with the department in which modified work was available.

---

[20] D. Buchwald *et al.*, "Sleep Disorders in Patients with Chronic Fatigue" (1994) 18 (Supp. 1) Clinical Infectious Diseases at 68-72; L. Krupp *et al.*, "Sleep Disturbance in Chronic Fatigue Syndrome" (1993) 37:4 Journal of Psychosomatic Research at 325-331; R. Morriss *et al.*, "Abnormalities of Sleep in Patients With the Chronic Fatigue Syndrome" (1993) 306 British Medical Journal at 1161-1163.

In summary, this multi-disciplinary approach to chronic fatigue syndrome rehabilitation did make a difference, and the gains in recovery appear to be sustainable. Some recommendations for future Chronic Fatigue Syndrome Rehabilitation Programs are:

- document baseline states so that progress can be measured;
- include a transitional period prior to discharge from the program so that participants can move towards self-sufficiency;
- build "Time Management" and "Achieving Balance Between Work and Family Life" sessions into the program;
- anticipate and investigate the possible presence of sleep disturbances so they can be treated;
- incorporate dietary counselling into the program, as it can help to reduce the underlying physical symptoms; and
- offer vocational counselling to promote employability once a return to full-time work has been achieved.

SUMMARY

Case management and rehabilitation of "hot illnesses", like chronic fatigue syndrome, are challenging processes. To result in a successful return to a productive lifestyle for the employee, a goal-oriented plan of action is required that encompasses a team effort, a multi-disciplinary approach and collaboration by all stakeholders.

CHAPTER REFERENCES

S.E. Abbey & S.D. Shafran, "Chronic Fatigue Syndrome: It's Real, It's Treatable" (1993) March Patient Care at 35-51.

D. Buchwald, "Current Concepts in Assessment and Treatment of Chronic Fatigue" (Understanding Chronic Fatigue Conference. Symposium conducted at Health Science Theatre, Medical Sciences, University of Calgary, October, 1994) [unpublished].

D. Buchwald *et al.*, "Sleep Disorders in Patients with Chronic Fatigue" (1994) 18 (Supp. 1) Clinical Infectious Diseases at 68-72.

S. Butler *et al.*, "Cognitive Behavior in Chronic Fatigue Syndrome" (1991) 54 Journal of Neurological and Neurosurgical Psychiatry at 153-158.

Canadian Diabetic Association (CDA), *Good Healthy Eating Guide, Resource Manual* (Edmonton: CDA, 1994).

Canadian Society for Exercise Physiology (CSEP), *Physical Fitness Testing: Certified Fitness Appraiser, Resource Manual* (Gloucester: CSEP, 1993).

Centers for Disease Control and Prevention, *Chronic Fatigue Syndrome* (2005), available online at: <http://www.cdc.gov/ncidod/diseases/cfs>.

D. Dyck, "Management of Chronic Fatigue Syndrome: Case Study" (1996) 44:2 AAOHN Journal at 85-92. Reprinted with permission.

Essi Systems, *Stress Map: A Personal Exploration* (Collingwood: The Centre for High Performance, 1987).

K. Fukuda, S. Straus, I. Hickie, *et al.*, "The Chronic Fatigue Syndrome: A Comprehensive Approach to its Definition and Study" (1994) 121:12 American College of Physicians at 953-59.

G.P. Holmes, J.E. Kaplan, *et al.*, "Chronic Fatigue Syndrome: A Working Definition" (1988) 108 Annuals of Internal Medicine at 387-9.

L. Krupp *et al.*, "Sleep Disturbance in Chronic Fatigue Syndrome" (1993) 37:4 Journal of Psychosomatic Research at 325-331.

R. Morriss *et al.*, "Abnormalities of Sleep in Patients With the Chronic Fatigue Syndrome" (1993), 306 British Medical Journal at 1161-1163.

J.K. Nelson *et al.*, *Mayo Clinic Diet Manual: A Handbook of Nutritional Practices*, 7th ed. (St. Louis: The C.V. Mosby Company, 1994).

Quichena Consulting Ltd., *Nuts Version 3.7* (Victoria: Quichena Consulting Ltd., 1992).

I.J. Russell, "Neurohormonal Dysfunction in Chronic Fatigue and Fibromyalgia (7th International Symposium of Physical Medicine Research Foundation on Repetitive Strain Injuries, Fibromyalgia, and Chronic Fatigue Syndrome, June, 1994) [unpublished].

M. Winther, "Essential Fatty Acid Therapy for Myalgic Encephalomyelitis" in *The Clinical and Scientific Basis of Myalgic Encephalomyelitis — Chronic Fatigue Syndrome* (Ottawa: Nightingale Research Foundation, 1992) at 628-633.

Chapter 10

Workplace Attendance Support and Assistance

INTRODUCTION

Companies are increasingly being challenged to meet the needs of customers, expectations of shareholders and obligations to the community at large in their daily operations. Meeting this challenge requires the commitment and support of every employee. For this reason, attention is being paid to supporting employee attendance.

Disability management involves assisting ill or injured employees in managing their medical absence and return to work, having policies and procedures in place, providing education to stakeholders, clarifying stakeholder roles and responsibilities in the process, having a graduated Return-to-Work Program and addressing workplace wellness (Chapter 1, Figure 1.1). Encouraging employees to attend work on a regular basis should be part of any organization's disability management efforts. To this end, many companies have chosen to assist their employees through the use of a formalized workplace attendance support program.

EMPLOYEE ABSENTEEISM

Employee absenteeism is defined as unplanned work absence due to illness, injury or personal reasons, or just failing to come to work. Some reasons for unscheduled absences, which can lead to chronic absenteeism, are:

- chronic medical conditions;
- personal problems;
- problems balancing work-family life demands;
- job dissatisfaction or disinterest;
- frequent illness/injuries;
- lack of awareness of attendance expectations;
- irresponsible work attitudes;
- medical, dental or personal appointments;
- poor quality of supervision; and/or
- decaying employee-employer relations.

WHY MANAGE EMPLOYEE ABSENTEEISM?

Employee absenteeism is a costly and complex problem for employers in all segments of Canada's economy. In the 1970s, when productivity was high, many employers chose to ignore employee attendance problems. Through the leaner years of the 1980s, 1990s and into the 2000s, the challenge for companies has been to ensure a consistent level of productivity and service in a climate of downsizing.

Employee absenteeism costs:

- In 2004, 7.6% of all full-time employees were absent from work for all or part of any given week. This is an increase from 1997 when about 5.5% of all full-time employees were absent.[1]
- In 1994 unplanned absences cost Canadian employers about $15 billion per year;[2] by 2001 this increased to $17 billion.[3] Today this number is much higher.
- In 1994 absenteeism cost American employers 1.3% of payroll;[4] by 2004 this increased to approximately $48 billion.[5]
- Direct costs of employee absenteeism in Canada in 1991 averaged $1,112 per employee per year.[6] Today it is approximately $1,462 per full time employee per year.[7, 8]
- Over the last 10 years, American companies experienced absenteeism rates ranging from a high of 2.9% in 1998 to a low of 1.9% in 2003. Likewise, the per employee costs ranged between $572 in 1997 to the all time high of $789 in 2002 (Figure 10.1).[9]
- Absenteeism costs approximately 2.8 – 4.7% of payroll.[10, 11]
- By managing absenteeism, a reduction of 30-50% or more can be realized.[12, 13]

---

[1] Statistics Canada, *Work Absence Rate* (Ottawa: Statistics Canada, 2005) at 7.

[2] D. Thompson, "The Dollars and Sense of Managing Absenteeism" (1995) 3:8 Group Healthcare Management at 17-21.

[3] J. Kranc, "Fact Check" *Benefits Canada* (March 2004) at 70, 86.

[4] CCH Incorporated, "The 11th Annual CCH Unscheduled Absences Survey" (2001) 521, Part 2 Human Resources Management: Ideas and Trends at 1-12.

[5] Commonwealth Fund, News Release, " 'Lost Labor Time' Costs U.S. $260 Billion Each Year" (31 August 2005), available online at: <http://www.cmwf.org/newsroom/newsroom_show. htm?doc_id=294188>.

[6] Peat, Marwick & Kellog, *Data Produced on 1991 Employee Benefit Costs in Canada* (1993), [unpublished].

[7] Statistics Canada, *Average Hourly Wages of Employees by Selected Characteristics and Profession* (5 January 2006), online: <http://www40.statcan.ca/l01/cst01/labr69k.htm>.

[8] *Supra*, note 1.

[9] CCH Incorporated, News Release, "2004 CCH Unscheduled Absence Survey: Unscheduled Employee Absenteeism Rises to Five-Year High" (7 October 2004), available online at: <http://www.cch.com/press/news/2004/20042007h .asp>.

[10] *Supra*, note 2.

[11] *Supra*, note 6.

[12] *Supra*, note 2.

[13] Aon Consulting, "The Case for Absence Management" (2005) Aon Workforce Strategies, available online at: <http://www.aon/us/busi/pdf/workforce_strategies/case_for_absence_mgmt.pdf>.

Some of the hidden costs associated with absenteeism are difficult to quantify. They include:

- replacement costs;
- overtime costs;
- supervisor time to rearrange work schedules;
- lowered morale;
- reduction in productivity;
- catch-up time for the returning employee;
- administration time and cost to deal with the absence claims and costs; and
- increased insurance premiums.

Figure 10.1: Rate and Cost of Absenteeism: United States of America

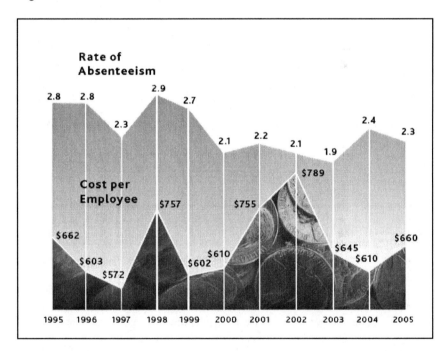

Source: Reproduced with permission, CCH Incorporated, 2005 Unscheduled Absence Survey.[14]

According to Lori Rosen, J.D., a CCH workplace analyst, and author of *HR Networking: Work-Life Benefits*, the tight economy seems to have:

---

[14] CCH Incorporated, "2005 Unscheduled Absence Survey" (CCH Incorporated, 2005).

...helped companies in holding the per-employee cost of absenteeism steady, but with the rate of unscheduled absences increasing, the overall out-of-pocket cost to employers rises accordingly. This trend makes it all the more important to closely examine why employees aren't showing up for work and what work-life and absence control programs can be used to help stem the tide.[15]

WHAT DOES AN ATTENDANCE SUPPORT AND ASSISTANCE PROGRAM INVOLVE?

There is no one "best" or "standard" way to manage absenteeism. Some aspects of absenteeism are within managerial control and some are not, depending on the type of absenteeism and its severity, frequency, concentration and causes. The Annual CCH Unscheduled Absences Surveys (1995 and 2004) determined that "sick time" is not the single leading reason for employee absence from work. The five main reasons for unscheduled absences are as follows:[16,17,18]

Figure 10.2: Reasons for Unscheduled Absences: 1995-2005[19]

Reasons	1995	1996	1997	1998	1999	2000	2001	2002	2003	2004	2005	Average
Personal Illness	45%	28%	26%	22%	21%	40%	32%	33%	36%	38%	35%	**32%**
Personal Needs	13%	20%	22%	20%	20%	20%	19%	21%	18%	18%	18%	**19%**
Family Issues	27%	26%	26%	26%	21%	21%	21%	24%	22%	23%	21%	**23%**
Entitlement Mentality	9%	15%	14%	16%	19%	14%	9%	10%	13%	10%	14%	**13%**
Stress	6%	11%	12%	16%	19%	5%	19%	11%	18%	11%	12%	**13%**

Using this data, personal illness seems to account for only 32% of unscheduled work absence while 68% of the absences are related to factors such as personal needs, family issues, entitlement mentality and stress.

Cultural absenteeism, which can be a self-fulfilling prophecy, is defined as employee absenteeism that is supported and nurtured by the beliefs of the work culture. If people perceive that attendance is of little concern to management and co-workers and that their attendance does not matter, cultural absenteeism will prevail.[20]

---

[15] *Supra*, note 6.

[16] CCH Incorporated, "The 7th Annual CCH Unscheduled Absences Survey" (1997) 412 Human Resources Management: Ideas and Trends at 121-122; CCH Incorporated, "The 11th Annual CCH Unscheduled Absences Survey" (2001) 521, Part 1 Human Resources Management: Ideas and Trends at 1-12.

[17] *Supra*, note 6.

[18] *Supra*, note 9.

[19] *Supra*, note 14.

[20] L. Kelly, *Absenteeism: Manual* (Kingston: International Research, 1991).

Coming to work is an important part of a person's normal activities. People gain intrinsic and extrinsic benefits from working. The intrinsic benefits include self-actualization, job satisfaction, pride in a strong work ethic and loyalty to co-workers and company. The extrinsic benefits are compensation, rewards and recognition for good performance.

A few suggestions to encourage and promote greater job satisfaction among employees are:

- strive to make jobs interesting and challenging;
- provide opportunities for personal achievement (*i.e.*, opportunities to make suggestions for improvement, special projects, *etc.*);
- ensure that employees are recognized appropriately for their achievements;
- encourage employee participation in setting organizational goals and solving problems; and
- maintain regular communication with all employees.

A number of companies have introduced attendance management programs only to learn that what has been implemented is negatively perceived by employees and unions. Programs with an "enforcement approach" have met with unanticipated resistance.

An Attendance Support and Assistance Program, on the other hand, is a pro-active approach to promoting and supporting employee attendance at work, or "work presenteeism". Although an attendance program can be called many different things, like attendance management, attendance support, employee wellness, workplace wellness, *etc.*, the term Attendance Support and Assistance Program will be used in this text.

Over the years, human resource personnel have come to realize that successful attendance program implementation requires:

- internal partnerships to address employee attendance;
- increased employee understanding of the impact lost work time has on the organization and its employees;
- standards involving regular work attendance;
- employee accountability for work attendance;
- fair and consistent treatment of employees;
- a focus on supporting and helping the employee attend work;
- the capacity to work with individual employees who are having difficulty maintaining regular work attendance; and
- workplace solutions to maintain regular employee attendance and reduce absenteeism.

To be successful, an Attendance Support and Assistance Program must be custom-made to fit the organization and the attendance problems identified. Although there is no such thing as a "standard" program, there are many common features of a successful attendance support program. The key functions of a successful Attendance Support and Assistance Program include:

- identifying the importance to the organization of employee dependability and responsibility, as demonstrated through good attendance;
- indicating the concern of the organization regarding excessive absenteeism for any reason;
- identifying the relationship between absence and performance management;
- defining culpable or "blameworthy" absences and non-culpable or "innocent" absences, and the measure for dealing with these separately, that is, progressive discipline for culpable absence and counselling or resource assistance for non-culpable absence;
- clearly outlining the rules of the organization on reporting absences, for example:

    (a) the frequency and direction of reporting;
    (b) when and if a medical certificate is required; and
    (c) the nature and frequency of any additional information required by the employer during a period of absence from work.

- being consistently enforced, while at the same time flexible enough to allow for some discretion on the part of the employer in the case of emergencies or unusual circumstances;
- providing guidance to managers on what information is required from the absent employee, and what type of information is necessary for tracking purposes; and
- ensuring that there is a method for documentation and follow-up in the management of absenteeism.

HOW CAN THIS BE DONE?

Commitment

Work together to build an attendance support policy that assists employees, while clearly outlining the consequences of chronic absenteeism. Of particular note, the name of the program can either make or break the program intent. For this reason, I suggest the title "Attendance Support and Assistance Program". It denotes support, and, as the acronym ASAP indicates, responsiveness.

Policy Development

As with any program, a policy statement is required. A sample policy attendance could be:

> **POLICY**
>
> The Company and its Unions recognize that a standard of excellence in service delivery can be achieved and maintained through the regular attendance of all employees.
>
> Employees have a duty to attend work as part of the job requirements for which they were hired. Employees encountering difficulties in maintaining their regular work attendance are encouraged to take advantage of the employee supports available. The Company and its Unions are committed to assisting employees who experience difficulty in attending work.

Definitions

Operative definitions are needed to ensure clarity. One of the key terms to define is excessive absenteeism. In Canada, excessive absenteeism is employee absence from work that exceeds two to three times the average absenteeism rate for the employee population within an organization. Another measure is employee absence that is in excess of the national standard for employee absenteeism.

Stakeholder Responsibilities

Of paramount importance is the task of defining the roles and responsibilities of each stakeholder in the proposed attendance program. Some examples will be provided later in this chapter.

Reporting an Absence

Clear instructions regarding the reporting practices must be provided. For example:

> The employee is to contact his or her direct supervisor as soon as possible, either via a designated contact person, or through the use of a voice recorded message. The information provided should cover the name, reason for the absence, the anticipated return-to-work date, and what provisions, if applicable, have been made to cover his or her duties.
>
> For an absence of greater than five consecutive workdays in duration, the employee will be required to produce a medical certificate and to submit it to the occupational health service.
>
> In a case of excessive absenteeism, the Company may request a medical certificate or a signed statement from the employee identifying the cause of absences of five or less days.

Measuring and Monitoring Attendance

One of the basic tools that supervisors require when implementing an effective Attendance Support and Assistance Program is a set of reliable statistics on sick leave usage. Supervisors must be aware of the overall absence records for their work group and for each individual employee. This need not be a complex process. Some companies put the onus on the employee to record absences in a logbook, on individual time sheets or in a computerized database. Other companies have administrative or clerical personnel collect this data and enter it into an absence tracking system.

Regardless of the practice, minimally, a company should record and summarize the following:

- absences of ten days or less;
- absences of more than ten days;
- absences due to illness at work, or for medical/dental appointments;
- absences due to an injury on duty (Workers' Compensation);
- absences due to long-term disability;
- absences due to tardiness; and
- unauthorized absences.

Reports

Plans should be made so that regular monthly reports are generated to assist employees, managers or supervisors, and human resource personnel in the administration of the Attendance Support and Assistance Program. Annual reports are also required to determine the overall effectiveness of the program.

Attendance should be monitored by the manager or supervisor. Employees with excessive absenteeism would be identified by the manager or supervisor. In these cases, it would be the manager or supervisor's responsibility to initiate the Attendance Support and Assistance Program Action Steps.

Action Steps

The action steps are designed for the:

(a)   early detection of employees experiencing work attendance problems;
(b)   provision of assistance;
(c)   encouragement of employees to address attendance problems; and
(d)   addressing of problem attendance issues in a fair and consistent manner.

The Attendance Support and Assistance Program Flow Chart (Figure 10.3) outlines the steps and actions that can be taken. It is the employee's responsibility to take charge of his or her attendance problems. However, support and assistance is consistently offered and available through the Employee Assistance Program, Disability Management Program or through human resources.

ATTENDANCE SUPPORT AND ASSISTANCE PROGRAM: AN INDUSTRY EXAMPLE

Concepts for an Attendance Support and Assistance Program

In very basic terms, the Attendance Support and Assistance Program should be based on the following concepts:

AWARENESS

- The supervisor should be aware of the exact level of attendance for the work unit and for each individual employee in the work unit. As discussed earlier, this necessitates comprehensive and effective absenteeism recording and analysis.
- The supervisor should pay regular attention to reviewing attendance information and examining all situations where absence is a concern.
- The supervisor should pay careful attention to pattern absences or increases in absenteeism.

EXPECTATIONS

- Employees must be aware that full attendance is expected. This expectation is to be communicated to all employees on a regular basis.
- The importance of regular attendance should be officially communicated to employees, discussed at regular meetings and performance reviews and reiterated to those whose attendance is of concern.
- The importance of regular attendance should be emphasized during a new employee's induction and during the probationary period.
- Misconceptions regarding attendance should be cleared up on an ongoing basis (*e.g.*, some employees feel that they are "entitled" to a certain number of sick days a year).

ROLE MODELLING

- Each supervisor sets the standard for attendance by his or her personal attendance. Role modelling good attendance is critical to promoting regular attendance by employees.

RECOGNITION

- Good attendance warrants as much attention as poor attendance. Recognize employees with consistent good attendance, as well as those who improve poor attendance. This may be done either orally or in writing, *e.g.*, with a copy to the employee's official file.

ATTENTION

- Some employees need more supervisory support than others, whether regarding job performance or regular work attendance record. It is important to meet with employees informally after periods of absence. More specific discussions are required with employees who are not meeting attendance expectations.

ACTION

- Some situations, particularly those involving chronic absenteeism, require other direct action by the supervisor.

Provisions for Authorizing or Not Authorizing Absences

COLLECTIVE AGREEMENT

- Usually, the applicable collective agreement clearly stipulates the work leaves available to employees.

TERMS OF EMPLOYMENT

- The terms of employment clearly stipulate the work leaves available to non-unionized employees.

DEPARTMENT RULES

- In line with providing quality service, rules are established to assist the organization in meeting the operational needs of the department, for example, service or operational hours are from 8:00 a.m. to 4:00 p.m. on weekdays, lunch hour is at 12 noon.
- Other rules may be required for the operational requirements of the organization or a department. Supervisors should ensure that employees are aware of these rules by direct communication, by posting the rules on bulletin boards and through reinforcement at employee meetings or when confronting an employee about a work absence.

Stakeholder Responsibilities

SENIOR MANAGEMENT RESPONSIBILITIES

Senior Management is responsible for ensuring that employees and customers have a safe and healthy environment in which to work. They are also charged with the responsibility of providing this service in an effective and cost-efficient manner using good business practices.

HUMAN RESOURCE DEPARTMENT RESPONSIBILITIES

Senior Management usually authorizes the implementation of an Attendance Support and Assistance Program, which helps employees understand the costs of uncontrollable absenteeism and enlists employee support for attendance management. In collaboration with the employees and administration, human resources is responsible for setting the Attendance Support and Assistance Policy and Program and the associated performance targets.

EMPLOYEE RESPONSIBILITIES

Every employee is responsible for maintaining an acceptable attendance record at work. Employees should also be aware of the provisions of the governing collective agreement, available sick leave or short-term disability benefits, and the Attendance Support and Assistance Policy and Program procedures around reporting absences, proof of illness and other workplace requirements relating to work attendance.

It is the employee's responsibility to:

- understand the intent of the various disability plan benefits;
- understand the obligation to perform, with regularity, the prescribed duties;
- be at work regularly and on time;
- be interested in their own health and well-being;
- make every effort to live and work safely;
- attend to personal affairs and obligations outside of working hours;
- make every effort to schedule medical appointments outside of working hours;
- follow the procedures set out for reporting illness or injuries;
- personally keep the supervisor informed on their recovery when absent due to illness or injury;
- report to the supervisor upon their return to work;
- provide any required documentation verifying the absence; and
- recognize the benefit of a formal rehabilitation program for recovering employees.

Expectations regarding work attendance need to be communicated on a regular basis. Efforts should not be focused only on problem or crisis situations. The following are examples of some opportunities to discuss attendance with employees:

- *During the orientation and training of a probationary employee* — This is an appropriate time to ensure employee's awareness of the Attendance Support and Assistance Program, the supervisory expectations regarding attendance and the requirements for reporting work absences.
- *During the performance appraisal cycle* — This is the ideal time to discuss and document expectations and to recognize good or improved attendance. For example, set specific attendance goals and document effects of the absence on the employee's performance.
- *When an employee reports an illness or injury* — This is an opportunity to discuss the reasons for the absence, the expected length of the absence, the value that the employee provides to the company and customers and any concern for the employee's well-being.
- *When an employee returns to work after an absence* — This is an ideal time to convey genuine concern for the person's health and well-being. Inquire in a positive and caring manner about how the employee is feeling. Let it be known that he or she was missed and that the workplace is glad to have him or her back.

THE ROLE OF THE UNION

In this model, the union is responsible for:

- supporting the Attendance Support and Assistance Policy and Program;
- assisting with the implementation of the Attendance Support and Assistance Policy and Program;
- promoting communication with employees as to the related attendance standards and expectations;
- identifying situations where an employee needs help;
- participating in attendance reviews, if required; and
- participating in the review of attendance targets and recommending changes at a department level.

SUPERVISOR RESPONSIBILITIES

It is the supervisor's responsibility to ensure the proper and efficient management of the employees in his or her department and to be accountable for managing acceptable attendance rates of all employees.

The supervisor's responsibilities include:

- provision of leadership and a positive attendance role model;

- application and administration of the Attendance Support and Assistance Policy and Program for employees;
- communication about the Attendance Support and Assistance Policy and Program;
- promotion of communication with employees as to the related attendance standards and expectations;
- tracking employee attendance;
- identification of situations where an employee needs help;
- implementation of regular attendance reviews with employees;
- reinforcement of good attendance with employees with exemplary attendance and encouragement for attendance improvement with employees who have poorer attendance records;
- investigation of barriers to regular work attendance;
- provision of a safe and healthy workplace;
- adherence to the set procedures for managing excessive employee absenteeism; and
- data management for reporting purposes.

REPORTING AN ABSENCE

The employee is to contact the department, or his or her direct supervisor, as soon as possible either via a designated contact person or through the use of a voice recorded message. The employee should provide his or her name, reason for the absence, the anticipated return-to-work date and what provisions, if any, have been made to cover his or her duties.

A medical certificate is usually not required for an absence of three days or less. However, the absence is recorded on a monthly basis and submitted to the human resource payroll system.

For an absence between three and ten days in length, the process is the same as above. However, the employee may be required to produce a medical certificate (Chapter 11, Appendix 3, Forms 2a and 2b).

For absences longer than ten days, the process is the same; however, the employee remits a medical certificate to the Disability Management Service for processing.

Reports and Monitoring Absenteeism

REPORTS

As already mentioned, various attendance reports are needed to assist employees, supervisors and human resources in the administration of the Attendance Support and Assistance Program. These reports should be prepared weekly/monthly for the department so that timely action can be taken by the supervisor. An annual report which reports attendance performance to the company along with any related recommendations is critical. It allows the organization the opportunity to assess employee attendance and the related costs.

MONITORING

Annual interviews regarding attendance are to be conducted by the supervisor with each and every employee. This is one way to reinforce good attendance and to address attendance concerns.

Employees with "excessive absenteeism"[21] are to be identified by the supervisors. It is the supervisors' responsibility to initiate the Attendance Support and Assistance Action Steps.

Attendance Support and Assistance Plan Action Steps: Preparation

When an employee's work attendance begins to cause concern, a supervisor must be prepared to discuss the matter with the person. During these discussions, the goal is for the supervisor to encourage and support the employee to achieve an acceptable level of work attendance.

Before entering into an employee interview, the supervisor should take the time to do the following:

1. Review the employee's attendance record. Have both the specific information about the employee's work absence and a summary of the past absences available. Identify any patterns of absences, such as Friday and Monday absences, extended vacation or holiday periods or seasonal absences. Consider any available information on the causes of the employee's absence and fitness to work.
2. Consider the employee's performance. Is it declining due, in part, to poor attendance? Are there other factors at play?
3. Determine if it is necessary or appropriate to meet privately with the employee. For example, if an employee with a good attendance record suffers a heart attack and is absent for a lengthy recovery period, a private discussion about absenteeism is inappropriate. However, if the employee has been inexplicably absent from work on many occasions and his or her work performance has deteriorated, meeting in private with the employee is appropriate.
4. Inform the employee when the discussion will be held and the reason for the discussion, preferably giving one to two days notice. The discussion should not be disciplinary in nature; rather it is an exploration of how the

---

[21] Excessive absenteeism is defined as absenteeism that exceeds either the corporate average for employee absence, or the Canadian national average of eight days (1998).

supervisor/company can assist the employee in regaining an acceptable level of work attendance.

When interviewing the employee, it is advisable to meet in a comfortable, private environment. Privacy is strongly recommended as the employee may choose to reveal information about themselves, the workplace or other work relationships that should be kept confidential between the employee and supervisor.

Always remember that the purpose of the meeting is to avoid intimidating the employee.

Attendance Support and Assistance Plan Action Steps: Implementation

STEP 1

An employee is absent for three days or less, but does not exceed the company's absenteeism standard:

- The supervisor briefly meets with the employee to acknowledge the absence.
- If the employee is off for more than four days, the supervisor contacts the employee to inquire as to his or her return-to-work status.

STEP 2

The absence exceeds the company's standard and is unrelated to a documented medical condition:

- The supervisor arranges for an interview with the employee on the day of his or her return to work, or as soon as possible thereafter.
- The supervisor advises the employee as to the reason for the interview.
- The supervisor and employee set realistic objectives for improvement in attendance, taking individual circumstances into account.
- The supervisor asks the employee if any assistance is required in order to meet the expected attendance standard. This will include a discussion as to the services available, which include the occupational health services or corporate programs such as the Employee and Family Assistance Program.
- The supervisor reinforces the impact of absenteeism on the department, students and co-workers.
- The supervisor completes an Attendance Support and Assistance Program Action/Status Initial Concern Letter (Appendix 1), and provides the employee with a copy. This letter forms part of the employee's personnel record.
- If required, a process of workplace accommodation may be initiated and supported by proper medical documentation.

- A follow-up meeting with the employee is arranged. The meeting is held three to six months after the Step 2 interview, depending on the situation. The supervisor continues to monitor the employee's attendance during this period. If required, the follow-up interview may be held earlier based on individual circumstances, or if the objectives are exceeded.

STEP 3

At the follow-up meeting with the supervisor, one of the following conditions will exist:

Case A. The Employee's Attendance Improves

- The supervisor gives a Letter of Congratulations (Appendix 2) to the employee with a copy sent to the human resource department. The letter forms part of the employee's personnel record.
- Attendance continues to be monitored by the supervisor.

Case B. The Employee's Attendance Meets the Objective but is Still Above the Company's Absenteeism Standard

- The supervisor gives a Letter of Recognition of Improvement (Appendix 3) to the employee.
- The supervisor clearly indicates that continued improvement is expected and new attendance objectives are set.
- The supervisor and employee agree to a follow-up meeting and repeat Step 3 (please note that some employees may be at Step 3 for several months as they continue to show improvement).

Case C. The Employee's Attendance Shows No Improvement

- The supervisor holds a meeting with the employee (and a union representative if requested by the employee).
- The supervisor reviews the employee's attendance statistics.
- The supervisor asks the employee if any assistance is required in order to meet the attendance expectations. This includes a discussion as to services available, including referral to the occupational health services or to corporate programs such as the Employee and Family Assistance Program.
- The supervisor establishes short-term objectives. While efforts are made to help the employee achieve the attendance expectations, attendance continues to be monitored.
- Employees are to be reminded that regular attendance is a condition of employment.
- The company may require additional information through medical documentation that may be utilized if workplace accommodation is required.

Appendix 4 illustrates two sample letters that can be used to request medical documentation — one designed for the unionized workplace and one for the non-unionized environment.

- The supervisor completes the Attendance Support Program Action/Status Advanced Concern Letter (Appendix 5), and provides the employee with a copy. This letter will form part of the employee's personnel record.
- A follow-up meeting occurs within three months of the Step 3 interview.
- If required, the process of accommodation may be initiated and supported by proper documentation.

STEP 4

At the follow-up meeting to Step 3, one of the following conditions will exist:

Case A. The Employee's Attendance Improves

- The supervisor gives a Letter of Congratulations to the employee with a copy to the human resource department. The letter forms part of the employee's personnel record.
- Attendance continues to be monitored by the supervisor.

Case B. The Employee's Attendance Meets the Objective but is Still Above Company's Standard

- The supervisor gives a Letter of Recognition of Improvement (Appendix 3) to employee.
- The supervisor clearly indicates that continued improvement is expected and new attendance objectives are set.
- The supervisor arranges a follow-up meeting and repeats Step 3 (please note that some employees may be at Step 3 for several months as they continue to show improvement).

Case C. The Employee's Attendance Shows No Improvement

- The Director of Human Resources and the supervisor meet with the employee. In a unionized workplace, the employee may have union representation if requested.
- The Director of Human Resources reviews the attendance statistics and asks the employee if he or she requires any assistance to achieve the expected level of attendance.
- The Director of Human Resources sets short-term targets and a follow-up meeting is held within three months.
- The Director of Human Resources may require the employee to bring in a medical certificate to substantiate every absence, and may use other

mechanisms deemed appropriate to guide the employee towards achieving the expected standard of attendance.

- Employees should be alerted to the fact that regular attendance is a condition of employment.
- The process of accommodation may be initiated if required and supported by proper documentation.
- A follow-up meeting is set for three months.

STEP 5

- The Director of Human Resources continues to follow up with the employee until he or she is satisfied that there is sustainable improvement. If the employee does not achieve the objectives within the allotted time period, and every effort has been made to assist the employee including accommodation (if necessary), the need to terminate the employment may arise. The Director of Human Resources and the supervisor should be very clear as to the expectations and objectives that are to be met in the given time period.

Figure 10.3 is a graphic depiction of how an Attendance Support and Assistance Program could function. As well, Appendix 1 contains sample letters that could be used at various stages of the Attendance Support and Assistance Program Action Steps.

SUMMARY

Assisting employees in attending work on a regular basis is critical to the success of any Disability Management Program. The process begins by clearly setting corporate expectations, and continues through an established action plan to address excessive employee absenteeism. Having a functional process in place allows for a supportive but fair manner in which to deal with absenteeism. As well, it promotes early assistance for "troubled" employees. In essence, it is part of the preventative aspects of disability management.

Employee attendance is crucial to the effective functioning of a company. Employee absenteeism is costly. By being proactive and addressing employee attendance in a supportive manner, employees are shown that the company cares about them. However, the corollary is also true:

> If people perceive that attendance is of no concern to a company, that it doesn't matter if they are at work or not, cultural absenteeism will prevail.[22]

---

[22] CCH Incorporated, "The 7th Annual CCH Unscheduled Absences Survey" (1997) 412 Human Resources Management: Ideas and Trends at 121-122.

Figure 10.3: Company XYZ: Attendance Support and Assistance Program (ASAP)

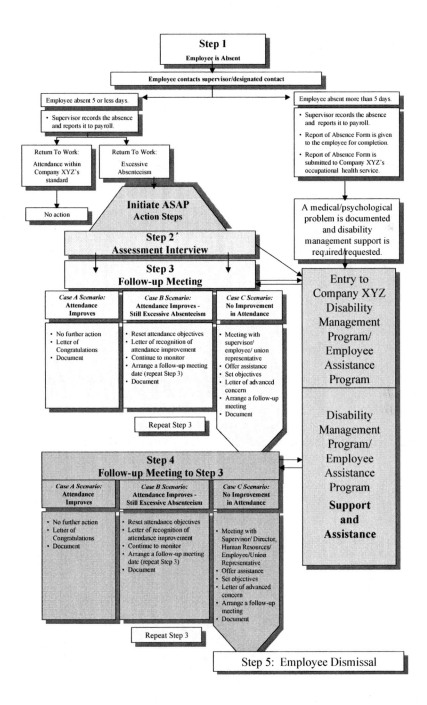

Step 1

Employee is Absent

Employee contacts supervisor/designated contact

Employee absent 5 or less days.

• Supervisor records the absence and reports it to payroll.

Employee absent more than 5 days.

• Supervisor records the absence and reports it to payroll.
• Report of Absence Form is given to the employee for completion.
• Report of Absence Form is submitted to Company XYZ's occupational health service.

Return To Work:
Attendance within Company XYZ's standard

Return To Work:
Excessive Absenteeism

No action

Initiate ASAP Action Steps

Step 2´
Assessment Interview

A medical/psychological problem is documented and disability management support is required/requested.

Step 3
Follow-up Meeting

Case A Scenario:
Attendance Improves

• No further action
• Letter of Congratulations
• Document

Case B Scenario:
Attendance Improves - Still Excessive Absenteeism

• Reset attendance objectives
• Letter of recognition of attendance improvement
• Continue to monitor
• Arrange a follow-up meeting date (repeat Step 3)
• Document

Case C Scenario:
No Improvement in Attendance

• Meeting with supervisor/ employee/ union representative
• Offer assistance
• Set objectives
• Letter of advanced concern
• Arrange a follow-up meeting
• Document

Repeat Step 3

Entry to Company XYZ Disability Management Program/ Employee Assistance Program

Step 4
Follow-up Meeting to Step 3

Case A Scenario:
Attendance Improves

• No further action
• Letter of Congratulations
• Document

Case B Scenario:
Attendance Improves - Still Excessive Absenteeism

• Reset attendance objectives
• Letter of recognition of attendance improvement
• Continue to monitor
• Arrange a follow-up meeting date (repeat Step 3)
• Document

Case C Scenario:
No Improvement in Attendance

• Meeting with Supervisor/ Director, Human Resources/ Employee/Union Representative
• Offer assistance
• Set objectives
• Letter of advanced concern
• Arrange a follow-up meeting
• Document

Repeat Step 3

Disability Management Program/ Employee Assistance Program

Support and Assistance

Step 5: Employee Dismissal

Appendix 1

Sample — ASAP Action/Status Initial Concern Letter

Date: _____

To: [EMPLOYEE] _____

From: Manager/Supervisor

Dear [EMPLOYEE]:

The purpose of this letter is to confirm our discussion of [DATE] regarding your attendance at work.

At that time, it was brought to your attention that the number of your absent days has reached a level of concern to the [DEPARTMENT].

The expectations of Company XYZ with respect to attendance were reviewed as well as the problems caused by your absenteeism.

The Company is willing to provide you with whatever assistance it is able to maintain your attendance at an acceptable level. It was noted that, should your absenteeism increase further, the Company will have to take further action.

Please note that neither our meeting nor this letter of communication is disciplinary.

Sincerely,

_____
Manager/Supervisor

cc: Union Representative (if applicable)
     Employee File

Appendix 2

Sample — Letter of Congratulations

Date: _____

To: [EMPLOYEE]_____

From: Manager/Supervisor

Dear [EMPLOYEE]:

Congratulations! You have made a significant improvement on your attendance record over the past [NUMBER] months.

As work absences cost us all in the long run, I thank you for your cooperation in this matter.

Please accept my best wishes for your good health as you strive for good work attendance.

Sincerely,

_____

Manager/Supervisor

cc: (Human Resources)
      Union Representative (if applicable)
      Employee File

Appendix 3

Sample — Letter of Recognition of Attendance Improvement

Date: _____

To: [EMPLOYEE]_____

From: Manager/Supervisor

Dear [EMPLOYEE]:

Congratulations! You have made improvements on your work attendance over the past [NUMBER] months.

Your goal is to increase your attendance target of [NUMBER] days this year. Company XYZ and I are willing to provide you with support and assistance in your endeavour. Our plan is to continue to monitor your work attendance and to review your progress in [NUMBER] months.

As absences cost us all in the long run, I thank you for your cooperation in this matter. Please accept my best wishes for your good health as you strive for good work attendance.

Sincerely,

_____
Manager/Supervisor

cc: (Human Resources)
     Union Representative (if applicable)
     Employee File

Appendix 4

Sample — Letter Requesting Medical Documentation

TWO EXAMPLES OF A LETTER REQUESTING REQUIRED MEDICAL DOCUMENTATION

Option 1 — For Unionized Employees

To: Dr. _____

Re: [EMPLOYEE]

The above named person is an employee of Company XYZ employed as a _____ in the _____ [DEPARTMENT].

It is our primary objective that [EMPLOYEE NAME] is healthy and able to attend work regularly. However, our concern is that the employee's absences over the past year have been significantly higher than the Company XYZ average for worker absenteeism.

During the past 12 months, [EMPLOYEE NAME] has been absent from work, for reasons of illness or injury, on _____ occasions for a total of _____ days.

The Collective Agreement between Company XYZ and the Union states that:

> Before payment is made under the foregoing provisions, the Employee may be required to provide:
>
> for illness of three (3) consecutive days or less, statement in a form provided by the Employer, signed by the Employee substantiating the illness;
>
> for illness of more than three (3) consecutive days, a medical certificate in a form approved by the Employer, from a qualified medical or dental practitioner.

(This will differ with each Collective Agreement.)

[EMPLOYEE NAME] has requested that you conduct this examination and release your findings to us. We are requesting that your examination and report address the following issues:

1.   The nature of the employee's illnesses or injuries and whether or not these are likely to continue to affect his or her ability to work now and in the future. This may require that you consult with other physicians who have treated [EMPLOYEE NAME].

2.   Your assessment of the employee's present abilities to perform the full duties of a [JOB TITLE].

In order to assist you, the following is a list of duties that [EMPLOYEE NAME] may be asked to perform.

[LIST DUTIES]

Company XYZ agrees to pay a maximum of $50 in medical fees for this examination. Please submit your report and invoice to the Company, Occupational Health Nurse, Company XYZ Occupational Health Centre.

Should you wish to discuss these duties more fully, please contact me at your convenience. If a visit to the workplace would aid you in reaching your prognosis or completing your report, I will arrange that at your convenience.

Sincerely,

_____

Manager/Supervisor

cc: Human Resources
     Union Representative
     Occupational Health Nurse
     Employee File

Option 2 — For Non-Unionized Employees

To: Dr. _____

Re: [EMPLOYEE]

The above named person is an employee of Company XYZ employed as a _____ in the [DEPARTMENT].

It is our primary objective that [EMPLOYEE NAME] be healthy and able to attend work regularly. However, our concern is that the employee's absences over the past year have been significantly higher than Company XYZ average for worker absenteeism.

During the past 12 months, [EMPLOYEE NAME] has been absent from work, for reasons of illness or injury, on _____ occasions for a total of _____ days.

Company XYZ has an Attendance Support and Assistance Policy which states that for an absence greater than five (5) consecutive workdays in duration, the employee will be required to produce a medical certificate and to submit it to the Occupational Health Service. It also states that, in a case of excessive absenteeism, a medical certificate may be requested for absences of five (5) days or less.

[EMPLOYEE NAME] has requested that you conduct this examination and release your findings to us. We are requesting that your examination and report address the following issues:

The nature of the employee's illnesses or injuries and whether or not these are likely to continue to affect his or her ability to work now and in the future. This may require that you consult with other physicians who have treated [EMPLOYEE NAME].

Your assessment of the employee's present abilities to perform the full duties of a [JOB TITLE].

In order to assist you, the following is a list of duties that [EMPLOYEE NAME] may be asked to perform.

[LIST DUTIES]

Company XYZ agrees to pay a maximum of $50 in medical fees for this examination. Please submit your report and invoice to the Company, Occupational Health Nurse, Company XYZ Occupational Health Centre.

Should you wish to discuss these duties more fully, please contact me at your convenience. If a visit to the workplace would aid you in reaching your prognosis or completing your report, I will arrange that at your convenience.

Yours sincerely,

_____

Manager/Supervisor

cc: Human Resources
      Occupational Health Nurse
      Employee File

Appendix 5

Sample — Attendance Support Program Action/Status Advanced Concern Letter

Date: _____

To: [EMPLOYEE]_____

From: Manager/Supervisor

Dear [EMPLOYEE]:

The purpose of this letter is to confirm our discussion of [DATE] regarding your attendance at work.

At that time, I referred to our earlier meeting of [DATE], at which time you were alerted to our concern with the number of your work absence days at that point.

You were notified that, since that discussion, the number of absent days has increased to the point where further action is now necessary and you are requested to attend a meeting with the Company, Occupational Health Advisor, on [DATE and TIME] for the purpose of discussing, in confidence, detailed reasons for your absenteeism and determining what you and Company XYZ can do to improve this situation.

You were reminded that should your absence record not improve, Company XYZ will have to take further action.

As well, please note that neither our discussion nor this letter of communication is disciplinary.

Sincerely,

_____
Manager/Supervisor
cc: Human Resources
     Union Representative (if applicable)
     Employee File

CHAPTER REFERENCES

Aon Consulting, "The Case for Absence Management" (2005), Aon Workforce Strategies, available online at: <www.aon.com/us/busi/pdf/workforce_strategies/case_for_absence_mgmt.pdf>.

CCH Incorporated, "The 7th Annual CCH Unscheduled Absences Survey" (1997) 412 Human Resources Management: Ideas and Trends at 121-122.

CCH Incorporated, "The 11th Annual CCH Unscheduled Absences Survey" (2001) 521, Part 2 Human Resources Management: Ideas and Trends at 1-12.

CCH Incorporated, News Release, "2004 CCH Unscheduled Absence Survey: Unscheduled Employee Absenteeism Rises to Five-Year High" (7 October 2004), available online at: <http://www.cch.com/press/news/2004/20042007h.asp>.

CCH Incorporated, "2005 Unscheduled Absence Survey" (CCH Incorporated, 2005).

L. Kelly, *Absenteeism: Manual* (Kingston: International Research, 1991).

J. Kranc, "Fact Check" *Benefits Canada* (March 2004) at 70, 86.

Commonwealth Fund, News Release, " 'Lost Labor Time' Costs U.S. $260 Billion Each Year" (31 August 2005), available online at: <http://www.cmwf.org/newsroom/newsroom_show.htm?doc_id=294188>.

Peat, Marwick & Kellog, *Data Produced on 1991 Employee Benefit Costs in Canada*, (1993) [unpublished].

Statistics Canada, *Average Hourly Wages of Employees by Selected Characteristics and Profession* (5 January 2006), available online at: <http://www40.statcan.ca/l01/cst01/labr69k.htm>.

Statistics Canada, *Work Absence Rates, 2004* (Ottawa: Statistics Canada, 2005).

D. Thompson, "The Dollars and Sense of Managing Absenteeism" (1993) 3:8 Group Healthcare Management at 17-21.

Chapter 11

Disability Management Practice Standards

INTRODUCTION

To assist Case Managers, many organizations and insurers have developed practice standards, or codes of practice, for disability management. Unlike disability guidelines, which advise on expected length of absences for various illnesses or injuries, these standards or practice codes outline the best practice rehabilitation strategies and steps the organization expects health professionals to follow.

Practice standards are stated approaches to care and practice based on recognized and accepted principles of clinical practice for planned processes, such as disability management. They form the guidelines and rules for the practice, provide the boundaries for the practice activity, clarify stakeholder roles and responsibilities and can act as a benchmark.

Practice standards can be beneficial because they:

* promote a consistent approach to case management;
* provide meaningful direction to the practice in question; and
* promote effectiveness and efficiency of practice through a reduction of errors, complications and costs.

To remain current and credible, practice standards must be regularly reviewed and updated.

RECOMMENDED DISABILITY MANAGEMENT PRACTICE STANDARDS

The key practice standards required for a Disability Management Program address issues such as claims management, case management, confidentiality and documentation. The following sections describe in detail each of these practice standards.

Some of the materials contained in these practice standard examples have been covered elsewhere in this book. However, the intent is to present each of the relevant Disability Management Practice Standards in a format that can be adapted for the reader's use.

DISABILITY CLAIMS MANAGEMENT STANDARD OF PRACTICE

Introduction

Claims Management is the service provided in administering income loss claims through employee benefit plans such as short-term disability, Workers' Compensation or long-term disability. This activity includes the determination of eligibility contained in the plan contract, collective agreement or contract of insurance; the facilitation of income loss replacement; and the processing of the claim towards a resolution or termination.

Claims Management Steps

DETERMINING ELIGIBILITY FOR INCOME REPLACEMENT BENEFITS

Workers Compensation Benefits (Occupational)

The Workers' Compensation system is designed to compensate ill or injured workers for work-related diseases and injuries. It is a no-fault insurance system funded entirely by the employers. The provincial Workers' Compensation Acts govern the functioning of the Workers' Compensation Board. It is important to remember that Workers' Compensation benefits are a worker's statutory right. An effective claims management system never attempts to prevent workers from receiving benefits to which they are legitimately entitled.

Workers

Workers employed in industries to which provincial Workers' Compensation Acts apply are protected from loss of earnings due to a work-related injury or disease. The provincial Workers' Compensation Acts generally define "worker" as a person who enters into, or works under, a contract of service or apprenticeship.[1] This contract can be written or verbal, express or implied, for manual labour or otherwise. This includes trainees, apprentices, clerks, sales staff, office staff and supervisors. It includes individuals employed on a part-time, full-time, casual or commission basis. It also includes any other individuals the Workers' Compensation Board deems to be a worker.

---

[1]   Alberta: *Workers' Compensation Act*, R.S.A. 2000, c. W-15, s. 1(1)(z); British Columbia: *Workers' Compensation Act*, R.S.B.C. 1996, c. 492, s. 1; Ontario: *Workplace Safety and Insurance Act, 1997*, S.O. 1997, c. 16, Sch. A, s. 2.

Contractors and Subcontractors

Individuals hired on a contract or subcontract basis are workers of the principal,[2] unless these individuals have a Workers' Compensation Board account or are incorporated as a limited company. The Workers' Compensation Board will determine if an individual is considered a worker of the principal, or required to establish his or her own account with the Workers' Compensation Board.

A contractor or subcontractor is not considered a worker when performing the work as:

- an employer;
- a worker of another employer;
- a director of a corporation;
- a proprietor with personal coverage; or
- a partner in a partnership with personal coverage.

The Workers' Compensation Board may, at its discretion, deem any or all persons (or classes of persons) performing work for the principal to be the principal's workers.

Before engaging a contractor, a company should check with the applicable provincial Workers' Compensation Board to determine if the contractor has an account in good standing.

Other Groups Considered by the Workers' Compensation Board to be Workers

Some other individuals or groups may be covered under provincial Workers' Compensation Acts, such as:

- proprietors;
- partners;
- individuals sharing labour;
- students on a work experience; and
- workers engaged in volunteer activities.

As provincial Workers' Compensation Acts vary, care must be taken to determine the applicable conditions for the organization.

---

[2] "Principal" refers to a contractor or subcontractor hired to perform work or services by a person or entity.

Compensable Illness or Injury

If an illness or injury occurs in the course of employment, the illness or injury is compensable unless there is evidence that the illness or injury was caused by factors extrinsic to employment.

A worker may be compensated when an illness or injury is progressive and occurs over a period of time rather than resulting from a specific incident. However, for an illness or injury to be compensable there must be evidence that the employment was a significant factor in producing the injury or illness. Speculation is insufficient to prove that the illness or injury is compensable.

Pre-existing Conditions

There are instances where a medical condition has reached a critical point, and that some immediate workplace activity triggered an injury. If it were not for a specific work-related activity or accident, a worker may not have experienced an injury. The Workers' Compensation Board may accept the initial acute stage of the disability, but may not accept the ongoing disability as it relates to the underlying, pre-existing condition. Claims of this type should be followed closely for cost-relief purposes.[3]

Sick Leave Benefits (Non-Occupational)

There are a number of short-term, non-occupational disability benefits in existence that tend to be uniquely defined by organizations in which they operate. Some typical plans are:

- *Casual Sick Leave* — coverage for a non-occupational absence that extends for less than five consecutive workdays.
- *Sick Leave/Short-term Disability* — income replacement for the employee while recuperating from a non-occupational illness or injury.
- *Long-term Disability* — an insurance program through which eligible employees may derive income replacement for long-term illness or injury.

INFORMATION REQUIRED TO SUPPORT A CLAIM FOR INCOME REPLACEMENT

The type of information required to support the employee's claim for income replacement varies with the benefit desired. The following are some common examples of required information:

---

[3]   Alberta: *Workers' Compensation Act*, R.S.A. 2000, c. W-15, s. 105(4); British Columbia: *Workers' Compensation Act*, R.S.B.C. 1996, c. 492, s. 47(2); Ontario: *Workplace Safety and Insurance Act, 1997*, S.O. 1997, c. 16, Sch. A, s. 21(3).

Workers' Compensation Benefits

- An employee is legally bound to report a work-related injury to the employer as soon as it is practical, and to submit a Worker's Report of Injury to the provincial Workers' Compensation Board. In most provinces, a copy of the Worker's Report of Injury form should then accompany the Employer's Report of Injury to the WCB. Refusal by the worker to complete the form can result in denial of the WCB claim.
- The employer is obliged to submit an Employer's Report of Injury to the provincial Workers' Compensation Board within a set time frame of becoming aware of the accident.
- The employee must consult his or her physician regarding the illness or injury. The physician is legally required to submit a medical report to the Workers' Compensation Board. Subsequent physician's progress reports are also sent to the Workers' Compensation Board as a means of monitoring the ill or injured employee's recovery.

Sick Leave Benefits

- The employee is to contact his or her direct supervisor as soon as possible, either via a designated contact person or through the use of a voice recorded message. The information provided should cover his or her name, reason for the absence, the anticipated return-to-work date and what provisions, if applicable, have been made to cover his or her duties.
- The supervisor should notify the appropriate department, either by a time recording system or telephone call, once the employee returns to work.

Short-term Disability

- For an absence of greater than five consecutive workdays in duration, the employee is required to produce a medical certificate and to submit it directly to occupational health services (if available), or human resources.
- The Report of Absence Form (Appendix 3: Form 2a and 2b) is to be completed by the attending physician and signed and dated by the employee. Additional information may be required by occupational health services.

Long-term Disability

- Typically, the long-term disability claim application must be initiated once the employee has been on short-term disability for half of the short-term elimination period,[4] or earlier if it is apparent that a long-term disability claim is inevitable.

- The insurance company's long-term disability claim forms should be completed as indicated.
- The insurance company's application for waiver of premium under life insurance should also be initiated.
- Additional information for the insurer may be requested from the employee or employer as required.

PROCESSING CLAIM FORMS

As with the type of information collected to support a claim, claim processing also varies. The following are the usual steps required for processing a claim for each type of disability benefit plan:

Workers' Compensation Benefits

Submit the Employer's Report of Injury and the Worker's Report of Injury on the required provincial Workers' Compensation Board forms to ensure that the Worker's Compensation Board Claims Adjudicator has the necessary information to appropriately adjudicate the claim.

An injury report must be sent to the Workers' Compensation Board if the injury results in medical treatment and/or subsequent time loss. Generally, if there is no time loss, there is no need to submit a report of accident to the Workers' Compensation Board. However, there are exceptions that do require reporting. These might include injuries requiring the modification of work duties beyond the day of accident, the need to purchase drugs and dressings, eyeglasses replacement, dental damage, chiropractic treatment and physiotherapy and motor vehicle accidents. If uncertain about whether or not to file a claim, the employer is advised to err on the side of caution and send one. There are provisions in the provincial Workers' Compensation Acts for a penalty assessment for late injury reporting.[5]

Sick Leave Benefits

- The employee phones his or her supervisor on the first day of absence.
- The absence is documented on the company payroll time accounting system.

---

4   The short-term elimination period is the time of illness/injury prior to applying for long-term disability benefits. This period of time varies in length depending on the long-term disability plan design. It may be 17 weeks, six months, 12 months or 24 months.

5   Cost Relief is defined as a reduction in a company's Workers' Compensation (WCB) claims costs as the result of a reassignment of those costs to the other industry members. This is done to spread out the costs so that an individual company is not overburdened by its WCB claims costs.

Short-term Disability

- The Report of Absence Form is generated by the employee and attending physician.
- The Report of Absence Form is reviewed by the occupational health nurse.
- The occupational health nurse then advises the company Claims Administrator regarding the employee's fitness to work.
- If unfit for work, then the employee is eligible for short-term disability in accordance with the employee's earned sick leave.
- If the employee is fit to work modified duties, the occupational health nurse advises the Claims Administrator of the employee's work capabilities.
- If the employee is fit to work, the occupational health nurse advises the Claims Administrator and short-term disability is denied.

Long-term Disability

- The company Claims Administrator initiates the long-term disability claim by contacting the long-term carrier.
- Complete the required insurance carrier's claim forms. These usually include:
    - an employee form;
    - a physician form; and
    - an employer form.

Claims Adjudication

Claims adjudication is the process of determining whether a claim is eligible under the terms of the benefit contract or plan for benefit coverage.

Claims Adjudication Steps

The claims adjudication process includes:

- Receipt and review of the claim.
- Establishment of the claimant's status and eligibility for benefit coverage. Is this a work-related claim? Is the employee applying for the proper coverage given the nature of the situation?
- Review of the eligibility requirements according to the contract/plan, and/or the collective agreement.
- Consideration of the issue of any limitations or exclusions. Limitations occur when the employee is eligible for benefits, but cannot receive payments for a specific cause. Exclusions occur when the employee cannot receive payment because the illness or injury resulted from a situation not covered by the plan. For example, for short-term disability coverage, exclusions would be appropriate for injury due to work-related accident, riot, war, *etc.*

- Consideration of pre-existing conditions. Pre-existing conditions are typically defined in the contract or plan as conditions of illness or injury that occurred prior to the employee being covered by the plan. Coverage for subsequent illness or injury, or a recurrence within a specific time frame, is not allowed.
- Consideration of the existence of specialized clauses that would preclude the claimant from benefit coverage. Policy holders can place additional exclusions in benefit plans or contracts, such as participation in risky events or sports.
- Determination for eligibility.
- Acceptance or rejection of the claim.

Figure 11.1 is a checklist which the claims adjudicator can use to assist with this process. This is not meant to be all-inclusive, rather a quick reference guide.

The Role of the Physician in Determining Disability

In determining an employee's eligibility to receive income replacement benefits, physicians are frequently put in the position of verifying a disability. The Canadian Medical Association and many provincial medical associations have produced position statements clarifying that the role of the physician is "to diagnose and treat the illness or injury, to advise the employer and support the patient, to provide and communicate appropriate information to the patient and the employer, and to work closely with other involved health care professionals to facilitate the patient's safe and timely return to work."[6] They support the shift towards using a variety of means to determine if an employee is fit to work or not. Ultimately it is the employer who determines the type of work available and whether or not the physician's recommendations can be accommodated.

The following position papers regarding the role of the physician in determining disability have been released:

- Ontario Medical Association — Ontario Medical Association (OMA), *Position Paper: OMA Position Papers in Support of Timely Return to Work Programs and the Role of the Primary Care Physician* (Toronto: OMA, 1994).[7]
- Alberta Medical Association — Alberta Medical Association (AMA), *An Information Sheet for Patients: Early Return to Work After Illness or Injury* (Edmonton: AMA, February 1994) still current, this information is available online.[8]

---

[6] Canadian Medical Association, *The Physician's Role in Helping Patients Return to Work After an Illness or Injury* (update 2000), available online at: <http://policybase.cma.ca/dbtw-wpd/exec/dbtwpub.dll>.

[7] Available online at: <http://www.oma.org/phealth/position.htm>.

[8] Alberta Medical Association (AMA, 1994), *An Information Sheet for Patients: Early Return to Work After Illness or Injury* (Edmonton: AMA, 1994) in the "Advocacy and Positions" section

- Canadian Medical Association — Canadian Medical Association (CMA), *The Physician's Role in Helping Patients Return to Work After an Illness or Injury* (update 2000). This position was reviewed by the CMA in February 2005 and found to still be relevant.[9]

These position papers imply that physicians can determine employee eligibility for benefits or level of work accommodation. Eligibility for a disability benefit (including short-term disability, long-term disability and Workers' Compensation Board) is a contractual decision determined by comparing the job requirements with the contract provisions and the impairment of the employee. It is the Claims Administrator who must determine whether the definition of disability is met.

Figure 11.1: Checklist for Claims Adjudication

- Appropriate physician completes the form/letter, *i.e.*, information is sent to the appropriate source.
- Work-related issues have been addressed. (This is not a Workers' Compensation Claim.)
- The evidence is objective.
- The employee is under treatment.
- Rehabilitation/resource initiatives have been implemented.
- File documentation supports a well-managed case, based on a well thought out process approach, *i.e.*, the problems are identified, actions implemented, results evaluated, costs and consequences considered.
- This is a work-related illness or injury.
- If information is insufficient to support disability, suspension or termination of benefits has been considered.
- If long-term disability is pending, medical information has been requested to support the long-term disability claim.

Claim Referral Triggers

As a claim is processed, certain triggers for referral may occur. These are listed as:

- short-term disability or Workers' Compensation Board claim is beyond duration of disability suggested in medical guidelines;
- nature of injury severe enough to warrant referral (*i.e.*, prognosis for return to work greater than six weeks);

---

[9] of the AMA's website, available online at: <http://www.albertadoctors.org/bcm/ama/ama-website.nsf/frmHome?OpenForm>.
Supra, note 6.

- history of frequent absences from work, multiple previous sick leave or Workers' Compensation Board claims;
- no contact from employee for past three weeks;
- claim goes beyond six weeks in length;
- claimant referred to Workers' Compensation Board Vocational Rehabilitation Caseworker;
- notification that treatment does not appear to be appropriate;
- notification of non-compliance with treatment;
- notification of no known diagnosis;
- notification of a vague diagnosis;
- notification that case is failing to progress.

Development of Claims Management Action Plans

Claims Management plans are tools designed to facilitate the disability management claim process by helping key players to focus their actions towards a claims resolution.

IDENTIFYING HIGH RISK CLAIMS

Some claims risk a more lengthy duration than others. Some characteristics associated with lengthy disability claims are:

- expected duration of disability exceeding one month;
- hospitalization greater than one week;
- a Workers' Compensation claim longer than one week;
- employee 50 years of age or older;
- stress as the diagnosis;
- diagnoses of cardiovascular, cancer, digestive, skeletal (repetitive strain injury), neurological or psychological conditions;
- multiple diagnoses;
- cases which fail just before the expected return-to-work date;
- presence of discipline or performance problems;
- presence of labour relations problems;
- presence of pending litigation associated with the injury; and
- employee with a high rate of absenteeism.

These claims should be referred to the occupational health nurse or Case Manager for case management and warrant careful claims management.

IDENTIFYING WORK LIMITATIONS

Fitness to Work

To determine employee fitness to work, two pieces of information are required:

- the physical and psychological job demands for the position; and
- the employee's work capabilities and limitations.

These two pieces of information are then compared to determine the gap between the employee's current level of functioning and the level of functioning required to safely and effectively do the job.

How is This Information Obtained?

The best way to gather information about an employee's work restrictions and abilities is to provide the attending practitioner (whether that is the physician, physiotherapist or chiropractor) with a job demands analysis that outlines the demands of the employee's job. If that is not available, ask the employer if a checklist outlining the job requirements could be completed by occupational health, the health and safety representative or supervisor. More detailed information can be obtained by referring the employee for a functional capacity evaluation.

While disability benefits are approved based on an employee's restrictions, the employee and employer should be focusing on work abilities. Gathering information about the employee's abilities by interviewing the employee and confirming information with the practitioner can be invaluable in paving the way for a modified return to work.

Physical Job Requirements

Physical job demands are the physical activities that the employee is required to do in the course of doing his or her job. These may include the ability to:

- sit, stand, walk, bend, climb;
- drive;
- lift, push, pull, twist, reach, crawl;
- write, handle small objects, pinch;
- see, hear, taste, smell;
- read;
- speak;
- travel;
- tolerate heat, cold, altitude; and/or
- other specific work-related physical activities or conditions.

Psychological Job Requirements

These are the cognitive and emotional demands of the job. They may include the ability to:

- comprehend and follow instructions;
- perform simple and repetitive tasks;
- maintain a work pace appropriate to a given workload;
- perform complex or varied tasks;
- relate to other people beyond giving and receiving instructions;
- influence people;
- make generalizations, evaluations and decisions without immediate supervision;
- accept and carry out responsibility for direction, control and planning of work; and/or
- deal with multiple tasks or activities.

Using Disability Guidelines

Comprehensive guidelines incorporate the background information about the medical condition, treatment regimes and estimated duration and established timelines for a return to work. Sources of information for disability guidelines include:

- ICDC-9 or 10 Codes;
- publications including *The Medical Disability Advisor, The Comprehensive Textbook of Modern Synopsis of Psychiatry II*, and the *Presley Reed Disability Advisor*;
- AMA and Workers' Compensation Guidelines;
- Millimand and Robertson, *Healthcare Management Guidelines*;
- Work-loss Data Institute;
- actuarial analysis and past claims experience; and
- consultation with occupational health professionals.

Disability Guidelines help the Claims Administrator:

- develop the expected absence duration for the average employee;
- determine when an independent medical examination or referral to a specialist may be warranted; and
- promote the use of consistent practices between Claims Managers (important for client satisfaction with services provided).

These guidelines are valuable but should not be used as the only basis for a decision on benefit eligibility. Other tools that can be used are second opinion, referrals, claims management action plans and case conferences.

Second Opinion Referrals

A second opinion regarding the employee's health status and functional capabilities is often required. This can be obtained through a number of avenues:

Independent Medical Examinations

The decision to request a second opinion, or independent medical examination, is based on several factors including:

- concerns about the duration of the claim;
- availability of adequate information to determine function;
- direction needed regarding prognosis or treatment;
- concerns about the validity of the claim;
- difficulty in obtaining information from the treating practitioner;
- inconsistent information submitted from different sources; and
- differences of opinion in the interpretation of medical information.

Functional Capacity Assessments

A functional capacity assessment may be chosen instead of, or in addition to, an independent medical examination for the following reasons:

- It provides more detailed information needed for the development of a rehabilitation plan;
- It clarifies prognosis for return to own job duties;
- It assists in identifying work abilities which may be needed to assess employability for other occupations; and
- It assists in outlining appropriate treatment.

Some of the terms used in this process are provided in Figure 11.2.

Figure 11.2: Definition of Terms

The following is a list of terms that may appear on the reports obtained:		
Physical Capacity Evaluation	—	An assessment of the functional abilities of an individual.
Work Hardening/Conditioning	—	Improving tolerance to perform a job.
Work Sample Evaluations	—	Simulates real jobs or tasks for the purpose of evaluation.
Ergonomics	—	A study of human interface with work.

Claims Management Action Plan

DEVELOPING CLAIMS MANAGEMENT ACTION PLANS

A claims management action plan is the planned approach for managing a specific claim. It includes:

- employee information;
- employee's current health status;
- an estimate of the likelihood of the employee returning to work;
- the proposed claims management action plans; and
- the claims and case management activity tracking.

A sample claims management action plan is provided in Appendix 1.

DOCUMENTATION

A claims management action plan should be documented and regularly updated. Documentation is crucial for effective claims management. It serves to provide:

- a profile of the claims status and the claims management services provided;
- a means of communication among members of the disability management team contributing to claims management;
- a basis for planning and for continuity of claims management for each case;
- a basis for review, study and evaluation of the claim;
- some protection for the medical and legal interests of both the employee and the company; and
- an audit trail of activities completed which can serve as a "due diligence" tool if required.

REVIEW/UPDATE ACTION PLANS

Claims management action plans should be regularly reviewed and updated. Actions and plans should be noted, assigned and completion dates established. Progress against these plans needs to be monitored and recorded.

COMMUNICATING ACTION PLANS TO KEY STAKEHOLDERS

All players in a disability management claim need to be kept current on the progress of the claim and the employee's fitness to work. How often this is done and to whom, depends on the complexity and chronicity of the case. Typically, weekly to bi-monthly reports need to be made.

CONFIDENTIALITY

All persons who collect, maintain, handle and use employee health information are required to protect the confidentiality of the information. To ensure compliance, human resource personnel involved in claims administration are bound by an oath of confidentiality (Figure 11.6). The oath is to be reviewed annually and the form dated, signed and witnessed.

ADMINISTRATION RESPONSIBILITY

Primary responsibility for the administration and update of this standard of practice rests with senior management.

DISABILITY CASE MANAGEMENT STANDARD OF PRACTICE

Companies and professionals involved in disability management should provide a planned approach to remove barriers so that employees can return to work as quickly as possible without risk to their health or the health of others. The purpose of this standard is to provide guidelines for disability case management.

Case Management

DEFINITION

A collaborative process for assessing, planning, implementing, coordinating, monitoring and evaluating the options and services available to meet an individual's health needs through communication and accessible resources to promote quality, cost-effective outcomes.[10] Case management promotes:

- safe and timely return-to-work efforts;
- early identification of disability claims for services and coordination of services, such as early intervention;
- maintaining contact with disabled employees;
- developing and monitoring modified/alternate work opportunities; and
- coordinating issues with the insurer and arranging for vocational rehabilitation when required.

---

[10] Case Management Society of America (CMSA), *Standards of Practice for Case Management* (Little Rock: CMSA, 1995).

GOAL

Case management is intended to assist ill and injured employees in reaching the highest level of medical improvement possible and to facilitate a return to work in the most cost-effective manner.

CASE MANAGERS

Case Managers ensure that appropriate rehabilitative care is underway with the employee, and that the goal from the onset of injury or illness is to return the employee to productive work as soon as possible.

QUALIFICATIONS

The qualifications necessary for a Case Manager are:

- Maintenance of current professional licensure or national certification in a health and human services profession, or both.
- Completion of a baccalaureate or higher level educational program in a health care related field of study, such as occupational health nursing, rehabilitation therapy, occupational therapy, *etc.*
- Completion of specific training and a minimum of 24 months of experience with the health needs of the population to be served.
- Demonstration of knowledge of occupational health, organizational behaviour, employee benefits plans and community health care services.
- Maintenance of continuing education appropriate to disability case management and professional licensure.
- Maintenance of case management certification. Certifications that are equivalent to case management certification (CCM) include the certified occupational health nurse (COHN), and certified insurance rehabilitation specialist (CIRS).

ROLE OF CASE MANAGER

The Case Manager:

- initiates and maintains contact with injured or ill employees, health professionals, the insurance carrier, the employer and other involved parties;
- reviews medical care of injured or ill employees and their response to treatment;
- facilitates and coordinates sharing of information among all involved parties;
- communicates and educates stakeholders regarding graduated return-to-work guidelines;

- facilitates graduated return-to-work strategies, including modified/alternate work opportunities;
- monitors modified/alternate work efforts;
- establishes vocational rehabilitation when required; and
- collects data to show cost-effectiveness of the Disability Management Program and any identified trends for illness or injury prevention.

Case Management Process

The Case Manager functions as the catalyst and liaison to facilitate the recovery of employees with non-occupational and work-related illness or injury in the most expedient and cost-effective manner. To accomplish this, the Case Manager utilizes the foundation of good business management coupled with good medical, nursing and disability management knowledge. Specifically, the Case Manager performs the following functions in an orderly manner:

ASSESSMENT

Disability management requires a comprehensive approach. The following are some of the factors that need to be assessed when determining the need for case management:

Physical factors, such as:

- physical capabilities;
- job demands;
- potential for job modification;
- potential for use of adaptive devices; and
- potential for worksite/environmental modifications.

Personal factors, such as:

- changes in the family since the onset of the illness or injury;
- the presence of a personal crisis compounding the disability (*i.e.*, legal, domestic problems, job insecurity, *etc.*);
- the health status of other family members; and
- how the family dynamics impact the current disability situation.

Vocational factors, such as:

- degree of job satisfaction;
- the occurrence of recent changes at work (*i.e.*, hours, assignment, performance, availability of work, *etc.*);
- any previous work activities and other marketable skills;
- the employee's vocational interests and aptitudes; and

- the supervisor's and human resource professional's promotion of a graduated return to work.

Medical factors, such as:

- diagnosis;
- prognosis;
- treatment plan;
- expected return-to-work date;
- employee confidence and satisfaction with medical treatment;
- potential residual limitations;
- presence of pain and coping skills;
- presence of other health problems; and
- independent practitioner, nutritional guidance, adaptive devices, aids to daily living, home help, and/or home care services, *etc.*

Psychological factors, such as:

- the employee's reaction to illness/injury;
- the employee's thoughts and feelings, level of self-esteem, outlook, locus of control and degree of personal power;
- cultural factors;
- the employee's interests and attitude about work and the illness or injury;
- reliance on alcohol and/or drugs;
- stress management needs; and
- the employee's willingness to try modified work/alternate work duties.

Performance issues, such as:

- the quality of the relationship between the employee and his/her supervisor;
- the quality of relationships with co-workers;
- employee's past and recent work performance; and
- past absenteeism.

Educational factors, such as:

- formal education; and
- specialized training.

Financial factors, such as:

- available employee benefits;
- income;
- financial assets/liabilities; and

• treatment/rehabilitation expenses.

Organizational factors, such as:

• willingness to host case management conferences to expedite a successful graduated return-to-work plan; and
• resources to meet the employee's rehabilitation needs.

Effective case management requires the appropriate assessment and evaluation of the employee's needs; of the availability and utilization of appropriate medical treatment; and of the factors that may impede the employee's successful recovery and reintegration into the workforce (Chapter 5, Figure 5.2). By providing parallel assistance with work and medical issues, return-to-work barriers can be eliminated.

PROBLEM IDENTIFICATION

Background

An overwhelming majority of injured, ill or disabled employees return to work without difficulty. For approximately 15% to 20% of employees on short-term and long-term disability and Workers' Compensation, disability provokes a constellation of personal, emotional and work-related issues that delay return to work. The existence of person-job mismatch, workplace discord and a performance problem usually indicates a prolonged absence from work.

Some factors associated with a delayed return to work are:

• the absence of a Graduated Return-to-Work Program;
• time lags in obtaining medical care or other forms of therapy;
• lack of knowledge on the part of the community practitioner about the workplace and what accommodations can be made for the disabled employee;
• disability insurance plans that promote a "reward" for being disabled;
• unreliable methods for tracking the ill or injured worker;
• employee fear of losing disability income if he or she attempts an unsuccessful return to work;
• physical pain;
• employee fear of relapse or re-injury;
• employee anxiety concerning poor job performance due to disability;
• decreased self-confidence;
• a work situation perceived as intolerable by the employee;
• a negative industrial relations climate;
• layoffs due to "downsizing";
• cultural differences in illness/injury response;

- a breakdown in communication between the employee and employer; and
- lack of understanding by all stakeholders of the real costs associated with disability.

The factors associated with a timely and safe return to work are:

- job satisfaction;
- respect for the worker;
- open communication between the employer and worker;
- existence of a modified/alternate work program; and
- use of a team approach (*i.e.*, employee, supervisor, union, insurance company, human resource professionals, physician, Employee Assistance Program counsellors, occupational health professionals, *etc.*) towards a graduated return to work with the employee being the key player.

Recent changes in the workers' compensation and human rights regulations in Canada demand workplace accommodation for the disabled worker. For larger companies, this can mean workplace and/or work duty modifications, or necessitate the development of alternate job positions.

CASE MANAGER ROLE

Case Managers identify cases, non-occupational or occupational in origin that will benefit the most from case management intervention. Criteria for early identification include:

- expected duration of disability exceeding one month;
- hospitalization greater than one week;
- Workers' Compensation claim longer than one week;
- employee 50 years of age or older;
- stress as the diagnosis;
- diagnoses of cardiovascular, cancer, digestive, skeletal (*i.e.*, repetitive strain injury), neurological or psychological conditions;
- multiple diagnoses;
- cases which fail just before the expected return-to-work date;
- presence of discipline or performance problems;
- presence of labour relations problems;
- presence of pending litigation associated with the injury; and
- employee with a high rate of absenteeism.

Outcome Identification

Case management is a goal-directed process. Information is gathered and evaluated to form an assessment of an injured or ill employee's needs. When these needs have been identified, the Case Manager, in collaboration with the medical care provider, employee, employer and other involved parties, identifies cost-effective and appropriate resources that can be utilized to facilitate the worker's recovery. For each identified resource, or intervention, the Case Manager must be able to report, in quantifiable terms, its impact on quality of care or quality of life in order to appropriately evaluate outcomes.

Planning Process

The Case Manager facilitates the planning of care and the selection of resources. This facilitation is not conducted in a vacuum but rather in partnership with the employee, management, union, physician, Employee Assistance Program counsellor and often the family. All of the factors identified in the assessment process are considered in deciding on appropriate care, the delivery of that care, and necessary resources, such as equipment, supplemental assistance, available Employee Assistance Programs (own and spousal) and extended health care plans.

A rehabilitation action plan is developed for each employee who can benefit from proactive intervention. This is accomplished by gathering data using the following techniques:

- *Job Analysis* — Job description and physical demand requirements are reviewed to identify capabilities, as well as limitations.
- *Attending Physician Support* — The purpose of the case management process is to work as a team to benefit the employee. This includes involvement of the attending physician. The Case Manager needs to explain the benefits and corporate support available for the employee to the physician, if appropriate.
- *Job or Worksite Modification* — The opportunity for job changes, or the reassignment of parts of a job, are considered so that the employee can return to work in a safe and timely manner. Once the employee's capabilities have been identified by an occupational health professional, the supervisor, union representative, Return-to-Work Coordinator and human resource personnel are usually the leaders of a modified/alternate work opportunity.
- *Employee Assistance Program Support* — The Case Manager should offer Employee Assistance Program support to the employee and family as appropriate. Many disabled employees need help to cope with a disability, work stress, personal issues, and any mental health component of the existent medical conditions.
- *Coordination with a Specialist* — When warranted, a Case Manager may arrange to obtain an earlier appointment for the employee. Under certain circumstances, it may be advantageous to fund a medical assessment, especially if it facilitates getting an earlier appointment.
- *Third Party Functional Capacity Assessment* — This may be sought to determine the employee's fitness to work.
- *Adaptive Devices* — Special clothing, devices, or equipment that allow adaptation of the work to the employee's limitations are considered where

possible. From the beginning, the disabled employee and supervisor are involved in selecting and learning how to use any device that assists in the workplace accommodation of the returning employee. The occupational hygiene professionals can be an excellent team resource in this area.

- *Job Finding* — Human resources should be advised as early as possible of the likelihood that the employee will not be able to return to his or her own job. In that way, an internal job search can be instituted.

- *Employee Education* — Resources may be used to help the employee understand and cope with his or her disability. This is important when trying to encourage a positive attitude towards illness or injury management. The employee must feel a sense of control over life if he or she is to successfully cope with the situation.

- *Case Conferences* — It is critical to invite all the relevant stakeholders to attend any required case management meetings. Specific goals and time frames are developed and communicated to the team, of which the employee is the key player. A decision tree, like the one provided in Chapter 3, Figure 3.3, can help the team remain focused. Another useful tool is the Rehabilitation Action Plan, (Chapter 5, Figure 5.5). In this way, all the stakeholders can review and address any identified rehabilitation or return-to-work barriers. This is particularly important if the employee will not be able to return to his or her own job.

Rehabilitation Action Plans should be regularly reviewed and updated to reflect the progress being made. The Case Manager documents the effectiveness of each step of the plan, identifies any unforeseen obstacles and prepares all participants in the plan for the subsequent steps. By involving the employee in case management decisions, the employee retains a sense of control over his or her life.

MONITORING AND COORDINATION

The Case Manager:

- provides for the assessment and documentation of quality of care and of services and products delivered to the employee;
- determines if rehabilitation goals are being met;
- determines whether the case management goals and the expected outcomes are realistic and appropriate;
- continuously monitors the rehabilitation process through good oral and written communication;
- ensures effective coordination of care and services for the injured or ill employee;
- documents the rehabilitation process;
- ensures a timely response to rehabilitation issues; and
- ensures prompt reporting to the management of any relevant workplace issues.

A Disability Case Management Flow Chart, like the one presented in Chapter 3, Figure 3.2, can be used by Case Managers to assess the employee's progress throughout the case management process.

Evaluation

Evaluation of the case's progress and outcomes is necessary to determine the effectiveness of the case management plan and the quality of medical care, services, and products from providers. Evaluation is most effective if metrics, or medical case measurements, are used. Comparing the results of a particular case management scenario against the case-plan metrics can be a valuable exercise when it comes to appropriately evaluating outcomes. Figure 11.3 is a listing of some of the possible Case Management Metrics.

Individual case management process and results are reviewed continually and process improvements sought. The Case Management Assessment and Evaluation Checklist (Figure 11.4) can be a useful evaluation tool for Case Managers.

Program results, costs, system concerns and recommendations are tabulated and reported annually to management and the Disability Management Program Steering Committee. Confidentiality of individual information is maintained as per the company's Disability Management Standard of Practice for Confidentiality of Personal Health Information.

Annual auditing of the Disability Case Management, peer review and self-auditing is recommended.

Figure 11.3: Case Management Metrics[11]

Metric	Best Practice
Diagnosis verified.	Diagnosis verified by appropriate test or observations. If diagnosis is not verified, Case Manager will challenge diagnosis until it is verified.
Evidence-based practice protocols.	Ten most common diagnoses will have practice protocols.
Existence of "red flag" alerts Case Manager to institute or increase case management.	Case Manager has established criteria or indicators for increased case acuity.
Case Manager has specific diagnosis-based disability-duration guidelines to follow.	Low variances from disability-duration guidelines.

---

[11] Printed with permission: D. DiBenedetto *et al.*, *OEM Occupational Health and Safety Manual* (Boston: OEM Press, 1996).

Metric	Best Practice
Resources used for hospital and ambulatory care.	Most appropriate resources are identified and used.
Average number of disability days per diagnosis.	Documented decrease in disability days.
Case cost with case management.	Decreased case cost with case management.
Case notes/documentation.	Well-documented treatment plan, decision making.
Hospitalization.	Low hospitalization rates (below 5%) coupled with good outcomes.
Re-admissions.	Low re-admission rate (below 1%).
Medical management.	Treatment process changes based on case management information.
Individual (worker/patient) satisfaction.	Improved patient satisfaction with case management (using a survey tool).

Figure 11.4: Case Management Assessment and Evaluation Checklist[12]

Information to be Obtained	Rationale
Age	Age affects recovery time and rate of rehabilitation.
Gender	Gender plays a role in the recovery time.
Years of service with the company	Raises the issue of motivation to return to work, interest in medical retirement, *etc.*
Length of time in the current job position	In-depth knowledge of position will aid in developing opportunities for modified work.
Previous workers' compensation injury	If yes, what is the employee's views towards return to modified work, litigation, *etc.*
Current injury, diagnosis and treatment	In addition to gathering the particulars, it is important to note any areas in which the employee, provider or adjuster lacks all the needed information.
Diagnostic testing	Determine what tests have been done and the results but also review what tests, which might be expected for a particular diagnosis, have not been done.

---

[12] *Ibid.*

Information to be Obtained	Rationale
Medications: (a) Appropriateness of use (b) Use of other personal medications (c) Outcomes of (a) and/or (b)	Some personal medications may have an addictive or negative combination effect. Patients may not be taking medication in the appropriate time frame or manner, thus delaying recovery. Medications that seem ineffective or have side-effects should be brought to the attention of the physician.
Physical medicine modalities and results	Modalities should be scientifically based, and if a patient is not showing progress after 4 to 6 weeks, a re-evaluation by the physician should be initiated.
Expectations of the disability duration	Expectations of disability duration by the physician, patient and family may subtly influence the recovery.
Psychosocial variables	Family and social issues may be incentives or disincentives in the recovery process. This is an area in which Case Managers may frequently uncover hidden agendas or issues that would have delayed recovery if not addressed.
Communication:	Employee's failing to receive a timely Workers' Compensation payment, or his or her uncertainty as to how the Workers' Compensation system works, has one of the highest correlations with the employee's initiation of litigation. The Case Manager fills a vital role as liaison with the employee, insurance providers, employer and third-party administrator.

Documentation

Refer to the Disability Management Standard of Practice — Documentation in Personal Health.

Consent for Handling

Disability case management requires information on the employee's physical and emotional capabilities and restrictions. Input from the employee's attending physician is essential.

According to Canadian legislation, an employer must obtain the consent of the employee before approaching the employee's physician for personal medical information. Thus the company, or its representative, must make efforts to obtain the employee's written consent before seeking such input from the employee's physician.[13]

Appendix 3 contains sample forms for this practice standard:

1.   Letter to Absent Employee
2.   Report of Absence Form
3.   Modified/Alternate Work Plan Notification
4.   Restricted Work Form
5.   Physician's Statement of Medical Status
6.   Return-to-Work Report
7.   Consent Form

Confidentiality

Refer to the Disability Management Standard of Practice — Confidentiality of Personal Health Information for information on maintaining the confidentiality of personal health information.

Administration Responsibility

Primary responsibility for the administration and update of this standard of practice rests with senior management.

DISABILITY MANAGEMENT STANDARD OF PRACTICE — CONFIDENTIALITY

Introduction

All persons who collect, maintain, handle and use personal health information are required to protect the confidentiality of the information.

This standard is based on the *Model Code for the Protection of Personal Information*[14] and the various pieces of provincial and federal privacy legislation. It details the procedures for collection, retention, storage, security access, disclosure, transmittal, reproduction and destruction of identifiable personal health information held by the company or organization.

All staff must comply with the Disability Management Standard of Practice document on confidentiality of personal health information when interpreting

---

[13]   A. Legault *et al.*, "How to Cope with Absenteeism, Part IV: Requesting a Medical Opinion" (1996) Focus on Canadian Employment and Equality Rights at 126–128.

[14]   CAN/CSA, *The Model Code for the Protection of Personal Information*, CAN/CSA - Q830-96, (Ottawa: CSA, 1996).

personal health information to the employer-client without divulging any privileged information.

General

The company or organization recognizes the individual's right to privacy in relation to personal health information collected.

The principles governing confidentiality are:

* personal health information is only used on a "need-to-know" basis;
* personal health information should be relevant to the purposes for which it is to be used;
* personal health information is restricted to the company or organization staff who sign a pledge of confidentiality and who are subject to a recognized professional code of ethics;
* upon request, an employee has the right to access all information regarding his or her health;
* personal health information is protected by reasonable security safeguards;
* documented personal and health information is the property of the company or organization entrusted to occupational health staff for safeguarding and protection; and
* compliance with this standard is the responsibility of the Case Manager.

Definitions

Collection — The act of gathering, acquiring or obtaining personal information from any source, including third parties, by any means.

Confidentiality — The maintenance of trust and the avoidance of invasion of privacy through accurate reporting and authorized communication.

Consent — The voluntary agreement with what is being done or proposed. Consent can be either express or implied. Express consent is given explicitly, either orally or in writing. It is unequivocal and does not require any inference on the part of the organization seeking consent. Implied consent arises where consent may reasonably be inferred from the action or inaction of the individual.

Designated Representative — Any individual or organization to whom an employee gives written authorization to exercise a right to access.

Disclosure — The act of making employee personal information available to others outside the organization.

Personal Health Information — An accumulation of data relevant to the past, present and future health status of an individual which includes all that the company or organization staff learn in the exercise of their responsibilities. It is the information about an identifiable individual that is recorded in any form.

Privacy — The claim of individuals, groups or institutions to determine for themselves when, how and to what extent information about them is communicated to others.

Application

These guidelines apply to all occupational health and disability management staff and include contract employees and all other support staff whether permanent, temporary or volunteers.

COLLECTION OF PERSONAL HEALTH INFORMATION

The primary purpose for collecting and retaining personal health information is disability management. All information collected is subject to confidentiality and must be treated with respect.

Knowledge and consent of the employee are required for the collection and disclosure of personal health data relevant to disability management. Figure 11.5 shows how personal information should be collected. In essence, personal health information is not to be collected indiscriminately. Only the personal health information relevant to disability management should be collected.

Figure 11.5: Collection of Information

- Request for information will be in writing and contain the following:
  - Name and address of recipient of information.
  - Purpose or need for information.
  - Full name, address and date of birth of person whose information is being requested.
  - Specific definition of the type and extent of information required.
- All requests will be accompanied by the appropriate "Release for Medical Information" form signed by the employee whose personal health record is being requested.
- A record of all requests will be maintained on the employee's personal health record.

Personal health information is collected using various methods, including interviewing, written documentation (*i.e.*, insurance claims, Workers' Compensation Board forms, *etc.*) and electronic data processing, all of which are subject to confidentiality. Appendix 2 provides standards for computerized employee health information management.

The personal health information collected relates to medical assessments, Employee Assistance Program treatment reports, illness and injury reports, personal and family history and consultant reports.

Personal health information is only collected by designated staff subject to a pledge of confidentiality (Figure 11.6). Personal health information should be as accurate, complete and current as possible.

Figure 11.6: Pledge of Confidentiality

- All personal health information related to an identified employee will be treated as confidential. This information may be in writing, oral, electronic or in any other form.
- Confidentiality extends to everything Company XYZ staff learns in the exercise of their responsibilities. It extends to both obviously important and apparently trivial information and includes the nature of the employee's contact with the staff, all information an employee discloses and all information learned from external caregivers.
- Personal health information related to the disability claim can be shared with occupational health professionals employed by Company XYZ *in privacy* to enhance continuity of care and a coordinated disability management approach.
- The dissemination of personal health information will be considered a breach of confidentiality and will be reported to Director, Human Resources and the CEO, Company XYZ. Disciplinary action will be taken up to and include immediate termination of employment *with cause*.
- Senior Management is responsible for ensuring that the Company XYZ staff involved in disability management are aware of the Pledge of Confidentiality and that they sign the pledge acknowledging this awareness.
- To acknowledge and emphasize the serious responsibility in safeguarding employee health information, all Company XYZ staff (permanent or temporary), or contract staff involved with disability management will be required to sign a pledge of confidentiality on the first day of work and annually thereafter, which will be worded as follows:

Pledge of Confidentiality

I have read and reviewed Company XYZ's Standard of Practice on Confidentiality of Personal Health Information. I understand that all employee personal health information, to which I may have access, is confidential and will not be communicated except as outlined in the Disability Management Standard of Practice.

Signed	Witness	Date

Signed	Witness	Date

Signed	Witness	Date

Note: This pledge is to be signed annually. The original form is to be sent to the staff member's file, Company XYZ HR Department. Copies are to be retained by the area Manager and the Company XYZ staff person.

RETENTION, STORAGE AND SECURITY

All personal health information must be stored separately from other employee information. The storage location is checked regularly and safeguarded from fire, water and other potential disasters.

All computerized health information must be secured using passwords and access codes.

All activities of employees and visitors to the company or organization offices must be supervised in order to protect the confidentiality of personal health information.

During active use, records and other personal health information must be kept in private offices, always ensuring that identifiable information is protected from the observation and the hearing of other individuals.

All personal health information must be retained for a period of seven years from the last date of contact.

Personal health records of employees who have left the company are retained as outlined in Figure 11.7.

Figure 11.7: Retention, Storage and Security

- The medical records of terminated employees are to be pulled from the active files, placed in a designated envelope marked "Confidential Personal Health Document: To Be Opened By Authorized Personnel Only", labelled and placed in a storage box. The box is to be numbered.
- A list of the medical files in the storage box is to be created. Three sets of this list are to be made: one copy to go with the storage box, another is to be sent to the employee, and a third is to be retained by Company XYZ.
- A system of archiving that links the file with the storage box is required.
- Files are to be stored in a location that is safeguarded from water, fire and access by unauthorized persons.

ACCESSIBILITY

Upon request, an employee is to be informed of the existence, use and disclosure of personal health information and is given access to that information.

Employees, former employees and other properly designated representatives have the right to inspect and copy, all or in part, personal health records. All such written requests are to be honoured within a reasonable time that should not exceed 15 days.

> **Note:** *The actual health record is the property of the company, however, the information contained in the record belongs to the employee.*

To the extent practicable, inspection of a personal health record is to be made in the presence of a representative of the company or organization, who endeavours to explain the meaning of the contents of the record to the employee. Rebuttal of information contained in the personal health record by the employee will be included in the record, signed and dated by the employee. The representative will add a note to the file concerning explanation and agreement, or disagreement.

The company or organization personnel may delete the identity of a family member, personal friend or fellow employee who has provided confidential information concerning an employee's health status from the requested health records.

It is recommended that employees:

- accept a summary of material facts and opinions in lieu of copies of the records requested; or
- accept a release of the requested information only to the family physician or other qualified health care professional.

Access to health information that may have an adverse impact upon the health of the employee will only be provided to a designated physician of the employee.

No other personnel, except designated staff, have the right to access health information unless disclosure obligations have been met.

DISCLOSURE INTERNAL TO THE EMPLOYER-CLIENT

Management Disclosure — Personal health information released to managers and/or supervisors is limited to the following:

- report of fitness to work following a mandated or statutory health assessment;
- determination that a medical condition exists and that the employee is under medical care. This could include the dates or follow-up appointments or referrals to specialists or treatment programs;
- time that the employee has been or is expected to be off work;
- medical limitations, if any, to carry out work in a safe and timely manner;
- medical restrictions, if any, regarding specific tasks; and/or
- estimated date for a realistic return to work, or a return to modified/alternate work.

However, if, in the opinion of a health professional, disclosure is necessary because of a *clear danger* to the employee, other employees, the workplace or the public at large, and:

- the employee consistently refuses to give consent; and
- a second opinion is obtained from the employee's personal physician when the concern is for the health of the employee or fellow employees-clients, or from the medical officer of health when the risk is to the public;

the appropriate staff member may make the disclosure to the appropriate manager after giving notice in writing to the employee, indicating that confidential information will be disclosed.

EXTERNAL DISCLOSURE

Subject to the exceptions specified below, the company or organization should not disclose personal health information regarding employees or former employees to external sources unless the individual has authorized such release by providing a signed and dated consent form for release of medical information or its equivalent. Disclosure will follow the checklist provided in Figure 11.8, and the Requirement for Informed Consent in Figure 11.9.

Figure 11.8: Disclosure of Information Checklist

- All requests for disclosure of information will be directed to the Company XYZ Disability Case Manager.
- Any authorization for release of information will be an original form and will specify the source, content, recipient, purpose and time limitations. The form will identify the:
  - Name of the individual or institution who is to disclose the information.
  - Name of the individual or institution who is to receive the information.
  - Full name, address and date of birth of the person whose information is being requested.
  - Purpose or need of information, unless included in accompanying request.
  - Extent or nature of information to be released, including date(s) of treatment or contact (blanket authorizations requesting "any" or "all" information will not be honoured).
  - Date that consent/authorization is signed which must be subsequent to the date of treatment or contact in question and within sixty (60) days of signature of person whose information is to be released, or that of his or her legally authorized representative.

- Information released to legally authorized persons is not to be made available to any other party without further authorization. The recipient will be so informed by including a copy of the following letter with the information:

Sample Letter

To Whom It May Concern:

The enclosed information is being forwarded to you from our records, which are the property of Company XYZ and managed by Company XYZ. Such copies are released only to persons authorized according to law and the policy of Company XYZ. In this way, we seek to uphold the trust vested in us by the individual and ensure that his or her wishes and best interests are served at all times. Accordingly, this information is released on the following conditions:

- That it not be further copied, transmitted or disseminated without further specific authorization of the person concerned;
- That it be used only for the purpose as outlined in your request; and
- That it be destroyed by shredding or incineration when the original purpose has been served.

Your cooperation and compliance with the above is appreciated.

Figure 11.9: Requirements for Informed Consent

- There is an obligation to ensure that sufficient information is provided to employees about the nature and consequence of the intended action to allow the employee to come to a reasoned decision.
- The employee is mentally competent, and has the ability to understand and appreciate the nature and consequences of the procedure.
- Consent is freely given.
- Consent is not obtained through misrepresentation or fraud.
- Consent cannot be given to the performance of an illegal procedure.
- Consent is in relation to the specific act contemplated unless the employee's life is immediately endangered and it is impractical to obtain consent.

Routine Request for Release of Medical Information — A written request by a physician, medical institution, another health agency, or insurance company, for abstracts or copies of part or all of the individual's health record is honoured when the consent form (Appendix 3, Form 7) or its equivalent is signed by the employee.

Release of Pertinent Medical Data to Appropriate Public Health Authorities — When it is determined that a public health issue or risk has been uncovered, as in the case of a reportable communicable disease, appropriate notification to provincial or municipal health authorities will be made in accordance with the statutory requirement.

Disclosure to Government Agencies — To preserve the confidentiality of employee health records, the company or organization usually requests government agencies for consent for release of medical information signed by the employee. However, government legislation may have the authority to require immediate access to employee and former employee medical information. Whenever access is necessary without the prior written consent of the employee, a government agency must present a written access order to the company or organization.

Disclosure to Designated Representative — The company or organization, upon presentation of a written consent by an employee or former employee, will release copies of the individual's medical record to the designated representative. With respect to medical information that may be deemed to have a detrimental impact upon the health of the employee, medical information will be provided only to the employee's family physician. Information received in confidence from external sources that is part of the health record will not be divulged to the employee's designated representative.

Disclosure of Subpoenaed Information — A company or organization should respond to a subpoena as follows:

- with the server present, the employee's name and the validity of the subpoena are verified;
- the Chief Executive Officer is notified;
- only the specific material requested in the subpoena is collected and photocopied;
- authorization to release information is given by the Chief Executive Officer and the Senior Counsel, Corporate; and
- without written authorization of the employee, subpoenaed records are not available for review by outside counsel prior to being established as evidence.

REPRODUCTION AND TRANSMITTAL

Reproduction of any individualized health information is to be done by designated staff in privacy.

Transmittal of individualized health records can be faxed to a recipient with a confidentiality notice. Information can also be mailed or couriered in envelopes clearly marked "Confidential: To Be Opened by Addressee Only".

Transmittal of individualized health records will be in sealed envelopes or boxes. The envelopes or boxes must be clearly marked "Confidential: To Be Opened by Addressee Only".

DESTRUCTION

When it becomes appropriate to dispose of health information, including formal health records, notes and messages pertaining to an individual employee, they will be rendered completely and permanently unidentifiable through destruction by burning, shredding or automated erasure.

When burning, shredding or automated erasure is not feasible, health information will be transmitted to the closest office with the ability to destroy such information.

Company or organization staff will personally transmit the information to be destroyed and remain with the information until it is destroyed.

MISUSE OF PERSONAL HEALTH INFORMATION

Any individual who becomes aware of an abuse of confidentiality of health information will document and report the incident to the Chief Executive Officer.

DISABILITY MANAGEMENT STANDARD OF PRACTICE — DOCUMENTATION IN PERSONAL HEALTH RECORDS

Introduction

This standard of practice is intended to provide guidance and direction to disability Case Managers in the initiation, maintenance and disposal of employee health records.

When completed properly, the personal health record can:

- provide a profile of the health status and the health care provided to each employee;
- provide a means of communication among members of the disability management team contributing to the case management of the employee;
- provide a basis for planning and for continuity of rehabilitation care for employees;
- provide a basis for review, study and evaluation of the case; and
- assist in the provision of protection for the medical and legal interests of both the employee and the company.

General

Case Managers are required to discharge their legal responsibilities by providing accurate and timely records of events and information affecting the health of the employee.

Information recorded in the employee health record is confidential. The Disability Management Standard of Practice — Confidentiality of Personal Health Information applies to all Case Managers documenting and handling employee personal health records.

Personal health records are to be cumulative and sequential. Filing in the chart is done in such a way that the most current information in each selection is on top when the file is opened.

Application

These guidelines apply to all professionals and contract employees who gather information for the purpose of disability case management.

PERSONAL HEALTH RECORD FORMAT

The employee's health record is kept in an appropriately labelled data file folder in a secured manner. The employee's name must appear on every page of the record.

Each record will contain the following information:

- reports of sickness and injury absences;
- reports of all medical examinations and consultations;
- record of all inquiries related to health problems, whether presented in person or by phone;
- copies of disability claim forms;
- correspondence with other health care professionals or agencies;
- copies of Workers' Compensation claims;
- memos or notes regarding discussions relevant to the case (*e.g.*, discussions between professionals, medical experts, Employee Assistance Program counsellors);
- record of communication with other health and safety related bodies (*e.g.*, Workers' Compensation Board, insurance companies and government agencies); and/or
- record of all communication with management, unions and employees. These signed notes should include time and date of call.

RECORDING

The general guidelines for recording are:

- all entries are to be recorded on the Disability Case Management Status Report (Figure 11.10);
- all entries should be dated and entered sequentially;
- every entry must be signed. The accepted format for a signature is the initial, surname and professional designation (if applicable);
- entries are to be made in ink or typed;
- entries should be made at the earliest opportunity following contact;
- writing in the record must be legible;
- entries should be continuous, do not skip lines between entries or leave space within an entry;
- entries in the record are permanent. Do not obliterate material on the record by scratching out, using correction fluid, felt tip pen or typewritten XXXs; and
- when content corrections are required, the following procedure is to be observed:
  - draw a single line through each line of inaccurate recording making certain it is still legible;
  - date and initial the line;
  - enter corrections in chronological order;
  - time the entry and sign;
  - make certain to indicate which entry the correction is replacing; and
  - in questionable situations, it is wise to have the corrected material witnessed by an occupational health colleague. Countersigning of the record is completed with the signature of the responsible party and the witness or counter-signatory (signature should be in the standard format).

ACCESS TO THE HEALTH RECORD

Refer to the Corporate Disability Management Standard of Practice — Confidentiality of Health Information regarding the topics of:

- accessibility; and
- internal and external disclosure.

RETENTION OF HEALTH RECORD

Refer to the Corporate Disability Management Standard of Practice — Confidentiality of Health Information regarding:

- retention, storage, security; and
- Retention of Inactive Health Records — Appendix B.

TRANSMITTAL OF HEALTH RECORD

Refer to the Corporate Disability Management Standard of Practice — Confidentiality of Health Information regarding:

• Reproduction and Transmittal.

DESTRUCTION OF HEALTH RECORD

Refer to the Corporate Disability Management Standard of Practice — Confidentiality of Health Information.

Figure 11.10: Disability Case Management Status Record

COMPANY XYZ
LOGO/ADDRESS

Employee Name _____
Company/Organization _____
Employee Number/Identifier _____

Date	Status	Signature

REVIEW OF HEALTH RECORD

Regular and periodic review of personal health records is conducted to ensure that policies and practices are implemented, and that forms and records continue to capture appropriate information without duplication.

ADMINISTRATION RESPONSIBILITY

Primary responsibility for the administration and update of this standard of practice rests jointly with senior management.

SUMMARY

These four disability management practice standards comprise the key elements of a responsible Disability Management Program. Companies that offer disability management services of any sort should have these safeguards in place. This is one way to protect against costly litigation, and to demonstrate "due diligence".

Appendix 1

Claims Management Action Plan Form

COMPANY XYZ
LOGO/ADDRESS

Claims Management Action Plan

Employee Information

Name: _____   Employee #: _____

Phone: (H)_____

       (W)_____

Job Title: _____   Manager: _____

Occupation: _____   Phone: _____

Return-to-Work Probability

Expected date of return to work: _____

     Likely to return to own job   ☐

     Unlikely to return to own job   ☐

     Job modifications necessary   ☐

Current Status

Last Day Worked: _____

Previous Work Absence in the Last Six (6) Months: _____ (Dates)

Functional Limitations:

Lifting	_____	Bending	_____
Sitting	_____	Reaching	_____
Standing	_____	Psychological	_____
Other	_____		

Comments:

_____

_____

_____

> COMPANY XYZ
> LOGO/ADDRESS

Employee Name: _____   Employee #: _____

Treatment Program:

_____

_____

_____

Able to Return to Work   □

Date: _____   Full-time □   Part-time □

Restrictions: _____

Unable to Return to Work □

Expected Date of Return to Work: _____

Next Case Management Assessment Date: _____

Action Plan
Claim Management Plan:

		Comments	Date Requested
□	Standard Physician Form	_____	_____
□	Diagnosis Specific Form	_____	_____
□	Attending Physician's Narrative	_____	_____
□	Functional Evaluation	_____	_____
□	Specialist Consult Report	_____	_____
□	Investigative Studies	_____	_____
□	IME (Independent Medical Evaluation)	_____	_____
□	Other	_____	_____

COMPANY XYZ
LOGO/ADDRESS

Employee Name: _____   Employee #: _____

Claims and Case Management Tracking

#	Date	Claim Action Plan	Rehabilitation Action Plan
1.			
2.			
3.			
4.			
5.			
6.			
7.			
8.			
9.			
10.			
11.			
12.			

Additional Comments:

_____
_____
_____
_____
_____

Appendix 2

Computerized Employee Health Information Management[15]

COMPUTERIZED EMPLOYEE HEALTH INFORMATION MANAGEMENT

Security of Computerized Health Information

1. Company XYZ recognizes the individual's right to privacy in relation to health information. Computerized health information is subject to the same security as written information:

   - Company XYZ has the property right to the computerized health information that is compiled.
   - All Company XYZ offices shall safeguard computerized health information against loss or unwarranted access.
   - All Company XYZ offices shall establish policies and procedures concerning the confidentiality and security of computerized health information.
   - The office policies and procedures for access to written information must serve as a minimum standard for computerized information.

2. It is recognized that a computerized health information system can be as secure as a paper system and should allow relative ease of use for authorized personnel while eliminating unauthorized access:

   - The issue of confidentiality shall not be used as a barrier to the implementation of computerized information systems.

3. An individual's access to his or her own computerized health information shall follow the guidelines on Accessibility of this Standard of Practice:

   - Management and employees shall be informed as to existence, purpose and type of information contained in the computerized health information system.

---

[15] Adapted from: Petro-Canada, "Confidentiality Code of Practice, Reference Number 130" in *Occupational Health Manual* (Calgary: Petro-Canada, 1994) at 12-14.

4. Information from computerized health information used or maintained to facilitate information exchange in support of employee care shall be accessible only to authorized persons.
5. Data security shall include data integrity. Steps must be taken to ensure the reliability of data input.

- Data shall be protected so that it cannot be altered or purged without the proper authorization.
- Principles of documentation and context of health information shall be adhered to in order that computer charting will meet legal and professional standards.

> **Note:** *Records should not be computerized without obtaining the advice of legal counsel to determine whether the "hard copy" will be acceptable as evidence, and whether the act of computerization conflicts with any provincial enactment regarding written or other traditional forms of records. Special care must be taken regarding confidentiality and errors. Since there is very little law on this matter, the computerization of records must be kept under constant review with respect to possible legal changes.*

Policies and Procedures Regarding Security of Computerized Health Information

1. Physical Protection — The facility must ensure:

- The physical protection of the system by guarding against threats from electrical failure/fluctuations, fire, flood and temperature variations.
- Terminals located in such a way that the screen cannot be viewed by unauthorized persons.
- Back-up copies of vital files are stored in a physically separated and secure area.
- Documented manual systems to enable ongoing operation during a down period of the computerized systems.
- Written agreements from computer vendors involved with health care data that specify methods by which information is handled and transported.

2. Access of Information in System — There shall be:

- Controlled access to terminals. Categories of personnel shall be identified to indicate authorized access to these terminals.
- Defined access, specifying information to which users may be granted access.

- A personal security passcode for each authorized individual.
- Immediate removal of passcode upon an individual's denial to access.
- A provision for change of passcode where access has been restricted or redefined.
- A policy for access to the system. It shall be available at every point of access.

3. General Administrative — Policies and procedures shall include:

- Development of, or change to any computerized health record and/or health information system governed by a committee of multi-disciplinary health professionals.
- Administrative responsibility for ensuring the security of the system which shall be designated to an individual and that responsibility shall be defined and documented.
- Appropriate security which must be inherent in the software when computer facilities are shared.

4. User Responsibility:

- The users are expected to guard their identification and passwords to prevent a breach of security.

Appendix 3

Disability Case Management Sample Forms

1. Letter to Absent Employee
2. Report of Absence Forms
    *   Sample (a)
    *   Sample (b)
3. Modified/Alternate Work Plan Forms
    *   Sample (a)
    *   Sample (b)
4. Restricted Work Form
5. Physician's Statement of Medical Status
6. Return-to-Work Report
7. Consent Form

Form 1: Letter to the Employee

```
COMPANY XYZ
LOGO/ADDRESS
```

Date _____

Dear _____
            (Employee)

RE: Disability

We have been advised by your supervisor that you are unable to work due to illness/injury. We sincerely hope that you will have an early recovery and wish to assist you wherever possible.

As part of our corporate Disability Management Program, we require the following:

* a completed attending physician's report (as attached); and
* a signed consent form for release of medical information to our Disability Case Manager(s), and our insurers/adjudicators (_____).

The attending physician report must be completed and returned to Company XYZ's Occupational Health Department within 3 working days. Your signed consent form must accompany this physician report.

Your supervisor will be in contact on a weekly basis to determine if there are any opportunities for modified/alternate work. We would encourage you to utilize the Employee Assistance Program should you require such services during your disability.

If there is any additional assistance the company can provide, please contact _____.

We look forward to having you return to your job in the very near future.

Yours truly,

_____

Supervisor

Form 2a: Report of Absence Form[16]

Sample (a):   For Organizations with Occupational Health Services:

REPORT OF ABSENCE FORM

EMPLOYEE AUTHORIZATION: *(To be completed by the employee)*

Name:		Employee Number:	
Address:		Home Phone Number:	
Work Injury ☐	Work Illness ☐	Work Phone Number:	
Non-work Injury ☐	Non-work Illness ☐	Start Date of Injury/Illness:	

Is your injury or illness related to your work? ☐ Yes ☐ No   If yes, please explain below:

I hereby authorize my insurer and attending physician to release any information related to this injury/illness, or copies thereof acquired in the course of examination or my treatment, Company XYZ's Occupational Health Service. I further authorize the Occupational Health Service to release to my insurer/employer any information required to determine my eligibility for short term disability benefits and any information related to the employment relationship. I understand that this information will be used to determine my eligibility for disability benefits, to assist with the management of my claim, and to remedy any work-related factors contributing to my illness or injury or my return to work. This consent is valid for 180 days.

Signature:		Date:	

COMPANY PHILOSOPHY

Company XYZ has a Disability Management Program designed to assist the safe and timely return of employees who are recovering from injury/ illness, or who have ongoing health problems. We would appreciate your assistance and co-operation. If you have any questions or suggestions about the Disability Management Program, and/or the placement of this employee, please contact at____.

Submit form to: The Occupational Health Service at above address, or in the confidential envelope provided, or by confidential fax **(XXX-XXXX)**. Thank you for the time and consideration you have provided to Company XYZ and this employee.

PHYSICAL WORK RESTRICTIONS: *(To be completed by the attending physician)*

Please check and complete either Section A or Section B:

Section A:	The employee will be able to return to **Regular Work** on:	Date:	
Section B:	The employee may return to **Modified Work** on:	Date:	
	And may return to Regular Work on:	Date:	

If Modified Work is required, please complete the following **Work Restrictions**:

☐	Lifting - from waist	(weight/frequency)	☐ Typing	(how long)	
☐	Lifting - from shoulder	(weight/frequency)	☐ Sitting	(how long)	
☐	Prolonged standing	(how long/frequency)	☐ Walking	(how long)	
☐	Working in the cold	(how long/frequency)	☐ Bending	(how long)	
☐	Working in the heat	(how long/frequency)	☐ Kneeling	(how long)	
☐	Working outdoors	(how long/frequency)	☐ Twisting	(frequency)	
☐	Repetition (hand/arm)	(how long/frequency)	☐ Crawling	(frequency)	
☐	Operating heavy machinery	(frequency)	☐ Working shift work		
☐	Climbing ladders	(frequency)	☐ Driving		
☐	Working at heights		☐ Climbing stairs		

Other Comments:

Temporarily reduced or gradually increasing hours are available. Please indicate any restriction of this type:

DIAGNOSIS: *(To be completed by the attending physician)*

Diagnosis of the *Present Health Condition*:

1.	Primary Diagnosis:			
2.	Pre-existing condition or complications that may affect the work absence:			

3.	Date of next follow-up visit	Day	Month	Year

4.	Is the present condition the result of, or complicated by, a pre-existing condition?	Yes ☐	No ☐

If Yes, please explain:

Date of Hospitalization (if applicable):		Date of Injury/Illness Onset:	
Nature of Treatment (e.g., surgery, physiotherapy):		Name of Specialist (if applicable):	
Duration/ Frequency of Treatment:			
Date of First Treatment:		Date of Last Treatment:	
Name of Physician:		Physician Phone Number:	
Address:		Physician Fax Number:	
Physician's Signature:		Date:	

Thank you for your assistance in supporting this employee through this injury or illness, and a timely return to work.

---

[16] Adapted from: L. Ydreos, "Medical Status Report Forms" (Presented at the Absenteeism and Disability Management Seminar, Toronto, 9-10 May 1995) [unpublished].

Form 2b: Report of Absence Form

Sample (b):   For Organizations without Occupational Health Professional Support

Return-to-Work Certificate

This must be completed and signed by an employee returning to work after an absence of 3 (three) or more days

Non-Work Related: ☐	Work Related: ☐
i.e., the flu, sports injury	*i.e.,* a possible Workers' Compensation claim

1.(a)   ☐   I have seen a physician and he advised me that I would be medically fit to work on this date: _____

(b)   ☐   To the best of my knowledge I am fit for work.

(check one)

2.   Specify any work restrictions recommended by your physician:

_____

_____

_____

Physician's Name and Address:

_____

_____

Employee Name: (please print)	Employee Signature:
_____	_____
Employee Number:	Date:
_____	_____

Return-to-work date:

_____

Form 3a: Modified/Alternate Work Plan Form — Sample (a)

COMPANY XYZ
LOGO/ADDRESS

Date: _____

To: _____

Department: _____

The following employee is to be placed in a Modified/Alternate Work Plan due to a medical condition:

Name: _____

Employee Number: _____

Title: _____

Company: _____ Department: _____

Work Restriction:
Length of
restriction: _____ days: _____ weeks: _____ months: _____

MWP begins (date): _____ (time): _____

THE EMPLOYEE WILL BE
RE-EVALUATED ON (DATE): _____ (TIME): _____

Please contact our office if you
have any questions at (telephone): _____

Completed by: _____ MD/OHN

Title: _____

Address (of contract provider): _____

_____

Form 3b: Modified/Alternate Work Plan Form — Sample (b)

COMPANY XYZ LOGO/ADDRESS

Modified/Alternate Work Plan:
[To be completed by the Disability Case Manager]

Employee Name:	
Last Day Worked:	Supervisor:
Regular Work Location:	Regular Occupation:
Information Provided by Employee:	

Modified/Alternate Work Requirements:

Permanent: ☐   Starting Date: _____

Temporary: ☐   Starting Date: _____   Expected Ending Date: _____

Modified/Alternate Work Plan Details:

Location:	Supervisor:
Modified/Alternate Work Description:	
Comments/Special Considerations:	
Next Medical Reassessment:	Next Review:

Signed: _____   Date: _____
       (Supervisor)

Signed: _____   Date: _____
       (Modified/Alternate Work
       Supervisor, if applicable)

Signed: _____   Date: _____
       (Employee)

cc: For WCB — Manager, Occupational Health
       All others — Manager, Employee Benefits

Form 4: Restricted Work Form[17]

COMPANY XYZ
LOGO/ADDRESS

Date: _____

Employee Name: _____

Employee Number: _____

Department: _____ Title: _____

Work Location: _____

Work Restrictions are: ☐ job-related (WC)   ☐ non-occupational
Explain physical limitations: (and reasons for them on the medical copy only)

_____

_____

_____

_____

_____

_____

_____

_____

_____

_____

Expected length of restriction/limitation: _____ days _____ weeks

Restriction is (check one):   ☐ Temporary   ☐ Permanent
Employee will be re-evaluated on: (date) _____

Signature: _____

Examiner: (print name) _____

Telephone No.: _____

Date: _____

_____

[17]   Adapted from: OEM Health Information Inc., "Restricted Work Form IB-21" in *OEM Occupational Health and Safety Manual* (Beverley, MA: The OEM Press, 1996).

Form 5: Physician's Statement of Medical Status Form[18]

COMPANY XYZ
LOGO/ADDRESS

Company   XYZ
Representative: _____   Department: _____
Title: _____   Telephone No.: _____
Address: _____

Instructions to the Attending Physician/Health Care Provider:
Please complete all information requested regarding your patient and return this form within 3 days to the Company Representative (address provided above). Thank you.

Date: _____
Employee Name: _____   Employee Number: _____
Job Title: _____   Department: _____
Date of Injury/Illness: _____   First Day out of Work: _____

Is this absence an occupational/workers' compensation ☐ or non-occupational/disability ☐ related diagnosis/condition
  (Please explain/list chief complaints, signs, symptoms): _____
_____
Date of first treatment for this condition: _____
Date of most recent treatment/diagnostic examination: _____
What were the findings of the above treatment/examination: _____

What treatment/therapy and medication regimen are you prescribing? Please indicate frequency and expected duration of treatment, *etc.*:
_____
_____

Physician's signature: _____   Date: _____
Physician's name (please print): _____   Telephone No.: _____
Address: _____   Fax No.: _____
Thank you for this information. It is essential to our efforts of safely returning employees back to work.

Company XYZ Disability Case Manager

---

[18]   Adapted from: OEM Health Information Inc., in "Physician's Statement of Medical Status, IB-16" *OEM Occupational Health and Safety Manual* (Beverley, MA: The OEM Press, 1996).

Form 6: Return-to-Work Report[19]
(For use by Occupational Health Professional)

COMPANY XYZ
LOGO/ADDRESS

Employee Name: (print last, first, middle) _____
Employee Number: _____

I hereby authorize my attending physician to release any information or copies thereof acquired in the course of examination or treatment for the injury/illness identified below to my employer or their representative.
Employee Signature: _____ Date: _____

To be completed by personal physician:
Employee diagnosis: _____

Date of first injury/illness: _____
Date of latest visit/treatment: _____
Date last worked: _____
Current medical status:
☐ Recovered (may return to work with no limitations on _____ date).
☐ May return to work with the following limitations:* _____

*These limitations   or until employee is
are in effect until: _____   reevaluated on: _____
                       (date)   (date)
☐ Employee remains totally incapacitated at the
   present time and will be reevaluated on: _____
                                              (date)
Physician's comments: _____

Physician's signature: _____ Date: _____
Physician's name: Telephone
(please print) _____   No.: _____
Address: _____ Fax No.: _____

Note: Both employee and physician must complete form.

---

[19]   Adapted from: OEM Health Information Inc., "Return-to-Work Notification: Report to Employer, IB-19" in *OEM Occupational Health and Safety Manual* (Beverly, MA: The OEM Press, 1996).

Form 7: Consent Form

```
┌─────────────────────────┐
│ COMPANY XYZ             │
│ LOGO/ADDRESS            │
└─────────────────────────┘
```

I hereby authorize all physicians, practitioners, hospitals and other institutions by this form or photographic copy thereof to give Company XYZ's representatives, The Occupational Health Services, for inclusion in medical files, any information they may have regarding the status of my health when I was under observation for my disability.

_____   _____

Employee Signature   Date

Please note that all information received will be kept in STRICT CONFIDENCE and will be used for adjudication, rehabilitation and return to work purposes.

CHAPTER REFERENCES

Alberta Medical Association (AMA), *An Information Sheet for Patients: Early Return to Work After Illness or Injury* (Edmonton: AMA, 1994), available online at <http://www.albertadoctors.org/bcm/ama/ama-website.nsf/frmHome?Openfrm>.

CAN/CSA, *The Model Code for the Protection of Personal Information*, (CAN/CSA - Q830-96) (Ottawa: CSA, 1996).

Canadian Medical Association (CMA), *The Physician's Role in Helping Patients Return to Work After an Illness or Injury* (update 2000), available online at <http://policybase.cma.ca/dbtw-wpd/exec/dbtwpub.dll>.

Case Management Society of America (CMSA), *Standards of Practice for Case Management* (Little Rock: CMSA, 1995).

D. DiBenedetto *et al.*, *OEM Occupational Health and Safety Manual* (Boston: OEM Press, 1996).

A. Legault *et al.*, "How to Cope with Absenteeism, Part IV: Requesting a Medical Opinion" (1996), Focus on Canadian Employment and Equality Rights at 126–128.

OEM Health Information Inc., "Physician's Statement of Medical Status, IB-16" in *OEM Occupational Health and Safety Manual* (Bevery, MA: The OEM Press, 1996).

OEM Health Information Inc., "Restricted Work Form IB-21" in *OEM Occupational Health and Safety Manual* (Bevery, MA: The OEM Press, 1996).

OEM Health Information Inc., "Return-to-Work Notification: Report to Employer, IB-19" in *OEM Occupational Health and Safety Manual* (Bevery, MA: The OEM Press, 1996).

Ontario Medical Association (OMA), *Position Paper: OMA Position Papers in Support of Timely Return to Work Programs and the Role of the Primary Care Physician* (Toronto: OMA, 1994).

Petro-Canada, "Confidentiality Code of Practice, Reference Number 130 in *Occupational Health Manual* (Calgary: Petro-Canada, 1994).

L. Ydreos, "Medical Status Report Forms" (Presented at the Absenteeism and Disability Management Seminar, Toronto, 9-10 May 1995) [unpublished].

Chapter 12

Prevention of Workplace Illness and Injury

INTRODUCTION

Organizations vary in the degree of coordination that exists between the Disability Management Program and other company programs such as the Employee Assistance Program, Occupational Health and Safety Program, Workplace Wellness Program and human resources management practices. Some function independently as "silos" while others are integrated to form a comprehensive workplace support system. This chapter supports the latter approach.

ROLE OF EMPLOYEE ASSISTANCE PROGRAMS IN THE PREVENTION OF WORKPLACE ILLNESS AND INJURY

Employee Assistance Program professionals can assist the employees and the organizations they serve by focusing on attendance and disability management. Work-related injuries, illnesses and disabilities drain millions of dollars from the Canadian economy, not to mention the toll exacted on individual employees and their families.

In Chapter 8, the role of the Employee Assistance Programs in disability management was discussed in detail. Chapter 10 described attendance support and required links to a company Employee Assistance Program. However, the Employee Assistance Program can provide other services such as:

- critical incident stress debriefing following a tragedy within the workplace or community;
- assistance with identifying and addressing the contributing causes of workplace accidents/injuries. Some contributing causes are employee fatigue, grief, preoccupation with personal problems or workplace discord, dysfunctional workgroups, substance abuse, *etc.*;
- development and presentation of both workplace and personal change management seminars;
- coaching clinics for supervisory staff on how to deal with the troubled employee, developing people skills or understanding the impact that home situations can have on employees and workgroups; and

- coaching clinics for management on the effect that various management practices can have on the workplace and employees.

ROLE OF OCCUPATIONAL HEALTH AND SAFETY IN DISABILITY MANAGEMENT

"Workers' compensation costs are significant, and there are substantial other costs that are incurred when an injury/illness occurs. The sum of these add directly to operational costs and hence profits".[1] For example, in 2001 the average workers' compensation cost for work-related injury in Ontario, Canada was $59,000. If a company has a 10% profit margin, it requires $590,000 in sales to cover these injury costs. The message presented in Business Results Through Health & Safety is that Occupational Health and Safety Programs have an important role to play in the prevention of workplace illness or injuries. Typically, prevention strategies are achieved through:

- developing occupational health and safety standards;
- providing occupational health and safety training for everyone in the workplace, particularly supervisors, managers and employers;
- providing and maintaining personal protective equipment and fit-testing;
- enabling ergonomic accommodations to be made;
- conducting worksite walk-through assessments;
- auditing workplace practices;
- responding, reporting and investigating occupational illness/injuries;
- tracking workplace illness/injuries; and
- enabling workplace safety to become part of the fabric of the work, as opposed to being seen as a program.

An effective Occupational Health and Safety Program can result in a "zero tolerance" for occupational injuries or illness. In addition, many elements of an Occupational Health and Safety Program are legislated, either federally or provincially. When an Occupational Health and Safety Program operates in conjunction with a Disability Management Program, synergies can be realized. For example, an existing Joint Health and Safety Committee can be used to address some Disability Management issues, such as return-to-work practices, modified work opportunities, and workplace hazard risk reduction.

Recently, occupational health and safety services have focused on off-the-job safety. This has been in response to the fact that for every workplace illness or injury, eight to 14 non-occupational illnesses or injuries occur. Some of the

---

[1] Workplace Safety & Insurance Board (WSIB), *Business Results Through Health & Safety* (Toronto ON: WSIB, 2002) at 3, available online at: <http://www.wsib.on.ca/wsib/wsibsite.nsf/ LookupFiles/DownloadableFileBusinessResultsThroughHealth&Safety/$File/Biz.pdf>.

off-the-job safety initiatives have included home safety, sport safety, water safety, cycling safety, fire prevention and sun safety.

ROLE OF WORKPLACE WELLNESS IN DISABILITY MANAGEMENT[2]

Workplace wellness can be viewed as having two key elements — organizational wellness and personal wellness. Organizational wellness involves managing both business functions and employee well-being in a manner that allows the organization to be more resistant to environmental pressures. Personal wellness involves managing both psychological and physical issues in response to environmental stress, including the work environment. These two forms of wellness are interdependent. For example, in companies where employee morale is low, the rates of unscheduled absence are 50% higher than in companies with good employee morale.[3]

Integration of Workplace Wellness

Some human resources leaders shy away from workplace wellness because of the vagueness of the topic and the anticipated extra costs. However, Canadian organizations tend to have most of the workplace wellness components in place. For example, over 80% of Canadian companies with 500 or more employees have Employee Assistance Programs.[4] In the United States, 85% of medium to large sized companies surveyed had smoke-free workplaces; 78% put out wellness newsletters; 76% had Health Risk Assessments (HRA) with blood pressure tests and cholesterol testing; 50% hosted health fairs; 48% had employer-sponsored sports; 41% had employer-owned fitness facilities; 39% had financial incentive programs for smoking cessation and weight control programs; 33% had discounted fitness facilities; and 25% offered HRA surveys to their employees.[5]

It is ironic that, although companies have some of these workplace wellness components, the various programs such as the Employee Assistance Program, Occupational Health and Safety Program and human resources supports tend to be disjointed, operating in isolation and focusing solely on individual goals. There is no overall scheme in place for workplace wellness with concrete

---

[2] Adapted from D. Dyck, "Workplace Wellness: What is Your Potential Return on Investment?" *Human Resources Association of Calgary: A Newsletter on Human Resources Management* (November 1998). Adapted with permission from D. Dyck, "Wrapping Up the Wellness Package", *Benefits Canada* (January 1999) at 16-20.

[3] CCH Incorporated, "Unscheduled Absenteeism Rises to Five-Year High", *Human Resources Management Ideas & Trends* (6 October 2005, Issue No. 616).

[4] Conference Board of Canada, *Compensation Planning Outlook* (Ottawa: Conference Board of Canada, 1997).

[5] Hewitt, "Health Promotion Programs on the Increase", *Aon Comments* (2 September 1996).

measures and expected targets. The opportunity for collective synergy and for demonstrating a return on investment is missed. The challenge for companies is not to find the resources to implement programs, but rather, to integrate the existing components under the umbrella of workplace wellness and to channel efforts and outcomes to meet business needs.

The following workplace wellness model (Figure 12.1) was designed by Aon Consulting Inc. and the City of Calgary to graphically display workplace wellness, what it involves, and how it functions.

In this model, organizational wellness, and employee and family wellness operate side-by-side and are linked through a partnership approach. Open communication, proactivity, timely interventions and ongoing measurement focus the Workplace Wellness Program on employee and organizational well-being. Outcome measures for both employee and organizational wellness are geared towards productivity, effectiveness, efficiency, "value addedness" and profitability and resource optimization.

Prior to the introduction of a Workplace Wellness Program, baseline data should be obtained for the outcome measures that are to be used. Targets based on health promotion research can then be set for each measure. Achievements should be assessed regularly to determine whether the process is meeting its established objectives. The Workplace Wellness Program should be aligned with and be part of the existing corporate business strategy. As well, the Workplace Wellness Program should have long-term, mid-range and short-term goals to justify and sustain its existence.

WHY CONSIDER IMPLEMENTING A WORKPLACE WELLNESS STRATEGY?

Companies that focus on reactive business health culture approaches (*i.e.*, dealing with attendance and disability rates and costs; accident rates and costs; Employee Assistance Program utilization rates and costs and/or staff turnover rates and costs), tend to focus resources and energies on "failure costs".

However, detective and preventive business health culture approaches can positively impact an organization's business outcomes. By definition, detection activities focus on identifying workplace concerns and issues before they become problematic. Organizational climate evaluation, health and safety audits, employee health risk appraisals, pre-placement screenings, and incident or "near-miss" investigations are some examples of detection activities.

On the other hand, prevention activities focus on addressing and eliminating the identified concerns and issues so that they do not lead to health problems. Traditionally, fitness programs, nutrition counselling, smoking cessation, stress management, on and off the job safety training, immunization and financial planning have been examples of workplace prevention initiatives. However, a study conducted by Aon Consulting in 1999 has shown that high performance leadership, communication, support of work-personal life balance, meaningful participation in and control over one's work and development of effective interpersonal skills can also help avoid workplace "failures" (*i.e.*, the failure of an employer to respond to the needs of its employees resulting in an accident).

In essence, organizations should approach health as an investment rather than a cost. Judicious investment in detection and prevention can significantly reduce "failure" costs. Research has shown that companies that focus on detection and prevention activities realize lower "failure" costs.[6]

Figure 12.1: Workplace Wellness Model

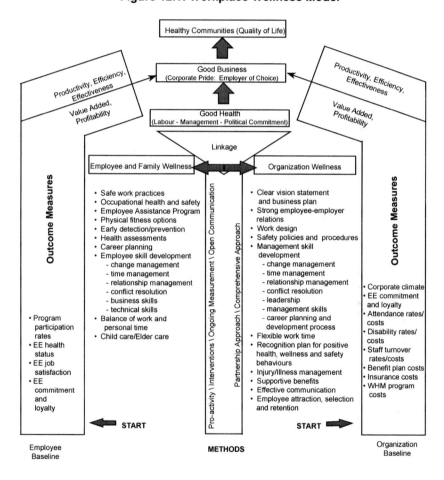

---

[6]   D. Pratt, *Competitiveness and Corporate Health Promotion: The Role of Management Control* (Graduate paper in Management Accounting, University of Western Ontario Business School, 1992) [unpublished].

A BUSINESS CASE FOR WORKPLACE WELLNESS

A business case for a Workplace Wellness Program should focus on demonstrating the positive impact that a Workplace Wellness Program can have on the "bottom-line". This means examining a number of outcome measures when establishing what return on investment a Workplace Wellness Program can offer. These outcome measures include:

- the status of the corporate climate/culture;
- level of employee commitment and loyalty;
- level of employee job satisfaction;
- participation rate in various programs;
- attendance rates and costs;
- disability rates and costs;
- staff turnover and costs;
- benefit costs;
- insurance premiums and costs; and
- costs required to implement a Workplace Wellness Program.

According to Danielle Pratt, President, Healthy Business Inc., Calgary, Alberta, the required themes in a business case for workplace wellness are:

- the impact of health, safety and wellness problems on the company's effectiveness;
- the projected impact of doing nothing to address problems and how doing nothing will affect future costs, organizational resilience, employee morale and corporate culture;
- the magnitude of the potential improvement, which can be achieved by implementing workplace wellness best practices; and
- the opportunity to achieve a level of excellence in employee health, safety and wellness. High organizational performance can be achieved.[7]

In his work on workplace health and well-being, Dr. Martin Shain, University of Toronto, reinforces the need to link workplace wellness with corporate business strategy.[8] He has developed a Business Health Culture Index (BHCI) which is based on the relationship between job stressors (demand and pressure versus effort and fatigue) and job satisfiers (recognition and reward versus control).

The BHCI is a summary indicator of the extent to which the *health culture* of an organization supports its *business objectives*. It provides a simple basis for conceptualizing workplace health cultures as "business-positive", "business-neutral" or "business-negative". Business-negative health cultures actively

---

[7] *Ibid.*

[8] M. Shain, "Managing Stress at its Source in the Workplace" (Presented at the Health Work and Wellness Conference '98, Whistler, BC, 27-30 September 1998) [unpublished].

obstruct the achievement of business objectives. Business-positive cultures facilitate the achievement of business objectives and business-neutral cultures have no impact on business objectives.

The BHCI has the potential to yield benchmarks. Internally it provides a baseline for action plans aimed at abating job stressors and enhancing job satisfiers. For example, a Workplace Wellness Program objective may be to move the organization from a BHCI of 0.96 to one of 1.5, signalling an important shift in the ratio between workplace stress and job satisfaction. Externally, the index can provide a basis for comparisons within industry sectors, such as municipalities, hospitals, school settings, manufacturers, *etc.*

Measurement tools, such as corporate climate surveys, employee commitment (loyalty) surveys, rates of program utilization/participation, job satisfaction surveys, benefit rates and costs can be used to demonstrate the Workplace Wellness Program's influence on an organization's business objectives.

INDUSTRY FINDINGS

Many companies in Canada and the United States are now reporting Workplace Wellness Program outcomes. The cost of workplace wellness per employee per year varies depending on whether a comprehensive approach or a single program is presented. As well, costs vary according to the formulae used and variables perceived to be program costs and can range between $12 and $1,000 per employee per year.

As for the benefits noted from Workplace Wellness Programs, the following are a number of outcomes reported by a variety of companies:

- Canada Life developed a health promotion program in 1978 and had it independently evaluated over a 10-year period. The program showed a return of $6.85 on each corporate dollar invested: "Reduced employee turnover, greater productivity and decreased medical claims by participating employees were primarily cited as the benefits contributing to this economic and health success".[9]
- A review of worldwide wellness studies indicated that Canadian Workplace Wellness Programs realize a return on investment of between $1.95 and $3.75 per employee per dollar spent.[10]
- British employees who feel little or no control at work have a greater risk of heart disease — 50% more than those with executive positions. This study was conducted with 7,372 male and female British civil servants from 1985 to 1993.[11]

---

[9]   R. Kirby, "The ROI of Health Workplaces", *Canadian HR Reporter* (20 October 1997) at 31.

[10]   R. Shepard, *The High Cost of Sedentary Lifestyle* (Toronto: Government of Ontario, 1996).

[11]   *Supra*, note 6.

- Employees who smoke cost Canadian companies between $2,308 and $2,613 more per year than non-smoking employees. This is due to increased absenteeism, lost productivity and increased health and life insurance premiums.[12]
- According to a 1996 Conference Board of Canada survey of 400 Canadian employers, recent government cutbacks have resulted in a 25% increase in the cost of benefits. This cost is greater for employers who have health benefits for retirees.
- In 1996, Dr. Roy Shepard noted the effects of wellness on productivity as follows: "Up to half of the burden of medical costs could be prevented by changes in personal lifestyle. Physical activity in particular has the potential to reduce both acute and chronic demands on the medical care system, with a reduction in employee turnover, an increase in productivity, a reduction in absenteeism and a decreased risk in industrial injury".[13]
- The recent Wellness Survey by Buffett Taylor, 1996,[14] cited the top ten success markers of a wellness program as depicted in the following graph (Figure 12.2).

Figure 12.2: Effectiveness of a Wellness Program:
Top 10 Success Markers by Industry Sector
maximum score = 2990

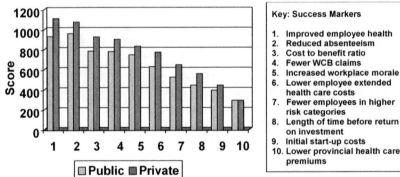

Key: Success Markers

1. Improved employee health
2. Reduced absenteeism
3. Cost to benefit ratio
4. Fewer WCB claims
5. Increased workplace morale
6. Lower employee extended health care costs
7. Fewer employees in higher risk categories
8. Length of time before return on investment
9. Initial start-up costs
10. Lower provincial health care premiums

THE ROLE OF THE HUMAN RESOURCE PROFESSIONAL

The Workplace Wellness Program model presented in this chapter (Figure 12.1) is a futuristic model. It was designed to encourage a partnership approach to employee well-being. Unlike past workplace health promotion models, it is

---

[12] *Supra*, note 9.
[13] Buffett Taylor, *The First Comprehensive Canadian Wellness Survey* (Toronto: Buffett Taylor & Associates Ltd., 1996).
[14] *Ibid.*

meant to encourage employee responsibility for wellness. The organization's role is to provide a receptive environment and support for positive health and well-being. However, the organizational goal is to achieve good business results through good health. In essence, workplace wellness is more than a service or a benefit, it is a management strategy.

Human resources personnel are well positioned to assist management with this business strategy. Human resources personnel can contribute to the Workplace Wellness Program by:

- determining the current status of workplace wellness efforts within a company;
- collecting objective outcome data (*i.e.*, attendance, staff retention, disability, benefit program and corporate culture data);
- influencing policies and procedures to improve employee and organizational health;
- developing a business case for workplace wellness; and
- evaluating the program outcomes.

Human resources personnel can also actively reinforce the idea that workplace wellness is a management issue — one that has cost drivers and expected outcomes.

CONCLUSION

For a Workplace Wellness Program to be effective it must:

- have "buy-in" by all stakeholders;
- be proactive in its approach;
- meet stakeholder needs;
- be aligned with the business strategy; and
- add value to the organization and employees in terms of effectiveness, efficiency, productivity and profitability (or resource optimization).

How companies implement a Workplace Wellness Program will vary depending on individual culture, business and needs. Regardless of implementation, workplace wellness has been demonstrated to be cost-effective and to be valued by employees and organizations alike. In short, "good health is good business".

POSITIONING OF THE DISABILITY MANAGEMENT, OCCUPATIONAL HEALTH AND SAFETY, EMPLOYEE ASSISTANCE AND WORKPLACE WELLNESS PROGRAMS

In most companies, the Occupational Health and Safety Program, Employee Assistance Program and Workplace Wellness Program tend to operate independently. These programs may be a mix of internally and externally resourced and operated programs. The result is a "silo" effect, with each program functioning in isolation and the opportunities to provide integrated services that can offer comprehensive programming and services, and to benefit from the activities and learning of each discipline and service are lost.

A few organizations have implemented integrated services. For example, The University of Calgary (1998) has combined the Staff Assistance Program (Employee Assistance Program), Managed Rehabilitation Program (Occupational Health Centre (OHC) dealing with attendance and disability management), and human resources support in its approach to wellness.[15] This service is integrated at a number of levels:

*   *Organizational Commitment* — support of key players (senior executive, leaders, unions, staff) and integration with policies and procedures.
*   *Team Approach* — appropriate sharing of information and cross referral of cases between OHC, Staff Assistance Program, human resources and the health care community.
*   *Case Management* — management of all cases associated with potential lost productivity (incidental absence, long-term disability, Workers' Compensation Board and short-term disability).

This approach has resulted in considerable savings for the University. In 1997, 3,785 days were saved with a $400,000 productivity recovery (cost avoidance). In 1998, 4,563 days were saved with a productivity recovery of $477,362. The return on investment (ROI) in the first year was roughly 1:1. However, for years two and three of this program, the ROI has been 2:1 — that is, for every dollar spent on the program $2.00 have been saved.[16]

Staff have responded positively to this approach, rating their level of satisfaction with the service as good-excellent (96.9%). As well, 100% indicated they would use the service again and would make referrals to peers, and 93.4% said that the presenting problem was improved.[17]

A second example is Petro-Canada. They have used an occupational health services model that integrates occupational health, disability management, occu-

---

[15] B. Daigle & G. Schick, "Early Intervention, Integration and Successful Resolution of Employee Health Issues" (Presented at the Health Work and Wellness Conference '98, Whistler, 27-30 September 1998) [unpublished].

[16] *Ibid.*

[17] *Ibid.*

pational safety, industrial hygiene, Employee Assistance Program, Workers' Compensation claims management and human resources practices for a number of years. The outcome is a comprehensive program that has low absenteeism and disability management costs.

Interestingly, more companies are integrating certain elements of their disability management programs. For example, in 2002, 62% of American employers reported using a consistent approach to managing occupational and non-occupational return-to-work programs. This was a 32% increase over 2001. Fifty-one percent had integrated their STD and LTD coverage, an increase of 39% from 2001.[18] As companies recognize the financial and administrative benefits of integrated services, the expectation is that they will opt for this approach.

ADMINISTRATION OF DISABILITY MANAGEMENT PROGRAMS

Typically, the Disability Management Program is operated independent of the Employee Assistance Program. This feature does not vary by industry sector, rather by the philosophies and preferred practices of the service providers involved.

The more progressive organizations link human resources, Disability Management Program and Employee Assistance Program services. Ideally, the human resources professional refers the employee to the Employee Assistance Program and the Employee Assistance Program assesses the attendance problem and either counsels the employee, or refers for appropriate assistance. If a health issue exists, then the Employee Assistance Program would refer the employee to the Disability Management Program for help. This arrangement will also work if the initial point of contact comes through either the Disability Management Program or Employee Assistance Program.

However, the following issues exist:

1. Not all Disability Case Managers are familiar or comfortable with attendance management practices and their potential role in the corrective counselling process. Disability Case Managers are well-positioned to support the employee and supervisors with health-related issues if they are part of the reason for the employee's absence.
2. Not all Employee Assistance Program, disability management, human resources personnel understand how to address an attendance problem. Many service providers need coaching on this practice.

---

[18]   Marsh Risk Consulting, *Workforce Risk: Fourth Annual Marsh Mercer Survey on Employers' Time-Off & Disability Programs* (2003), online: <http://www.marshriskconsulting.com/st/ PDEv_C_371_SC228135_NR_306_Pl_347745.htm>.

3.   Many organizations fail to have systems that allow for the Human
       Resources-Disability Management Program-Employee Assistance Pro-
       gram linkages. To function, a workable structure, process and method of
       outcome measurement is needed. This translates to a system in which
       there is clarity of roles and processes; availability of consents for informa-
       tion exchange; identified performance measures and targeted outcomes;
       and follow-up mechanisms.

There is less of a difference in program structure by nature of the industry
sector than there is by level of awareness of an organization's attendance and
disability rates and costs. Organizations that know the cost of employee absence
and disability tend to be far more interested in using an integrated approach to
managing employee attendance and disability.

LINKS TO MANAGEMENT PRACTICES AND HUMAN RESOURCE MANAGEMENT THEORIES

Until recently, organizations have focused on program issues when trying to
understand attendance and disability management program outcomes. However,
current research indicates that management practices and human resource management theories can have a significant impact on Disability Management Program outcomes. This section will deal with the relevance of management practices and human resource management theories in attendance and disability
management.

Stress Risk Management in the Workplace: Research by Dr. Martin Shain, University of Toronto[19]

Job-related stress results from human interactions in the workplace. It needs to
be managed like production and operational activity. It is up to management to
address job stress at the source instead of dealing solely with the symptoms of
job stress through the Employee Assistance Program, Disability Management
Program and Occupational Health and Safety Program. This can best be
achieved by balancing the organizational and programmatic approaches to stress
risk management.

The key ingredients for good employee mental health in the workplace are:

*   mutual respect and appreciation;
*   employee's feeling heard and appreciated;
*   open communication;

---

[19]   M. Shain, "Managing Stress at its Source in the Workplace" (Presented at the Health Work and
       Wellness Conference '98, Whistler, 27-30 September 1998) [unpublished].

- freedom from feelings of hostility and anger; and
- a sense of self-worth and confidence.[20]

The work factors that threaten employee mental health and physical safety and contribute to workplace stress are:

- work overload and time pressures;
- lack of influence over daily work;
- too many changes within the job;
- lack of training and/or job preparation;
- too little or too much responsibility;
- discrimination;
- harassment;
- poor communication;
- lack of quality supervision/management; and
- neglect of legal and safety obligations.[21]

Excess workplace stress can erode employee self-efficacy and social supports — both key elements to employee well-being. In their book *Healthy Work: Stress, Productivity and the Reconstruction of Working Life,*[22] Robert Karasek and Tores Theorell identified the combination of high pressure (too much work in too short a period of time) and lack of influence over day-to-day work as a key contributor to cardiovascular disease. This "deadly duo" also threatens people's health by making it harder for them to take care of themselves. Getting too little exercise, smoking and drinking too much, poor nutrition, insomnia or hypersomnia and sleeping badly and feeling generally out of control and miserable are a few of the signs that stress is becoming disruptive.

A 24-year study of workers found that workers in low-control jobs are 43% more prone to premature death; likewise those in jobs lacking meaningful content tend to take greater risks. This study is consistent with the Whitehall studies of British civil servants. Workers with less decision-making latitude died sooner from heart disease and other similar ailments.[23]

Overwhelming pressure and lack of influence do not occur by chance. They result directly from how work is organized (*i.e.*, the allocation of work and relationship between employees) and how it is designed (the structure and content of work). The organization and design of work are dictated by both the job's technological requirements and human decisions. These two factors determine how employees relate to one another and to their jobs; they also contribute to the increase

---

[20] *Ibid.*

[21] *Ibid.*

[22] R. Karasek & T. Theorell, *Healthy Work: Stress, Productivity and the Reconstruction of Working Life* (Toronto: Harper Collins, 1992).

[23] Editor, "Low-control jobs are hazardous to health", *O.H.S. Canada* (July/August, 2002).

or decrease of stress levels and have an important impact on mental and physical health (Figure 12.3). When stress from other sources — especially the home — is thrown into the equation, health is even more likely to be adversely affected.

Figure 12.3: Organization and Design of Work[24]

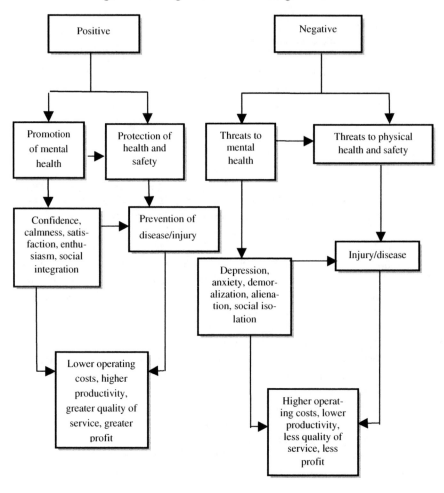

It is not simply a matter of benefiting the "weak" by increasing their resiliency to stress. It is an issue of work conditions that can be modified to manage the risks of job-related stress.

[24] M. Shain, "A New Take on Stress: Strategies that Work", *Health Policy Forum* (November 1997) at 12.

In April 1998, the Families and Work Institute released a study that supports Dr. Shain's work.[25] It found that productivity is far more likely to be hurt by job-related stress than by family problems. Until recently, organizations tended to focus on helping employees to address family problems to improve productivity. The Families and Work Institute study revealed that pay and benefits are far less important to workers than the quality of work and supportiveness of the organization.

A study by MacMillian-Bloedel, British Columbia[26] showed that job stress due to high employee effort and low reward, coupled with home stress can lead to anger and a sense of unfairness. This anger can manifest in two ways: overtly in the form of conflict (*e.g.*, workplace/home violence, road rage, sabotage); or covertly in the form of substance abuse. Anger caused by the discrepancy between effort and compensation can cause workplace injuries. Workplace injuries will occur if the employee perceives that he or she is unable to control or avoid hazards. Overt and covert anger due to work conditions end up increasing employee absenteeism and disability.

An organization can have a positive influence on the workforce and workplace outcomes by promoting good mental health and protecting employees from injury and illness. This is described as an "upstream" approach — dealing with the root causes instead of the symptoms of the problem.

Dr. Shain notes that management can have a positive influence on the health and well-being of employees as well as the Occupational Health and Safety Program outcomes.[27] Dr. Shain calls the influence of management on well-being the Zone of Management Discretion, which is not paternalistic towards employees, but rather focuses on prevention (Figure 12.4).

Dr. Shain also supports management recognition and control of threats to employee well-being such as high energy and effort output, high job demands, low recognition for work done and little control over the job. The last two conditions are easily changed. Employees should actively help the organization lower risks and increase mental health benefits. Being part of the problem helps people to determine workable solutions and to own the remediation when introduced.

---

[25] M. Jackson, "Worker Squeeze: Employee Stress Cuts Productivity, Study Declares", *Calgary Herald* (15 April 1998) A5.

[26] M. Shain, "Stress, Satisfaction and Health at Work: Tuning for Performance (Presented at the Health & Wellness Conference '99, Vancouver, 24-27 October 1999) [unpublished].

[27] *Ibid.*

Figure 12.4: The Health Differential[28]
Technological Determinants Versus Management
as Influences on Employee Health

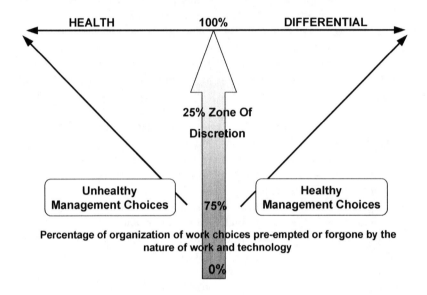

Dr. Shain promotes management prevention of the harmful consequences of stress. He presented a Best Practice model at the 1998 Work, Health and Wellness Conference (Figure 12.5).

Most human resources managers are unaware of the magnitude of stress risk and hazards in the workplace. By identifying stress risks, they can then have a positive impact on reducing employee absenteeism and disability. To improve employee health, managers must:

- encourage two-way communication with employees;
- articulate and communicate a clear vision for the future;
- train employees in new competencies and capabilities for success;
- articulate the desired organizational culture;
- re-engineer work processes to meet current demands;
- encourage employees to challenge the status quo;
- develop change management competencies of leaders; and
- educate managers/supervisors to be more sensitive to employee concerns.

---

[28] *Supra*, note 19.

Figure 12.5: Physical and Psychosocial Hazards[29]
(A Combined Forces Approach to Hazard Abatement)

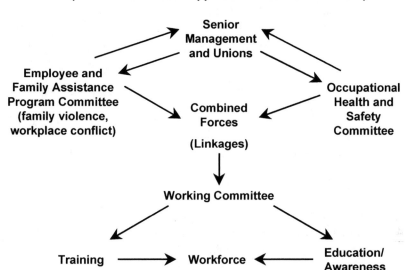

Supportive Versus Punitive Attendance Management Programs

Attendance management programs that are more punitive than supportive in their focus of regular employee attendance tend to fail at meeting the anticipated program outcomes.

Dr. Lawrence Kelly[30] recommends attendance management programs that focus on employee well-being and support regular attendance. This means having employee assistance, ergonomic, return-to-work, eldercare, childcare, and flex time programs in place to assist the employee in balancing work and home life issues and responsibilities.

The concept of a supportive attendance program is described in more detail in Chapter 10.

Recognition of the Importance of Personal and Family Life

In 2000, Aon conducted the *Canada@Work*[31] study to investigate the organizational factors and conditions that build strong workforce commitment. This

---

[29] *Ibid.*
[30] L. Kelly, "Attendance Management" (Presented at the Alberta Occupational Health Nurses 21st Annual Conference, Calgary 24-26 May 1998) [unpublished].
[31] Aon Consulting Inc., *Canada@Work* (Chicago: Aon Group, 2000).

survey provided a unique source of information on employees and the effectiveness of various human resources and organizational practices. A similar study was produced a year earlier in the United States – *America @ Work.*[32]

Employees who give their best to an organization and help to meet the business goals are characterized as *committed*. How are they recognized? The survey found that these employees:

- work hard to improve themselves, increasing their value to the employer, and make personal sacrifices to ensure the organization's success;
- recommend their company as a good place to work, and their employer's products and services as valuable; and
- believe that their workplace is one of the best around, and intend to stay.

What are the drivers of employee commitment? The study found the following:

- employees who believe that management recognizes the importance of their personal and family lives are committed employees;
- most committed employees believe they have benefits that meet their needs and are fairly paid;
- employers of committed employees communicate more effectively about a variety of topics: employee benefits, compensation and change initiatives; and
- employers of committed employees provide training to help employees remain current with the increased technical demands of today's jobs.

The study also noted that stress plays a major role in reduced employee commitment. Stress can be attributed to the difficulty in balancing the conflicting demands of work and personal and family life. An appreciation of the importance of employee personal and family life will result in increased productivity and the resulting increased profitability.

FAMILY-FRIENDLY POLICIES

Attracting, retaining and motivating the best people is a challenge for most organizations. For this reason programs need to be created that recognize the needs of individuals and diverse family situations. Employers note that flexible scheduling is one of the most important recruiting tools. Studies indicate that flexible work programs lower employee stress levels.[33] As well, providing

---

[32]   Aon Consulting Inc., *America@Work: An Overview of Employee Commitment in America* (Chicago: Aon Group, 1999).

[33]   Conference Board of Canada, News Release, "Eldercare Taking its Toll on Canadian Workers", (10 November 1999); HRM, "Flexible Working Reduces Absenteeism" (12 July 2001), online: <http://www.HRM.co.uk>.

support for employees and families can translate into decreased absenteeism and tardiness.

Women, who are a significant part of today's workforce, have traditionally been the caregivers in their family. Although men are assuming more childcare responsibilities today, women remain the major caregivers. The pressure of juggling work and family tasks is strongly associated with the stress employees perceive in their lives. In general, work-family stress stems from two sources:

- *role interference* — the roles played by individuals overlap and conflict; and
- *role overload* — the daily work-family tasks are simply too much for one individual to handle.

Role interference and role overload can make life very difficult for the employee and, indirectly, for the employer.

A study done in the early 1990s by the Conference Board of Canada indicated that nearly one third of employees reported experiencing stress or anxiety as a result of balancing work and family life responsibilities. At that time, Statistics Canada estimated that stress-related disorders due to overwork cost Canadian businesses $15 billion per year. However, data from the 1999 CCH Unscheduled Absences Survey shows a significant increase in absenteeism due to worker stress. Personal illness and family issues were the most cited reasons for last minute absences.[34] In 1999, a Health Canada study reported that 40% of working Canadians experienced high levels of work-family conflict. For women, this conflict was especially acute.[35] However, work-life programs, flexible work hours, and paid time off programs had positive effects on reducing last minute absences.[36]

Obviously, a workplace that affords employees the flexibility to balance work and personal commitments can significantly reduce stress while enhancing business objectives.

OPTIONS FOR THE FAMILY-RESPONSIVE WORKPLACE

Making the workplace family-friendly involves much more than implementing a set of programs designed to address one or two issues. Helping workers cope with work and family demands involves a strategic commitment to engage in a comprehensive transformation of the workplace culture.

This reconfiguration of the workplace involves changes in attitude as well as clearly articulated program goals, preferably linked to the organization's strategic plan. Achieving this *is no easy task and the process takes time.* Although

---

[34] CCH, "Special Report: 1999 CCH Unscheduled Absences Survey" (1999), 467 Human Resource Management: Ideas and Trends at 149-155.

[35] Human Resources Development Canada, Labour Program, "Business Case for Work-Life Balance (Benefits & Costs)" (2002).

[36] *Ibid.*

research shows that there are positive relationships between work and family programming and the bottom line, such evidence fails to convince leaders who do not believe in this new role for business. This can require a quantum leap in management attitudes and belief systems.

In order to create a family-responsive workplace, management must:

(a)   determine employee needs; and
(b)   tailor incentives to meet those needs.

Although this sounds elementary, many Canadian employers (over 60%) have not created family-responsive workplaces.

What can an employer do to help employees balance work and family life? In general, offer or promote:

- flexible work arrangements;
- flexible work time — job sharing, compressed work week, shorter work week, shorter workday;
- changes where employees work;
- childcare assistance — information and referral assistance, on-site daycare, family home care, emergency/sick-child care, daycare subsidy;
- eldercare assistance;
- Employee Assistance Program;
- a change in the corporate culture — the attitudes, practices, values and relationships within the organization that impact family-friendly practices. This includes belief in the legitimacy of work-family policies and practices as part of the workplace, available policies and procedures, supervisory understanding of the issues, flexibility in dealing with situations, to name a few.

There is an incontestable relationship between work and family-related stresses, and workplace productivity, absenteeism and staff turnover. For example, a recent survey on workplace absence showed that absence rates fell from eight to 6.5 days per employee when companies introduced flexible annual leave, flexible work hours and the ability to work from home occasionally.[37] Organizations can realize improvements by making decisions on specific options and methods of implementation that will help employees alleviate some of these pressures.

Supportive Infrastructure for the Disability Management Program

A supportive infrastructure is the system and environment within which a Disability Management Program operates. It encompasses the corporate culture,

---

[37]   HRM, "Flexible Working Reduces Absenteeism" (12 July 2001), available online at: <http://www.hrmguide.co.uk/flexibility/flexibility_absenteeism.htm>.

attendance and disability-related policies and procedures, benefit plans and linkages between the Disability Management Program and other organizational resources.

CORPORATE CULTURE

The corporate culture consists of learned values, assumptions and behaviours that convey a sense of identity for employees and management. It acts to encourage employee commitment, organizational stability and desired behaviours.

Depending on the nature of the corporate culture, employees and management may be receptive to:

- helping each other;
- looking for innovative ways to accommodate recovering employees back into the workplace;
- taking risks on certain workplace rehabilitation approaches; or
- implementing benefit plans that encourage a return to employability for the ill/injured employee.

As well, the corporate culture dictates what type of Disability Management Program model will be adopted. For instance, a paternalistic culture tends to adopt a model that is more organizational-operated and directed. Here, the onus for the person's successful return to work is assumed by the organization. This is typical of the more traditional models of attendance and disability management. On the other hand, a democratic corporate culture tends to encourage employee responsibility for absence and successful return to work. In this model, the organization works with the employee to affect a successful rehabilitation plan leaving the employee ultimately in control of his or her situation. This is exemplified by the direct case management model for attendance and disability management.

In a more subtle fashion, the corporate culture affects occupational bonding. As already mentioned, occupational bonding is a mutually beneficial relationship between the employee and the employer. When an organization has a corporate culture that promotes pride in belonging to the organization and that adheres to a strong work ethic, employees are more likely to see personal value in belonging to the social group and in working for the organization. They are less likely to be absent, except for valid reasons, and more likely to return to work as soon as possible. In this instance, the occupational bond is difficult to break.

However, the reverse can also be true. When employees do not experience corporate pride, a sense of belonging, or a feeling of adding value to the organization, the occupational bond is easy to break and remaining off work on disability is more likely.

To attain a successful attendance and Disability Management Program, the corporate culture should value the employee and convey the message that all employees are valuable and that absence from the workplace is of great concern.

Policies and Procedures

Corporate policies and procedures reflect management's attitude and values regarding attendance and disability management establish the parameters for the attendance and disability management practice and promote equal treatment for all employees. They are designed to facilitate the achievement of the established program goals. Chapter 3 addresses the required infrastructure for a Disability Management Program.

SUMMARY

By linking an organization's disability management efforts with its Employee Assistance Program, Occupational Health and Safety Program, and Workplace Wellness Program, and by recognizing the impact that management and human resource management theories can have on a workforce and workplace wellness, the opportunity to significantly reduce illness or injury incidence and impact exists. The challenge is to act on that knowledge in a proactive manner.

CHAPTER REFERENCES

Aon Consulting Inc., *America @Work: An Overview of Employee Commitment in America* (Chicago: Aon Group, 1999).

Aon Consulting Inc., *Canada@Work* (Chicago: Aon Group, 2000)

CCH, "Special Report: 1999 CCH Unscheduled Absences Survey" (1999) 467 Human Resource Management: Ideas and Trends at 149-155.

CCH Incorporated, "Unscheduled Absenteeism Rises to Five-Year High", *Human Resources Management Ideas & Trends* (6 October 2005, Issue 616).

Conference Board of Canada, *Compensation Planning Outlook* (Ottawa: Conference Board of Canada, 1997).

Conference Board of Canada, News Release, "Eldercare Taking its Toll on Canadian Workers" (10 November 1999).

B. Daigle & G. Schick, "Early Intervention, Integration and Successful Resolution of Employee Health Issues" (Presented at the Health Work and Wellness Conference '98, Whistler, 27-30 September 1998).

D. Dyck, "Workplace Wellness: What is Your Potential Return on Investment?" *Human Resources Association of Calgary: A Newsletter on Human Resources Management* (November 1998).

D. Dyck, "Wrapping Up The Wellness Package", *Benefits Canada* (January 1999).

Editor, "Low-control jobs are hazardous to health", *O.H.S. Canada* (July/August, 2002) at 23.

Hewitt, "Health Promotion Programs on the Increase", *Aon Comments* (2 September 1996).

HRM, "Flexible Working Reduces Absenteeism" (12 July 2001), available online at: <http://www.hrmguide.co.uk/flexibility/flexibility_absenteeism.htm>.

Human Resources Development Canada, Labour Program, "Business Case for Work-Life Balance" (Benefits & Costs) (2002).

M. Jackson, "Worker Squeeze: Employee Stress Cuts Productivity, Study Declares" *Calgary Herald* (15 April 1998) A5.

R. Karasek & T. Theorell, *Healthy Work: Stress, Productivity and the Reconstruction of Working Life* (Toronto: Harper Collins, 1992).

L. Kelly, "Attendance Management" (Presented at the Alberta Occupational Health Nurses 21st Annual Conference, Calgary, 24-26 May 1998) [unpublished].

R. Kirby, "The ROI of Health Workplaces", *Canadian HR Reporter* (20 October 1997) at 31.

Marsh Risk Consulting, *Workforce Risk: Fourth Annual Marsh Mercer Survey on Employers' Time-Off & Disability Programs* (2003), online: <http://www.marshriskconsulting.com/st/PDEv_C_371_SC_228135_NR_306_Pl_347745.htm>.

D. Pratt, *Competitiveness and Corporate Health Promotion: The Role of Management Control* (Graduate paper in Management Accounting, University of Western Ontario Business School, 1992) [unpublished].

M. Shain, "A New Take on Stress: Strategies that Work", *Health Policy Forum* (November 1997) at 12.

M. Shain, "Managing Stress at its Source in the Workplace" (Presented at the Health Work and Wellness Conference '98, Whistler, BC, 27-30 September 1998) [unpublished].

M. Shain, "Stress, Satisfaction and Health at Work: Tuning for Performance" (Presented at the Health and Wellness Conference '99, Vancouver, 24-27 October 1999) [unpublished].

R. Shepard, *The High Cost of Sedentary Lifestyle* (Toronto: Government of Ontario, 1996).

Workplace, Safety & Insurance Board (WSIB), *Business Results Through Health & Safety* (Toronto, ON: WSIB, 2002) at 3, online: <http://www.wsib.on.ca/wsib/wsibsite.nsf/LookupFiles/DownloadableFileBusinessResultsThrough Health&Safety/$File/Biz.pdf>.

Chapter 13

Toxic Work Environments: Impact on Employee Illness/Injury[1]

INTRODUCTION

Over the years, occupational health and human resource personnel have witnessed the effects of organizational stressors on employee and manager health. Workers who perceive themselves as being "stressed":

- report making more mistakes;
- feel angry with their employers for creating the stressful situation; and
- resent their coworkers who they feel are not working as hard as they are, which can lead to a desire to leave the job.[2]

Overstressed workers also cost their employers 50% more in terms of health care expenditures, lost workdays, staff turnover costs[3] and accident costs.

Typically, the response is "What can we do? Things have been this way for years". The purpose of this chapter is to encourage understanding of the impact that a stressful, toxic work environment can have on both the employee and organization, and to present a plausible argument for initiating realistic workplace changes to help "break the cycle" of workplace stress and contain disability costs.

The bottom line is that workers vary in their tolerance of workloads. What is desirable for one worker is an intolerable level for another.[4] It is important for managers to understand the drivers of stress and to respect the individual differences of each employee in the workplace.

---

[1] Excerpts taken from: D. Dyck & T. Roithmayr, "Organizational Stressors and Health: How Occupational Health Nurses Can Help Break the Cycle" (2002), 50:5 AAOHN Journal at 213-219. Reprinted with permission from the AAOHN Journal.

[2] L. Duxbury & C. Higgins, "Wrestling with Workload: Organizational Strategies for Success", *Conference Board of Canada, Report* (May 2005) at 3.

[3] *Supra*, note 2 at 5.

[4] *Ibid.*, at 1.

HAVE ORGANIZATIONS BECOME TOXIC TO HUMAN LIFE?

In too many workplaces, the following things have happened, or are happening:

- Too many and conflicting priorities	- Employees experiencing frequent headaches, workplace accidents, anxiety attacks, ulcers, or high blood pressure	- Poor employee morale
- Lack of understanding about how performance is measured	- Employees reporting insomnia	- Workplace tension
		- High absenteeism
- Poor communications	- Employees experiencing irritability, anger, or depression	- Staff turnover
- Little or no feedback and recognition for work done	- Increased drug or alcohol abuse	- Rising employee benefit plan costs
		- Disappointing financial results

These three lists are causally-related and this relationship tends to have a destructive cycle. The cumulative effect of a multitude of organizational stressors manifests in deteriorating employee health, lost productivity and escalating disability and employee group benefit plan costs.[5]

For example, Dr. Martin Shain reports that employees who experience high stress due to high work effort and low reward (recognition), and high strain due to high work demands and limited control over their job, suffer a threefold increase in the incidence of heart problems, back pain, work/family conflicts, substance abuse, infections, mental health problems and injuries; and a fivefold increase in the incidence of certain cancers like colorectal cancer. Other studies have shown that employees who experience chronic low job control are more prone to premature death. The primary cause was cardiovascular in nature.[6]

The Conference Board of Canada's *Survey of Canadian Workers on Work-Life Balance* reports that high stress levels due to the difficulty of balancing the demands of work and personal commitments is associated with health problems and work absence. Respondents experiencing high stress miss twice as much work time as those who report being in low stress situations (7.2 versus 3.6 days absence).[7]

---

[5] R. Karasek & T. Theorell, *Healthy Work: Stress, Productivity and the Reconstruction of Working Life* (New York, NY: Basic Books Inc., 1992).

[6] J. Siegrist, "Adverse Health Effects of High-effort/Low-reward Conditions" (1996) 1:1 Journal of Occupational Health Psychology, at 27-41; B.B. Marmot *et al.*, "Contribution of Job Control and Other Risk Factors to Social Variations in Cardiovascular Heart Disease Incidence" (1997) 350 (9073) Lancet at 235-239; J. Johnson, "Long-term Psychological Work Environment and Cardiovascular Mortality among Swedish Men" (1996) 86:3 American Journal of Public Health at 324-331; A. LaCroix, *Occupational Exposure to High Demand/low Control Work and Coronary Heart Disease Incidence in the Framingham Cohort* (Ann Arbor, Mich: University of North Carolina, UMI Dissertation Services, 1984).

[7] Conference Board of Canada, *Survey of Canadian Workers on Work-Life Balance* (Ottawa: Conference Board of Canada, 1999).

According to a Health Canada survey (2003), employees who perceive that they have "too much to do in too little time" are:

- 5.6 times more likely to report high levels of job stress;
- 3.5 times more likely to experience high absenteeism rates due to emotional, physical or mental fatigue;
- 2.3 times more likely to report the intent to leave their current job; and
- 1.6 times more likely to have high absenteeism rates and to miss six or more days per year.[8]

Stress-related absences cost Canadian employers approximately $3.5 billion annually.[9] Workplace stress contributes to:

- 19% of absenteeism costs;
- 40% of staff turnover costs;
- 55% of Employee Assistance Program costs;
- 30% of STD and LTD costs;
- 60% of occupational incidents; and
- 10% of prescription drug plan costs.[10]

So what can be done? How can organizations eliminate or mitigate the impact of organizational stressors? Experts in the field recommend eliminating stress at its source:[11] "to achieve high levels of employee productivity, efficiency and morale, leading executives have learned that they need to address workplace health and wellness in an integrated fashion".[12] This can be done effectively by focusing on the environment in which the work is being done.

The following model provides insight into how to create a healthy and productive workforce through an integrated approach that enables employees to do their job and gain enjoyment and growth from the experience.

---

[8] L. Duxbury & C. Higgins, *Work-life Conflict in Canada in the New millennium: A Status Report* (prepared for Health Canada, Healthy Communities Division) (Ottawa: Health Canada, 2003), available online at: <http://www.phac-aspc.gc.ca/punlicat/work-travail/report2/>.

[9] Canadian Policy Research, reported in *IAPA: Creating Healthy Workplaces Everywhere – Healthy Workplace Week* (19 October 2005), available online at: <http://www.newswire.ca/en/releases/archive/October2005/19/c3209.html>.

[10] Chrysalis Performance Inc., reported in *IAPA: Creating Healthy Workplaces Everywhere – Healthy Workplace Week* (19 October 2005), available online at: <http://www.newswire.ca/en/releases/archive/October2005/19/c3209.html>.

[11] M. Shain, "Managing Stress at its Source in the Workplace" (Presented at the Health Work & Wellness Conference 1998, Whistler, B.C., 27-30 September 1998) [unpublished].

[12] K. Bachmann, *More Than Just Hard Hats and Safety Boots: Creating Healthier Work Environments* (Ottawa: Conference Board of Canada, 2000) at 1.

THE PERFORMANCE MAXIMIZER™ MODEL

We will start with some of the fundamental aspects about human performance in the workplace. To sustain success, organizations must provide a supportive environment that enables and supports employee performance in a variety of ways. Using The Performance Maximizer™ (Figure 13.1), we will examine the nature of a supportive work environment. This tool focuses on the factors that shape optimal human performance in the workplace. It describes, in a simple and memorable way, the conditions that exist when successful human performance occurs in the workplace.

Figure 13.1: The Performance Maximizer Model[13]

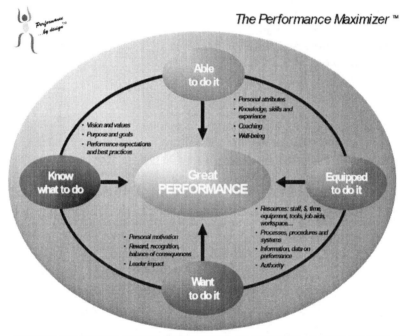

Simply stated, employees and work leaders need to jointly create conditions whereby everyone will:

- *Know* what to do
- be *Able* to do it
- be *Equipped* to do it
- *Want* to do it

---

[13]   T. Roithmayr, The Performance Maximizer™ (Calgary, AB: Performance by Design) available online at: <http://www.performance–bydesign.com>.

In the absence of these conditions, "organizational stressors" develop which cause problems with employee health and on-the-job performance, and ultimately, impact the organization's bottom line. The premise is that by focusing on the leading indicators for creating great human performance, lagging indicators such as employee absence, disability-related costs, reduced productivity and poor profits will gradually decrease.

ORGANIZATIONAL STRESSORS AND HEALTH

The essential elements of Organizational Stressors and Health are presented in Figure 13.2.[14] It describes a situation that requires human performance improvement techniques to solve formidable and serious business problems. Intuitively, we recognize that a causal relationship exists among the elements presented below. But, how does this model actually work?

The cycle begins and ends with organizational stressors, defined as the absence of the conditions that enable performance. (For a comprehensive list of stressors, see items 1 through 26 in the Organizational Stressors Survey, Figure 13.4). Following the arrows, the model illustrates how organizational stressors impact individuals and then, ultimately, organization performance.

Figure 13.2: Organizational Stressors and Health: Breaking the Toxic Cycle

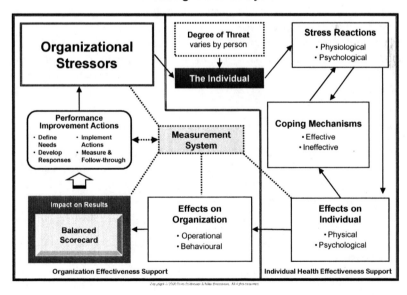

---

[14] T. Roithmayr, *Performance by Design* (2000).

Explanation of the Model

The cycle begins and ends with organizational stressors. Organizational stressors are defined as the absence of conditions that enable maximum performance. Starting with the individual (the employee), the elements include:

DEGREE OF THREAT

Sustained exposure to organizational stressors can impact even the most resilient of individuals.[15] The more stressors there are and the longer the duration of the exposure, the more likely that detrimental effects will occur.

In general, personal impact depends on individual strengths and social supports — personality, the degree of self-confidence, level of self-esteem, emotional well-being and personal support system all play a role in mitigating the effects of workplace stressors.

STRESS REACTIONS

Workplace stress produces stress reactions. Physiologically, there may be changes in blood pressure or cholesterol levels, heightened awareness of the environment, or increases in muscle tension. Psychologically, judgement may be impaired. The person may experience irritability, anxiety, anger, an inability to concentrate, or short-term memory loss.

Today, the estimate is that employees process 190 messages per day (voice mail, e-mail, faxes, *etc.*). This constant information processing and overloading can lead to increased stress.[16] As well, life in general is deemed to be more stressful that it was 30 years ago.[17]

A recent study indicates that 62% of workers report experiencing "a great deal of stress" at work. For 34% of workers, "stress has been so overwhelming that it has made me physically ill at times".[18] This is consistent with previous studies.[19]

COPING MECHANISMS

Everyone has individual ways of dealing with everyday stressors. Good communication and problem solving skills, regular exercise, relaxation and social sup-

[15]   R. Karasek & T. Theorell, *Healthy Work: Stress, Productivity and the Reconstruction of Working Life* (New York, NY: Basic Books Inc., 1992).

[16]   Conference Board of Canada, News Release, "Workplace Solutions for Stressed Out Workers" (7 September 1999).

[17]   B.A. Cryer, "Neutralizing Workplace Stress: The Physiology of Human Performance and Organizational Effectiveness" (Presented at the Psychological Disabilities in the Workplace: Prevention, Rehabilitation and Cost Control Conference, Toronto, 10-11 June 1996) [unpublished].

[18]   Aventis Pharma-Canada, *The Aventis Healthcare Survey* (2001).

[19]   *Supra*, note 15.

ports, as well as a variety of personal interests can serve to lessen the effects of stress. However, when stress is prolonged, many people respond in ineffective ways: avoidance, withdrawal, panic, or aggressive behaviour — even an increased use of drugs and alcohol. These ineffective coping mechanisms can temporarily help an individual deal with the stress of the moment, but can seriously impair physical and emotional health in the long run.

EFFECTS ON INDIVIDUALS

For years, health professionals have recognized the symptoms of workplace stress: headaches, ulcers, infections, hypertension, cardiovascular disease, substance abuse, anxiety, hostility and clinical depression.[20] However, society is just now beginning to appreciate the tremendous costs associated with workplace stress: productivity losses; human suffering; increased disability management and employee group benefit plan costs; and the enormous burden on our health care system.

Organizations are not solely responsible for the negative effects of organizational stress. However, when the average worker spends as much as two-thirds of his or her waking hours at work, or with concerns of work, it begs the question: What is the appropriate level of organizational responsibility?

- Three million Canadians suffer depressive episodes in any 12 month period
- One in four cases are detected and diagnosed
- Less than 7% are being properly treated
- North American price tag for direct costs and productivity losses is $60 billion annually[21]

INDIVIDUAL HEALTH EFFECTIVENESS SUPPORT (HEALTH AND WELLNESS PROGRAMS)

Our organizations and institutions are not typically uncaring, nor do they choose to deliberately ignore stress-related problems. Many of the workplace leaders are themselves affected. In response, organizations have put supportive services in place to help employees develop effective coping mechanisms, for example:

- Employee Assistance Programs (EAPs);
- Flexible Benefit Plans;

---

[20] Health Canada, *Best Advice on Stress Risk Management in the Workplace* (Ottawa: Minister of Public Works and Government Services Canada, 2000); J. Siegrist, "Adverse Health Effects of High-effort/Low-reward Conditions" (1996) 1:1, Journal of Occupational Health Psychology at 27-41.

[21] Centre for Addiction and Mental Health (2001), Research, CAMH homepage, available online at: <http://www.camh.net>.

- flexible work hours;
- Disability Management Programs;
- fitness centres or subsidies;
- exercise and relaxation programs;
- Child Care Services;
- Elder Care Services; and
- education programs.

ARE WE TREATING SYMPTOMS INSTEAD OF ROOT CAUSES?

No doubt, these good and very necessary employee support services do help the individual. However, should organizations address the "root causes" of workplace stress instead? We maintain that a significant causal factor is the organizational environment in which the employee works. In essence, many workplace environments are "toxic to human life".

In support of this premise, we will examine below the second part of this model, the organizational elements.

Effects on Organizations

The cost of workplace stress is not borne by employees alone. Organizations pay a huge price for the emotional mismanagement of their human capital (employees) in the form of increased operational and benefit expenses, and productivity losses.[22] Low morale, lack of cooperation, workplace conflict, apathy and hostility are some of the behavioural outcomes. The operational outcomes of this stressors cycle include high rates of employee absenteeism, staff turnover, productivity losses and increased employee benefit plan costs. In the final analysis, the overall result impacts the organization's "bottom line".

Measurement

Dealing with the causes can break this unfortunate "cycle of harm". To achieve this, an organization must truly understand what is going on. Measurement is the key.

Measurement enables an organization to make evidence-based decisions about which remedies will produce the desired improvements. This is not only about tracking EFAP usage, or monitoring drug plan usage, or counting union grievances, or determining the number of absent employees. Measurement must

---

[22] M. Shain, "Stress, Satisfaction and Health at Work: Tuning for Performance" (Presented at the Health & Wellness Conference '99, Vancouver, B.C., 24-27 October 1999) [unpublished].

track all the components of the cycle illustrated in Figure 13.2 and bring the data together to form a holistic picture of the relationships active within the cycle.

"If you don't measure it, you can't manage it!

If you can't management, you can't control it."

Measurement provides information about:

- The degree to which stressors are being experienced by employees.
- The physical and psychological effects on individuals.
- The effects on the organization:
  - behavioural outcomes; and
  - operational results.
- The financial or 'balanced scorecard' results of the organization.[23]

Performance Improvement Actions

Performance and Organizational Effectiveness consultants have the "soft technology" for improving human performance in the workplace — by dealing with the "organizational stressors" as the root causes they are. Occupational Health Nurses and Disability Managers can assist Performance and Organizational Effectiveness consultants in:

1. conducting needs assessments;
2. analyzing the "root causes" of the problems;
3. selecting and implementing interventions; and
4. tracking results and evaluating the outcomes.

Through an effective organization analysis, remedies such as the following can be utilized:

- **Education:** provide comprehensive briefings to top executives and senior management using both external and internal data to illustrate the business case associated with workplace stress and enhancing employee health and well-being.
- **Measurement system:** develop and implement measurement that includes indicators for "stress toxicity" as well as individual health and financial results.
- Promote **access** to and the use of a Wellness program (Individual Effectiveness Support).

---

[23] D. Pratt, *Employee Wellbeing, Learning and Growth: The Root of the Balanced Scorecard* (1999), available online at: <http://www.healthyscorecard.com>.

- Improve the capacity of management to **recognize** and respond to causes of workplace stress and employee distress.
- **Performance Support Practices:** become better at managing people. The most effective and enduring remedy is to implement and sustain performance support practices that focus on the "four Es" of people management:

  - Establish purpose
  - Enable performance
  - Expect results and
  - Encourage success

The importance of effective people management is not a new proposal. We realize it is not just "nice to do", but essential to creating an environment that fosters employee loyalty and in the long-term, sustainable success.

USE OF GOOD PERFORMANCE SUPPORT PRACTICES IS GOOD BUSINESS

Dennis Kravetz studied the correlation between people management practices and financial success. He developed an index for rating an organization's performance in people management practises (PMP score). In 1996, he published a study that looked at the correlation of PMP scores to financial performance over a 10-year period. The following chart (Figure 13.3) compares companies having low PMP scores with companies having high PMP scores:

Figure 13.3:   Comparison of Companies with High and Low PMP Scores [24]

Financial Factors	Companies with High PMP Scores	Companies with Low PMP Scores
Sales growth	16.1%	7.4%
Profit growth	18.2%	4.4%
Profit margin	6.4%	3.3%
Growth (earnings/share)	10.7%	4.7%
Total return (stock appreciation + dividends)	19.0%	8.8%

---

[24] D. Kravetz, *People Management Practices and Financial Success: A Ten Year Study* (Bartlet, Illinois: Kravetz Associates, 1996).

Establish Purpose

* help employees understand the organization's vision, values, goals and business strategies; and
* guide the development of individual performance and learning plans that will achieve organizational goals.

Enable Performance

* align resource allocations with performance expectations;
* coach employees to overcome difficulties and build skill and knowledge;
* foster and maintain effective work groups; and
* resolve performance issues and remove barriers that are beyond the control of individuals and teams.

Expect Results

* facilitate the measurement of progress, contribution and development; and
* hold people accountable for delivering agreed upon results.

Encourage success

* sustain communication that maintains focus, fosters commitment and facilitates implementation; and
* recognize and celebrate progress, development and the achievement of desired results.

ORIGINAL RESEARCH

An informal survey (Figure 13.4) was conducted to measure the degree of organizational stress in one Canadian city. The survey looked at specific factors within the conditions we know are needed to foster and sustain successful performance.[25] The results suggest that significant organizational stressors exist in some workplaces.

In general, the number of people who responded "disagree" or "strongly disagree" is low on most items. It is a concern that few people can say "this is not a stressor" for most items.

Highlights from the survey are organized below into the "four conditions for great performance".[26] In choosing the highlights, focus was placed on the percentage of combined "agree" and "strongly agree" responses and the percentage of combined "disagree" or "strongly disagree" responses. The numbers in brackets that appear below refer to the item numbers in Figure 13.4.

---

[25] T. Roithmayr & D. Dyck, "The Toxic Workplace" 25:3 *Benefits Canada* (March 2001).
[26] *Ibid.*

KNOW WHAT TO DO

- 72% of the respondents said employees are faced with conflicting priorities and demands (item 2).
- 42% of the respondents reported that employees are unclear about how their performance is measured (item 5).
- Less than 25% of the respondents reported goal alignment (items 1 & 4).

ABLE TO DO IT

- Half the respondents reported that employees do not get the coaching and learning support they need (items 6 & 7).

EQUIPPED TO DO IT

- Few (10%) of the respondents believed that employees get measurement data about their progress (item 12).
- Few (7%) of the respondents believed that employees have clear and effective work processes and procedures (item 19).
- 63% of the respondents reported that employees do not have the time to do the work required of them (item 21).

WANT TO DO IT

- Half the respondents said that employees lack the recognition they need to stay motivated while only 5% indicate that they do receive recognition (item 22).
- 15% reported that employees get positive feedback while only 10% say they get helpful corrective feedback (items 23 & 24).

The 44 respondents who completed this survey acknowledged the proposed "cycle of harm".[27] Their work experience supports a causal relationship among organizational stressors, health and operational results (items 27, 28 and 29).

This finding is consistent with research reported in 1998 by Dr. Martin Shain, University of Toronto.[28] He advocates dealing with workplace stress at the source in terms of "work design, work control, work demand and work effort" as opposed to trying to address the negative outcomes — *i.e.*, workplace injuries, increased operational costs, human suffering and increased employee group benefit plan costs.

---

[27] *Ibid.*

[28] M. Shain, "Managing Stress at its Source in the Workplace" (Presented at the Health Work & Wellness Conference '99, Vancouver B.C., 24-27 October 1999) [unpublished].

On a positive note, 83% of the survey respondents believed that organizations can reduce or eliminate organizational stressors while maintaining or growing their business results (item 30).

These survey results can be compared with the *Top Ten Sources of Workplace Stress* reported by the Global Business and Economic Roundtable on Addiction and Mental Health (2001):

1. Treadmill Syndrome: too much to do at once requiring a 24-hour workday.
2. Random work interruptions.
3. Doubt: employees unsure what is happening, or where things are headed.
4. Mistrust: vicious office politics that disrupt positive behaviour.
5. Unclear company direction and policies.
6. Career/job ambiguity: things happen without employees knowing why.
7. Inconsistent performance management: employees get raises without a performance review and positive feedback and then get laid off.
8. Feeling unappreciated.
9. Lack of two-way communication between employees and management.
10. Experiencing a feeling of not contributing and having lack of control over the work and workplace.

Figure 13.4: Organizational Stressors Survey

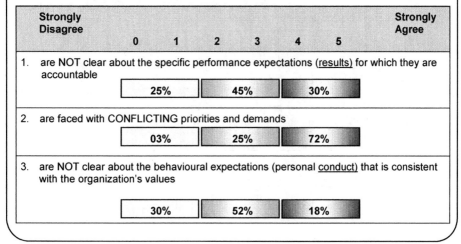

	Strongly Disagree					Strongly Agree
	0	1	2	3	4	5

4. are NOT clear about how their individual work will contribute to the goals of the organization

22%	55%	23%

5. do NOT understand the standards for their success and how their progress and contributions will be measured

13%	45%	42%

6. do NOT get the coaching they need to succeed in their current roles

08%	40%	52%

7. do NOT get the learning support they need to further develop their capabilities

20%	32%	48%

8. are in jobs that do NOT match their own personal interests and attributes; do NOT find their work meaningful

28%	65%	07%

9. are often involved in POOR working relationships

33%	50%	17%

10. encounter workplace situations in which they feel emotionally or psychologically VULNERABLE

22%	48%	30%

11. encounter workplace situations in which they feel physically UNSAFE

68%	32%	00%

12. do NOT get measurement data about their progress

10%	63%	27%

13. do NOT get sufficient communications about developments in the organization or information that affects their job

33%	47%	20%

14. have little or NO involvement in decisions that affect their work

20%	45%	35%

15. do NOT have the necessary autonomy and discretion to successfully deliver on their accountabilities

27%	53%	20%

Strongly Disagree						Strongly Agree
	0	1	2	3	4	5

16. feel they have NO influence over things that happen to them at work

26%	52%	22%

17. feel their roles are UNCLEAR or are in conflict with the roles of other employees

27%	43%	30%

18. do NOT have access to the tools, equipment, job aids or other resources they need to succeed in their jobs

35%	52%	13%

19. feel encumbered with unclear or ineffective work practices or procedures

07%	63%	30%

20. feel their physical work environment is NOT conducive to working efficiently or effectively

22%	48%	30%

21. feel they lack sufficient time to do the work required of them

05%	32%	63%

22. do NOT get the recognition they need to stay energized and motivated in their work

05%	47%	48%

23. get little or NO positive feedback on how they do their work

15%	45%	40%

24. get little or NO helpful corrective feedback on how they do their work

10%	55%	35%

25. believe they are not treated with fairness, trust and respect

40%	43%	17%

26. believe that how well they perform DOES NOT really matter — that there are NEITHER positive consequences for good performance NOR negative consequences for poor performance

37%	40%	23%

No Effect At All		Somewhat Detrimental				Highly Detrimental
	0	1	2	3	4	5

27. In your experience, to what degree do "organizational stressors" have detrimental physical and psychological effects on individuals?

00%	18%	82%

28. In your experience, to what degree do "organizational stressors" have detrimental operational and behavioural effects on organizations?

03%	30%	67%

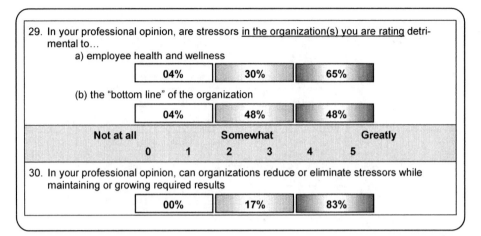

SUMMARY

Based on the experience of Occupational Health, Human Resources, and Wellness professionals, unmanaged organizational stress leads to increased employee stress, failing employee health, decreased productivity, increased absence and disability costs, and lowered financial results. However, the task is to prove this statement. To our knowledge, not enough data is available to tie all the elements described in this article into a holistic framework of cause and effect.

Organizations want to make evidence-based decisions regarding the allocation of their limited resources. To do this, a commitment is needed to:

- implement a measurement system to track the entire "cycle of harm";
- implement evidence-based actions to reduce or eliminate stressors;
- track progress for three to five years and share the results publicly in order to motivate others to follow suit.

Through the use of a multi-disciplinary approach, occupational health, human resource and organizational effective professionals can take action and find workable solutions to mitigate organizational stressors and the resultant employee illness/injury.

CHAPTER REFERENCES

Aventis Pharma-Canada, *The Aventis Healthcare Survey* (2001).

K. Bachmann, *More Than Just Hard Hats and Safety Boots: Creating Healthier Work Environments* (Ottawa: Conference Board of Canada, 2000) at 1.

Canadian Policy Research, reported in *IAPA: Creating Healthy Workplaces Everywhere – Healthy Workplace Week* (19 October 2005), available online at: <http://www.newswire.ca/en/releases/archive/October2005/19/c3209.html>.

Centre for Addiction and Mental Health, (2001).

Conference Board of Canada, *Survey of Canadian Workers on Work-Life Balance* (Ottawa: Conference Board of Canada, 1999).

Conference Board of Canada, News Release, "Workplace Solutions for Stressed Out Workers" (7 September 1999).

B.A. Cryer, "Neutralizing Workplace Stress: The Physiology of Human Performance and Organizational Effectiveness" (Presented at the Psychological Disabilities in the Workplace: Prevention, Rehabilitation and Cost Control Conference, Toronto, 10-11 June 1996) [unpublished].

Chrysalis Performance Inc., reported in *IAPA: Creating Healthy Workplaces Everywhere – Healthy Workplace Week* (19 October 2005), available online at: <http://www.newswire.ca/en/releases/archive/October2005/19/c3209.html>.

L. Duxbury & C. Higgins, *Work-life Conflict in Canada in the New millennium: A Status Report* (prepared for Health Canada, Healthy Communities Division) (Ottawa: Health Canada, 2003), available online at: <http://www.phac-aspc.gc.ca/punlicat/work-travail/report2/>.

L. Duxbury & C. Higgins, "Wrestling with Workload: Organizational Strategies for Success", Conference Board of Canada Report (May 2005).

D. Dyck & T. Roithmayr, "Organizational Stressors and Health: How Occupational Health Nurses Can Help Break the Cycle" (2002) 50:5 AAOHN Journal, 213-219.

Health Canada, *Best Advice on Stress Risk Management in the Workplace* (Ottawa: Minister of Public Works and Government Services Canada, 2000).

J. Johnson, "Long-term Psychosocial Work Environment and Cardiovascular Mortality among Swedish Men" (1996) 86:3 American Journal of Public Health at 324-331.

R. Karasek & T. Theorell, *Healthy Work: Stress, Productivity and the Reconstruction of Working Life* (New York, NY: Basic Books Inc., 1992).

D. Kravetz, *People Management Practices and Financial Success: A Ten Year Study* (Bartlet, Illinois: Kravetz Associates, 1996), www.kravetz.com.

A. LaCroix, *Occupational Exposure to High Demand/low Control Work and Coronary Heart Disease Incidence in the Framingham Cohort* (Ann Arbor, Michigan: University of North Carolina, UMI Dissertation Services, 1984).

B.B. Marmot *et al.*, "Contribution of Job Control and Other Risk Factors to Social Variations in Cardiovascular Heart Disease Incidence" (1997) 350 (9073) Lancet at 235-239.

D. Pratt, *Employee Wellbeing, Learning and Growth: The Root of the Balanced Scorecard* (1999), available online at: <http://www.healthyscorecard.com>.

T. Roithmayr, *Performance by Design* (2000).

T. Roithmayr, The Performance Maximizer™ (Calgary, AB: Performance by Design) available online at: <http://www.performance–bydesign.com>.

T. Roithmayr & D. Dyck, "The Toxic Workplace" 25:3 *Benefits Canada* (March, 2001).

M. Shain, "Managing Stress at its Source in the Workplace" (Presented at the Health Work & Wellness Conference 1998, Whistler, B.C., 27-30 September 1998) [unpublished].

M. Shain, "Stress, Satisfaction and Health at Work: Tuning for Performance" (Presented at the Health & Wellness Conference '99, Vancouver, B.C., 24-27 October 1999) [unpublished].

J. Siegrist, "Adverse Health Effects of High-Effort/Low-Reward Conditions" (1996) 1:1 Journal of Occupational Health Psychology at 27-41.

Top Ten Sources of Workplace Stress, Global Business and Economic Roundtable on Addiction and Mental Health (2001).

Chapter 14

Marketing Disability Management Programs[1]

INTRODUCTION

The shortfall of most Disability Management Programs is that although they exist and function, few people know about them until they need to use them. In essence, attention to program marketing is missing. This chapter addresses the concepts of program marketing and how they can be applied to promoting a Disability Management Program.

CORE MARKETING CONCEPTS

Marketing is defined as a social and managerial process through which individuals and groups obtain what they need and want by creating and exchanging products or services and value with others. The components of marketing are discussed below.

Customer Needs, Wants and Demands

Customer needs, wants and demands must be taken into account when producing products or developing services to be delivered. This means that program developers need to know what each stakeholder needs, wants and expects from the program. In terms of marketing a Disability Management Program, the program leaders must demonstrate how the program and its services meet those specific needs, wants and expectations.

Products or Services

Products and services involve anything that can be offered to a market to satisfy a customer need or want. This includes both tangible (products) and intangible items (services). Disability Management Services provided to employees and workplace operations fall into this category.

---

[1]   D. Dyck, "Disability Management Program: Communication Plan & Marketing Strategy" (Presented as a class offering in the Fundamentals of Disability Management Course, University of Alberta, Calgary, Alberta, 2002) [unpublished].

Product Value, Consumer Satisfaction and Product Quality

Consumers buy based on their perception of the value the product or service offers. Satisfaction depends on the product or service's perceived performance relative to buyer expectations. When the product or service quality meets or exceeds customer expectations, the customer is satisfied. This means that for employees and managers to view the Disability Management Services as valuable, they must perceive that they have received more value than what they initially expected. For Disability Case Managers, the message is not to over-promise and under-deliver, but rather to keep your promises realistic regarding what you can do.

Exchange

The exchange is the actual delivery of the product or service. How the product or service is made available to the customer is important. It can be either a negative or positive experience. This is where customer service principles come into play. The strategy is to provide the right product or service to the right person at the right time and for the right price.

Market

The market is the potential customers for whom the product or service has been designed. In a Disability Management Program, this would include the employees, management, unions and various external stakeholders like health care providers, insurers and family members.

MARKETING MANAGEMENT

Effective marketing can be equated to effective marketing management. Marketing management involves managing customer demand which, in turn, involves managing customer relationships. Marketers need to build long-term relationships with valued customers, distributors, dealers and suppliers.

Disability Management Managers and Disability Case Managers can promote their programs by nurturing strong relationships with program champions and those employees who have benefited from the services offered. Union leaders, line managers and human resource personnel can be valuable allies. They are well positioned to help market the program and its services.

Key Marketing Concept

Marketing management involves a thorough understanding of a key marketing concept. Successful marketing depends on determining customer needs and wants, and delivering the desired services more effectively and efficiently than one's competitors. What does this mean to the promoters of a Disability Management

Program? Simply stated, *"demonstrate what the program and its services can offer to each of the stakeholders involved"*.

The following are some general principles that can be followed so that this key marketing concept can be operationalized:

PROMOTE THE BENEFITS OF THE DISABILITY MANAGEMENT PROGRAM

Articulate to stakeholders the benefits that the Disability Management Program can offer to each of them. For example:

1. Employee regains income and a chance to remain in the workplace.
2. Union able to protect the employability of members while retaining rights and principles.
3. Employer retains a valuable employee and realizes decreased disability costs.

These benefits can be broadly stated, or specifically defined. Some general statements that can be made are:

Corporate Benefits

For the organization, the Disability Management Program allows for:

- Risk Management:
    - at any time, 8-12% of the workforce are off due to a disability;
    - employee absenteeism costs the employer about 250% of the employee's salary; and
    - reduces rate of injuries.
- Fewer lost days and lower Workers' Compensation claims.
- Cost-containment of approximately 19% can be realized through:
    - lower disability costs;
    - lower insurance premiums and rates; and
    - lower Workers' Compensation rebates.
- Higher level of employee productivity.
- Reduced costs associated with hiring replacement workers.
- Enhancing accident prevention.
- Supporting a healthy workforce.
- Meeting the organization's legislative obligations.

Union Benefits

For the Union, the Disability Management Program affords the union members an opportunity to:
- contribute to company profitability and competitiveness;
- problem-solve addressing areas of mutual interest and concern;
- interact and build relationships;

- protect employability of its members;
- maintain labour rights and principles; and
- promote employee well-being.

Employee Benefits

The employee (and his or her family) benefits from the Disability Management Program because the personnel and services:

- encourage a speedy rehabilitation;
- allow the employee to maintain contact and support from co-workers;
- reduce the time for optimal recovery;
- enable the employee to maintain self-identity and respect;
- enable the employee to remain current in his or her field; and
- result in the illness/injury experience being less disruptive in normal family/workplace relationships.

As one employee who went through a lengthy illness and Disability Management Program support stated:

> *This program was great and it allowed me to:*
> - *concentrate on getting better and to not worry about my financial and vocational future;*
> - *keep a regular routine despite medical appointment interruptions;*
> - *maintain a sense of self-worth;*
> - *make a contribution to the company;*
> - *work at regular duties for as many hours as I could tolerate;*
> - *keep my work contacts;*
> - *remain current with the changing work duties and responsibilities within my department;*
> - *remain current with changing technology;*
> - *gradually re-adjust to full-time work; and*
> - *return to work without upgrading.*

BE PREPARED TO ANSWER SOME TOUGH QUESTIONS

Promoters of the Disability Management Program must know how to answer the following questions:

1. Why is a DMP needed in our company?
2. What are the benefits to the company and the various stakeholders?
3. What data are required to build a business case that promotes the existence of this program?
4. What are the real costs related to employee disability?

5. What savings can be realized due to having a Disability Management Program?
6. What return on investment (ROI) can be realized?

To effectively answer these questions, the promoters have to do some internal and external research and legwork. To assist with this process, the following facts may prove helpful (Table 14.1):

Table 14.1 Relevant Facts

- The total cost of time off and disability programs in 2002 averaged 14.9% of company payrolls.[2]

- National Institute of Disability Management & Research (1997) worker disability costs eight cents for every dollar earned in British Columbia, Canada. The breakdown of costs is as follows:

  - 35% of the cost borne by employers
  - 27% borne by employees
  - 38% borne by government agencies

- In the first six months of a disability:

  - 1 in 3 employees experience an additional disability
  - 1 in 3 employees experience marital problems
  - 1 in 4 employees experience financial problems
  - 1 in 5 employees experience a clinical depression
  - 1 in 6 employees become involved in substance abuse

- Each of these outcomes results in an additional cost for those paying for the disability.

- The cumulative weight of evidence supports a strong link between health & productivity.

- Increasingly, employers are recognizing that the manner in which they integrate their employee benefit systems (linking medical care, disability management, and return to work) is important to their future productivity and ongoing competitiveness.

---

[2]   Marsh Risk Consulting, *Workforce Risk: Fourth Annual Marsh Mercer Survey of Employers' Time-Off & Disability Programs* (2003), online: <http://www.marshriskconsulting.com/st/ PDEv_C_371_sc_228135J_NR_306_Pl_347745.htm>.

BUILD A BUSINESS CASE FOR THE DISABILITY MANAGEMENT PROGRAM

The business case for the Disability Management Program must demonstrate the benefits and return on investment that could be realized by having the program in place. This is important when initiating the program and should be repeated regularly thereafter. Stakeholders need to know the rationale for initially supporting the program and then why they should continue to offer that support.

Some suggestions that can be made to garner support from the various stakeholders are:

For the Organization:

The Disability Management Program is a management tool for:

- managing employee medical absenteeism and the related costs;
- identifying the reasons for medical absences through data collection and trend analysis;
- preventing employee illness/injuries; and
- containing disability-related costs.

Selling the program as such can help management to see the value it can provide to the company

For the Union:

An opportunity to:

- promote employee well-being;
- maintain labour rights and principles;
- protect the employability of members;
- demonstrate the union's "due diligence" in terms of helping injured workers to return to work;
- interact and build relationships;
- problem-solve mutual concerns and issues; and
- contribute to the company's profitability and competitiveness.

For Employees:

The Disability Management Program enables the employee to:

- have a speedy rehabilitation;
- maintain self-identity and respect;
- maintain social supports;
- remain technically competent;
- sustain financial and vocational stability;
- minimize family disruption; and
- maintain a sense of self-control.

DEVELOP A COMMUNICATION STRATEGY AND PLAN

To begin with, determine the communication goal for the Disability Management Program. This goal will vary as the program evolves. Initially, it may be as follows:

Disability Management Program: Sample Communication Goal

All stakeholders are to be knowledgeable about the Disability Management Program (DMP) and of their roles and responsibilities in regards to the program.

From that point, strategies to enable the realization of this goal can be developed. These are the steps that the program promoters would take to move towards the completion of the goal. Some examples may be:

Disability Management Program: Sample Communication Objectives

By January 2007, 100% of the stakeholders will know about the DMP and their specific roles and responsibilities as evidenced by their level of program awareness and/or their level of participation in the program.

By June 2007, all the key stakeholders will have an in-depth knowledge about the DMP and be able to enact their specific roles and responsibilities, as evidenced by their level of program awareness and their participation in the program.

These objectives can be operationalized by:

1. Achieving the overall endorsement of the Disability Management Program (DMP).
2. Providing general education about the program to all.
3. Providing specific education for key players in the program (Supervisors/Managers, Union Reps, OHN and DMC).
4. Provision of introductory and regular communication about the program.
5. Providing ongoing education about the DMP to all.
6. Provision of introductory and regular communication with external stakeholders (physician, insurers & EAP).
7. Development of regular reports on the DMP outcomes (quarterly/annual).
8. Implementation of a mechanism for communicating employee fitness to work between relevant stakeholders.

The next step is to create a communication plan and the accompanying tools to tell the key stakeholders about the program. As in the development of a Disability Management Program, a plan of action is required. This means determining what message to provide to each stakeholder group. The following is a graphic representation of a sample communication plan for a Disability Management Program.

Disability Management Program: Sample Communication Plan

Communication Plan

Stakeholder	What?	How?	When?	Accountability?

For each stakeholder, determine the desired message to be delivered, the appropriate approach and timing, the best medium and who will be accountable for delivering the message.

Different stakeholders have different informational needs. For example, senior management will be interested in how the introduction of the Disability Management Program will allow for the fair and consistent management of employee illness/injury, save money and demonstrate compliance to the applicable legislation. The financial officer for the company will want to hear about the objective measures about the program and the expected return on investment from the Disability Management Program. Line managers will be interested in outcomes such as increased employee attendance, lowered sickness and accident costs and increased productivity. Employees will want to know how the Disability Management Program will provide them greater access to medical and vocational support, timely income continuance payments and a speedy return to a productive lifestyle. Occupational health and safety personnel will value information on how the program will enable them to enhance employee health and wellness and how workplace injuries can be reduced. Lastly, union personnel will want to know what the Disability Management Program will offer to their members in terms of fair and equitable treatment for ill/injured members and job security.

The following are some sample communication plans that were industry-created:

For Employees

Stakeholder	What?	How?	When?	Accountability?
Employees	— History of the sick leave, STD, LTD, and the WCB experiences; the effects of doing nothing — Overview of the DMP — Benefits (direct and indirect) of the DMP — Future plans re: — Sick Leave — STD — LTD — WCB	— Overview of the DMP; presentations using real examples; explain the business case — Training re: disability management and DMP: • Introductory • Ongoing — Scheduled union meetings (shift employees) — Handouts	— Scheduled meetings (introductory, follow-up, new-hire orientation)	— Union Reps — Management — Advisory Council — HR — Home department

For Senior Management and Corporate Directors

Stake-holder	What?	How?	When?	Account-ability?
Senior Management	Knowledge of DMP; understanding of the purpose; understanding of the benefits; gain support for DMP; seek endorsement of DMP and its goals	— Presentation: overview outlining issues, implications, business plan — Entire program document	— After ratification by union	Person's Name
Corporate Services & Human Resources	Knowledge of DMP; understanding of DMP	Status Reports (1 page briefing notes)	Monthly	Person's Name
Board of Directors	Knowledge of DMP to level of application; understanding	— Review entire document — Overview presentation	End of April (next draft available)	Person's Name
— Senior Management — Board of Directors	Program outcome data (ongoing reports)	Slides (graphs) trends	— Annually — Quarterly	Person's Name

Through the use of similar communication plans, a plan of action for promoting the Disability Management Program to each stakeholder is developed. Typically, these are:

- Senior Management /Board of Directors
- Employees
- Managers/Supervisors
- Union Executive Officers/Shop Stewards
- Healthcare Providers

As part of the communication plan, the Disability Management Program promoters have to develop communication tools. These can be presentations, a Disability Management Program web site, company newsletter announcements and articles, paycheque inserts or brochures. The following is a sample brochure designed to promote the Disability Management Program and explain the services offered.

Disability Management Program: Sample Communication Tool (Brochure)

A sample brochure marketing the Disability Program is contained in Appendix 1. Key to producing such a brochure is to ensure that:

- the message contained is accurate;
- contact personnel are included to enhance user access of the service;
- the tool is attractively presented and aligned with company branding and other marketing techniques; and
- the reading level is at a grade 6-8 level so all employees can understand the message contained.

SUMMARY

For Disability Management Programs and services to remain visible and viable, they must be promoted within the organization. In return, the program promoters must demonstrate that the program is adding value to the organization. This information must be reported back to all the stakeholders in order for them to understand that the program is providing them with what they value the most. Thus, they will support the implementation and sustainability of the Disability Management Program.

Appendix 1

Disability Management Program Brochure

At COMPANY XYZ, employees are our most important assets. COMPANY XYZ is committed to providing programs and services to support employee wellness and regular work attendance. We support initiatives to assist employees experiencing a diminished work capacity and to help ill/injured employees to return to work.

THE DISABILITY MANAGEMENT PROGRAM

COMPANY XYZ's Disability Management Program is designed to:

- Support employees and business operations during an employee illness/injury period
- Promote employee health and recovery
- Assist employees to return to work in a safe and timely manner
- Lower the costs associated with employee absence
- Promote a healthy work environment

HOW DOES IT WORK?

The ill/injured employee notifies his/her immediate supervisor of the medical absence.

The Line Manager notifies the Disability Management Coordinator who initiates the claims submission process.

The Disability Management Coordinator contacts the employee to assess the situation, identify the need for employee supports and determine the anticipated length of the absence.

The Disability Management Coordinator may request the employee's written consent to have medical information released by their family physician, specialist or other health service provider. Information released to the Disability Management Coordinator is used to aid in the evaluation of the employee's fitness-to-work status.

Confidential medical information about the employee is not shared. What is disclosed is the source of the injury/illness — work-related or not — as well as the employee's fitness-to-work status, the identified work limitations and capabilities and a realistic return-to-work date.

Case management meetings involving the Return-to-Work Team may occur at any time throughout the Disability

Management process. The aim is to address any barriers to a safe and timely return to work that the employee may be experiencing.

THE DISABILITY MANAGEMENT TEAM

COMPANY XYZ's Disability Management Program uses a coordinated team approach for facilitating the employee's safe and timely return to work following an illness/injury. The team may include any or all of the following:

- Employee
- Line Manager
- Union Representative (if applicable)
- Attending Health Care Providers
- COMPANY XYZ's Disability Management Services
- Employee and Family Assistance Service provider
- COMPANY XYZ Employee Services
- Rehabilitation specialists
- Insurance company representatives

BENEFITS OF THE DISABILITY MANAGEMENT PROGRAM

For the Employee:

- Encourages a timely recovery
- Maintains contact and support from co-workers
- Decreases the risk of relapse
- Offers the ability to maintain self-identity and respect
- Lessens the disruption in normal family and work life
- Supports a return to work in a safe and timely manner
- Reduces the associated financial hardships

For the Employer:

- Supports and promotes a healthy workforce
- Maintains valuable employees within the workplace
- Meets legislative obligations
- Manages illness/injury costs effectively

NEED MORE INFORMATION?

If you require more information, please contact one of the following:

- COMPANY XYZ Intranet
- Your Line Manager
- Your Union Representative
- COMPANY XYZ Disability Management Coordinator
- COMPANY XYZ Employee Services

CONTACTS:

Disability Management Coordinator, Employee Relations — Health
Address

Phone: [insert number]
Cell: [insert number]
Fax: [insert number]

Union Offices
UNION. – [insert number]
UNION. – [insert number]

CHAPTER REFERENCES

D. Dyck, "Disability Management Program: Communication Plan & Marketing Strategy" (Presented as a class offering in the Fundamentals of Disability Management Course, University of Alberta, Calgary, Alberta, 2002) [unpublished].

Marsh Risk Consulting, *Workforce Risk: Fourth Annual Marsh Mercer Survey of Employers' Time-Off & Disability Programs*, Workforce Risk (2003), on-line: <http://www.marshriskconsulting.com/st/PDEv_C_371_sc_228135_NR_306_Pl_347745.htm>.

Chapter 15

Outsourcing Disability Management Services

INTRODUCTION

Disability management services can be provided to an organization through an in-house occupational health service or through a contract service arrangement with an external service provider. Each option has its advantages and limitations. Organizations must decide which option is best suited to their particular disability management and business needs. Once the decision to use an external service provider is made, the next step is to determine a "best fit" between the organization's Disability Management Program, business approaches and corporate culture, and the services offered by available external service providers.

In today's marketplace, the plethora of disability management service providers makes determining a "best fit" a difficult task for organizational leaders. This chapter examines the relevant issues in outsourcing disability management services and how to address them effectively.

WHY OUTSOURCE?

Companies must first decide whether to outsource their disability management services or keep it in-house. After examining their business practices, many large organizations decide that internal disability management services are not within the scope of their core business practices or competencies. For smaller companies, having an in-house disability management service may be impractical and too costly.

However, before going to the marketplace, an organization should identify and understand their reasons for potentially outsourcing disability management services. It is paramount to know why and how the decision to outsource was made. In this way, attention can be paid to addressing the issues that were originally identified as drivers for outsourcing the disability management services. Without understanding why outsourcing is necessary, service providers and contracted services can be positioned in a manner that fails to address the reasons for seeking external services in the first place.

Decision-making Process

According to Jane Hall, a comprehensive process is needed to make sure that all aspects of the decision-making process have been considered. The necessary steps are listed below:

1. Identify the desired changes and the reasons behind making those changes.
2. Explore the possibility of alternative service delivery options.
3. Obtain stakeholder input into what they want from a future disability management service.
4. Develop a communication strategy to explain the need for change, and describe the new disability management service that is ultimately selected. According to Hall, "ineffective or inadequate communication of change is a prime reason for implementation failures".[1]
5. Establish value criteria for deciding on a suitable service provider.
6. Define the nature of the desired service provider arrangement. Is the organization seeking service/product delivery, or a partnership arrangement to deliver disability management services?

Some of the reasons organizations choose to outsource disability management services include:

*   *Lack of internal expertise* — By the time the reader reaches this chapter in the book, he or she will appreciate that disability management services require a level of expertise lacking in many organizations. Without occupational health support, case management is difficult if not impossible. Likewise, claims management expertise is required to effectively and efficiently process employee disability claims.
*   *Lack of internal resources* — Resources, facilities and funding are needed for a successful internal Disability Management Program to operate. The type and amount of resources required varies depending on the size of the organization. In general, office space and equipment, file cabinets, support personnel and a budget for rehabilitation services are key to providing efficient internal disability management services.
*   *Insignificant number of services required* — If an organization experiences only a few absences per year, having an internal disability management service can be a costly venture. This is often the major reason for outsourcing disability management services on an "as needed" basis.
*   *Desired benefits of economies of scale* — This reason ties into the one provided above. By accessing disability management services from a service provider that works with many other organizations, the organization can benefit from the infrastructure and services already in place. Theoretically,

---

[1]   J. Hall, "The Decision to Vendor and Vendor Management: A Tool for Occupational Health and Workers' Compensation Management" (1997), 11:5 The OEM Report at 45.

this type of arrangement can provide quality disability management services at a lower unit price than the organization could manage internally. Companies value economies of scale and often seek disability management service arrangements that can offer savings through a contracted service arrangement.

- *Specialty expertise is required to achieve a cultural shift within the organization* — Some organizations desire extensive changes in their service practices over a short period of time. To achieve such an aggressive goal, they need the help of an external service provider. Getting there on their own would take too much time, resources and money. This is often seen when a shift from a traditional to a more business and people-oriented approach to disability management is sought.

- *Geographically complex services are desired* — In some instances, organizations choose to keep the majority of their disability management services in-house except for those services that are remote and better provided by a local service provider. These mini-contract arrangements are common and usually purchased as "one-off" situations.

- *Seek a method to deal with fluctuating service demands* — Disability management service demands can be unpredictable. Theoretically, service providers are better positioned to handle the peaks and valleys of servicing.

- *Desire to purchase current skills* — Remaining current in an emerging field like disability management can be difficult, particularly for smaller organizations. By purchasing disability management services from a service provider whose core business is disability management servicing, current disability management service practices and expertise will be obtained.

- *Desire to transfer assets and people to a third party manager* — Organizations that have in-house occupational health service may *wish* to outsource the personnel and resources that provide disability management services. The intent is often to keep only "core" business functions in-house, and to outsource the rest.

For the above reasons, an outsourced disability management service option is often sought. However, to be successful the service provider arrangement must be well planned, implemented and evaluated.

PREPARATION FOR OUTSOURCING

For organizations to attain a suitable disability management service provider, a number of preparations must be made prior to going to the marketplace. They are discussed below.

Development of a Disability Management Program

First, develop the type of Disability Management Program that the organization wants to have in place. This important first step can be likened to house shopping. Prior to meeting with a realtor, the purchaser must decide what type of house is required. Will it be a starter home, large family home or a retirement residence? The same holds true for seeking a disability management service provider. The organization must determine the extent of the disability management services required and the framework within which they are to be delivered.

This is a vital step to a successful service provider arrangement. By having a Disability Management Program in place that is known to all stakeholders, the participants are aware of their roles and areas of responsibility. As well, there is an established structure within which the service can function. Trying to operate without a framework will result in confusion. Service expectations and perceptions will become divided and poor service quality will result. This is one of the major reasons for disability management service provider failures.

Determination of the Preferred Customer-Service Provider Relationship

The organization must identify the preferred customer-service provider relationship desired. Some options include:

(a)   a service that functions independently and is separated from other organizational activities (*i.e.*, service/product delivery only);

(b)   a service that is integrated with the rest of the corporate programs and that is expected to provide and receive organizational data relevant to the Disability Management Program and various prevention strategies (*i.e.*, a partnership); or

(c)   a service that is not only integrated, but comprehensive in the approach to disability management (*i.e.*, an enabler arrangement). This includes providing disability management services, and participating in the long-term planning for employee/organizational health and well-being.

In summary, the continuum ranges from a completely outsourced service with minimal involvement by the purchaser, to a service provision that enables the organization to offer a comprehensive Disability Management Program with an internal feel.

Before choosing the desired service provider arrangement, the organization must explore the differences between the following three options:

Option 1: the provision of a service/product is not only the least involvement that a service provider can have with the organization, but it is also the least time-consuming, risky and costly option for them.

Option 2: a partnership arrangement takes more time, energy and expertise for the service provider to deliver. It involves building relationships, knowing about the organization and its employees, and seeking ways to provide effective and efficient disability management services.

Option 3: an enabling relationship is the most comprehensive in nature. It involves partnering, as well as enabling the organization to move towards illness or injury prevention. To achieve this level of service provision, the service provider must fully understand the organization, its people, the business strategies, service demands, work environment and challenges. This takes the most time and expertise, and involves risk-taking. In essence, it requires making personal investment in the organization and its issues. This is also the most costly of the three options provided.

Service gaps occur when the organization believes the service purchased is a partnership or enabling agreement, and the service provider has contracted for service delivery only. Service gaps can cause an outsourcing disaster.

Determination of the Nature of Services Required

The next step is to decide what parts of the Disability Management Program will be kept internally and which ones will be contracted. Some organizations design their Disability Management Program so as to keep all the program management and return-to-work activities in-house. In this type of program, only the disability management clinical services are contracted out. Others seek the provision of a complete Disability Management Program — program management, provision of clinical services and return-to-work responsibilities — from a service provider.

An awareness of the services required, and the ability to articulate them clearly are essential to outsourcing Disability Management Program services. The organization should not only list the desired services, but also clearly describe the nature of the services, desired service quality, required turn-around times and preferred reporting mechanisms for the services provided. Also, linkages for these services back into the organization have to be outlined.

The positioning of the desired client-service provider relationship is also important. Some organizations want their service provider to operate within the confines of the organization and to provide consulting services to employees, work groups and the organization as a whole. Others prefer a completely external service, with an "arm's length" relationship and very little input into the organization's business and operational practices.

Establishment of Service Criteria

Organizations must decide what service criteria of the disability management service provider will be expected. What quality of service, service reliability, proven track record, level of expertise, nature of the service facility, data management and reporting capabilities and cost savings are expected? How will these be assessed and evaluated?

The organization should rate the value placed on each service criterion. For example, the organization should prioritize the value of service quality responsiveness and cost, data management capabilities, comprehensive servicing, provision of integrated services, service provider solvency as a business entity and the features of the service facility. This critical step influences how the bidders' response to the Request for Proposal for service provision will be evaluated.

Establishment of Desired Funding Arrangement

Funding arrangements for the disability management service can vary. The typical arrangements are fee-for-service, capitation or a fee-for-service arrangement with a per capita retainer for administration services.

Companies that have set budgets and little margin for budgetary overruns often choose the per capita option. It is also the funding option of choice for mature Disability Management Programs with predictable service demands and outcomes.

The fee-for-service option can be suitable for organizations with new or changing Disability Management Programs. Since the organization only pays for the services used, they can establish what yearly costs are incurred and then, if desired, they can establish an appropriate per capita pricing arrangement.

A mixture of fee-for-service and capitation can work well in situations where the corporate services and the care services for the organization are funded under a per capita scheme, while the business units (operational) services are paid on a fee-for-service arrangement. Thus, the combination of funding can meet an organization's various demands.

Establishment of a Desired Payment Arrangement

Once a desired funding arrangement is selected, the next step is to establish a payment arrangement. The options may include a set fee per month or a variable fee based on the services rendered. Again, depending on the organization's needs, available cash flows and budgetary constraints, a suitable funding arrangement can be determined.

Determination of the Desired Performance Criteria and Measurement Techniques

As with any service contract, performance criteria and measurement techniques for the disability management service provider contract must be set. These should be established in concert with the selected service provider. However, it is critical for the organization to decide on the performance criteria and to document the measurement techniques to be used.

Some typical performance measures are:

- service response time;
- service provision turn around times;
- satisfied employees or business units;
- compliance with legislative requirements;
- short-term and Workers' Compensation disability durations;
- the percentage of short-term disability cases that progress to long-term disability;
- the percentage of disability cases that include modified work opportunities;
- the average duration of disability cases; and
- the cost-benefit ratio per disability case.

SERVICE PROVIDER MARKET SEARCH

A disability management service provider search is a relatively new approach to determining a suitable organization-service provider match. The key is to find a suitable arrangement that meets all the organization's required criteria.

Steps

DEVELOP A REQUEST FOR PROPOSAL (RFP)

The RFP should describe the organization, its business and people needs, the Disability Management Program and the services sought. Typically, the approach is to provide background information on the organization, the corporate values and beliefs, and its products or services, size and locations. A description of the organization's Disability Management Program and commitment to employee well-being should be provided. Other available employee support services and how they link with the Disability Management Program also warrant explanation. The current service provision arrangements should be included, along with the reasons for seeking the current request for quotation for services.

The requested disability management plan design must be fully described. What are the services sought? What is the expected standard of service required, and how will these be demonstrated?

RFP questions must be asked in a format that will elicit bidder responses that can be compared. Comparison of bidders is facilitated using a questionnaire. In this way, all bidders are asked the same questions and their responses can be rated according to pre-determined value criteria.

Submission information must also be included in the RFP. It should describe to the bidders the scope of the project, the procedure for the bidder to acknowledge receipt of the RFP, the format for the proposal, the terms for proposal response submission, the terms for proposal response rejection, the length of time for bid acceptance, the potential method for proposal clarification and the confidential manner in which bidder information will be handled. For ease of processing, the required response letters to be used by the bidders should be included, along with a sample service agreement contract. Bidders are asked to document their level of agreement with the contract format and terms.

SELECT SUITABLE SERVICE PROVIDERS

The organization has to decide whether to seek an invited or open bid for services. The invited bid to tender is a request for proposal from a selected number of potential service providers. The open bid is a general invitation for any service provider to respond to the RFP.

For many organizations, an open bid situation is just too cumbersome to conduct and manage. As well, the responding service providers may be unable to meet the organization's needs. More and more, organizations are choosing to pre-screen potential service providers, and then, conduct an in-depth examination of the individual service capabilities of each service provider.

DISTRIBUTE THE RFP

The RFPs should be sent out in enough time to allow the service providers to adequately respond. RFPs can take over two weeks to prepare. As well, time should be allowed for mailing and delivery. A minimum of three weeks is recommended between issuing the RFP and the deadline date for bidder response.

It is important to clearly restate in the accompanying cover letter the preferred method of submission and the closing time and date. As well, bidders should be reminded that any late responses will be considered invalid and returned to the sender unopened. Likewise, it is critical for organizations to abide by this statement.

RFPs should be sent out with a self-addressed, return envelope that ensures that the bid response gets to the appropriate department or person for processing. One tip is to have an identifier of some sort put on the envelope to indicate that a returned bid is enclosed. In this way, the recipient of the RFPs within the organization knows it is a returned bid and refrains from opening it until the RFP response time has elapsed. Then all the bids can be opened at once.

DATA COLLECTION AND COLLATION

Each RFP response is reviewed in its entirety. Then, all the RFPs are dissected in terms of their responses to each of the questions asked. A standard approach is to use a spreadsheet to list the RFP questions and the individual bidder responses to each question. The spreadsheet helps compare the individual bid responses to each question.

ANALYSIS OF THE **RFP** RESPONSES

The RFP response analysis process can take a number of formats. One is to score each question based on the value for each service criterion established by the organization. For example, if the organization pre-determines that it values quality of service first, service cost second, data management capabilities third, comprehensive servicing fourth and business solvency fifth, then scores of five points would be given to the questions that deal with service quality, four points for service cost questions, three points for data management capabilities, two points for comprehensive servicing and one point for business solvency. In this way, each question can be objectively scored. The outcome is an overall score for each bidder, and in this instance, high scores are good.

A second approach is to decide which of the RFP questions are "show-stoppers", and to rate each bidder response on those questions. The service providers with the best responses to all the critical questions are then identified as candidates for a final presentation.

With any scoring or rating system, it is important to pre-determine whether the responses will be rated against each other, or whether an "all or nothing" scoring system for each question will be used. As well, plans should be made for how to deal with instances where all respondents score equally on a question. This allows for a consistent approach to the scoring technique.

Once the questionnaire responses are scored, service costs are addressed. Typically, bidders are asked to provide per capita and fee-for-service price schedules for the services requested. By applying the fee-for-service prices to the disability management utilization rates for a former year, a comparison can be made between the fee-for-service and capitation models quoted for each bidder. Bidders are also compared respecting the services *excluded* from their respective capitation models.

Other areas for in-depth examination are:

* staffing levels;
* staff qualifications;
* service facilities;
* service provider network;
* service capabilities; and
* client references.

SELECTION PROCESS

Once all the responses are analyzed, the findings are reviewed by the organization's decision-makers. In addition to the items noted above, other factors like accessibility, fit with the corporate culture, service responsiveness and service nature (reactive versus proactive, service provider versus partnership arrangement) are discussed. Based on the "fit", the decision-makers then select the service providers that they want to interview.

Finalist presentations are designed to permit the organization to meet the potential service providers and to learn more about their services, philosophies and plans to provide the disability management services requested. Typically, these are formal presentations in which the service providers describe their business, service capabilities, staff qualifications, provider network, facilities, data management systems, past successes and future plans. Presentations should include discussion of how the provider plans to deliver the requested disability management services, various funding options and the nature of the potential working relationship.

To facilitate the interview, the organization should develop a list of questions for the service providers to answer. This allows for the further exploration of a potential business relationship, as well as adding rigour to the comparison process of the finalist presentation.

The responses to the prepared questions provided by the two or three finalists can be assessed and rated using the decision matrix tool which rates responses in order of merit. Similar rating systems can also be used. It is of prime importance to keep the reasons for originally going to the marketplace, the pre-determined value criteria, the desired service outcomes and the need to find a suitable service provider in mind.

The interview is usually the most revealing part of the selection process. On paper, many service providers sound great. However, in person the match between the organization and service provider tends to become apparent.

RESPONSE TO BIDDERS

Successful and unsuccessful bidders expect a decision regarding the success or failure of their RFP responses. Service providers spend considerable time and resources developing RFP responses and out of professional courtesy, they deserve a response letter, regardless of the bid's success or failure.

SERVICE CONTRACT DEVELOPMENT

The development of the service contract begins at the onset of the project. By knowing the value criteria, services required, desired funding arrangement and duration of the contract, the procurement officer for the organization can begin to craft a service contract document.

Many organizations have standardized service contract templates. These can be used and modified to meet the needs of the proposed disability management service contract. Regardless of the form used, the following elements should be included:

- description of services to be provided;
- expected level of service quality;

- required levels of reporting and communication;
- mutually agreed upon service performance measures;
- responsibilities of each party;
- pricing agreement;
- duration of the contract;
- payment schedule;
- legal compliance;
- hold harmless clause; and
- required business insurance coverage.

VENDOR MANAGEMENT

Vendor management is a key aspect of a successful disability management outsourcing arrangement. Having a comprehensive service agreement contract is only the first step in this process. Other strategies need to be in place to ensure that the outsourced service is in alignment with both organizations' needs and wants.

Recommended Strategies

PARTNERING

Partnering is a method of accomplishing the mutual goals of the organization and the outsourced service in a planned and pre-described way. It involves jointly establishing service goals, objectives and procedures. The intent is to have open communication and a solid working relationship, which foster the accomplishment of the desired goals.

QUALITY ASSURANCE AND CONTINUOUS IMPROVEMENT

Programs and disability management services are established to address needs. As needs change, so must the programs and services. This can be successfully accomplished by keeping the two concepts of quality assurance and continuous improvement in mind.

Quality assurance involves the determination that the desired quality of service is indeed being attained. There are a number of evaluation techniques that can be used. However, even before any of those can be employed, the contracting organization must establish the standard of disability management servicing that will be expected of the service provider or vendor. These standards should be clear; valid in their rationale and intent; based on research; specific to the area of disability management best practices; and measurable. Chapters 3, 7 and 11 of this book address some of the possible standards of practice for disability management programs.

A number of quality assurance techniques are provided by Jane Hall,[2] and include:

- *Cat in the Corner* — visiting and observing first-hand the services provided by the service provider to employees. The intent is to evaluate the services offered.
- *The "I Don't Understand" Tool* — asking the service provider to explain a process, or practice of concern.
- *Checking Out the Competition* — scanning the marketplace and comparing the various services and practices available.

Organizations should closely scrutinize the service provider's activities and make sure that the agreed upon service demands and service quality are being met.

PERFORMANCE MEASUREMENT

The service agreement contract should stipulate the expected levels of performance for both the hiring organization and the service provider. Once in place, the onus falls on both parties to monitor the performance levels exhibited. This includes the regular measurement of the service quality and outcomes delivered.

The measurement criteria and the techniques spelled out in the service agreement contract should be followed. A review of the results should involve both parties. Here, the partnership arrangement becomes important. Both parties should be cognizant of the issues or problems and should work together to arrive at feasible solutions.

Performance measurement is an ongoing process — not an event. Regular measurement is key to the success of the outsourced arrangement. It allows for the identification of issues or problems, development of action plans and solutions, establishment of short and long-term goals, trend analysis and identification of proactive approaches to illness or injury prevention. Without regular performance measurement and open communication of performance issues, an outsourced service arrangement can fail. This is often the reason for tension between organizations and service providers, which is all too common, and can easily be prevented. As Yogi Berra once stated, "If you don't know where you're going, you'll end up someplace else". In any service arrangement, the organization and service provider have to work together. Performance measurement is one tool to enable this to successfully happen.

---

[2]   *Ibid.*, at 44-47.

SERVICE PROVIDER REPORTING

Regular reports on the service provided and the outcomes achieved are another important element to a successful contract arrangement. This feedback should be timely and should address all the requirements stated in the service agreement contract.

COST-CONTAINMENT

The costs associated with the outsourced disability management services require monitoring and cost-containment. Both parties should regularly review the projected costs stated in the service agreement contract. Knowing where cost savings and cost overruns occur will help to deal with the service costs experienced or anticipated. In this way, contingency plans for the disability management service costs can be developed, if required.

REGULAR MEETINGS

Regular meetings between both parties should be held to discuss the successes and limitations of the outsourced servicing. This is one way to promote open communication; to identify problems before they escalate; to determine which services are working well and those that require more attention; to identify any noted service trends; and to build a solid working relationship.

These six strategies are but a few examples of vendor management practices that can be implemented to ensure a successfully operated disability management service. Partnering, open communication, regular monitoring and measurement of performance and continuous service improvement are key aspects of a comprehensive service agreement contract.

SUMMARY

Disability Management Programs and services can be outsourced in whole or in part. Regardless of the arrangement, the sponsoring organization must remain actively involved in managing the service agreement contract. Organizations can contract out services, but not liability and accountability for the provision of those services. This means that they must think strategically and act responsibly: "An organization's decision to outsource or retain a particular service should be a well-thought-out process encompassing all the ramifications of the decision".[3]

---

[3] *Ibid.*

CHAPTER REFERENCES

J. Hall, "The Decision to Vendor and Vendor Management: A Tool for Occupational Health and Workers' Compensation Management" (1997) 11:5 The OEM Report at 44-47.

Chapter 16

Disability Management: Ethical Practice

INTRODUCTION

Disability management is based on relationships and trust. It impacts corporate plans and costs; individual/family well-being, vocational aspirations and finances; and employee culture and morale. In dealing with such an important topic, ethical considerations must be addressed. The following discussion deals with the key ethical theories and their implications for disability management practitioners.

ETHICAL CONSIDERATIONS

By Bonnie Rogers

Ethics is defined as *the science of morals, a system of principles and rules of conduct,*[1] the study of standards of right and wrong, or having to do with human character, conduct, moral duty and obligations to the community.[2] It is the moral reasoning that humans possess.

Ethical theories and principles guide us in making ethical decisions. The major ones include the *teleological theory — utilitarianism*, which focuses on the consequences of an action and gauges the value of that action by the end results, rather than by the means to achieve the results. It concentrates on providing the greatest good (or the least harm), for the greatest number of people. In this context, policy formation based on cost-benefit analysis, wherein the greatest benefit is achieved by the most, but not all, for the lowest cost, is a good example of utility.

The *deontological theory* deals with action and asserts that "rightness" and "wrongness" are measured by means, rather than by consequences of an action. So, the nature of an action is more important than the outcomes. By way of comparison, the deontologist would assert that confidentiality of employee health information must always be maintained; whereas the utilitarian might

---

[1] B. Kirkpatrick, ed., *The Cassell Concise English Dictionary* (London, England: Cassell Publishers Ltd., 1989) *s.v.* "ethic".

[2] *Ibid.*

hold that if keeping certain kinds of health information secret would cause more harm than good, then confidentiality should be broken.

Ethical principles extend from the deontological theory, and the most widely observed principles are autonomy, nonmaleficence, beneficence and justice. *Autonomy* is a form of personal liberty whereby the individual is regarded as having the right to self-determination. This means that the individual's values and goals must be considered in major decisions that affect his or her welfare, and precludes paternalistic decision-making (when one claims to know what is best for another person), as well as requiring informed consent when decisions are made. Health professionals or others who are making decisions for employees without the employee's input and consent would be in violation of this principle. The inclusion of the employee in making disability care choices is important to upholding the autonomous principles.

The second principle, *nonmaleficence*, is often referred to as the "no harm" principle. It is the foundation of most professional codes of ethics. For example, an employee with a known disability, such as a hearing loss, should not be placed in a job situation that would further compromise his or her hearing. In addition, returning an ill or injured employee to work too soon could compromise his or her continued recovery and potentially harm the employee. Here, the health care professional must guard against having divided loyalties to the employee-organization, and remain an advocate for the employee. Conducting return-to-work examinations is one way to provide protection for the health of the employee, as well as for the well-being of the organization, co-workers and public at large.

Beneficence, the third principle, requires that health care professionals act in the best interest of the employee. The identification of potential health hazards through routine worksite "walk-throughs", the identification of employees at increased risk for illness or injury, and making recommendations for risk reduction, represent a positive occupational health intervention. Positive occupational health intervention is aimed at employee protection thereby preventing a potential disabling event from happening. For example, the development of a back injury prevention program for employees with a previous history of back injury would be a beneficent action. In addition, assuring the disabled employee that he or she will receive quality case management is critical to this principle.

The fourth principle, *justice*, is directed towards treating employees fairly, equally, and without discrimination. This includes providing equal opportunity for disabled persons regarding job availability and promotion; and assuring that individuals are not discriminated against because of a health condition, such as HIV, or another chronic disorder, when they are able to perform the job safely. This concept is embodied in Canadian human rights legislation. Another example is treating employees equally with regard to access to modified/alternate work opportunities within an organization.

In many instances, ethical principles provide us with a guide with which to weigh the risks and benefits with respect to individual health and welfare, and the development of policies and procedures to safeguard individual rights and protect health. It is incumbent upon the Disability Manager, in particular occupational health nurses and physicians, to examine the situation with respect to these guiding principles and to assure that the benefits of their actions clearly outweigh the risks.

ETHICS AND CASE MANAGEMENT[3]

By Jane Hall

Professional bodies and organizations establish professional codes of ethics. Occupational health professionals and Case Managers are bound to uphold the codes of the professional disciplines. Professional behaviour will be held accountable to the standards, regardless of feelings, personal beliefs or views.

In professional practice, particularly when delivering case management services, we speak of "autonomy", or the right of the employee to determine as much as possible the direction of his or her care. Autonomy is critical to keep in mind during problem solving or advocacy, especially if the employee's desires are in conflict with those of the health care providers or employers.

The other ethical principles to consider are truthfulness and justice — that is, what is right versus what is wrong in a given situation. The term "ethical dilemma" comes into play when two apparent truths are in conflict with one another. For example, an ethical dilemma may arise when a legal situation regarding a medical matter is in conflict with a religious belief. A moral wrong may not be illegal, but could be unethical. A clear legal parameter may be at odds with the moral-judgement consensus. Ethics, then, is a philosophical issue rather than a scientific one. In case management, evaluation and weighing of the ethics of a case must be done in an unemotional manner so that decision-making is rational and based on facts rather than the emotional issues attached to the decision at hand.

An everyday definition of ethics would be: "Doing the right thing, at the right time, for the right person, in the right way and knowing why it is the right thing, at the right time, for the right person, in the right way".

---

[3] Adapted and reprinted with permission from J. Hall, "Ethics and Case Management" (1999) 13:2 The OEM Report at 13-16.

Common Ethical Case Management Considerations

PERSONAL BELIEFS VERSUS PROFESSIONAL EXPECTATIONS

Culture, experiences, belief systems and academic persuasions influence Case Managers. As human beings, we react emotionally as well as intellectually to situations. To deny that case management activities are prone to influences from our background and beliefs is to bury your head in the sand. What is required is "physician know thyself" imperative. Case Managers must take the time for introspection and examination of their beliefs, values, biases and prejudices. Only when we have acknowledged to ourselves where we stand on various issues can we put those issues aside and deal with the factual realm, which is the professional case management standard.

CONFIDENTIALITY VERSUS RIGHT TO KNOW

Confidentiality has to do with credibility and with legality. A Case Manager should be clear with employees that theirs is not a legally supported confidential relationship like the relationship between physician and patient, lawyer and client or priest and parishioner. The Case Manager is bound to share information with other stakeholders who need to know about information pertinent to the individual case. It is strongly recommended that the Case Manager have a frank discussion with the employee at the onset of the relationship to disclose what his or her role and responsibility entails. A client who starts a sentence with, "I don't want you to tell", needs to be stopped, counselled about the case management role and told that confidentiality cannot be promised.

On the other hand, it is not ethical for a Case Manager to share information with anyone else who does not need to know the information. Shoptalk is a common breech of confidential employee information. Sharing a dilemma with a supervisor, however, is an appropriate method of communication.

Another example of appropriate sharing of information is when the Case Manager realizes that the employee is non-compliant with treatment. The employee may request that the Case Manager not tell his or her physician. The Case Manager should attempt to determine why the employee is being non-compliant, but cannot agree to the request of non-disclosure to the physician. Such an action may prevent needed adjustments to the treatment regimen.

INDIVIDUAL WISHES VERSUS FAMILY OR LEGAL CONSTRAINTS

Case management never occurs in a vacuum. Physicians and other health care providers, claim adjusters, employers, co-workers and family members frequently contribute to the employee's assessment and rehabilitation plans. The manner in which the Case Manager obtains and uses the information must be carefully thought out and planned, keeping in mind the employee's best interests and wishes. The Case Manager should avoid becoming entangled in legal issues.

Once again, the guidelines used to affect this should be sought in the standards for case management practice. If a legal decision is rendered, the Case Manager is bound to obey the law. If this presents an ethical dilemma for the Case Manager, then the Case Manager's supervisor and/or lawyer should be consulted. In some cases, a Case Manager may need to withdraw from a case rather than compromise the principles of case management.

Tools for Determining Ethical Case Management Practices

DISCUSSION WITH SUPERVISORS

Also known as the "when in doubt, check it out" philosophy, this method of dealing with ethical issues is recommended as the first step in acknowledging and confronting a problem. It is appropriate because in most situations the supervisor is accountable for the actions of individual Case Managers that they supervise. Presumably, they have attained their supervisory position on the basis of greater knowledge and experience. Also, being more removed from the situation, they may possess more rationality and wisdom in case management practices.

LEGAL COUNSEL

Most organizations have access to legal counsel. In ethical situations related to occupational health, legal counsel is likely to be a labour lawyer. If a Case Manager seeks legal counsel, it is appropriate to remember that there is usually some bias by the attorney(s) towards the organization's position on the situation. The Case Manager should consider the legal opinion as well as any other opinions as representing part of the picture in a specific case.

SELF-APPRAISAL

Self-appraisal is a difficult tool, but by examining our rationale, motives and emotions as Case Managers we can gain an understanding of what we believe and why we believe what we do. In that way we can gain some self-insight so that we can act on our client's behalf in an informed and non-judgemental manner.

RESOURCES

Seldom is there a situation in which the critical ethical issues have not been raised before. Thus, it is helpful to search for other similar cases and examine them for any pearls of wisdom that may apply.

ETHICAL DECISION-MAKING

By Dianne Dyck

There are numerous ethical conflicts and dilemmas that can arise in today's work environment, including issues such as confidentiality of employee health records, worker notification of "right to know", substance abuse, employee screening for health indices[4] and "whistle-blowing". Ethical dilemmas often arise, such as cost containment versus the quality of health care; conflicting loyalties of the health care professional between the employee and the organization; and returning a worker to a safe work environment.

Ethical Dilemma

An ethical dilemma exists when two core values that the person upholds come into conflict, making it difficult for the person to decide how to move forward. In the fields of occupational health and workers' compensation, ethical issues are more likely to centre on matters of confidentiality of employee medical records, employee "right to know", action regarding potential workplace hazards and human resource issues that conflict with human rights legislation and the duty to accommodate. As well, psychological issues often come to the attention of the Case Manager, and issues of roles and responsibility may arise. Case Managers can easily find themselves in the middle of "hot issues" and may be called upon to advocate for an employer rather than the employee. In such situations, the Case Manager needs to carefully assess the situation and all the issues, both medical and ethical; utilize the available resources and tools; and ultimately make conscious, carefully thought-out decisions before taking any action.[5]

Although there is no magic remedy to resolve ethical dilemmas, there are a number of ethical decision-making models that can be used. The following is a discussion on two such models:

ETHICAL FITNESS™ MODEL[6]

Developed at the Institute for Global Ethics, this ethical decision-making model assumes that human beings have universal core values that cross religious, cultural and geographic boundaries. It serves as a decision-making guide, helping the individual to move from ethical dilemma recognition to resolution.

---

[4] Health indices are the measures used to establish "normal" or "abnormal" health conditions, such as body temperature, blood pressure, pulse, neurological functioning, *etc.*

[5] Adapted and reprinted with permission from J. Hall, "Ethics and Case Management" (1999) 13:2 The OEM Report at 13-16.

[6] R.M. Kidder, *How Good People Make Tough Choices: Resolving the Dilemmas of Ethical Living* (New York, NY: Fireside Books, 1995).

For example, as a Disability Case Manager, you are aware that an employee has multiple sclerosis. She is being considered for a promotion that will include long hours, high service demands and extensive travel. A couple of months ago, this employee was off work for two weeks due to an exacerbation of her medical condition. She is fine now, but her manager has come to ask you if you know of any reason why this employee should not be considered for this new position within the company. You have a good relationship with this manager and would like to tell him that you are concerned that the employee will not be able to handle the stress and rigours of this job due to health reasons. However, in your role as Disability Case Manager, you are bound to uphold the medical confidentiality entrusted to you. This is an ethical dilemma for you.

The critical step is recognizing that an ethical dilemma exists, followed by identifying which of the core values are in conflict. Once achieved, the Disability Case Manager, or Occupational Health Nurse, can apply the following steps of the Ethical Fitness™ Model:

a) *Awareness: Determine the moral issue* – First recognize that an ethical dilemma exists.

b) *Actor: Determine the actor* – Decide who is experiencing the conflict in values.

c) *Facts: Get the details* – Gather all the facts and assess what you learn. There may or may not be an actual conflict at hand.

d) *Determine if the moral issue is "right vs. wrong"* – Could this simply be an issue of "right and wrong" and not an ethical dilemma? To determine this, you can use five tests:

(i.)	The legal test	— Does the action or choice contravene any laws?
(ii.)	The front page test	— Would this action/decision stand the test of public scrutiny?
(iii.)	The gut feeling test	— What does your "gut" tell you about this decision: is it right or wrong?
(iv.)	The role model test	— How would you feel about someone you respect knowing you took this action or made this decision?
(v.)	The professional standards test	— Would your action/decision align with your professional standards?

e) *Test for "right" by assigning one of the four dilemma paradigms* – With facts in hand and the assurance that an ethical dilemma exists, determine which core values are in conflict and why. The ethical decision-making paradigms are:

Figure 16.1: Ethical Decision-making Paradigms

Ethical Decision-making Paradigms[7]	
Truth versus Loyalty	Disclosure versus Confidentiality
Justice versus Mercy	Fairness versus Compassion
Short-term versus Long-term	Immediate individual needs versus Conservation for future needs
Individual versus community	Autonomy versus Collective rights of the larger community

f) *Apply resolution principles: Ends-based, Rules-based, or Care-based* – Examine the dilemma using the three resolution principles:

   (i) *Ends-based Principle* – What is the end result of the action or decision made? Which choice would result in the greater good for the largest number of people?
   (ii) *Rules-based Principle* – What is your obligation here? If you have a duty to uphold medical confidentiality, then that is what you must do.
   (iii) *Care-based Principle* – This principle is based on the Golden Rule: "do unto others as you would have done unto you". In essence, show the level of compassion that you would like shown if the roles were reversed.

g) *Identify if a third option exists* – Is there another action or decision option that could be adopted? If so, could it allow the players to reach that "win-win" plateau that we all strive for?

h) *Decide* – Once all the options have been considered, it is time to decide. As Egdar[8] notes, procrastination can be a decision – the decision to choose not to decide. Usually, it is not a recommended resolution tactic.

i) *Evaluate the decision* – Looking back on actions taken or decisions made is worthwhile. It serves to help prepare the Disability Case Manager for future instances of ethical decision-making.

---

[7] P. Edgar, "Resolving Ethical Dilemmas: Applying the Institute for Global Ethics' Ethical Fitness™ Model to Occupational and Environmental Health Practice Issues" (2002) 50:1 AAOHN Journal, at 40-45.

[8] *Ibid.*

MODEL FOR ETHICAL DECISION-MAKING IN A PROFESSIONAL SITUATION[9]

For health care and disability management professionals, ethical dilemmas abound. This is compounded by being in a position of trust: the person whom you have agreed to help trusts that you will act as their advocate and provide them reasonable guidance during a vulnerable period in their life. According to Parsons, two ethical guidelines for caregivers in a professional situation are:

- the needs of the client come first and foremost; and
- the practitioner must recognize his or her own needs and biases and avoid situations in which these might negatively impact client care giving.

The steps that Parsons recommends for ethical decision-making are:

a) *Parameters of the situation* — What are the facts and issues in this situation and who are all the players?

b) *Ethical-legal issues* — Identify all the legal issues and then all the ethical ones. By separating them out, it helps to clarify the situation and what action to take.

c) *Would legal guidelines help* — Consult the applicable legal guidelines and determine if they would lead to the resolution of the issue.

d) *Stakeholder rights, responsibilities and welfare* — List the stakeholders, how they are involved, their rights, responsibilities and welfare.

e) *Alternate Decisions/Actions* – Develop a list of alternative decisions possible for each identified issue.

f) *Consequences* — Assess the consequences of making each decision. Evaluate the short-term, ongoing and long-term consequences of each possible decision.

g) *Assessment* — Present any evidence of the likelihood that the various consequences or potential benefits may occur.

h) *Decision* — Make the decision and monitor the outcome.

---

[9] R.D. Parsons, *The Ethics of Professional Practice* (Needham Heights, MA: Allyn & Bacon, 2001).

DISABILITY MANAGEMENT STAKEHOLDERS: CONFLICTING GOALS

By Dianne Dyck

In any organization, the interests of the various players or stakeholders can be in opposition with each other. The area of disability management is no exception. To explain this issue, two case studies will be presented — one to demonstrate conflict at the individual level; another to illustrate conflict at a management level.

Case Study A — Goal Conflict at the Individual Level

Andrew worked for a large company that was nine months into a major project. Like Andrew, employees from throughout the organization were selected for this top priority project. The project was to last two years, involve intense periods of work and require total employee dedication. The corporate goal was to have the desired product within two years.

The project leaders were challenged to motivate the team to work as a unit, dedicating 50 to 70 hours per week to a long-term task. For them, the goal was a successful project completed on time and on budget.

Unfortunately, Andrew became very ill and the heavy project demands were believed to be the prime cause. He had a young family and an active community life. The project's extreme time demands became too much and he was unable to cope. However, given that the project was designed to function within a strong team milieu, Andrew continued to struggle. At that point, he did not want to let his team members down and his short-term goal was to survive.

Eventually, the strain became too great and Andrew needed to seek professional help. His desire to be a "team-player", to "pull his weight" and to do a good job could no longer be achieved in this setting. He sought support and guidance from the Employee Assistance Program and occupational health professionals. Their focus centred on getting Andrew the appropriate medical treatment.

Andrew needed time off work to rest, recover and re-evaluate his situation. The action plan was to put him on short-term disability until he recovered enough to be able to make a rational decision about his future. Family support was deemed critical to a successful recovery. For that reason, some of his family members were enlisted to be part of the case management and treatment processes. At that point, Andrew's wife's goal was to help her husband to regain his health, and be able to work towards putting their family life back together.

After a few weeks of intensive treatment, Andrew recovered. However, the issue of whether or not to return to the environment that contributed to his illness loomed. For career advancement, returning to the current project would have been a wise move. Andrew's support was needed for the project team. He was a key person and the team was missing his expertise and guidance. However, for his personal well-being, Andrew decided that he would be better off to return to his former job outside of the special project. He enjoyed his former job and he could work successfully within that environment.

As an added note, his co-workers were also individually concerned about their respective well-being. They did not know what was wrong with Andrew, and they were concerned that he may have a contagious condition that they would eventually experience. For them, two serious issues existed:

1. A valuable player had been lost to the team and his support was sorely missed.
2. Could they end up like Andrew?

The competing goals in this scenario were as follows:

Figure 16.2: Competing Stakeholder Goals and Conflicts

Stakeholder	Goal	Conflict
Company	To attain an important product within two years.	Andrew and his wife's goals and well-being/needs.
Project Leaders	To motivate and guide the team to complete the project as planned.	Corporate goal, team goals, and employee well-being/needs.
Employees	To function success-fully within a team en-vironment and do the job expected of them.	Corporate and Project Leader goals.
Co-workers (team)	To function cohesively and do the job expected of them.	Corporate goals, Project Leader goals and individual goals.
Andrew	To function in a com-petent manner.	Corporate goals, Project Leader goals, team goals, personal goals and his wife's goals.
Wife	To have a happy and healthy husband and family	Corporate goals, Project Leader goals, and team goals.

In summary, there can be a number of conflicts within an individual disability case that need to be recognized and managed.

Case Study B — Goal Conflict at the Management Level

Brenda was a long time employee with a manufacturing firm. She had joined the company early in her career and had remained doing relatively the same job ever since. Her skill sets, although compatible with the original job placement, had not adapted to the radical technological advancements in her area. However, everybody liked working with Brenda.

Brenda's work group experienced significant change during a corporate restructuring. A new manager entered the scene, along with a number of new employees. Brenda, feeling quite threatened by all the changes and by the technical ability of the new people, became sullen and passively aggressive with everyone. This evoked a variety of responses from her co-workers; the older ones supported Brenda while newer employees were quite vocal in their belief that management needed to deal with her. The outcome was a divided, non-productive work group, and a disgruntled employee.

The new manager, being involved in a number of projects, viewed the issue as a "worker problem" and one that the employees would "sort out for themselves". He was quite surprised when the employees came to him requesting that he take immediate action.

After a number of months of group anarchy, Brenda became ill and went on short-term disability. She was clinically depressed — not sleeping, eating or able to concentrate. She came to the occupational health centre a distraught, angry, confused and tearful person. Employee Assistance Program counselling and a medical consultation were arranged.

It took a number of weeks before the root of Brenda's problem could be unearthed. In the meantime, the work group had moved on and was beginning to function as a team. The manager was pleased with the progress and felt that his "laissez-faire" approach had worked well. He also decided that having Brenda out of the group had a positive effect on the group dynamic. His goal was to keep things this way.

Senior management in this company upheld an early-return-to-work policy. So, in the normal course of case management, the occupational health nurse began to work with Brenda and the manager to prepare for a gradual re-entry to the workplace. However, resistance to the idea was encountered with each attempt to initiate the process, resulting in an employee who was even more hurt and confused. Her goal was to get back to "the good old days", and to the working arrangement she knew and enjoyed.

The occupational health nurse began to identify a number of significant barriers to an early return to work for Brenda. Quickly, it became apparent that senior management and line management goals were at odds. One supported early return-to-work actions, while the other was using the employee's absence as a means for dealing with an unpleasant workplace situation.

As time passed, Brenda recovered from her depression and was ready to return to work in a modified work capacity. However, with her manager unwilling to entertain the idea, progress in this direction was impossible.

Having identified the goal conflict, the occupational health nurse adopted a new approach. A meeting was arranged with senior management and the line manager regarding the situation at hand, along with health-related and management issues. The former was being addressed, but the latter issue needed attention.

The occupational health nurse, along with senior management, helped the line manager understand the impact of the management style that has been adopted. The group examined the workplace issues, and explored a variety of ways in which the problem could be resolved. Senior management did not relieve the line manager of his responsibilities; rather they offered guidance and support to address the situation through the company's human resource department.

This is an example of goal conflict at a management level. If unresolved, the absent employee would remain out of the workforce for a protracted period of time and at added cost to the organization.

Conclusion

Case management is essential to manage and resolve goal conflicts at the individual and management level. A highly recommended approach to resolving goal conflicts includes the following steps:

1. identify and understand the underlying issues;
2. hold a case conference with the key players;
3. identify and address the issues as a group;
4. seek solutions to rectify the situation;
5. implement the plan;
6. evaluate the outcomes; and
7. communicate the outcomes to the interested parties.

SUMMARY

To reiterate, ethics is the science of morals, a system of principles and rules of conduct, the study of standards of right and wrong, or having to do with human character, conduct, moral duty and obligations to the community. It is the moral reasoning that humans possess.

The ethical principles covered in this chapter provide us with a guide with which to weigh the risks and benefits with respect to individual health and welfare, and the development of policies and procedures to safeguard individual rights and protect health. In case management, evaluation and weighing of the ethics of a case must be done in an unemotional manner so that decision-making is rational and based on facts rather than the emotional issues attached to the decision at hand. In short, it is "Doing the right thing, at the right time, for the right person, in the right way and knowing why it is the right thing, at the right time, for the right person, in the right way".

CHAPTER REFERENCES

P. Edgar, "Resolving Ethical Dilemmas: Applying the Institute for Global Ethics' Ethical Fitness™ Model to Occupational and Environmental Health Practice Issues" (2002) 50:1 AAOHN Journal at 40-45.

J. Hall, "Ethics and Case Management" (1999) 13:2 The OEM Report at 13-16.

R.M. Kidder, *How Good People Make Tough Choices: Resolving the Dilemmas of Ethical Living* (New York, NY: Fireside Books, 1995).

B. Kirkpatrick, ed., *The Cassell Concise English Dictionary* (London, England: Cassell Publishers Ltd., 1989) *s.v.* "ethics".

R.D. Parsons, *The Ethics of Professional Practice* (Needham Heights, MA: Allyn & Bacon, 2001).

Chapter 17

Disability Management: Legal Aspects

INTRODUCTION

Disability management is a management response to legislation which upholds that:

- disabled employees cannot be discriminated against on the basis of a physical or psychological disability (Canadian human rights legislation, *American Disabilities Act*);
- employers must provide work accommodation for workers recovering from an illness/injury (Workers' Compensation Acts, *Canada Labour Code*, Canadian human rights legislation, *American Disabilities Act*); and
- workers must be accommodated up to the point of undue hardship (Canadian Human Rights legislation).

In this chapter, legislative changes and their impact on disability management efforts; the duty to accommodate; and confidentiality requirements will be discussed.

THE IMPACT OF CHANGING LEGISLATION ON DISABILITY MANAGEMENT EFFORTS

By Sharon L. Chadwick

All stakeholders in the disability management process must be aware of the relevant legislation that may impact on the disability management processes. Such legislation may include, but is not limited to, occupational health and safety, human rights, Workers' Compensation, employee and labour relations, employment standards, and freedom of information and the protection of privacy legislation. As interpretation and application of the different regulatory requirements is varied and complex, it is also recommended that employers developing Disability Management Programs obtain the advice of a legal consultant.

In this section, some of the issues and considerations related to disability management will be discussed as they relate to occupational health and safety, human rights and freedom of information and the protection of privacy legislation. As these acts vary somewhat from province to province and from provincial to federal jurisdiction, it is imperative that stakeholders review the legislation that applies to their specific area.

Workers' Compensation Legislation

A number of Canadian Workers' Compensation Boards have enacted legislation that mandates employers to return ill/injured employees back to work. For example, sections 88 to 89.4 of Newfoundland's *Workplace, Health, Safety and Compensation Act,*[1] require that all employers and workers are obligated under the Act to co-operate in the worker's early and safe return to suitable and available employment with the injury employer. This may involve modified work, ease back to regular work, transfer to an alternate job, or trial work to assess the worker's capability.

In addition, employers in New Brunswick, Nova Scotia, Ontario, Prince Edward Island and Quebec are obliged to re-employ injured workers unless the worker refuses the job.

Occupational Health and Safety Legislation

In Canada, each province has its own occupational health and safety legislation, and organizations under federal jurisdiction are under the *Canada Labour Code.* Although the specific acts and regulations vary, the general principles remain the same: employers are responsible for maintaining the health and safety of employees at their work sites. Employees also have a responsibility to work safely and protect the health and safety of themselves, their co-workers and the general public where applicable. It is imperative that occupational health and safety programs be linked to disability management processes, especially in the area of illness and injury prevention and safety risks.

Areas generally covered in the occupational health and safety legislation include, but are not limited to:

- chemical hazards;
- physical hazards;
- noise;
- general work safety;
- radiation;
- ventilation;
- working alone;
- workplace violence; and
- first aid.

---

[1] R.S.N.L. 1990, C. W-11, ss. 88-89.4.

Within these regulations there may be specific requirements for pre-placement medical examinations, periodic medical surveillance and follow-up, as well as requirements for safe work practices and personal protective equipment. As this legislation is reviewed and updated, employers and occupational health and safety professionals should maintain communication with government occupational health and safety departments to ensure that they are informed of the latest changes.

Human Rights Legislation

Canadian human rights legislation has a major impact on the way employers treat employees, and in particular disability management processes. Although each province is covered by its own human rights legislation, and federal organizations are under federal human rights legislation, the human rights principles expressed in this legislation are fairly consistent.

The application and interpretation of individual human rights cases is complex and varies depending on the individual circumstances of the case. There are no black and white answers to questions in this arena — all cases must be assessed on their own merit, and much of today's awareness and understanding of human rights issues is based on case law. Even so, there is a great deal of variability, and employers are advised to obtain legal counsel when setting up policies and procedures which may have human rights implications, or when assessing difficult cases.

Generally, the principles of human rights legislation in relation to disability management include the following:

DISCRIMINATION

Human Rights legislation prohibits discrimination in employment practices such as hiring or retaining employees. For example, subsection 7(1) of the Alberta *Human Rights, Citizenship and Multiculturalism Act* states:

> 7(1) No employer shall:
> (a) refuse to employ or refuse to continue to employ any person, or
> (b) discriminate against any person with regard to employment or any term or condition of employment,
> because of the race, religious beliefs, colour, gender, physical disability, mental disability, marital status, age, ancestry, place of origin, family status or source of income of that person or of any other person.[2]

This impacts the employer for both pre-placement and return-to-work fitness requirements. Human rights legislation is based on the principle of individual assessment — persons should be evaluated on their *ability*.

---

[2] *Human Rights, Citizenship and Multiculturalism Act*, R.S.A. 2000, c. H-14, subs. 7(1).

The British Columbia Council of Human Rights advises employers to:

- concentrate on a person's capabilities and not disabilities;
- assess persons as individuals, not as members of a group;
- avoid making generalizations about disabilities;
- define specific employment needs according to business priorities;
- clearly state the essential components of the job; and
- establish reasonable standards for evaluating job performance.[3]

DUTY TO ACCOMMODATE

Employers are required to make reasonable accommodation for persons with a physical or mental disability. Duty to accommodate is a tripartite effort with responsibility resting with:

- *The employer* — has the primary duty to originate and implement a solution as he or she is in the best position to assess how the employee can be accommodated without undue interference in the operation of the business.
- *The union* (if applicable) — has a joint responsibility to assist in accommodating disabled employees. Unions must cooperate in the search for and implementation of accommodations as well as considering modifications or waiver of collective agreement provisions if necessary for accommodations of a particular case.
- *The employee* — has a variety of obligations in the process of seeking and sustaining a workable solution to accommodating their disability. The employee has the duty to inform the employer of their need for accommodation and of the effectiveness of the measures taken to accommodate. The employee is also required to provide to the employer information regarding their expected return-to-work date and any limitations or restrictions. The employee has a duty to take reasonable steps to facilitate the implementation of proposed workplace accommodations.[4]

Employers and unions are required to accommodate employees with disabilities (both physical and mental) to the point of "undue hardship". This includes the return to work of ill or injured employees. Basically, the employer must be able to demonstrate that they have made reasonable attempts to accommodate the employee to the point of "undue hardship".

The development of a comprehensive Disability Management Program with clear policies and procedures, as well as clearly defined roles and

---

[3] British Columbia Council of Human Rights, *Disability and the Human Rights Act* (Victoria: British Columbia Ministry of Labour and Consumer Service, 1998).

[4] Centre for Labour-Management Development, "Accommodation Guidelines" (Presented at the Illness and Disability: Claims in the Unionized Workplace Conference, Edmonton, Alberta, February 1999) [unpublished] at 69.

responsibilities, will ensure that the duty to accommodate is applied consistently for all employees, and will assist stakeholders in demonstrating that appropriate steps have been taken to accommodate disabled employees.

According to the Centre for Labour-Management Development outlines:

> Where the disability prevents the employee from performing some or all of the functions of a particular position, possible accommodations may include the provision of sedentary, light or modified duties, elimination of physically difficult or hazardous duties, modification of the work environment in a manner which permits the employee to continue to carry out his or her duties, alteration of shift schedules or hours of work, *etc.*
>
> While the nature of the employment may affect the content of the duty in a particular case, an employer is not relieved of its duty to accommodate simply because the disabled employee is a temporary employee.[5]

UNDUE HARDSHIP

The concept of "undue hardship" is flexible and not clearly defined. The exact interpretation and determination of "undue hardship" will depend on the individual circumstances of the case. Generally, the concept will include considerations of such factors as:

- financial cost;
- disruption of the collective agreement;
- employee morale;
- interchangeability of the work force and facilities;
- size of the employer's operation; and
- safety concerns.[6]

Regarding safety concerns, the seriousness of risk is assessed considering four factors:

- *The nature of the risk* — What could happen that would be harmful?
- *The severity of the risk* — How serious would the harm be if it occurred?
- *The probability of the risk* — How likely is it that the potential harm will actually occur? Is it a real risk, or merely hypothetical or speculative?
- *The scope of the risk* — Who will be affected by an event if it occurs?[7]

---

[5]   *Ibid.*, at 59.

[6]   *Ibid.*, at 73.

[7]   L. McDowell, *Human Rights in the Workplace: A Practical Guide* (Toronto: Carswell, 1998) at 7-43.

BONA FIDE OCCUPATIONAL REQUIREMENTS

Placement of employees both on hiring, and on return to work from an absence, should entail matching the tasks of the job to the person's abilities. In order to require that an employee "perform" a specific task, it must be demonstrated by the employer that the task is a Bona Fide Occupational Requirement. If the employee is unable to perform a task that is a requirement, they may not be placed in that position. For example, subsection 7(3) of the Alberta *Human Rights, Citizenship and Multiculturalism Act* states:

> Subsection (1) does not apply with respect to a refusal, limitation, specification or preference based on a bona fide occupational requirement.[8]

The term Bona Fide Occupational Requirement is not defined in the legislation. Basically, it means that the employer must show that the specific task is "essential" to the performance of the job.

Human Rights and Substance Abuse Policies

Employers who are considering the development and implementation of workplace substance abuse policies and procedures should be aware of the human rights implications related to these programs.

Alcohol and drug addictions are generally accepted as "disabilities",[9] the same as any other physical or mental disability. Employers have a duty to accommodate employees with substance abuse problems:

*   *Offers of assistance* — including arranging entry into treatment, providing counselling, and referral to an Employee Assistance Program.
*   *Time off for treatment* — with or without weekly indemnity, use of vacation entitlement, sick leave, or indefinite suspension.
*   *Modified work hours* — to accommodate attendance at follow-up counselling.
*   *Bearing the cost of monitoring the employee's compliance* — with the terms of agreed-upon treatment, managing morale problems of co-workers and perhaps altering the employer's position to remove safety sensitive responsibilities and duties.[10]

The issue of substance abuse testing remains controversial. In Canada, there is no specific legislation related to drug and alcohol testing in the workplace, and these cases are generally addressed under human rights legislation. Employers considering the implementation of these programs must ensure that they

---

[8]   *Supra*, note 4.
[9]   C. Sefton & B. Speigel, "Alcoholism Ruled a Handicap" (1995) 11:5 OH&S Canada at 16-17.
[10] R.D. Parsons, *The Ethics of Professional Practice* (Needham Heights, MA: Allyn & Bacon, 2001), at 97.

research this area and work closely with legal counsel. It is imperative that these programs are not discriminatory. The need for such a program should be thoroughly researched based on the specific requirements of the company and safety risks involved.

Recent Developments in Canadian Human Rights

A recent human rights case, *British Columbia (Public Service Employee Relations Commission) v. British Columbia Government and Service Employees' Union*,[11] involved fitness-for-work testing for firefighters and the interpretation of a specific fitness standard as a Bona Fide Occupational Requirement.

The recommendations from the review of this case have implications for the future assessment of human rights cases. It has been recommended that a three-step test should be adopted for determining whether an employer has established, on a balance of probabilities, that a *prima facie* discriminatory standard is a Bona Fide Occupational Requirement (BFOR).

First, the employer must show that it adopted the standard for a purpose rationally connected to the performance of the job. The focus at the first step is not on the validity of the particular standard, but rather on the validity of its more general purpose.

Second, the employer must establish that it adopted the particular standard in an honest and good faith belief that it was necessary to the fulfilment of that legitimate work-related purpose.

Third, the employer must establish that the standard is reasonably necessary to the accomplishment of that legitimate work-related purpose. To show that the standard is reasonably necessary, it must be demonstrated that it is impossible to accommodate the individual employees sharing the characteristics of the claimant without imposing undue hardship upon the employer.[12]

PRIVACY LEGISLATION[13]

By Kristine Robidoux

As with occupational health and safety and human rights legislation, privacy legislation has both provincial and federal statutes that govern the collection, use and disclosure of personal information. Again, it is important to be familiar with the legislation in the relevant jurisdiction and to know what bodies or organizations are covered under this legislation.

Public sector bodies are generally bound by provincial Freedom of Information and Protection of Privacy legislation (FOIP). This type of legislation is generally intended to increase government accountability by ensuring that individu-

---

[11] [1999] S.C.J. No. 46, 176 D.L.R. (4th) 1.

[12] *Ibid.*, at paras. 57-62.

[13] K. Robidoux, LL.B., Principal, ComplianceWorks (Calgary, Alberta, November 2005).

als have rights of access to information in the custody or under the control of government or public bodies. FOIP legislation has been developed to grant access to public documents that may be of interest to specific groups or individuals, and to protect the privacy and limit the use of individual personal information by public bodies, including medical information.

In the private sector, there are different statutes that govern British Columbia, Alberta and Quebec. All have private sector privacy legislation that balance the rights of individuals and employees of organizations to have their personal information protected while ensuring that the needs of private sector organizations to collect, use and disclose personal information for business purposes are reasonable. Federally-regulated works, undertakings and businesses, as well as private-sector businesses that are outside of British Columbia, Alberta or Quebec, are all subject to the federal statute, the *Personal Information Protection and Electronic Documents Act.*[14] Notably, the federal statute does not apply to the personal information of employees of private sector businesses in jurisdictions without provincial private sector privacy laws, but does apply to employees of federal works, undertakings or businesses.

This analysis is critical in order to determine whether privacy law applies to the personal information relating to the disability of the employee in question, and if so, which statute in particular. It can be a tricky determination to make.

In 2004, Alberta and British Columbia each enacted largely similar Personal Information Protection Acts[15] ("PIPA"). These two statutes provide that private sector organizations in those provinces may only collect, use and disclose the personal information of individuals and employees for purposes that are reasonable, and to the extent that is reasonable to carry out the purposes. An important exclusion contained in the PIPA statutes allows organizations to collect, use and disclose "personal employee information" without the consent of the individual in some cases: if the information is reasonably required by an organization and is collected, used or disclosed solely for the purpose of establishing, managing or terminating the employment relationship. This exclusion can be important as an organization determines its conduct and strategy in respect to an injured worker.

As discussed at length in previous chapters of this book, the assurance of confidentiality of medical information is essential in performing effective disability management processes, especially in the area of case management. Health care professionals are bound by professional ethics to maintain confidentiality, but this can be a challenge in the workplace setting, and the health care professional must be extremely stringent in maintaining confidentiality. These obligations are also reiterated in the privacy laws: personal information *must* be safeguarded with security that is appropriate for the relative sensitivity of the information. It must be protected against such risks as unauthorized access, collection, use,

---

[14] S.C. 2000, c. 5.

[15] S.A. 2003, c. P-65 (Alberta); and S.B.C. 2003, c. 63 (British Columbia).

disclosure, copying, modification, disposal or destruction. All stakeholders in the disability management process should be aware of privacy legislation in their jurisdiction and the impact this has on the processes of their programs.

Conclusion

It is important to stress that disability management processes are impacted by a variety of legislation. This legislation may vary from province to province and from provincial to federal jurisdiction. The most important thing to note is that stakeholders in disability management *must* be:

- aware of the current legislation in their locale; and
- aware that specific acts and regulations are constantly changing and that they should obtain legal counsel to ensure they have the most current and up to date case law information when setting up programs or when dealing with specific human rights cases.

Remember — *Ignorance of the law is never a valid excuse!*

PRIVACY LEGISLATION: THE APPLICATION

By Kristine Robidoux and Dianne Dyck

Canada's federal private sector privacy legislation, the *Personal Information Protection and Electronic Documents Act*[16] (PIPEDA), came into effect on January 1, 2004. This statute governs the collection, use and disclosure of personal information by federal works, undertakings and businesses (such as the federally-regulated banks, telecommunications, airlines, *etc.*), as well as by private sector businesses in provinces of Canada that have not enacted their own legislation that is substantially similar to PIPEDA. Therefore, any province without its own privacy legislation must follow the federal legislation.

British Columbia, Alberta and Quebec have enacted provincial private sector privacy legislation that governs the treatment of personal information of individuals and employees of private sector organizations in those provinces. Specifically in British Columbia and Alberta, the *Personal Information Protection Act*[17] (PIPA) provides the requirements for how organizations may collect, use, disclose and protect personal information, which may include personal health information of individuals as well as company employees. Under PIPA, individuals and employees have the right to:

---

[16] *Supra*, note 14.
[17] *Supra*, note 15.

- know why personal information is being collected, used or disclosed;
- expect the organization to collect, use or disclose personal information in a reasonable and appropriate manner;
- know who in the organization is accountable for the organization's compliance with privacy laws and practices;
- expect the organization to use the appropriate security measures to protect the information;
- expect that the information is accurate and complete;
- request corrections if required;
- complain to the organization about how it collects, uses or discloses personal information;
- appeal to the Privacy Commissioner if a dispute over personal health information cannot be resolved using the above measures; and
- access their personal information that is in the custody or under the control of the organization, unless one or more of the exceptions under PIPA apply.

In terms of the field of Disability Management, this legislation:

- requires employers to advise employees about the nature of personal information collected, used and disclosed, along with why, how and when, unless one of the enumerated exceptions applies;
- restricts the amount of personal information that may be collected;
- requires employee consent for the collection, use and disclosure of personal information, unless the personal information is reasonably required by the organization and is collected, used or disclosed solely for the purposes of establishing, managing or terminating the employment relationship;
- limits the free flow of employee personal health information between healthcare providers and the employers;
- reaffirms the need for "information firewalls" between occupational health personnel and the workplace;
- obligates Disability Management Coordinators to ensure that the employee personal information is accurate and complete; and
- requires employers to ensure that employee personal information is collected, used, retained, disclosed and destroyed in an appropriate manner (for more information refer to Chapter 11, Disability Management Standard of Practice – Confidentiality).

Management of Employee Personal Health Information

REQUEST FOR EMPLOYEE PERSONAL INFORMATION

Company representatives who try to obtain employee personal health information without informed consent from the employee have acted in violation of privacy legislation if it is found that the information was not reasonably required by the organization and collected solely for the purposes of establishing, managing or terminating the employment relationship. If the personal information does not meet this definition, then the consent of the individual is required.

Since the privacy laws were enacted (in Alberta, the *Health Information Act*[18] in 1998 and the *Personal Information Protection Act* in 2004), employer rights to collect employee personal health information have clearly changed. Before collecting personal information, employers should ask:

- "Is this information reasonably required?"
- "Is it fair?"
- "What will the information be used for?"
- "Is there heightened security around this information?"
- "Is there informed consent?"

To complicate matters, in certain circumstances it may not be proper to ask for consent from an employee to collect, use or disclose their personal information. For example, if the company wants to access information that would disclose the presence of a mental health condition, the privacy rights that the employee is being asked to waive are highly protected. The relationship that exists between a manager and employee is a power relationship that can be heavily weighted in favour of the manager. It cannot be assumed that the employee knows his or her rights in this respect. If there was any coercion or duress, or if the impression was given that the employee has no choice but to consent or else face adverse employment action, asking for employee consent may be contrary to the law. Consent must be informed and may not be obtained by providing false or misleading information about the proposed collection, or by using deceptive or unlawful practices.

There is a heightened security of personal health information when dealing with a mental health condition versus a physical one. There is far less social stigma attached to a fractured hip than to mental illness. As a result, more vigilance is required to protect this information.

PROTECTION OF EMPLOYEE HEALTH INFORMATION

Many companies outsource their disability case management services. In the course of their work, the internal Occupational Health professionals or Disability Management Coordinators have greater access to employee personal health information than does the rest of the company. To uphold the privacy of this information, "firewalls" must be in place (Figure 17.1).

---

[18] S.A. 1999, c. H-4.8.

Figure 17.1: Protection of Employee Health Information

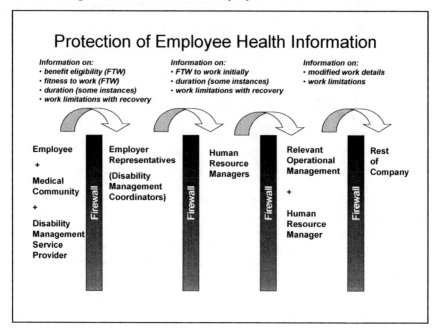

In essence, there are four privacy firewalls:

- Between the employee, health care providers and the Disability Management Service Provider and the internal employer representatives (the Disability Management Coordinators): the information that can be disclosed is limited to benefit eligibility, fitness to work (FTW), absence duration and work limitations.
- Between the Disability Management Coordinators and Human Resource Managers: there is a smaller amount of information disclosed and it is limited to fitness to work initially, duration of absence (in some instances) and anticipated work limitations with recovery.
- Between the Human Resource Managers and the relevant Operational managers: the disclosed information centres on the modified work details and work limitations.
- Between the relevant Operational manager and the rest of the company: the disclosed information is scaled down to a need-to-know basis.

DISCLOSURE OF EMPLOYEE HEALTH INFORMATION

The level of detail that Disability Management Coordinators are allowed to disclose to company managers is limited (Figure 17.2). In the acute phase of the illness/injury, only medical information exists which cannot be provided to company representatives without the employee's informed consent. As a result, the information released is limited to the employee being unfit to work, on a suitable treatment regimen and the nature of the health condition (work-related or non-work-related). This information supports the validity of the claim. In the recovery phase, details on work restrictions can be provided so that return-to-work plans can be made.

Figure 17.2: Stages for the Release of Personal Health Information

Stages for Release of Personal Health Information

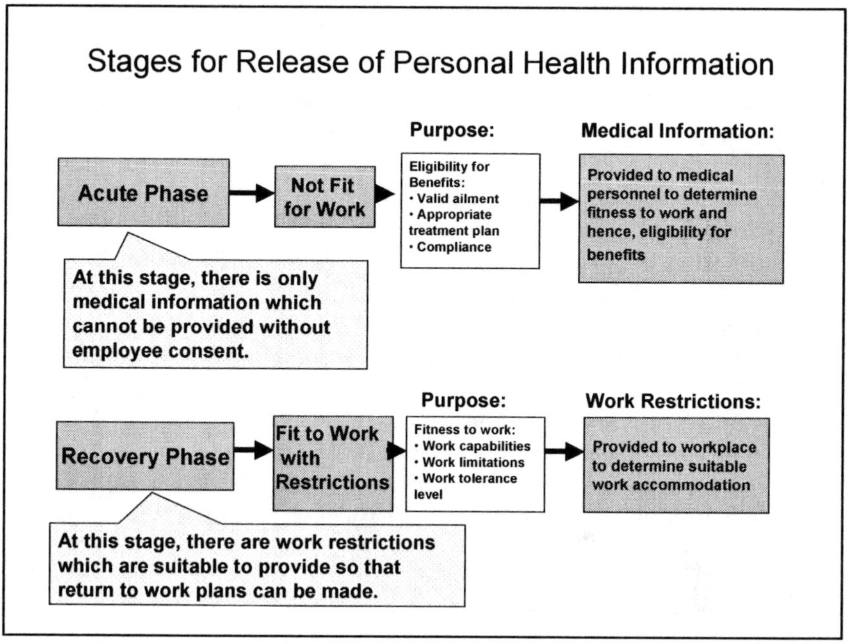

Often Disability Management Coordinators are pressured to provide more information. When this occurs, ask the question: "Is this information *reasonably required* for the sole purpose of maintaining the employment relationship?" If an employee is on STD and eligible for benefit coverage as established by the Disability Management Service Provider, asking for specifics about the employee's health condition could be a violation of privacy legislation.

If the Operation Manager claims that the information is *reasonably required* because he or she wants to know what area of practice the physician is engaged in, this may also be an unlawful collection of personal information. Where the nature of the medical practice would, to a reasonable person, reveal the nature of the ailment, the manager would be able to indirectly access information that they could not otherwise directly access.

If it is deemed *reasonably required* because the Operational Manager is seeking to take employment action, other aspects of employment law come into play. Employment action cannot generally be taken if the employee is lawfully on medical leave.

The Occupational Health professionals or Disability Management Coordinators are permitted to access some personal health information about the employee's condition in order to assess whether or not the external Disability Management Service Provider is fulfilling its contractual commitments to the company, or to ascertain the company's next steps in the work accommodation and reintegration process. Companies can challenge the external Disability Management Service Provider's findings by requesting an independent medical evaluation (IME). In such instances, company representatives are generally not entitled to medical reports, but rather to knowledge of the general nature of the employee's ailment.

Although privacy legislation is relatively new, recent court decisions are fairly clear that employers are required to ensure that:

- Medical information collected to administer an employee benefit plan is legitimately required.
- The medical information submitted by the employee is held in strictest confidence by qualified medical practitioners (PIPEDA, Case Summary #226).
- Appropriate security safeguards are in place to protect sensitive personal medical information from unauthorized access (PIPEDA, Case Summary #226).
- Employees are aware as to how to submit medical information so that it goes to a qualified medical professional (PIPEDA, Case Summary #226).
- Employee requests to review their personal health information are honoured within 30 days of receipt of the written request (PIPEDA, Case Summary #284).[19]

WORK ACCOMMODATION: THE APPLICATION

By Dianne Dyck

Work accommodation means a work opportunity offered to the recovering employee that allows for re-entry and participation in the workplace and which is aligned with the employee's rehabilitation goals and the employer's business needs. It involves:

1. consideration of ways in which the employee's job can be modified;
2. consideration of other available appropriate work within the company;

---

[19] Case Summaries 226 and 284 are available on the homepage of the Privacy Commissioner of Canada: <http://www.privcom.gc.ca/cf-dc/2003/index2-3_e.asp>.

3. the ability to offer rehabilitation and training programs if doing so will enhance the employee's ability for successful re-entry within a reasonable time frame; and
4. the employer taking a lead role in this process.

The duty to accommodate does not mean that companies have to create jobs (*McAlpine v. Econotech Services Ltd.*)[20] to tolerate excessive innocent absenteeism (*Desormeaux v. Ottawa–Carleton Regional Transit Commission*)[21] or to maintain the employment relationship at any cost (*Coulter v. Purolator Courier Ltd.*[22]).[23]

The following is a discussion on the employer and employee's responsibilities in work accommodation.

Employer — Employee Responsibilities

The process of determining reasonable and appropriate accommodation is a shared responsibility. The employer and employee each have key roles to play.

The employee is responsible for letting the employer know that he or she is fit for some level of work. The information must include documented medical support for the modified work along with work limitations. Once the employee is offered work that is appropriate to the identified work limitations, he or she must accept that work and endeavour to make it successful. The employee is also obligated to advise the employer if the work accommodation is suitable, as well as to update the employer on his or her ongoing fitness to work. So as the employee recovers, the work accommodation changes accordingly.

The employer is obliged to:

- ask for relevant information about the employee's medical condition and fitness to work. This means getting the appropriate consents to release medical information, respecting the privacy of the employee's medical information and complying with the applicable privacy legislation;[24]
- determine if suitable work accommodations exist;
- obtain, if required, expert advice on the employee's fitness to work;
- respond to the employee's request for work accommodation within a reasonable time frame;
- document the process and actions taken;
- protect the employee's right to privacy;
- assume all the related costs;

---

[20] [2004] B.C.J. No. 589, 2004 BCCA 111, 32 C.C.E.L. (3d) 165.
[21] [2004] F.C.J. No. 2172.
[22] [2004] C.H.R.D. No. 25.
[23] D. Cory, "Duty to Accommodate – Update (2005)" (Presented to the 23rd Annual Labour Arbitration Policy Conference, June 9, 2005, Toronto, Ontario) [unpublished].
[24] *Ibid.*

- monitor the suitability of the work accommodation opportunity, making changes as required; and
- should an offer of work accommodation be deemed impossible, the employer is obligated to explain to the employee why and be prepared to substantiate the decision.

In terms of the union, the Duty to Accommodate legislation takes precedence over any collective agreement clause that would appear to be discriminatory. The union must be supportive of the work accommodation efforts and facilitate the process up to the point of undue hardship.

SUMMARY

Managing disabilities brings with it many potential pitfalls and legal challenges. Disability management practitioners and employers need to be well versed on their legal obligations and ensure compliance with the applicable laws. Establishing and following Disability Management Standards can lessen such risks.

CHAPTER REFERENCES

British Columbia Council of Human Rights, *Disability and the Human Rights Act* (Victoria: British Columbia Ministry of Labour and Consumer Service, 1998).

Case Summaries 226 and 284, Privacy Commissioner of Canada, online: <http://www.privcom.gc.ca/cf-dc/2003/index2-3_e.asp>.

Centre for Labour Management, "Accommodation Guidelines" (Presented at the Illness and Disability: Claims in the Unionized Workplace Conference, Edmonton, Alberta, February 1999) [unpublished].

D. Cory, "Duty to Accommodate – Update (2005)" (Presented to the 23rd Annual Labour Arbitration Policy Conference, June 9, 2005, Toronto, Ontario) [unpublished].

Coulter v. Purolator Courier Ltd., [2004] C.H.R.D. No. 25.

Desormeaux v. Ottawa–Carleton Regional Transit Commission, [2004] F.C.J. No. 2172.

Health Information Act, S.A. 1999, c. H-4.8.

Human Rights, Citizenship and Multiculturalism Act, R.S.A. 2000, c. H-14, s. 7.

L. McDowell, *Human Rights in the Workplace: A Practical Guide* (Toronto: Carswell, 1998).

McAlpine v. Econotech Services Ltd., [2004] B.C.J. No. 389, 2004 BCCA 111, 32 C.C.E.L. (3d) 165.

R.D. Parsons, *The Ethics of Professional Practice* (Needham Heights, MA: Allyn & Bacon, 2001), at 97.

Personal Information Protection Act, S.A. 2003, c. P-6.5.

Personal Information Protection Act, S.B.C. 2003, c. 63.

Personal Information Protection and Electronic Documents Act, S.C. 2000, c. 5.

K. Robidoux, LL.B., Principal, ComplianceWorks (Calgary, Alberta, November 2005).

C. Sefton & B. Speigel, "Alcoholism Ruled a Handicap" (1995) 11:5 OH&S Canada at 16-17.

Workplace, Health, Safety and Compensation Act, R.S.N.L. 1990, C. W-11, ss. 88-89.4.

Chapter 18

Future Challenges in Disability Management

INTRODUCTION

Disability management came into vogue in the late 80s. It was born out of necessity. Organizational leaders realized that employee medical absences were costly, and that disability-related costs involved "after tax" dollars. This meant that organizations had to sell more gas, televisions, cars, goods and services to cover the cost of employee absenteeism and disability.

As organizations became more sophisticated in measuring employee absence and disability costs, they realized the need to manage medical absences and to facilitate early return-to-work opportunities for recovering employees. The adopted approach was to develop disability management programs that assist employees in returning to work.

Given that disability management was, and still is, an emerging field, there has been some confusion as to what it is, how it is implemented and by whom and what the best practices are. As well, much of what has been learned since the late 80s has been learned by trial and error. This book has been an attempt to compile that knowledge. However, there remain a number of challenges yet to be addressed. This chapter is a multi-author discussion on some of the future challenges in the field of disability management.

CLIENT CONFUSION REGARDING DISABILITY MANAGEMENT

By Heidi Börner

Disability management was typically offered as part of the duties of the occupational health professionals. However, as interest in the area of disability management grew, many new players became involved, each offering unique services to corporate clients. Confusion reigned. A discussion on the various service providers in disability management follows to assist individuals involved in disability management.

The potential for personal and economic savings through disability management instead of leaving illness/injury situations to take their own course has been recognized by the business world. Many service providers have sprung up of late claiming to be able to save companies huge amounts of money. Many of them can help companies save money, but how does an employer choose the one that is right for the organization? What capabilities and qualities should a service provider demonstrate before a potential employer should even consider bringing them into their organization?

Before choosing a service provider to deliver disability management services, the employer should have a good idea as to why their organization wants to manage disability. Is it to save money? To improve workplace relations with employees or unions? To retain valuable employees? A mixture of reasons? Knowing what is wanted from the disability management service, the employer can determine which service provider would be right for the organization. The beauty of disability management is that doing it right *does* result in saved resources for the organization — time, expertise, experience *and* money.

There are universal characteristics of effective disability management — ethics, knowledge, motivation, professionalism, respect, trust, confidentiality, communication, diplomacy, understanding of systems, reporting and record-keeping. In order to handle disabilities effectively, the service provider must have and use all of the skills and possess all of the qualities needed to operate according to the established principles. This is what makes disability management both a science and an art.

An ethical disability manager operates honestly, truthfully and consistently according to professional practice standards and recognized policies and procedures. As well, they must strive to create "win-win" situations, that is, a "win" for the company and a "win" for the injured or ill employee. Many service providers operate only by creating barriers for the injured or ill employee, believing that money will be saved by blocking employee access to insurance or Workers' Compensation benefits. While that may be true, managing claims in this manner not only creates undue hardship for the injured or ill employee in terms of financial, or medical care resources, but it can also be an illegal practice. Most organizations do not want this type of "win-lose" situation for their employees. They consider employees to be the company or organization's greatest resource. They have insurance plans in place because they want to assist employees in returning as productive members of the organization. Most organizations want also to be seen as good employers that offer a caring work environment. In choosing a service provider, or hiring one internally, ask them what their primary motivation is for providing disability management services. A good service provider's motivation is aligned with the sponsoring organization's culture and goals.

A service provider's ethical beliefs motivate their disability management efforts. Is the service provider in business solely to make money? If so, they are not necessarily good Disability Managers. Good Disability Managers are in business because they have the expertise to assist both the organization and the employee in getting through the disability period and to returning to productive work, or an optimal level of functioning. They are there to help both the organization and the employee. This sound and basic management principle can save resources for the organization. Ask for the service provider's mission statement. If they don't have one, find out what their motivation is to do this type of business. Being knowledgeable about potential service providers will help narrow your search.

Good communication is a key attribute for a Disability Manager. Communication occurs in several areas — between the Disability Manager and the employee; the Disability Manager and employer; the Disability Manager and community resource agencies; the employee and employer; the employee and co-workers; the Disability Manager and insurance companies; the employee and health professionals; the employer and unions; and the employee and unions — to name a few. The Disability Manager must have the ability to recognize what communication is taking place in the course of a claim, and be able to relate effectively with each party.

Proactive communication with all parties in the form of defining roles and responsibilities early in the case allows the disability management process to proceed without confusion. It is important to know how the disability management service provider plans to handle each step of a claim. By asking for a disability management process flowchart, the lack of consistent processes would be evident. Endless time and money can be wasted on poor or ineffective communication processes. Therefore, it is important to thoroughly investigate how the potential service provider plans to do both claims and case management.

The ability to communicate with diplomacy, empathy and understanding to the injured or ill employee and family is critical. Not only should the claims process reflect communication between all parties involved in the claim, it should also demonstrate respect and understanding for the ill or injured employee and his or her family. A therapeutic relationship can only be created when there is mutual understanding, respect and trust. When interviewing a potential disability management service provider, ask for real and specific examples of how difficult claims are handled; what makes those claims difficult; and what results can be expected.

An effective Disability Manager acknowledges that they have encountered difficult claims, and demonstrates effective problem solving techniques. What's more, the body language of the prospective service provider usually reflects just how committed they are to the human element. If the prospective service providers appear dismissive and tell you that they have never had a difficult claim, they should be regarded as suspect. A potential service provider who warms to the topic and displays a sense of accomplishment at a successful resolution gets marks for showing appropriate motivation.

Also, determine if the potential service provider conducts client satisfaction surveys, and ask to see the results. Verify the information obtained from the service provider against the client references supplied. Many service agreement contracts are not renewed due to deficiencies in this area; so be sure to check them out thoroughly before entering into a service agreement.

Disability management service qualifications are poorly defined. Certified occupational health nurses, occupational therapists, physiotherapists, kinesiologists and physicians all could have the proper qualifications. However, a good Disability Manager must have connections with both the medical and rehabilitation world. Without these connections, it becomes very difficult to refer employees to the appropriate community resources.

Make sure that the potential service provider can describe an employee's health status and history in medical terms; that the right information is recounted; and that effective rehabilitation plans are developed. Also knowledge of the terms required for the completion of Workers' Compensation Board, and third party insurance forms is essential to ensure that full and appropriate claims information is communicated. Knowledge of human anatomy, physiology and treatment modalities makes the Disability Manager a recognized part of a rehabilitation team, rather than an outside challenge or threat to health care providers.

Disability management service providers must adhere to a code of professional ethics, especially around the issue of confidentiality. Each health science professional has a code of ethics and process of confidentiality. Failure to adhere to the specific code of ethics can result in dismissal. Thus, it is important to determine what qualifications the prospective service provider's staff have, especially those handling the initial intake call to the service, and those involved in claims and case management.

Ask the service provider what information they disclose and to whom; what processes they use in obtaining the employee's consent to release medical information; and who has access to their patient records. Employers should only be receiving information from the Disability Manager who determines the ill or injured employee's fitness to work, and/or work restrictions. Anything more requires a signed consent to release personal health information.

Education in occupational health and safety is fundamental to the disability management process. Gathering the appropriate information regarding job demands, and translating that information into medical implications of an illness or injury, requires education in toxicology, human anatomy and physiology, environmental hazards and stressors, occupational safety and business practices. The Disability Manager must be able to demonstrate competence in translating medical terminology into business terms, and work demands into implications for care.

A service provider's list of client references can help to identify his or her level of competence. Ask the service provider's clients if they feel that they know and clearly understand what their returning employees can do upon re-entry to the workplace. Also, establish what information for improving the workplace health and safety practices is communicated to the client-organization.

An organization's reporting and record-keeping requirements should be decided before interviewing a prospective service provider. Organizations need to be able to quantify both the related disability management costs and savings in order to measure the performance of the Disability Management Program, and to celebrate the success of the program. Justifying the program's existence at budget time becomes that much easier if this information is available. Ask the service providers what kind of reports they can generate; how they track data and report illness or injury and recovery trends; and how they determine the total costs of a disability management program as well as the associated return on investment.

Service performance is not just measured in terms of dollars and cents. Service performance should reflect the universal disability management principles covered in Chapter 1 of this book. Ask the prospective service provider how you will know if they have delivered the services promised. Know what you want them to report to you and within what time frames. Ask how quickly they are able to respond to an employee in crisis; how many "lost time" days they usually save for their clients; how satisfied employees using their program/service are with the service; what rating they get from their clients for their staff being respectful, helpful, friendly and/or appropriate; and what measures they use to maintain client confidentiality. There are many ways to measure service performance. A responsible service provider will work with you to set up an evaluation program that meets both your needs.

Lastly, choosing a service provider should not be a hasty move. It requires introspection, planning and commitment from all levels of the sponsoring organization. It also requires internal preparation for the management of the activities or functions that the service provider cannot be expected to deliver. Even the best service provider cannot be effective in an organization that has no time, resources or interest in a Disability Management Program. The sponsoring organization must identify the internal and service provider roles; establish the areas of accountability; set performance measurement standards for each party; clearly define the measurement techniques and schedules; and ensure that the lines of communication remain open. By working together, the service provider and organization can effectively manage employee disability. The payoffs, for each, are definitely worth the effort required.

IMPACT OF RISING HEALTH CARE COSTS ON DISABILITY MANAGEMENT PROGRAMS

By Sharon Blaney

The delivery of health care in Canada is primarily the responsibility of the provincial and territorial governments. The funding, however, comes from a mix of public and private sources. The public sources include taxes and federal transfer payments. The private component is made up of employer-sponsored health care benefit plans, privately purchased health care insurance and direct charges.

To receive the federal transfer payments, a province must uphold the principles of the *Canada Health Act* — accessibility, portability, universality and comprehensiveness. Between 1991 and 1996, the public share of total Health Canada expenditures dropped from 74.6% to 69.9%.[1] This reduction of public funding is having a direct impact on disability management programs and their cost.

The impact on the reduction of public funding for health care has led to a number of cutbacks. These cutbacks resulted in longer waiting periods to see specialists, increased waiting time for hospital admissions, shortened hospital stays, cutbacks in diagnostic test procedure availability due to lack of equipment, and reduction or adjustments to pharmaceutical prescribing powers. These initiatives by the health care community, which have been driven by the need to reduce costs, have also increased employer costs for employee absenteeism and health care benefit plans. The challenge for Disability Management Programs is to turn these increasing costs of extended absence into real savings for the organization.

The increasing lengths of time for hospital admission or diagnostic testing cost companies money. This occurs in a number of ways. The longer an employee is off the job, the less likely he or she is to return. The average waiting time for hospital admission is between eight and 12 weeks. To compound this situation, hospital admissions cannot even be considered until after the specialist's review and diagnostic testing have been completed. On the other hand, statistics show that after an absence of three months, an employee is only 50% likely to return to work.[2]

A number of corporations have taken matters into their own hands. They recognize that the longer an employee is away, the less likely it is that he or she will return to the workplace. They realize that accessibility to specialist, diagnostic equipment and hospitalization continues to be difficult and prolonged. Employers also know that the cost to the corporate bottom line for employee absenteeism is steadily increasing. For example, in 1998, Health Canada estimated the cost of absenteeism to be in the neighbourhood of $10 billion.[3] By 2001, these costs increased to $17 billion.[4] Today, it is believed that this cost is much higher.

To overcome some of these issues, Canadian corporations are bypassing the national health care system. Frustrated by extended delays, employers are expediting specialist appointments, diagnostic tests and rehabilitation programs by

---

[1]   Conference Board of Canada, *From Payer to Payer: The Employer's Role in the Canadian Health Care System Report #246-98* (Ottawa: Conference Board of Canada, 1998) at 3.

[2]   J. Cowell, "Fitness to Work" (Presented at The Conference on Workers' Compensation, Calgary, 1996) [unpublished]. National Institute for Disability Management and Research (NIDMAR), *Strategies for Success: Disability Management in the Workplace* (Port Alberni, B.C.: NIDMAR, 1997) at 2.

[3]   Health Canada, "Lost Work Cost Placed at $10 Billion Dollars", *Vancouver Sun* (2 September, 1999).

[4]   J. Kranc, "Fact Check", *Benefits Canada* (March 2004) at 70 and 86.

paying for these services up front. This "fee for service" or "front of the line" approach is resulting in earlier diagnosis and treatment of employee health problems. This is translating to an earlier return to work by employees, and reduced absence costs for both employees and employers. Using this approach, one company estimates that the average saving per case for their early return-to-work program was approximately $20,000.[5] This approach, however, is not without dilemmas.

To begin with, arguments exist for and against the ethics of "jumping the cue" by accessing third party "fee-for-service" health care. Some of the dilemmas include the following:

- Are we creating a two- or three-tier health care system?
- How does the organization decide who to assist and who not to assist?
- Are employees being treated in a fair and consistent manner?

Another issue is cost, and assumption of cost. For example, many of the new costly pharmaceutical products and treatment modalities may not be covered by provincial health care plans and employee benefit programs. The arguments that exist involve the decisions regarding the cost of the treatment versus the savings to the organization. In essence, does the cost outweigh the projected savings? As organizations venture into the area of disability management, these costs can continue long past the employee's return-to-work date. An example of this is the new treatment for HIV. The cost for the medication cocktail is approximately $2,000 per month. This treatment regime is not designed to cure the disease, but merely to arrest its progress. Are these costs covered by the employee benefit drug plan? If not, who pays the bill? If the Disability Management Program picks up the costs, how long should these costs continue to be under the program's domain?

In this section, a number of future dilemmas for Disability Management Programs have been introduced. The answers to these issues remain unknown. However, as we move beyond the management of individual medical problems and enter into the era of disease state management, we will have to find answers to these and many other ethical-business situations.

---

[5] BCTel, *BCTel Evaluation of Occupational Health 1998 Program Costs* (British Columbia: BCTel, 1999) [unpublished].

IMPACT OF FOUR GENERATIONS IN THE WORKPLACE ON DISABILITY MANAGEMENT PROGRAMS

By Dianne Dyck

For the first time in history, there are four generations working in today's workplaces. This unique situation raises questions like:

- What impact will each of these generations have on employer absenteeism and disability management efforts?
- How will the inter-generational differences impact absenteeism and disability rates and processes?

The Four Generations

The following are broad descriptions of the four generations:

1.   VETERANS OR DEPRESSION GENERATION

Workers born between 1927 and 1945 make up this cohort. Now aged 61-79 years old, Veterans are approaching retirement, or have retired and returned to the workforce. The issue that employers face with these workers is that they are not sure how to use these very experienced older workers who are now taking the low-end service jobs away from young workers. Although employers value the Veterans' work ethics, reliability and wealth of experience, these workers are absorbing the "first jobs" typically held by workers entering the workplace — jobs that set the foundation for the building of work ethics.

Veterans, having been greatly influenced by the stock market crash and the Great Depression, World War II, the Atomic Bomb and the Cold War, display traits such as:

- patriotic values;
- a prudent approach to life and spending. They tend to save their money to pad their "nest-egg";
- when spending, they value quality and nationally-made products;
- a willingness to make personal sacrifices for delayed gratification;
- strong religious beliefs;
- strong company loyalty;
- value work relationships;
- participation in team work provided they lead the team;
- acceptance of hierarchical leadership;

- value chain of command;[6]
- respectful of authority;
- view work performance feedback in terms of "no news is good news";
- a black and white world view;
- unable to understand the need for work/life balance;
- struggle with the concept of leisure and recreation time; and
- reluctance to exercise.

Their work values include loyalty, dependability, persistence, hard work to get ahead, authoritarian leadership, and wisdom and experience over technical knowledge.

2. BABY BOOMERS

Born between 1946 and 1964, these workers are the heart and soul of today's workforce. This very large generation, which is now between the ages of 42 and 60 years, has shaped the face of the North American work scene for a number of years.

Influenced by Civil Rights, War on Poverty, Atomic Age, Race to Space, Vietnam, political turmoil of assassinations and impeachment, this cohort has challenged the existing social institutions, conventions, and assumptions through the use of protests. Dubbed the "whiners", they are today viewed as a disenchanted group because the promise that they bought into was that they would not be working as hard as they are at this time in their careers or lives. They want lots of control in their lives and perceive that they do not have it. The result is that many Boomers go to work, but are not really fully engaged in the work.

The traits of this generation are:

- idealistic;
- extremely competitive;
- crave stability and dislike change;[7]
- cling to revolutionary values;
- strong consumers;
- buy goods partly because they like them, but mainly to impress others;
- tend to buy foreign goods for prestige reasons;
- heavily into personal gratification;
- known as the true "Sandwich Generation" with responsibilities to aging parents and children;
- view religion as a "hobby";

---

[6] J. Duchscher & L. Cowen, "Multigenerational Nurses in the Workplace" (2004) 34:11 Journal of Nursing Administration at 493-501.

[7] S. Calhoun & P. Strasser, "Generations at Work" (2005) 53:11 American Association of Occupational Health Nurses at 469-471.

- perceive exercising as a duty;
- value profitability and their reputation;
- prefer leadership by consensus;
- value participatory leadership and coaching;[8]
- have a "love/hate" relationship with authority;
- work hard, play hard — they invented the term, "workaholic";
- tend to lack realistic views of their abilities and stamina;[9]
- tend to worry lots about money; and
- prefer yearly feedback work performance and with documentation.

Their work values include acceptance of stress, team-oriented, high regard for title and status symbols, demand respect and sacrifice from subordinates, workaholics, value job security and very competitive with others.

3.   GENERATION X OR BABY BUST

Deemed the "slackers", these workers were born between 1965 and 1985. Their values differ greatly from those held by the Boomers. They grew up with self-immersed,[10] workaholic parents.[11] Being latch-key children who watched their parents being "laid off" after years of hard work and personal sacrifices for "the company", this cohort tends to display great skepticism, independence and re-sourcefulness. In addition, they were impacted by increased technology, video games, cultural diversity, homelessness, nuclear threat, rap music, anti-child society, the fall of the Berlin Wall and AIDS.

Other characteristics of Generation Xers are:

- skeptical;
- cynical;
- nonconformist;
- possess an attitude of "I like it and I don't care what you think";
- reluctant to commit to a relationship (trial marriages);
- strongly value work/life balance and they want it *Now*;
- work hard provided work does not interfere with their play plans;
- willing to sacrifice some personal life for advancement;
- not into established community groups like the Lions Club or Rotary, or religion;
- value exercise for the well-being of their mental health;
- like inner-city living;
- seek stimulation, balance and feedback from their work world;

---

[8]   *Ibid.*, at 469.
[9]   *Ibid.*, at 469.
[10]   *Supra*, note 6.
[11]   N. Pekala, "Conquering the Generational Divide" (2001) 66:6 Journal of Property Management at 30-38.

- value leader competence;
- neither unimpressed nor intimidated by authority;
- good at saving money;
- want regular feedback on their work performance; and
- value recognition for their achievements.

In terms of work, they are determined to manage their own time. They value minimal supervision, a flexible work schedule, participatory leadership and coaching.[12]

4.　Baby Boomlet (also referred to as Nexus and Millennial)

This last generational group, born between 1984-2002, is currently four to 22 years of age. However, they are a big generation and are expected to make significant changes to society and the work scene.

Being the largest generation of "have and have nots", this group has been impacted by the breakdown in the nuclear family, environmental concerns, violence and bullying, terrorism, and being "wired" to technology. Baby Boomlets are the first generation to grow up without the expectations of a nuclear family — less than 33% lived in homes with two parents.[13] As well, this generation tends to use on-line technology to forge relationships. Reportedly, 35% of them report having found their "best friends" on-line.[14]

These children were raised by parents who involved them in a whirlwind of extra-curriculum activities. Because their parents did not, and do not, know how to deal with their hyperactivity, Baby Boomlets have the distinction of being the most medicated generation ever. In fact, some socialists feel that these children are growing up with a form of post-traumatic stress disorder.

The specific traits of this generation are:

- optimistic;
- "Gap" shoppers;
- value inclusive relationships;
- desire flexibility in their daily routine;
- willing to participate in community endeavours;
- unable to relate with religion;
- heavily into playing sports;
- like living with their parents;
- value cultural diversity in the workplace;
- appreciate the support systems afforded by the workplace;

---

[12] *Supra,* note 7.

[13] *Ibid.*

[14] J. Jamrog, "The Perfect Storm" (Presented at a CHRP Seminar, Calgary, Alberta, September 15, 2005) [unpublished].

- view leadership as "pulling together" for a cause;
- value collaboration and relationship-oriented leadership;[15]
- polite towards authority figures;
- work towards getting good grades in school;
- value saving money; and
- seek and demand feedback on their work performance. They are used to getting feedback at the touch of a button.

The Baby Boomlet worker is characterized as having short attention span, expecting things to happen quickly, and seeking variety in life and work. They want balance in their lives and strongly dislike organized groups like labour unions.

Impact on the Workplace

The world of work has changed. Loyalty and commitment to employers has vanished. Being at work on time has decreased in importance. Sick leave abuse is common. Job security and high pay are not the motivators they once were. Why? Young people have watched their parents remain loyal to their employees, only to witness them experience downsizing and layoffs.

Today, young workers are seeking jobs in which they can make a valuable contribution, work at a variety of tasks, and learn new marketable skills. They demand intellectual stimulation, team environments, transferability of work experiences, and salaries that match the rising cost of living. Interestingly, they do not believe they should have to "pay their dues" and bide their time for job advancement. Because they "work to live" and not "live to work", they refuse to be the workaholics that their parents were.

Older workers are working their way towards retirement; however, some, for a variety of reasons, are choosing not to retire as soon as was once predicted. Likewise, some older workers who have retired, are back doing entry level jobs.

With four generations in the workplace, each with their own beliefs, values, wants and needs, employers face the daunting challenge of trying to meet worker expectations. For example, meetings are viewed by Veterans and Baby Boomers as "busy work". They prefer short meetings, speedy decisions, and only want to meet when there is an urgent need. Generation Xers and Baby Boomlets tend to value the interaction and view meetings as a way to reach a solution to an identified problem.

Veterans and Boomers value rules and regulations. Generation Xers and Baby Boomlets have been known to ignore rules, policies and chain-of-command. Baby Boomlets live in a world of advanced technology. They are techno-wizards who embrace technology as a normal element of their lives. Veterans and

---

[15] *Supra*, note 7.

Boomers had to learn to adapt to technology and for some, there remains a healthy "distrust of these new tools".

IMPLICATIONS FOR THE DISABILITY MANAGEMENT COORDINATOR

Disability Management Coordinators working with these four generations need to appreciate the individual characteristics of each generation. For example, older workers tend to be away from work more days per year due to illness or personal reasons than are younger workers. If injured, older workers require much longer off work than do younger workers to recover. However, older workers have a strong work ethic and therefore are amenable to a variety of re-turn-to-work options. Unfortunately, many of them have vocational limitations in terms of their cross-transferable skills.

Some Baby Boomers are disenchanted with their lot in life and are trying to decide what their "golden years" might look like. They tend to overestimate their abilities and stamina, and are seeking to control their life and destiny. Such unrealistic goals tend to predispose them to an increased incidence of mental health problems. However, they are a generation where admission to having mental/nervous health problems remains "taboo", and therefore they tend to "struggle on" without seeking professional help until they "crash". For them, recovery can be difficult because to seek help, they first have to overcome a number of long-standing values and beliefs.

Younger workers, on the other hand, are less likely to succumb to illness, but are more likely to get injured in sport-related incidents or other risk-taking ac-tivities. Given they tend to challenge authority, company rules, and policies, these workers will be looking for adequate explanations of the Disability Man-agement Program and processes. They will be seeking innovative rehabilitation plans and modified work opportunities. They value competence and expect Dis-ability Management Coordinators to provide quality, competent services. Luck-ily, younger workers tend to have strong computer skills and technological capa-bilities that align well with many modified work opportunities.

Intergenerational Conflict

When four groups with different beliefs, attitudes, values, needs and wants exist in a workplace, misunderstanding and conflict can occur. In the past, workplace policies, programs, and benefits were designed to meet the beliefs, attitudes, values, needs and wants of the majority. Clearly, that approach of "one size fits all", is no longer effective.

For Disability Management Coordinators, challenges might arise in the fol-lowing scenarios:

1. the Veteran employees working with Generation X or Nexus employ-ees;
2. the Baby Boomer employee supervising the Generation X employee;

3. the Baby Boomer Human Resource manager working with a Nexus employee; or
4. the Baby Boomlet working in a traditional workplace where company loyalty, lines of authority, work rules, vertical career ladders and linear advancement are strongly valued.

From the descriptions already provided, one can imagine any number of conflicts that could arise when they are communicating, problem solving, working together, or trying to address differences of opinions.

Motivational Differences

While no two people are motivated in the same way, motivators tend to be generational-based. This means that managers need greater insight into age-related issues and what motivates workers. For example, Baby Boomers strive for money, title, and the "corner office with the rug". Generation X workers want freedom and job security; whereas the Baby Boomlets want a job that has meaning for them. The Veteran, on the other hand, is baffled as to why these other workers need any more recognition than the pay cheque they get every two weeks.

To motivate Veterans, the manager needs to opt for formality, such as communicating face-to-face or by phone as opposed to communicating through e-mail or voice mail. As well, it is important to explain the logic behind the actions proposed or taken. As for recognition, the traditional forms of recognition, such as plaques, certificates or photos with top executives are appreciated.

Boomers are motivated by goals that have been set by their managers. They value having the objectives established and the desired results stated in people-centred terms. Team participation is important. For them, recognition is being mentioned in the company newsletter, having their name on a parking spot, or receiving a promotion and title.

The Generation Xers prefer to be told what needs to be done; not how to do it. They like multiple tasks and the freedom to determine their own work priorities. Frequent and frank feedback is expected. As for their work preferences, they like flexibility, dressing casually, having fun and enjoying a healthy work/life balance.

Motivating the Baby Boomlets differs. They seek opportunities for continuous learning and enhancement of their work skills. Their managers need to appreciate the Boomlets' personal goals and respond by linking the assigned tasks to these goals. Baby Boomlets respond to a positive work environment and prefer their manager to be more of a coach and less of a boss. For them, informal communication such as casual chats in the hallway, e-mails, or voice mail, will suffice. Their preferred form of recognition is to be given bonus days off work.

Other Differences

Worker expectations and communication styles vary by generation. The Veterans do not seek much feedback. Their credo is "No news is good news". The Boomers prefer to receive feedback on their work performance once a year and in writing. Both the Generation X and Baby Boomlets want immediate and frequent feedback, only the Boomlets want it daily.

In terms of work/life balance, the Veterans want help to shift the work/life balance. The Boomers seek help to balance their work and family life. Generation Xers want work/life balance now. For the Boomlets, work isn't everything. They want the flexibility to balance their lives and activities. Family life and travel opportunities are highly valued. They are often willing to give up a job to return to school or to travel for extensive periods of time.

The perspectives on job change radically differ. For the Veterans, a job change carries a stigma. The Boomers perceive job change as a "glitch" in their career path. To the Generation Xers, job change is necessary — it is part of their career development and path. The Boomlets feel likewise, but they expect job change to happen many times in their careers.

Recommendations to Disability Management Coordinators

Disability Management Coordinators must continue to use a holistic approach when dealing with ill/injured workers. This means understanding the characteristics of these four generations, and adapting disability management services to meet their respective needs. Disability management programs, like other employee benefits, need to be "cafeteria style", providing flexibility and variability in the offerings and services.

Disability Management Program communications should appeal to all four generations. Multi-media approaches that include the traditional written documentation (brochures, newsletters, worker packages *etc.*) should be combined with more interactive media approaches (webpages, electronic message boards, *etc.*). Solicit feedback about the program and its services using a variety of techniques namely hardcopy and electronic surveys, focus groups, chat boxes, *etc.*

Disability Management Program marketing messages need to be tailored. The Veterans, who tend to possess strong company loyalty, value money and work relationships and have strong work ethics, respond well to the message that disability management helps them and their coworkers to remain active in the workplace. The Boomers on the other hand, tend to be workaholics. They work and play hard. They also perceive exercise and staying physically fit as their duty. They respond well to the sports analogy that one would never put a recovering athlete back into a game situation before providing rehabilitation and a period of participation in game workouts. Modified work is the same. It provides an opportunity for work hardening aimed at enabling the employee to return to his/her regular job. Additionally, they value money and perceive modified work as worthwhile if there is a pay differential over being on STD coverage.

Generation Xers perceive exercise as essential to their well being. For them, the sports analogy would also work, however they will expect frequent feedback on their recovery progress and recognition for their modified work efforts. The Baby Boomlets are similar on both the above issues, however, they may respond better to the message that modified work is one way of helping their work team to continue to operate through the disability period.

The choice of modified work duties is another area for consideration. Boomers, Generation Xers and Baby Boomlets who are technologically savvy, are well suited for modified duties involving office work, working at home and alternate job duties. Veterans who work in primarily labour positions pose an interesting challenge. Although knowledgeable and experienced, they may be unwilling to do modified duties that are outside of their comfort zone, or deemed to be lesser jobs.

Worker response to support services differs. As already noted, Veterans and Baby Boomers perceive mental/nervous health conditions in a negative manner. To them, the stigma of mental health disorders remains alive and well. Generation Xers and Baby Boomers are much more tolerant about human frailties. As a result, one would expect younger workers to be more receptive to using EAPs and other company supports. Boomers, Generation Xers and Baby Boomlets all value exercise and the benefits participation affords. Physiotherapy and reconditioning efforts would be better received by them than by the Veterans who view exercise only as a "necessary evil".

These are but a few of the generational differences that a Disability Management Coordinator will have to face. The key recommendation is to know your clientele, respect their unique differences, and be flexible and innovative in your approaches.

DISABILITY MANAGEMENT: DIVERSITY CONSIDERATIONS

By Dianne Dyck

"Today's workforce is highly diverse. It ranges from single men and women of various cultural backgrounds with no dependants, to those married with children and caring for elderly parents."[16] Each has different values, beliefs, needs and expectations on life and work. By effectively managing diversity, organizations can enhance their competitive advantage in the Canadian labour market.

---

[16] T. Buller, "A Flexible Combination", *Benefits Canada* (November 2004) at 99, online: <http://www.benefitscanada.ca>.

Diversity Types

THE OLDER WORKER (OVER AGED 60 YEARS)

Older workers have many work qualities that make them a valuable asset to any workplace. They are described as experienced, loyal, possessing strong work ethics, and willing to try a variety of roles.

Society as a whole, tends to be gerontophobic (fear of the aging process) and as such, tends to be prejudiced against older workers. Some of this is perpetuated by the media, and some by older workers themselves. For example, many older workers view themselves as being too old to start a new career or to tackle a new business endeavour. Having spent their entire career in one line of work, many believe that they could not do anything else. And some view themselves as being overqualified to do a less demanding job.

In terms of hiring the older worker, employers question the required training and development investment given that the older worker may not be with the company all that long. Employers also view these workers as being physically slower, less physically able, less productive, more set in their ways, unable to adapt to new technology, and more likely to get hurt.

Older workers do face a number of challenges that comes with the aging process. For example, 23% of Canadian workers experience illness/injuries that negatively impacts their ability to function in the workplace. By age 65, the prevalence of disability increases to 42%.[17] Some other noted conditions that are associated with aging are hearing loss, visual deficits, slower reaction times, problems with shift work, increased susceptibility to lengthy absences if injured and increased prevalence of chronic health conditions. However, these can be mitigated by a supportive lifestyle and being realistic with the work assignments.

In terms of work-personal life conflict, older workers are often involved in providing care for an older, dependant relative. Working and shouldering this type of responsibility can lead to caregiver strain — the stress of caring for an elderly dependant. Older women are particularly susceptible, especially when they have additional caregiving responsibilities for grandchildren.

Today, many older workers are holding down a variety of jobs that range from entry-level to key knowledge positions. Employers appreciate the dedication and expertise that they bring, and therefore, are willing to shoulder any associated risks and costs.

WOMEN

Women have been in the workforce for many years, but still experience a certain degree of systemic discrimination. For example, although they hold managerial and professional positions, many earn less income than men. Women who are

---

[17] K. Williams, "Returning to Work After Disability: What Goes Wrong?" (Presented at Canadian Human Resource Planners event, May 15, 2003, Calgary, Alberta) [unpublished].

trying to get into, or are employed in male-dominated occupations, continue to face many barriers. Other aspects like different communication styles, relationship styles, primary caregivers responsibilities, absence of mentoring programs, and the need for flexibility on work assignments, set women apart from men.

In terms of well being, women over age 40 years experience more stress than men or younger women. This phenomenon is believed to be related to balancing work and family issues. From a work perspective, the higher the amount of work interference with family duties, the greater the amount of stress experienced by women. For example, business travel, which requires making alternate child and elder care arrangements, is more stressful for women than for men. From a home perspective, the amount of caregiving that the woman is committed to provide is directly proportional to the amount of strain experienced. Additionally, as women age, they tend to be more involved in additional caregiving activities (aging parents, children and grandchildren).[18]

Women differ from men in the nature of the disabilities experienced. For example, they are more likely to suffer mobility problems, pain-related disabilities, and vision problems, whereas men tend to have more hearing and speech problems.[19] Some of these conditions tend to worsen with age.

Companies that have a predominantly female workforce are advised to provide family-friendly workplaces. Supportive policies and programs such as flexible work hours, flex days, childcare and eldercare information, daycare, EAP, family days, *etc.*, help women to balance their work and family commitments, thereby enabling them to meet company performance expectations.

OTHER CULTURES

Immigration is on the increase in Canada and the United States. In the past five years, immigration has accounted for 70% of the growth in Canada's labour force.[20] This translates to multicultural workforces with different views on life and approaches to work and life events. To better explain this phenomenon, a comparison of three dominant cultures found in Canada is provided (Figure 18.1).

---

[18] L. Duxbury & C. Higgins, *Report Four: Who is at Risk? Predictors of Work-Life Conflict* (Ottawa: Public Health Agency of Canada, 2005) at 7, 9 and 10, online: <http://www.phac-aspc.gc.ca/publicat/work-travail/report4/index.html>.

[19] Statistics Canada, *A Profile of Disability in Canada, 2001* (Ottawa: Statistics Canada, 2003), available online at: <http://www.statscan.ca/english/freepub/89-577-XIE/index.htm>.

[20] L. Duxbury, "Managing a Changing Workforce", presented in Calgary, Alberta (2004) [unpublished].

Figure 18.1: Cultural Viewpoints on Life, Approaches to Work and Life Events

Business Aspect	Western Perspective	First Nations Perspective	Asian Perspective
Meetings	The focus is on completing tasks and achieving goals. Time considerations are usually a driving force.	Interpersonal relations and affiliations are important when starting a discussion. The outcome is a prolonged discussion with the task being secondary.	The desire is to keep the conversation smooth and harmonious. Issues, circumstances and relationships are as important as the work.
	Agendas, deadlines and schedules are specifically set out.	Meetings may not be scheduled; dealings and accomplishments are based on need, attendance and consensus.	Meetings, agendas, schedules and punctuality are handled with regard for the individuals involved. In essence, human relations play an important role.
	Punctuality is valued.	Punctuality is not expected.	
Individual versus Group Importance	Individual importance is valued over the group.	Group importance is valued over individual importance.	Group importance is valued over individual importance.
Competitiveness	Competition and confrontation are accepted and individual initiative is valued.	Co-operation brings the best results; harmony and personal humility are important in the process.	Conversations are harmoniously conducted. This means refraining from open disagreements, asking difficult questions of superiors, publicly embarrassing a person, or saying things that will cause problems. Differences are best worked out quietly.
	Criticism and confrontation are accepted in order to "get the job done". Criticism and opposition may be used to expose the full picture.	Personal and group honour and dignity are valued and preserved. Criticism, disagreement or unsolicited suggestions are avoided.	

Business Aspect	Western Perspective	First Nations Perspective	Asian Perspective
Goal Achievement	Tasks are compartmentalized and considered one at a time.	Information and ideas are dealt with in the widest possible context.	Decisions are made by consensus.
	The facts directly related to the issue are presented with an emphasis on reaching a solution. Clarity is expected.	Several suggestions may be offered simultaneously and all are considered. This prolongs and enriches the process of problem solving.	The context of where and how comments are heard can be more important than what was said. Communication is indirect and implicit
	Rational, logical, linear problem solving is valued.	Problem solving is intuitive, creative and holistic.	Problem solving is handled with regard for the individuals involved.
	Accuracy and perfection are expected.	Inaccuracy and error are accepted.	Accuracy and perfection are expected.
	Timelines and completion expectations are required to achieve the desired goals.	While completion is at times important, time elements are seldom considered.	Timelines and completion expectations are required to achieve the desired goals.
	Problems are solved by the leader or when a group vote decides a course of action.	Group decision making prevails, conflicts are resolved through consensus after divergent ideas are debated.	Decisions are made by consensus.
	Ruthless measures may be taken to attain results.	Loss of dignity and disharmony is avoided.	Behaviours are directed primarily to maintaining congenial relations and affiliation within the group.
Directing Work	Direct orders and instruction are readily given.	Rather than direct orders, suggestions are better received.	Direct orders are avoided.

Business Aspect	Western Perspective	First Nations Perspective	Asian Perspective
Performance Feedback	Aversion to criticism, heeding advice, soliciting feedback may be viewed as a lack of commitment, motivation, confidence, enthusiasm or knowledge.	Criticism, advice, confrontation and emotional outbreaks are viewed as a lack of maturity or respect.	Self-disclosure and frankness about one's emotions are viewed as inappropriate.
Leadership	Male dominance presides.	Women are expected to assume a leadership role in families and are highly regarded in tribes where they often sit as elders.	Elders are revered.
Knowledge	Knowledge is for controlling peace and order.	Knowledge is for the sake of living in harmony with nature.	Knowledge is for the sake of living in harmony with nature and man.

In essence, "Cultures are like icebergs — some features are apparent to anyone not in a fog, while others are deeply hidden and are so far beneath the surface that they are hard to recognize."[21]

Recommendations to Disability Management Coordinators

One challenge for employers is to adopt the "Platinum Rule": Treat people as they wish to be treated, not like you want to be treated.[22] This requires a change in mindset, something that many companies will struggle to achieve.

In the field of disability management, instead of trying to force workers to adapt to an established practice, consider redesigning the practice so that it adopts some of the workers' cultural beliefs/practices. Create a culture of inclusion. Involve workers in the design of the Disability Management Program and accommodate cultural differences where possible. Listen to the workers and show trust in them by seeking their opinions on the things that matter to them.

---

[21] E. Winters, *Cultural Issues in Communication* (2002), online: <http://www.bena.com/ewinters/culiss.html>.

[22] *Supra*, note 7.

When planning the worker's return to work, the Disability Management Co-ordinator should consider factors such as:

- the impact of cultural attitudes towards illness/injury;
- the role of the family in the illness and recovery process;
- relationship development within the culture;
- the preferred communication style;
- the cultural aspects that could impact the return-to-work process;
- the mechanisms of problem-solving and goal-setting;
- the potential for cultural conflicts between the Disability Management Co-ordinator and worker;
- the potential for the worker to freely express concerns or issues about the return-to-work process; and
- presence/absence of language barriers.

Recognize that not all diversity is visible. Be aware that disability brings many diversity issues to light. Seek understanding and offer your respect. Try to look at the situation through the eyes of the ill/injured person and determine where the challenges for recovery and return to work exist. Most of all, promote responsibility for the problems and solutions.

EFFECTIVE MANAGEMENT OF MENTAL HEALTH DISABILITIES

By Dianne Dyck

The incidence of mental health disorders and claims is on the rise.[23,24] The World Health Organization estimates that 25% of the population will be affected by a mental health disorder at some time in their lives,[25] and by 2020, depression is predicted to be the leading cause of disability worldwide.[26]

Despite all the advances made in medicine, mental health disabilities remain poorly understood and stigmatized. Workers suffering from mental health disorders tend to try to work through their condition, which often goes unrecognized

---

[23] Watson Wyatt Worldwide, *Staying @ Work 2005* (2005), available online at: <http://www.watsonwyatt.com/research/resrender.asp?id=w-860&page=1>.

[24] Marsh Risk Consulting, *Workforce Risk: Fourth Annual Marsh Mercer Survey of Employers' Time-off and Disability Programs*, (2003), online: <http:www.marshriskconsulting.com.st/ PDEv_C_371_SC_228135_NR_306_PI_347745.htm>.

[25] World Health Organization (2005), reported in NQI, *So What Are Canadian Organizations Doing to Improve Mental Health? With Some Exceptions, Not Enough* (9 September 2005), online: <www.nqi.ca/articles/articles_details.aspx?id=532>.

[26] OMA Committee on Work and Health, *Return to Work for Patients with Mental Disorders* (January 2005), online: <http://www.oma.org/pcomm/omr/jan/05returntowork.htm>.

and untreated. Most physicians find it a challenge to help these workers return to gainful employment.[27] Likewise, it is frustrating for employers to understand why a worker, who looks fine, needs to be off work for extended periods of time.

To gain a better understanding of this situation, consider some of the following facts. Depressive disorders rank as the second most common reason for visiting a Canadian physician.[28] The person dealing with depression experiences difficulty in maintaining their level of productivity both at home and at work. Fewer than 20% of the people who need mental health treatment actually get it. Serious depression can result in a workplace absence of 40 or more days.[29] As well, returning to work after weeks of disability leave can be a "punishing experience".

Depression is a physical condition that is centred in the brain, but affects the whole body. It can strike early in the person's life creating life-long problems and costs. The manifestations of depression are:

- slumping home and work performance;
- poor timekeeping;
- increased substance abuse;
- frequent headaches and backaches;
- withdrawal from social contact;
- demonstrations of poor judgement;
- indecisiveness;
- constant fatigue or lack of energy; and
- unusual displays of emotion.

Depression is also associated with other conditions like diabetes, hypertension, asthma, heart disease and stroke.

So who is at "high risk"? According to the Global Business and Economic Roundtable on Addictions and Mental Health, the workers most vulnerable to developing depression are those who are in their prime working years; employees with 10 to 15 years with the same company; and workers new to the workforce.[30] As well, women over 40 years of age experience more stress than any other worker age group due to combined work and home stress and the inability to effectively balance the two.[31]

---

[27] *Supra,* note 7.

[28] OMA Committee on Work and Health, *Mental Illness and Workplace Absenteeism: Exploring Risk Factors and Effective Return to Work Strategies* (April 2002), available online at: <http://www.oma.org/pcomm/omr/apr/02returnwork.htm>.

[29] Global Business and Economic Roundtable on Addiction and Mental Health, "Roundtable Roadmap to Mental Health Disability Management in 2004-05" (Working document prepared 25 June 2004), available online at: <http://www.mentalhealthroundtable.ca/june_2004/monitor_june2004.pdf>.

[30] *Ibid.*

[31] CCOHS, "Stress Higher Among Working Women Over Forty, Study Finds" *CCOHS* (5 September 2005) at 5.

Employee Mental Health: Social Capital Theory

To better understand the issues that employees with mental health disability face, consider disability in terms of the Social Capital Theory. The Social Capital Theory holds that a person's willingness to do something to help another person is dependant on their belief that "good" will come back to him or her.[32] Applying this theory to the workplace, the concept is that employees have a "bank" of individual social credits (goodwill) that they accumulate based on their degree of involvement and commitment to the workplace and to other employees. Throughout their employment, employees collect these banked credits and draw on them as required.

Employees who are active team players; who invest in the interests of the company and other workers; who work with and assist other employees; and who shoulder their share of the work and responsibilities tend to earn lots of social credits. In times of hardship like illness, they are the ones that other people rally around and are willing to help them to successfully recover and return to work.

Employees, who are less engaged in the company, its activities and its people; who are withdrawn or lack social skills; who are viewed as insubordinate and difficult to manage; and/or who are frequently absent tend to have few, if any, social credits. In fact, they may be in a deficit position for social credits. These employees are the ones, who when ill/injured, go unsupported by the workplace. The validity of their absence is questioned. Questions about whether or not they really belong in this workplace emerge. Return-to-work issues occur, making the return-to-work experience feel more like a "punishment" than a rehabilitation effort.

Employees with mental health conditions often fit into this latter category. It is important for Disability Management Coordinators to recognize this and understand that the challenge is not only to re-integrate the employee, but also to help him/her mend some of the "bridges burned" prior to the disability absence. Also to enable them develop the skills needed to earn social credits that would help them to better fit into the workplace.

Managing Mental Health Disabilities

With workers tending to work though mental/nervous health disorders, crossovers between unrecognized symptoms and emerging performance and relationship problems often occur. Symptoms of mental/nervous health conditions are frequently mistaken for the employee being insubordinate or possessing a poor work attitude. Given that many managers/supervisors are unfamiliar with the signs and symptoms of mental health disorders, the need for early intervention often goes unnoticed.

---

[32]   *Supra*, note 17 at 469.

Key principles for managing mental health disabilities have been provided by the Global Business and Economic Roundtable on Addiction and Mental Health, 2004-05.[33] They include recommendations for companies to:

- Use performance management to detect job stress and mental health issues. The "Rule-out-rule" approach of performance management can be used to separate mental health symptoms from work performance and relationship problems (Figure 18.2). This approach aligns well with the Management of Personal Health Problems (Figure 3.4) discussed in Chapter 3.

Figure 18.2: Performance Management using the "Rule-Out-Rule"[34]

Rule-Out-Rule

When an employee is experiencing work performance problems, management needs to determine if the deterioration in performance is due to health problems. The recommended approach is to:

1. Educate management on how to verify if health problems are impacting the employee's work performance.
2. Encourage the employee to consult with his/her family physician or another health professional to rule out any related health issues.
3. Defer discussing work performance until the medical review has been completed and a fitness-to-work clearance has been received.

- Regular performance management combined with empathetic communication between the employee and supervisor can help to identify the symptoms of depression in a timely manner.
- Throughout the absence and return-to-work processes, maintain contact and communication between the workplace and employee to promote a safe, timely and supportive return to work. Isolation deepens depression and worsens the situation.
- Adopt a system of clear communication among the major stakeholders that ensures both the employer and employee needs are identified and addressed. The Roundtable recommends the use of the Green Chart (Figure 18.3),[35] which has been developed by this author into a sample chart (Figure 18.4). The Green Chart, that is designed for use by Occupational Health professionals and treating physicians, promotes dialogue on the relevant workplace concerns and employee performance issues. The intent is to identify

---

[33] *Supra,* note 20 at 25.
[34] *Ibid.*
[35] *Ibid.,* at 17.

the current state of affairs so that appropriate treatment and return-to-work plans can be developed and implemented. It also enables the workplace to put forth their concerns so that healthcare providers can appreciate the magnitude of the challenges faced by the employee and employer.

Figure 18.3: Green Chart[36]

Green Chart

Goal:

Facilitate a safe, timely and supported return to work for the employee suffering from a mental health problem.

Approach:

Implement the use of a chart like the one provided in Figure 18.3 to house:

1. Information that the attending physician needs in order to clearly understand the implications of the mental health disorder on the individual's ability to function in the workplace. It would include:
    *   The employee's job and functions;
    *   The required skills such as technical skills, planning skills, attention to critical details, interpersonal skills, organizational skills, ability to concentrate, retention of information, time management, *etc.*; and
    *   The work demands: pace, dynamics, need for interpersonal exchange and features of the work environment.

2. Information the employer needs to support the employee's recovery and return to work, such as:
    *   The nature of communication recommended between work to home and home to work; and
    *   The information the employee needs in order to understand, participate and "own" the return-to-work plan.

---

*   Defer the management of "relationship issues" left over from the pre-disability period until after the employee is successfully back to work.

---

[36]   *Ibid.*, at 17. Developed by Diane Rogalski for the Global Business and Economic Roundtable on Addictions and Mental Health, and endorsed by Dr. Bruce Rowat, Medical Director, Sun Life of Canada and the Bank of Montreal; and Dr. Sol Sax, Global Medical Director, Dupont Inc.

In terms of the last bullet, there may be some workplace issues that need to be clarified as part of the return-to-work plan. For example, employees who have threatened, bullied, or physically assaulted other employees have to know that upon their return to the workplace, this type of behaviour will not be tolerated. Under the various provincial and federal Occupational Health and Safety Acts, employers have a "duty of care" to protect all workers. However, this can be done in a constructive manner by setting the parameters around acceptable work behaviours at the return-to-work meeting.

Figure 18.4: Company XYZ Green Chart

Employee Name: _____

Onset Date of Short Term Disability:_____

Expected Return-to-Work Date: _____

Employee's Job Title:_____

Regular Job Functions and Duties Include:

_____

_____

_____

_____

Job Demands Include:

_____

_____

_____

_____

Requisite Skills Include:

_____

_____

_____

_____

_____

Information to Support a Safe, Timely and Supportive Return to Work:

1.   **Work-to-home Information:**

_____

_____

_____

_____

_____

_____

2.   **Home-to-work Communication:**

_____

_____

_____

_____

_____

_____

> **3. Return-to-Work Plan** (attach with duties, roles and timeframes indicated)
>
> _____
>
> _____
>
> _____
>
> _____
>
> _____
>
> _____

SUMMARY

The field of Disability Management will continue to be fraught with interesting challenges. To practice effectively, Disability Management Coordinators need to be equipped with current knowledge; sound disability case management principles and standards; honest and open communication skills; good relationship building and nurturing skills; and regular practice evaluation techniques.

CHAPTER REFERENCES

BCTel, *BCTel Evaluation of Occupational Health 1998 Program Costs* (British Columbia: BCTel, 1999) [unpublished].

T. Buller, "A Flexible Combination", *Benefits Canada* (November 2004) at 99, online: <http://www.benefitscanada.ca>.

S. Calhoun & P. Strasser, "Generations at Work" (2005) 53:11 American Association of Occupational Health Nurses, at 469-471.

CCOHS, "Stress Higher Among Working Women Over Forty, Study Finds" *CCOHS* (5 September 2005) at 5.

Conference Board of Canada, *From Payer to Payer: The Employer's Role in the Canadian Health Care System Report #246-98* (Ottawa: Conference Board of Canada, 1998) at 3.

J. Cowell, "Fitness to Work" (Presented at the Conference on Workers' Compensation, Calgary, 1996) [unpublished].

J. Duchscher & L. Cowen, "Multigenerational Nurses in the Workplace" (2004) 34:11 Journal of Nursing Administration at 493-501.

L. Duxbury & C. Higgins, *Report Four: Who is at Risk? Predictors of Work-Life Conflict* (Ottawa: Public Health Agency of Canada, 2005) at 7, 9 and 10, online: <http://www.phac-aspc.gc.ca/publicat/work-travail/report4/index.html>.

L. Duxbury, "Managing a Changing Workforce" (Presented in Calgary, Alberta, 2004) [unpublished].

Global Business and Economic Roundtable on Addiction and Mental Health, "Roundtable Roadmap to Mental Health Disability Management in 2004-05" (Working document prepared 25 June 2004), online: <http://www.mentalhealthroundtable.ca/june_2004/monitor_june2004.pdf>.

J. Jamrog, "The Perfect Storm" (Presented at a CHRP Seminar, Calgary, Alberta, September 15, 2005) [unpublished].

J. Kranc, "Fact Check" *Benefits Canada* (March 2004) at 70 and 86.

"Lost Work Cost Placed at $10 Billion Dollars", *Vancouver Sun* (2 September, 1999).

Marsh Risk Consulting, *Fourth Annual Marsh Mercer Survey of Employers' Time-off and Disability Programs* (2003), online: <http://www.marshrisk consulting.com/st/PDEv_C_371_SC_228135_NR_306_PI_347745.htm>.

National Institute for Disability Management and Research (NIDMAR) *Strategies for Success: Disability Management in the Workplace* (Port Alberni, B.C.: NIDMAR, 1997)

NQI, *So What Are Canadian Organizations Doing to Improve Mental Health? With Some Exceptions, Not Enough* (9 September 2005), online: <http://www.nqi.ca/articles/articles_details.aspx?id=532>.

OMA Committee on Work and Health, *Return to Work for Patients with Mental Disorders* (2005), online: <http://www.oma.org/pcomm/omr/jan/05returntowork .htm>.

OMA Committee on Work and Health, *Mental Illness and Workplace Absenteeism: Exploring Risk Factors and Effective Return to Work Strategies* (April 2002), online: <http://www.oma.org/pcomm/omr/apr/02returnwork.htm>.

N. Pekala, "Conquering the Generational Divide" (2001) 66:6 Journal of Property Management at 30-38.

Statistics Canada, *A Profile of Disability in Canada, 2001* (Ottawa: Statistics Canada, 2003), online: <http://www.statscan.ca/english/freepub/89-577-XIE/index.htm>.

Watson Wyatt Worldwide, *Staying @ Work 2005* (2005), www.watsonwyatt.com.

K. Williams, "Returning to Work After Disability: What Goes Wrong?" (Presented at Canadian Human Resource Planners event, May 15, 2003, Calgary, Alberta) [unpublished].

E. Winters, *Cultural Issues in Communication* (2002), online: <http://www.bena.com/ewinters/culiss.html>.

World Health Organization, (2005), reported in NQI, *So What Are Canadian Organizations Doing to Improve Mental Health? With Some Exceptions, Not Enough* (September 2005), online: <http://www.nqi.ca/articles/articles_details.aspx?id=532>.

Index

Best practices — *cont'd*
- integration of disability management efforts, 196–197
- joint labour-management support and commitment, 199–200
- linkage between program and external services, 210–211
- management of metal health disabilities, 220
- measurement of program, 216–217
- medical consents and certificates, 214–216
- monitoring of program, 216–217
- policies and procedures, 217–218

Blaney, Sharon, 5, 451–453

Bona Fide Occupational Requirement, 31, 434, 435

Borner, Heidi, 5, 447–451

Bowater Pulp and Paper Mill, 40

British Columbia Council of Human Rights, 432

British Columbia (Public Service Employee Relations Commission) v. British Columbia Government and Service Employees Union, 435

British Columbia Workers' Compensation Board, 26

Building a Stronger Movement at the Workplace, 41

Business Health Culture Index (BHCI), 350

Business Results Through Health & Safety, 346

Business skills. *See* **Core management/ business skills**

C

Canada Health Act, 452

Canada Life, 351

Canada Labour Code, 429, 430

Canada Post, 17

Canada@Work study, 361–362

Canadian Auto Workers (CAW), 41

Canadian Human Rights Act, 32

Canadian Insurance Association, 225

Canadian Life and Health Insurance Association Guidelines, 215

Canadian Labour Congress Convention, 40

Canadian Medical Association, 296

Cantor, Alan, 19

Capitation, 406

Care-based principle, 422

Caregiver survey tool, 175–192

Case conferences, 310

Case coordination, 131

Case management. *See* **Disability case management**

Case managers. *See* **Disability case manager**

Cash benefits, 60

Casual sick leave, 292

Centralization of responsibility, 198

Centre for Labour-Management Development, 432

CEP/IWA, 40

Chadwick, Sharon L., 5, 429–435

Challenges of disability management, 1–2

Change management, 100

Changing disabilities, 112

Chronic fatigue syndrome
- daily activity log, 254
- described, 241
- diagnosis, 242
- dietary assessment, 252–253
- early return to work, 257
- fitness tests, 250
- functional assessment, 253
- holistic approach, 255
- improved quality of life, 255–256
- management, 243–245
- optimal functioning level, 255–256
- other names for, 241